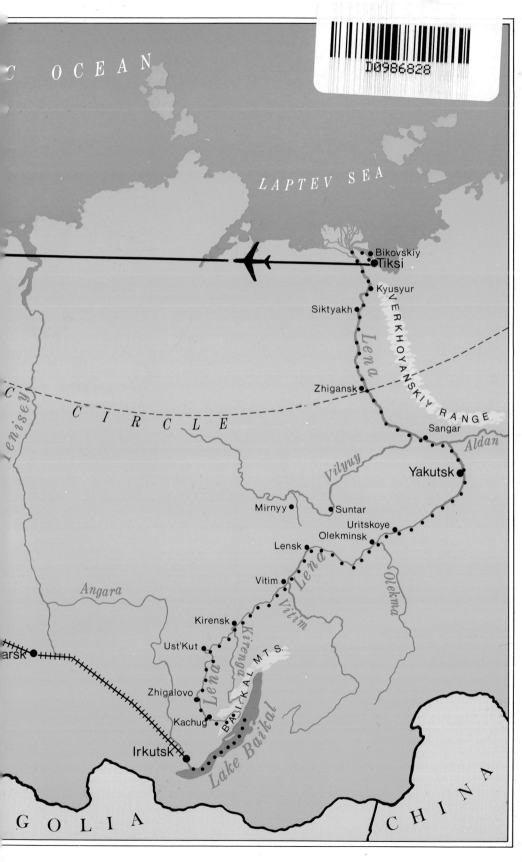

A GREAT CURRENT RUNNING

For Cerry —
good luck + best wishes!

[signature]

8/20/09

Also by C.W. Gusewelle:

A Paris Notebook

An Africa Notebook

Quick as Shadows Passing

Far From Any Coast

A GREAT CURRENT RUNNING

THE U.S.-RUSSIAN LENA RIVER EXPEDITION
WITH **LENA REUNION**

By

C.W. GUSEWELLE

THE LOWELL PRESS, INC. / KANSAS CITY
1994

Jacket design, maps and line art by Dorothy Day
Front jacket photograph by Talis Bergmanis
Back jacket photograph by Anne Gusewelle

First Edition

Library of Congress Catalog Card Number 94-077272
ISBN 0-932845-66-5

ACKNOWLEDGEMENTS

In the sequential accidents that taken together compose a life, the pattern, if there is one, can be seen more clearly from a little distance.

If Isachenko had not come to dinner, it's certain I would not have seen Siberia the first time in the way and in the company I did, and might never have had a passion to go there again. If James H. Hale had not been the publisher of *The Kansas City Star*, or had not been willing to support this project through its earliest development and, with others, to its very end, the Lena expedition could not have advanced beyond the stage of dreaming.

If luck had not led me to Natasha Alova, and through her to Andy Ostroukh, and through him to Valery Tishkov, failure would not just have been likely. It would have been guaranteed.

Without the encouragement of my wife, Katie, I could not have endured the worries that came crowding in the darkness of so many nights.

Without a friend like Patrick Dolan, there's every chance I would have given up, defeated, in those last desperate weeks before the river.

I have lived in one town, and spent a career writing for one newspaper. That may be a provincial design for a life. But except for it, I doubt that I would have had the nerve to go to men I respect and ask their sponsorship of an undertaking that could benefit them in no tangible way, and for which the only argument was that it seemed a thing worth doing.

And finally, had chance not dealt us Russian comrades as capable, as amiable, as resourceful and brave as Victor, Valera and Volodya, it's inconceivable we could have made it to the river's end.

Besides *The Star*, the expedition's sponsors were Hallmark Cards, Incorporated; Sprint; Kansas City Southern Industries; W. P. Dolan and Associates; Morton and Estelle Sosland and Wilbur F. Coen, Jr.

The Coleman Company of Wichita, Kansas, was generous in its support, supplying most of the durable outdoor gear for the journey, including canoes. Other indispensable equipment was provided by Eastman Kodak (film), Yamaha Motor Corporation (outboard motors), Katadyn USA, Inc. (expedition water filter) and The Peruvian Connection (warm, nearly indestructible sweaters).

Many U.S. companies made available quantities of their products to be given as gifts to the people we met along the Lena. Among them were Avon Products, Inc.; Brown & Williamson Tobacco Co.; Buck Knives; John Middleton, Incorporated, and Phillip Morris Company.

My friend, Dr. Ken Hoff of Rochester, Indiana, assembled the extensive kit of medical supplies that was our only insurance against illness or injury. Janet Frizzle, representative of KLM Royal Dutch Airlines, was a kind of guardian angel—seeing to our comfort in passage, worrying about us on the river and in those frantic days in Moscow at the end, and even meeting the plane that delivered our tired, disheveled party home.

I want to thank finally my long-time colleague and friend, David Zeeck, who critiqued this manuscript with such care, and Katie Ingels Gusewelle, always my most demanding editor, who saw it through its many drafts.

To each of these individuals and companies great credit is owed—credit of a kind that I'm afraid is not bankable, but which made the journey on the Lena as much their adventure as it was ours. I have accumulated heavy debts of gratitude. What follows is an attempt to pay them in some small part.

The Sponsors of The Lena River Expedition

This book is for those who rode the
current with us and who were friends.
And for good people met at the river's edge.

And most of all for Katie, my brave
comrade on the longer journey.

CONTENTS

Foreword. A Line on a Map (1973-1987) 1

I. Into the Maze (1988-1990) 17

II. The Matryoshka (Fall 1990) 41

III. Acts of Faith (Winter-Spring 1991) 77

IV. Divisions (early June, 1991) 105

V. A World of Shattered Stone: The Upper River 153

VI. Deep Into Summer: The Middle River 183

VII. On to the Polar Sea 311

VIII. The Current Sweeps Clean 379

Afterword 400

Lena Reunion 403

There was…one river especially, a mighty big river, that you could see on the map, resembling an immense snake uncoiled, with its head in the sea, its body at rest curving afar over a vast country. As I looked at it in a shop-window, it fascinated me as a snake would a bird—a silly little bird.

—Joseph Conrad

FOREWORD
A Line on a Map (1973-1987)

In the early spring of 1974 I received from Irkutsk an envelope that had been several months in the mail. It contained a
Christmas greeting from Leonid Monchinski, written in ball-point
pen on the back of a photograph of himself.

It is a wonderful snapshot, taken out-of-doors after the
Siberian snows had deepened. Monchinski's normally cheerful
face is arranged in the heroic scowl of the hunter who wants there
to be no mistake about the importance of the moment being
recorded by the camera. His jaws are clenched, making the mus-
cles in his cheeks stand out squarely. He is wearing a wolf's-fur coat
and hat, and carrying across his shoulders a large lynx that he has
shot. Behind him is a ragged line of forest, starkly black against the
snow. Seeing him in the photo brought fresh to mind the good
days we'd spent together the summer before.

I had gone for my newspaper on a long reporting and learning trip through East Germany, Czechoslovakia, Hungary, Poland
and the Soviet Union, interviewing officials of the governing
regimes where possible, talking with the few ordinary citizens I was
able to meet, filling my notebook with such dependable facts as I
could gather and also a traveler's hasty observations. It is the curse
of journalists to have to write too much, too often, on too many
subjects they know too little about.

The Soviet Union was the last stop on the journey, and I had

1

five weeks to perfect my knowledge of an empire flung out across 11 time zones from Europe to the eastern edge of Asia, and occupying one-sixth of the land area of the planet. We and the Soviets, in that year, were trying to grope our way toward some safer, more civil way to regulate our competition as the world's two most dangerous powers. The American tragedy in Vietnam was drawing finally toward its end. The Soviet tragedy in Afghanistan had not yet begun, and the 1968 outrage of the invasion and occupation of Czechoslovakia was long enough past to be expediently disremembered. In fact, at the very time I arrived in Moscow, Leonid Brezhnev and Richard Nixon were back-slapping and drinking toasts at Camp David—chummy but essentially hollow theatrics by two leaders untrusted by the people they governed.

Extensive travel in the U.S.S.R. was not easy for an American journalist that long ago, but the way was smoothed for me by a Russian friend. Some years before, Georgi Isachenko had come to Kansas City as a representative of his embassy, accompanying one of the first groups of Soviet professionals to visit our town. He'd stopped with the visitors for a meeting at the newspaper office and, never having had a chance to know a man from the "other side," I asked him home for dinner. He accepted immediately. I put on the outdoor grill one of those leathery cuts that underpaid journalists spoke of as steak, opened a bottle of bourbon, and by the time I drove him back to his hotel that night we'd poured the footings of a friendship that has lasted to this day.

The next week, a couple of dour fellows who identified themselves as agents of the FBI knocked at doors along our street, asking in a general way what the neighbors knew about my politics. The Cold War, you know, had to be prosecuted on every front. Isachenko—George, as he wanted to be called—had spent much of his career in Washington, where he was counselor of the embassy, editor of *Soviet Life* magazine, and head of the Soviet information office. The information service was staffed by Novosti Press Agency, "a peculiar organization," as I have heard it called. Novosti's activities had less to do with journalism than with propaganda, polishing the Soviet image in the world, and it was said to be connected in some way—exactly how or how closely I didn't know, and still don't—with the KGB.

But if George ever was an agent, certainly he was a benign one. In all the years I've known him, the only favor he ever asked was when he called to see if he might spend a weekend with us in Kansas City. Over that weekend, according to Monday's papers, several of his embassy colleagues had been expelled from the U.S. in one of those tit-for-tat indignities our governments used to impose on one another. Maybe his visit was a coincidence. Or maybe not. The only favor I ever asked of George was help with permission and arrangements for my 1973 reporting trip, and he gave it freely. By then he had been posted back to Moscow as the head of Novosti's North American department.

He made no attempt to stage-manage my Soviet travels. I drew up the schedule of places I wanted to go. He arranged the necessary clearances. And I made my way around the country largely alone, although at every stop—Leningrad, Moscow, the Ukraine, the Georgian Republic, Central Asia—the local Novosti correspondent met my train or plane, handed me his card and announced himself at my disposal in any way he might be helpful.

Siberia was the last stage of the journey, and I boarded the night flight from Tashkent to Irkutsk without enthusiasm.

I had logged too many miles and lived too long out of my suitcase. I had heard my quota of outlandish boasts of productivity from the managers of factories full of rusted machines and collective farms where women crept on their knees between the rows, pulling weeds by hand from fields that bent over the horizon. I had seen the drabness and dull-eyed resentment of too many badly used people, walking stooped past absurd slogans written large on building walls. What's more, I had lost nearly 30 pounds and was only beginning to recover from a dysentery I'd gotten from a salad in the Hotel National in Moscow, and might have perished from except for a large, brown, dusty-tasting tablet of unknown properties given me by an Uzbek taxi driver in Samarkand.

But itineraries in that country, once approved, were graven in stone. No deviation was allowed. Siberia was unavoidable, and so I went, in a spirit of grudging obligation, carrying with me that grim baggage of images the very name of the place evokes—images of cold, oppression, pain, brutality and the rest. And make no mistake: most of those images are well-enough founded in Russian history, from the Czars through nearly the whole period of Soviet power. They are one of the inescapable realities of Siberia.

The propeller plane droned and shuddered for what seemed an eternity across the vastness of Soviet Asia. Then, just as the sun was well up, it tipped steeply down, all of us passengers clutching our ears and groaning aloud—the pressurization system was crude, and comfort did not rate high among Aeroflot's concerns—and deposited us in the principal city of the region, Irkutsk.

Leonid Monchinski was George's correspondent there, a cheerful and vigorous young man, eager to show a visitor his corner of the world. And eager, above all, for me to understand how far Siberia was from European Russia, not only in distance but also in state of mind. Some of those differences were immediately striking. The people seemed to walk with a lighter step. They and their city had grace and style, and there were fewer doctrinaire slogans painted on the walls. In the other places I'd been, the two major events in modern Soviet history were spoken of formally as if reciting a catechism: *The Great October Revolution*, or *The Great Patriotic War*. In Siberia, if they were mentioned at all, they were simply the revolution, the war.

At the hotel, the woman who sat at the floor desk seemed pleasant and eager to make a visitor comfortable, unlike the hefty dragons in Moscow who manned their stations with about as much cordiality as warders in a reformatory. In Moscow, Leningrad or Kiev, getting fed was a project that could take upwards of two hours. First there was the argument with the uniformed restaurant door guard, who contended doggedly that there was no place available in the visibly empty dining room. Then, after a shouting scene, you were shown to a table and, after a considerable passage of time, a sullen waiter flung down an elaborate, 12-page menu, and slouched away, not to be seen for another quarter hour, leaving you to try to guess unaided which two or three of the 50 dishes listed might actually be available that day.

In Irkutsk, you just walked in, found a place, made your selection from a single mimeographed sheet. And in no time the food—plain fare, but tasty—was set before you by a smiling young woman who wished you "Good appetite," and seemed to mean it.

Monchinski was about the best company anyone could want. In his antique jeep-style military vehicle, and, when that wouldn't run, in a variety of rattletrap taxis, we saw as much of the Irkutsk region together as my ten days there allowed. Summer was coming on, and one hot afternoon we drove along a rough track bordered by wild rose and giant columbine in bloom, into the shadow of the great larch forest to visit a gamekeeper Leonid knew. The track opened into a little clearing with a log hut and a corral built of birch poles. Three giant red deer, the first I'd ever seen, grazed in the enclosure. The friend wasn't there. But the gamekeeper's wife, a friendly woman in a bright head scarf, greeted us pleasantly, and brought out a clay jug of *kvass*, the slightly effervescent drink made by fermenting black bread, for us to refresh ourselves before turning back to Irkutsk. The jug was beaded cold on the outside from evaporation. A breeze rustled coolly through the dark of the forest. There was a feeling we'd been transported back a century in time.

Another day, we took the road along the Angara River to Lake Baikal, the blue jewel of Siberia, so that I could meet with the director of the Baikal Limnological Institute, Dr. Galazy Ivanovich, a noted scientist and self-appointed father-protector of the lake.

Bounded by splendid mountain ranges on the east and west, Baikal is 400 miles long and 50 miles wide on average—surface dimensions that are not exceptional when compared, say, to the Great Lakes of North America. But it lies in a fault in the Earth's crust, and is slightly more than *a mile deep*. Some 300 rivers and streams pour into it. Only one, the Angara, flows out. Baikal is said to contain one-fifth of all the fresh water on Earth and, unlike the rift lakes of Africa, is oxygenated to its bottom by the churning action of the annual freezes and thaws. More than 2,000 species of plant and animal life found in the Baikal ecozone exist nowhere else. Among them are rare orchids that bloom but once every several years, and the *nerpa*, the world's only population of freshwater seals.

Rather than just speak about the wonders of Baikal, the director took us out in the Institute's motor launch so that I could get a sense of the lake firsthand. For two hours we cruised northward on the glassy waters, in which it's claimed a brass kopek, the smallest Soviet coin, can be seen clearly at a hundred feet. On either shore the mountains rose up darkly, with white capes of snow on their high shoulders. We were chilly, in spite of the sun. Baikal freezes so solidly in winter that, during the civil war, a track was laid for trains to pass across it. Even after the thaw, it radiates its memory of cold far into summer.

At midday, Dr. Ivanovich stopped the launch, took from his coat pocket a feathered hook on a line, jiggled it over the side and in no more than a minute pulled up a 20-inch whitefish. He produced a paper sack with a loaf of black bread, a bottle of vodka and three tumblers. Then he gutted the fish, washed it clean in the frigid water and cut it in three equal chunks. Pouring the tumblers full to their tops, he broke and passed the bread.

"Now we eat," he said. He peeled back the skin and bit with much satisfaction into the raw fish, being careful about the bones. With vodka and bread, especially the vodka, I found it was possible.

Dr. Ivanovich was fiercely good-natured, with a missionary's passion for what he considered *his* lake. For years he had been fighting the central regime in Moscow to reduce the effluent from a paper pulp plant on Baikal's shore, and seeking to organize opposition to the construction of others. This in a time when only the bravest or most reckless dared to put themselves in the way of the regime's central planners. Now, his collar open at the throat, the remnants of our lunch on a newspaper spread between us, he let his eyes run over the spectacle of pristine nature at every hand. Finally he could contain himself no longer.

"So you see!" he cried out—a shout of exultation, as he flung wide his arms to embrace it all. "Baikal is not just a Soviet treasure. *It is a global treasure!*"

From Irkutsk, Monchinski passed me on to a colleague, the Novosti correspondent in the town of Bratsk, north and west on the Angara 300 miles by small plane. Alexander Gurevich was his name, but friends—even friends just met—called him Sasha. He was a tall, powerful fellow, and a contemporary of mine. The hair on both our heads was starting to show a trace of gray, though his was wild and curly, and he had more of it.

He had studied to be a journalist at university in the Ukraine. In 1957, the year he took his degree and just two years after I was graduated from a small college in central Missouri, the party issued a call for the strongest, the most courageous young men of the Union to come as volunteers for the building of what would be the world's largest hydroelectric power station at Bratsk, which until then had been only a wilderness settlement of hunters and fishers on the Angara's bank.

"Well, I thought 'Why not?'" Sasha told me, as we drove up a winding gravel road to the high bluff that overlooked the river. "We were young. We had all our hair. The women loved us. *We went!*" — his voice singing with the memory of it.

For two years, he worked as a driller and dynamiter, cutting into the river-flanking hills the sheer walls of stone to which the ends of the great dam would be joined. In winter, he and his fellow laborers shivered in tents and railroad camp cars while the temperature fell away to minus-70 degrees Fahrenheit.

"There were only eighty days in the year when the temperature did not go below freezing. Winter lasted seven months. Then there were two months that were not winter, not summer, not spring. On June 22 the midges came. We called them the fascists, because our war with the German fascists began on June 22 and always the midges came on that day." The clouds of them rising from the river were so pestilential that laborers had to wear gauze masks to keep from suffocating on bugs.

He remembered the hardship almost fondly, his eyes alight as he told it, and I spoke of the enduring power of his enthusiasm.

"Enthusiasm," he said, "is the main construction material in the building of Siberia." He was remembering, then, a poem by Walt Whitman that he had read in school. He thought its title was "I Dreamed a Town" (although I could not later locate it by that name), about the poet's vision of a city rising out of wilderness. That had been the life experience of Siberians. "Every person in Bratsk built something," Sasha said.

When his voluntary term ended, he had returned to journalism and gotten on with his life. But it never occurred to him, he said, to leave Siberia.

He braked the car atop the bluff, and we got out. Far below was the vast impoundment, the Bratsk reservoir, running away south and eastward to the horizon and beyond. But the dominant feature of the landscape was the dam itself. It was the largest man-made construction I had ever seen, although larger ones have since been built. Across the face of the enormous dun-colored barrier that blocked the Angara's flow a train was passing on its track, the track invisible and the train a slender, slow-moving black worm, small and curiously out of place.

Above us on the bluff's rim were great steel pylons supporting the power cables that ran from the dam's turbines and away into the wilderness, carrying millions of volts to power the machines and lights over a nearly mapless region of Siberia that neither of us might ever see. The lines were a hundred feet aloft, or maybe more, but the field of static electricity as we stood under them was so intense it caused the hair to stand straight up on our heads.

Sasha's voice, when he spoke, had in it some of the same wonder I'd heard in the limnologist's when he spoke of the marvel of Baikal.

"I can always know," he said softly, "that I was a part of making this."

We went down afterward to have a tea together before my evening plane. Bratsk had grown into a modern, but raw and rather gray, Soviet town of 200,000 souls—dominated by forbidding concrete apartment blocks—created in less than 20 years where only the riverine village had been. A paved main street ran through it, then ended abruptly, a foot thick, as if cut by a giant knife. Beyond was a little grassy children's playground, with slides and a teeter-board.

And beyond that only the dark forest, through which one might walk half a thousand miles straight south and on into Mongolia, meeting no sign of man except the right-of-way of the Trans-Siberian Railway. Just then a fellow strode out of that forest leading a full-grown bear on a chain and together, man and bear, they disappeared around a building corner into the town.

⚜

S O, WHILE EVIL HISTORY is one of Siberia's realities, there are at least two others just as powerful.

The first is the warmth and energy of so many of the region's people. They live on one of the last great frontiers. They are generous, outspoken, independent-minded and enormously likeable—as different in style and temperament from their European countrymen on the other side of the Ural Mountains as American Midwesterners are from the inhabitants of Washington and New York. Irkutsk is five time zones east of Moscow. Siberians wish it were farther. To them, Moscow is another and dangerous world, to be ventured into cautiously and only if it cannot be helped.

The other reality, even more astonishing, at least to me, was that Siberia—provided you go there by choice, and especially if you go in a sweet season—is one of the jewels of creation.

The vast Central Asian steppe rolls up out of Mongolia to the south in mounting, verdant undulations, a sea of grass almost beyond imagining. Then the steppe gives way to the greatest northern forest of the planet, the *taiga*, as Russians call it—home of the wolf, moose, bear, wild reindeer and sable. Siberians speak of their *taiga* with pride and a tone of respect, Muscovites with foreboding and dread.

That forest zone, greater in expanse than the whole continental United States, is carved by mighty rivers, upheaved by mountain ranges whose names you've never heard. In its northernmost parts, in the Arctic region, forest begins finally to yield to tundra and largely unpeopled barrens, as Siberia curves toward the top of the world and the polar sea.

What a wonder it would be to try to write about, I thought, after Leonid Monchinski had put me on the 5 a.m. plane for the all-day flight back to Moscow. And I spoke of it again that night to my friend, George Isachenko, as we took a last walk together. I was leaving the next day for the States.

Coming out of the National Hotel we turned right along Marx Prospekt, past the main offices of Intourist, the government tourist agency. That building, which once housed the American embassy, had a sign on its top that said "Communism Will Win" in ten-foot neon letters, and was painted the same yellow as the Lubyanka, the KGB's headquarters and prison just a short way across Dzerzhinsky Square.

"So you liked Siberia," George said. He seemed pleased.

The next block of gray buildings had once been part of Moscow University. He stopped a moment, and pointed up to a dark window on the second floor. "In that classroom, behind that same window, I studied law," he said, sounding surprised and sad at how quickly so much of a life can pass. We walked on a block or two in silence.

"Who knows what will be possible?" he said after a while. "Everything could be. It all depends."

"On what?" I asked him.

"On what happens now between our countries. It is an important time, not just for work. I am thinking, too, of our daughters." Mine still were in their cribs, but George had started earlier. His daughter was 17, and just the other day had come home with the first pair of shoes she had selected for herself. Boys were coming to visit now, he said, and one of them he liked.

"What happens now," George said, "could decide what kind of world they will live in."

"Or whether."

"Yes. Or whether."

The Watergate scandal was worsening, and it was becoming clear even to the Russians that Nixon might be brought down. Brezhnev's health was rumored to be bad. There was no guessing how durable or how fragile the present thaw might prove to be.

❦

THESE WERE SOME OF the memories that came freshly back when the mail, the next spring, brought Monchinski's late Christmas greeting from Irkutsk and the picture of himself. And the idea of doing a long piece of writing about Siberia—though it still was a vague and unformed notion—stirred again.

I bought a map of the Soviet Union and spread it out, and the problem immediately became apparent. A subject as great as Siberia presents awful difficulties for a writer, unless, like James Michener, he is used to swallowing whole continents in a gulp. Somehow the topic had to be drawn to finer focus, but how? Over the next several months, I opened and closed that map until I wore it out and had to buy another.

Eight years later, in 1982, I was on my third map, and that one was getting fuzzy at the folds, when it struck me that the real impediment was not Siberia's size but my own lack of clear purpose. What gives point to most of the writing done about the ocean—and Siberia is, literally, oceanic in its scale—is what men have learned about it, and about themselves, by trying to cross it.

You can dip a sample from the edge, carry it to the laboratory and analyze it until you know everything there is to know about its chemical properties, and you will not know an ocean.

You can go down to the shore and look at the onrushing ranks of breakers, stretching away to that blurred line where water meets sky. And no matter how long you stand there, feet rooted securely on the sand, you cannot understand the ocean's bigness.

Only by crossing it, deliberately, with a route and a purpose— being tested by it and taking what it gives you along the way—is it possible to know what an ocean really means, and how little you mean to it. I say that as someone who has crossed the Atlantic once on a great, safe steamer and two dozen times or so flown over it by plane, and who therefore can't pretend to have even the first inkling of all that an ocean might really be.

With this new perspective, I looked at the map again. And almost immediately I saw a river.

Its name was the Lena, and from the map I could see that it rose almost at Siberia's southernmost edge, near the Mongolian border, somewhere up in the mountains that form the western rim of the cup holding Lake Baikal. From there, its course bent a little south and west, then north and slightly eastward again—the threadlike blue line widening and getting bolder, until it became the most prominent feature on the map. Recurring a last time, the river rushed northward to its end above the 72nd degree north latitude, some 500 miles beyond the Arctic Circle.

Discounting tributaries, the Lena is the longest of all that country's many great rivers, measured by Soviet geographers as 2,732 miles from its source to its mouth—the fifth longest river on Earth. It begins in the glacial seeps and spring snow-melt in a high valley of the Baikal range. After receiving the contributions of many hundreds of other watercourses, several of them great rivers in their own right, it pours its gatherings into the polar sea in such volume that its discharge is expressed in *cubic kilometers*, and with such force that the spiral ocean currents generated at its mouth have been photographed from space.

But most of this specific information I came by later. What I saw that first afternoon was only an immense blue snake uncoiled south to north across the whole expanse of Soviet Asia, the thread-like line at the bottom its tail, the fan delta of the Lena where it emptied into the Arctic Ocean the snake's head.

An idea began to find its shape in that moment—an idea that would cost more in time and risk and difficulty than I could guess. Rivers are linear, I thought, and so are stories. At least they both travel from a known starting place to a fixed destination. Mightn't it be possible to get at the subject of Siberia by riding the current of the greatest of Siberia's rivers from its beginning to its very end?

I put the suggestion in a letter to my friend Isachenko, who since I last saw him had finished his tour in the home office and been back several years at his old Washington job. It would be his last assignment in this country, George said. He and his wife, Musa, intended to go back soon to Moscow and stay there until he retired. Their daughter, married now, had given them their first grandchild and they couldn't bear to miss any of the boy's growing up.

In a few weeks I was to leave for Poland to write a series of articles about that country under martial law, and would be passing through Washington on my way out to Warsaw. While I was in town, Isachenko suggested, I could stop at the Soviet embassy to talk about the river idea. And afterward Musa, an inspired cook, would make a real Russian dinner at their apartment.

The May evening was coming on when I finished my other appointments and got to the forbidding old chancery on Sixteenth Street. I'd been there in past years a time or two, and always had been struck by the strained silence of the place, the sense of institutional unwelcome. Sitting with George and one of his younger colleagues in a small upstairs conference room, I spelled out the project I had in mind—to travel the whole length of the great Lena, and then to do a largely nonpolitical piece of writing about that remarkable part of our world, so little known to readers in the West.

The younger man heard out my spiel with an amused smile, as though I were proposing a journey to one of the remoter planets.

"I think it cannot be done," he said immediately.

"Why not?"

"Because some of that river is closed. For reasons of security."

Security, even in that fairly recent year, could be translated to mean forced labor camps.

"And also I believe it would be a difficult thing," George said. "Siberia is very hard. I have been there. And it must be a wild river in some parts. And who knows the possibility of a boat?"

"Why not travel the Volga?" the younger man said. "Or the Ob River. *National Geographic* magazine made a nice story about the Ob."

"Yes, I read it. But that's the wrong river. Look, I don't have any clear idea how I'd do this. I don't know anything about the difficulty or the boats. But all that could be looked into. What I need at this point is your help."

"What help?"

"In finding a partner on your side."

"In Russia," the younger man said, "there are many nice rivers. Why do you insist on this Lena?"

We talked until it was full dark outside the windows, and nothing was settled. Then we went with George in his car to the elaborate dinner Musa had prepared with help from the younger man's wife. The subject came up only once again in the whole evening, just before we moved from the buttered rolls, caviar and vodka in the living room to the table to begin the meal.

"I believe the Lena could be possible," George said. "But only if you go part of the time on the river, and let us take you by helicopter around certain of the places we consider sensitive. What do you think?"

I turned it in mind, but only briefly. It seemed to me that to hopscotch along the Lena as he proposed would not only destroy the integrity of a continuous river journey, but also would change in a fundamental way the character of the whole experience. *I have time*, I thought, with the arrogance of a man still in his 40s. *I'll out-wait you.*

"No, it needs to be the whole river," I said to George. "Or none of it."

And in an eye-blink, most of the rest of a decade would pass.

The repression in Poland, which I went to see firsthand, and the deepening Soviet embroilment in Afghanistan, wrote an end to the fragile thaw. Ronald Reagan branded the Soviet Union "the Evil Empire" and began developing his Star Wars missile umbrella. Moscow cranked up the volume of its propaganda against "militaristic U.S. imperialism," and intensified its global support of anti-American mischief-making. Leonid Brezhnev's terminal illness no longer could be hidden from the Russians or from the world. A crisis of Soviet leadership was in the offing, compounded by a deepening economic crisis. The winds of the Cold War had begun to blow briskly again.

Meantime, there were other projects. In 1984 and '85, I went with my wife, Katie, and daughters Anne and Jennie, then 14 and 15, to live in Paris for a year and write my newspaper column from there. Again the next year, we spent several months together in Senegal, while I wrote a set of essays on life in Africa.

The Lena was not quite forgotten. Each time we came home from somewhere, I would take from my desk file the fuzzy-edged map, held together now with plastic tape, and spread it to look again at that great curving blue snake of a river, running from the map's bottom almost to its very top. But subconsciously, I think, the idea already had been filed away among life's grand but unrealized intentions—those things that might have been wonderful if one had found the time or luck to do them.

I was 55 years old. It no longer seemed reasonable to think that I ever would set eyes upon that greatest of Siberian rivers, or write the book I'd hoped to write. Nor could there have been any way to guess, even if by some luck I finally were to get there, that the season spent on the mighty, north-flowing current would also be the season of another and even more powerful current that would change the possibilities for Russians and the world.

But here is how it happened.

I

Into the Maze (1988-1990)

ONE

"Good morning," said the heavily accented voice at the other end of the telephone line.

It was a Saturday in late August, 1988, and I had come into the newspaper office to clean up some last work before leaving for a month as a guest lecturer in the journalism department of a university in Texas.

"My name is Oleg Benyukh, and I am calling from the embassy of the Union of Soviet Socialist Republics. We are very excited about this proposal on the Lena River."

Excited? I thought. *Man, it's been six years!* But if you want to do a thing badly enough, you take the excitement whenever it comes. Evidently Mikhail Gorbachev's *glasnost,* and the rapidly improving climate of U.S.-Soviet relations, had let the Lena project back out of the deep freeze. The river expedition, and the book that would result from it, should be of interest not only to American but also Soviet readers, Benyukh said.

His telephone call set off a six-month exchange of optimistic correspondence. Then, early in the next year, a strange thing happened. Benyukh suddenly stopped replying to my letters. His telephone in Washington rang without an answer. The one promising contact was mysteriously broken. The Lena file became just another dusty folder somewhere in the labyrinth of the gray embassy.

And another year was lost.

Finally, at the turn of 1990—out of patience and running out of time—I called a friend in the U.S. government and asked if she could put together a meeting at her office with a couple of people from the Soviet embassy. That February 1990, carrying bound copies of the proposal (the Russians are charmed by documents that look official), I went to Washington for the meeting. Two junior officers of the embassy appeared. I laid out the plan.

"Say '*Da,*'" I told them, "or say '*Nyet.*' But in the name of heaven say *something!* I've been preoccupied with this for most of a decade, and it's time now either to do it or forget it and get on with other things."

Clearly, one of them replied, my passion to travel the Lena was very great. I had to understand that no such decision could be made in Washington, but he promised to take the matter up again "at a higher level" in Moscow. As the meeting ended, one of the Russian embassy men asked if I would autograph his copy of the proposal.

"Some day," he said, "it could be a valuable document." I took that for a hopeful sign.

The next month, in March, while I was traveling on a family vacation in the southwestern U.S., the paper tracked me down by phone to say word had been received from the embassy that I should prepare to go to Moscow in early April to discuss details of the project.

I could be forgiven, perhaps, for imagining then that the goal was all but in hand.

TWO

SATURDAY, APRIL 7, 1990.
Sherametyavo airport, Moscow, morning. My suitcase is missing at the end of the flight from New York. There's a milling crowd of people and tangle of crates, rope-tied valises and other peculiar luggage at the conveyors that work only sporadically. Then all clear out, and I'm still without mine—in rough travel clothes. No suit, not even a toothbrush, for the week of discussions ahead. I wait the whole day at airport for the next Aeroflot inbound. Not on that one, either. A young woman in a uniform takes a description, says maybe it will come tomorrow.

Through the rainy evening to the Ukraine Hotel. Try to place a call home. The hall woman on the floor says maybe it will be possible to order a connection *by Tuesday*. My hotel room has a small parlor with sleeping alcove. The room is cold. I have a blinding headache in a town where it's impossible to find an aspirin. The head throbs worse when I lie in bed. I record these miseries in a letter to Katie that I will carry back with other notes to her, then sit up

the whole night in chair, wrapped in a blanket from the bed, trying
to read in the cold and the weak light from one ceiling bulb.

D AYLIGHT SUNDAY, AND HEADACHE better. Hotel breakfast buffet crowded
with foreigners, mainly Americans and English, all shouldering like
me through glasnost's open door. Scholars on exchanges. Preachers
hoping to missionize. Businessmen planning deals. I go back to airport, and miraculously the bag is there. It came in on the morning
flight and is stored with other foundlings in a wire cage. I want to
kiss the young woman in the uniform, but might be misunderstood.

I rehearse the way by Metro to the office for tomorrow's
meeting, copying in my notebook the Cyrillic letters of the station
changes. Rainy and cold, sometimes snow showers. The place is in a
far district. Wander lost a long time, then finally locate it with help
from a woman who speaks a little English. It's a large, unkempt
square building at 7 Bolshaya Pochtovaya Street. By late afternoon,
brief interludes of pale sun slant through the chilly drizzle. In a little
plaza outside the Metro station, people stand in line at an ice cream
stall.

❧

T HE MAITRE D' OF THE hotel dining room stepped nimbly to block
the doorway with his tuxedoed body. He wagged his finger in
reproach.

"No place," he said.

I looked past him. There was a noisy company of diners
inside, tables crowded with plates and bottles of champagne. But I
could see there were places free.

"I'm staying in the hotel."

He continued to waggle that imperious finger.

"Maybe try buffet."

"But I want to eat a regular meal."

He squared his body in the door, and made a shrug with his
eyebrows and mouth. My effrontery at needing to eat seemed to

sadden and offend him. Too tired for a war, I turned and started away.

"Do you have cigarettes?" a man asked. He was a young man in his 30s, olive-skinned.

"Yes," I said, thinking he wanted a smoke.

"Then you can eat. Give me the package." He stepped smiling toward the maitre d'. "A table for my friend and me," he said. They shook hands warmly, and the maitre d' put his hand, and my cigarettes, in his pocket.

"Where you like," he said. We sat at a table with some other people. A waiter appeared, and my olive-skinned friend spoke to him in Russian.

"I ordered you some salad, a cutlet, smoked fish. Is that all right?"

"Fine," I said.

"There's a menu, but it's useless. I know this place."

He said he was from Turkey and had been seven months in Moscow for business. I didn't ask what kind of business. Seven months was a long time, he said, and he was eager to get out.

"You can live well enough here, once you learn how. It is the most corrupt city I know. And you can make good business in Moscow. But it tires you out to deal with it."

A pretty woman from Swiss television took an empty place at our table and began to talk about her day. She'd been in Moscow only a week, and said that by the second night she already had begun dreaming of Zurich. You get the feeling that foreigners huddle together here like survivors of a train wreck.

"How do I get the check?" I asked him when I'd finished.

"There isn't one."

"How much is it, then?"

"What's the difference? At six rubles for a dollar—or thirty if you buy them on the street—the money is worth nothing." He raised his hand to call the maitre d' to the table.

"Give him twenty-five rubles," he told me. "It's enough."

The tuxedoed one ducked his head in a little bow, and folded the notes into his pocket.

"He'll pay the waiter what he wants to, and keep the rest."

"What about the restaurant?"

"The restaurant gets nothing. It's how this place works."

As I went out, the Turk had his arm on the back of the chair of the Swiss broadcaster and had begun explaining how she could live well in Moscow. I don't think she was much interested, since she was on a television expense account, and anyway she was leaving on the next day's plane.

⚜

STARTLED UP FROM THE desk and my notes to Katie by a great clanging sound that rings all through the hotel, as if someone had dropped an enormous church bell from the roof to the street below. Throw open the window, and there's a repetition of it, with pulses of light showing around the cornice outside the room. Then, all across the misty, sullen city rockets can be seen going up and exploding in a vast fireworks display—not as grand as the Bastille Day detonations in Paris, or as long, but surprising and merry all the same.

I rush downstairs, but it's over. Can still smell the faint perfume of gunpowder from the portico of the hotel. One man says he thinks it's a celebration of the Day of the Air Defense Forces. Other people seem unclear about it, and generally indifferent.

Coming back inside, I notice the refreshment bar of the hotel still is open. Get big cup of good coffee and a nice sweet roll for one ruble (15 cents), tip the two ladies another ruble and establish my reputation there as a big spender. Panic and the awful feel of smallness and helplessness are being replaced by excitement and confidence, possibly unwarranted. An absolute rule: one must allow a full two days here for physical and psychological adjustment before attempting *anything*.

THREE

T HE LITTLE COFFEE HOUSE across the street from Novosti Publishing was noisy with its Monday morning crowd. They were mostly young, and could have been newspaper or writing people anywhere—reading the morning paper, making jokes, flirting, arguing. Then they pulled up their coat collars and crossed the wet street in the rain. I had a second coffee, waiting for it to be 9 o'clock, then followed them across.

The meeting had been arranged as the Russians have a genius for doing—with four of them shoulder-to-shoulder on one side of the table, me alone on the other. Alexei Pushkov, the director, sat in the center, flanked by his deputy editor-in-chief, whose name was Likutov. The others' names I didn't get. I distributed copies of the bound proposal, although I knew they would have gotten the text from the embassy in Washington.

Pushkov riffled the pages with his thumb, but did not bother to open his copy.

"So you want to travel the Lena," he said through the interpreter. "Why?"

My spiel had become practiced by now, and I delivered it with conviction, pausing to let the interpreter work. I could tell from their expressions as I spoke that certainly Likutov, and probably Pushkov, understood English perfectly. About the others I wasn't sure. Pushkov was a man in his 60s, gray-haired, who exuded awareness of his authority. Likutov, younger, dark-haired, seemed more congenial. When I finished speaking, they were silent for a moment.

Then Pushkov said, "That is all quite interesting. But really there are only two subjects to discuss. One is the possibility of doing it. The other is the money."

He smiled for the first time—or, rather, he displayed his teeth in what was meant to represent a smile.

"It will be difficult," he said. "All that is *taiga*, so there is danger. Danger from animals, and maybe from people. Security will be a problem. And there is the question of having permission, which we will have to get for you. And the boat is another problem—a big problem. It may be a boat will have to be taken over the mountains from Lake Baikal to the river."

"But you think it's possible?" I asked him.

"Possible, yes. But it will be a big expense."

"My budget is in the proposal." It was a budget of $110,000, a hypothetical sum that I didn't have and, if the project went forward, would have to raise from sponsors. In the Soviet Union, I knew perfectly well, a hundred thousand dollars was a great deal of money.

"Yes, I've seen it," Pushkov said. "But you are asking us to cooperate in something that is unique—something that has not been done before. And so the cost must increase. Likutov has made some research into the expense."

The younger man opened a notebook and read from a list of items and numbers.

"The biggest expense will be for the main expedition boat. The amount is two thousand four hundred rubles a day, for sixty-five days. The other costs will be for state security, for the airplanes you say you will rent, and for interpreters."

He read the sums, in rubles, for each category. I noted them, and did my hasty division.

"You bring all food and other equipment from the U.S.?" Pushkov asked.

"All of it. And we leave everything behind, for use by Russian scientific expeditions."

"Yes. Of course."

I totaled up the sums Likutov had quoted, and tried to keep a poker face. The numbers looked very good.

"That's within my budget," I said. "You can see in the proposal I planned thirty thousand dollars for the main ship. If it's less, that means we can use more helicopter time for photography."

"How do you mean, *less?*" Pushkov's pretense of a smile went away.

"Well, when I divide the total by six and one-half rubles to the dollar—"

"I'm sorry," Pushkov said. "It's your mistake. We have different rates of exchange. Six and one-half is a special rate only for foreign tourists. This is an official arrangement, and so we will use the official rate which is *point* six five for one dollar."

I felt dizzy. The pad of numbers spun before me. In a blinding instant, all the sums had been multiplied by a factor of 10. For the boat alone, not counting any personnel or use of aircraft, the amount was nearly *a quarter of a million dollars.* Including equipment, food and air travel, it suddenly had become an expedition of more than $400,000. My legs under the table felt strange and weak. I turned to the interpreter.

"Tell him I only want to hire the boat, not buy it."

The interpreter hesitated. He was not in the habit of making jokes to the director.

"Go ahead," I said. "Tell him."

But Pushkov had understood me well enough in English, and wasn't amused.

"Finally," he said, "there is the matter of an incentive. There must be something for all of our trouble." Something *under the table* was what he meant. "I am thinking of an amount of fifty thousand dollars. Possibly you are able to leave with us a check."

I must have been pale. I know my hands were shaking as I stared speechless across the table at that smooth, outrageous bureaucrat who could let me go—or not go—to the river, at his pleasure. Likutov, sitting beside the director, seemed a little embarrassed at the mention of an "incentive."

"I'll have to think about it," I told Pushkov. But it was a humiliated bluff. There was nothing to think about.

"Of course. And you will come back on Friday and we can discuss again."

I collected my papers to leave.

"It is a surprise to me," said Pushkov, "that you don't make this for *National Geographic* or for one of your American television networks. We have had experience arranging travels for such organizations. With them, money is not a problem."

I'd come to Moscow for what I thought would be a week of serious discussions, and the talking effectively had ended before noon on the first day. I stumbled out onto Bolshaya Pochtovaya street, with its broken curbs and muddy ooze, and found my way back to the Metro station. I felt somehow ashamed, like a stupid provincial who had overreached himself in a way not important enough to be tragic, only silly.

There was no one to whom I could confide my misery. The Muscovites on the subway car all were lost in reading newspapers and paperback books. They were better dressed and less beaten looking than I remembered them from years before. I almost envied them. Whatever the troubles in the country or in their lives, I was thinking, not one of them could have had a morning more calamitous than mine.

⚜

CHANGE TO WALKING CLOTHES. Set out afoot to try to compose myself—first to Red Square, remembering it with Katie 17 years ago. Then down past the National Hotel where we stayed, and past what was the Intourist building, which no longer has the "Communism Will Win" sign on the roof. It would, in such times, be a dismal joke (though Communism certainly has beaten me this day).

A sad note. I discover back at the hotel that the room maid is taking aspirin from my bottle above the wash basin. Just a few at a time. Nothing else has been touched. The desperation at every level is pitiful. My head's fine now, and I hope hers is better for it. She's a tired lady. The plumber came while I was out to fix my shower so it will work.

Sit up late, writing another of my desperate, unmailed night letters to Katie. Then, still too anxious to sleep, spend three hours more—until after 3 a.m.—working and reworking the numbers, always to the same result. Even if Pushkov were to halve all his costs, the amount still would be twice what I could raise. It's finished. I have the rest of the week to consider how I will explain to *The Star*'s publisher, when I go home on Saturday, that I have spent my time and some of his money on a folly.

Next day, on Tuesday, I set out to see if I can understand better what sort of broth I've fallen into, since plainly I'm out of my depth. No help, and barely even courtesy, at the fortress U.S. embassy. Or at the embassy's commercial office down the street. I telephone the bureaus of several U.S. news organizations, but the correspondents all are out.

Early evening, my first luck. At the office of the Associated Press, I meet a striking dark-haired woman named Natasha Alova, a former teacher at Moscow State University, who is working now as an assistant to the AP bureau chief. The scramble for news out of the Soviet Union, she says, plus the greed for dollars, has turned Novosti from a publishing/journalistic/intelligence/propaganda organization into a hard-currency extorter, selling access to the foreign press.

⁂

"THE PEOPLE YOU'RE DEALING with like to pretend they still have a monopoly. But you must understand that *there are no more monopolies in this country now*. It's all breaking down.

"If I were you," said Natasha Alova, "I would just leave those people—forget them."

It was a breathtaking notion, since they were the ones I'd come to talk with, the ones I'd dealt with for years.

"I would go in some completely new direction. Maybe the academic world."

"I'm leaving Saturday," I told her. "That's only three more working days. I'll need the best interpreter I can find."

"There's a young man who was a student of mine at the university. His name is Andrei Ostroukh. If I can reach him, I will have him telephone to your hotel tonight."

At 10:30 the phone buzzed in the room at the Ukraine.

"Hello," said a voice so unaccented it could have been from my Middle Western street.

"This is Andy. Tell me how I can help you."

FOUR

ANDY COMES FOR BREAKFAST at the hotel. He's a slender, humorous young man, about 30. I ask him a bit about himself. He's married, with a small daughter. For a while, he says, he was a teacher. But two years ago he gave up regular work, put his job passbook on his bookshelf and had cards printed. He hands me one. *Andrei Ostroukh, Free-Lance Interpreter and Translator.* "I work for ten dollars an hour," he says, "hard currency only. I have a West German bank account, and when there is enough money in the bank, I'm out of here." The room is crowded for the breakfast buffet, but he doesn't seem to care who might be listening.

In past years, there was an actual offense in Soviet law called "unauthorized contact." That is, if an ordinary Soviet citizen met with a traveler from the West, and it were observed, there could be serious consequences. It's clear that Gorbachev's reforms, whatever else they've accomplished, have swept that fear away.

I fill him in on the project and lay out the desperate situation. We set off first to Moscow State University, its spire looming gray on the Lenin Hills. Through crowds of students, looking young and harried as students anywhere, and up an elevator to the office of the dean of the geography faculty. Andy is as bold as he is humorous. He banters with the secretary in the outer office, charms her, gets in to see the dean. It's an interesting project, the dean says—very interesting. But they are a teaching faculty. They don't do expeditions. Why don't we try the Academy of Sciences? Andy gets a name, we ride in his jeep-type Lada to another building. "Shouldn't we call ahead for appointments?" I ask him. "No," he says, "we Russians don't trust the telephone. We just knock on doors."

An official of the Academy of Sciences, with whom Andy speaks briefly, also thinks the proposal for a source-to-mouth journey on the Lena has merit, but directs us on to yet another stop, the Academy's Institute of Ethnography.

"First we'll eat," says Andy. He steers through a labyrinth of narrow streets, then down an alley and pulls the car into a cindered niche beside a low, ugly, unmarked building. Finding restaurant food outside a hotel—or even inside—defeats a foreigner. Food is short, and many small eateries have gone out of business. But Andy, a hedonist, knows the places. Behind the drawn curtains of that ugly building is a very nice Vietnamese restaurant, which only Muscovites, and maybe not many of them, could know. He orders for us, and we eat a stupefying meal of five courses. When I pay, the bill for both of us is three dollars and change.

Then out into the early afternoon, which has turned sunny and fine—a lovely Moscow spring day. And on to what will be the greatest luck of all.

The Institute of Ethnography is in a flaking wreck of a building on Dm. Ulianov Street, set back from the road behind a little screen of trees. Old wooden floors, worn stairways, smelling of mice and mildew and old paper. Men scurry though the hallways important-ly—men you'd take for scientists anywhere—many of them with wild hair and full beards, carrying worn leather briefcases and sheaves of documents under their arms. Andy climbs the stairs to an upper floor, and this time the door we knock on is the right one.

⁂

THE SMALL MAN WITH thinning hair and close-cropped black beard turned the bound proposal in his hands, while Andy, reading from his copy, summarized its contents. He was listening to Andy, interrupting from time to time to ask a question, but he was inspecting me with friendly curiosity.

He spoke to his secretary at her desk across the room. She stepped out, and came back a few minutes later with a pot of tea and plate of cookies.

"Please," the little man said in English, and indicated the cookies.

Andy finished explaining. The little man sat quietly a moment, eyes owlishly magnified behind his glasses. Then he replied, a long reply, looking first at one then the other of us as he spoke.

"What does he say?"

"He says—well, anyway the main point—he says that you may be like a star fallen from the heaven."

The little man nodded vigorously.

"Is that good or bad?"

"For them maybe good. They have very little resources. As you may know, science is well-funded in this country—*rocket science.* But for other kinds of science not much. He says they have no money to make big expeditions. For Russian scientists to travel the whole Lena, and to make notes on the country and the people they pass… It could be a wonderful opportunity for them."

"You explained about the budget?"

"Yes, but I will explain again." He opened his copy to the page and began down the list. The Institute man interrupted, waving the issue aside.

"He says it all will have to be discussed, but the amount seems to him sufficient. I told him about your problem, and he says they are not greedy like those other people. It could be enough that you leave the equipment afterward and that there should be some small amount for the Institute, for its later work."

The little man spoke again.

"He says that he is only an administrator of the Institute. And of course the decision will depend on the director, who is traveling out of Moscow now, and on the scientific staff. A meeting must be arranged."

"But it's already Wednesday. Tell him I leave to the U.S. on Saturday. There isn't time."

"He means a meeting *now*, today."

The little man got up, spoke to Andy, and left the room.

"Wednesday is 'library day'—for study and research, without any classes to teach. So they all are here, except the director. He will try to get the assistant director."

Fifteen minutes later I was at another conference table. But this time it wasn't a confrontation. All of us sat around the table together. The little administrator spoke, then the assistant director, a spare, scholarly man from his place at the table's head. Then I held forth with the recitation I'd already delivered, uselessly, so many times before.

Across from me were Dr. Yuri Simchenko, ethnographer and writer, and Dr. Alexander Oskin, ethnographic filmmaker. Both were large men—Simchenko white-haired and easy in his manner; Oskin, his bullet head nearly hairless and his expression guarded, reminding me of a retired wrestler. From the deference they received from the others, even the assistant director, I guessed that those two were the critical audience.

"Why the Lena?" Simchenko asked when I'd finished. "Why not the Yenisey?" (I would learn later that most of his research had been among the people of that river.)

"Because for ten years it's the Lena I've wanted to travel."

"The Yenisey is very interesting."

"I'm sure it is. But I am like a man who has been in love for a long time with a certain woman."

His eyes crinkled as he smiled.

"Sometimes a man loves the wrong woman," he said. But he wasn't angry.

Thus far, Oskin, the bullet-headed one, had only listened. Now he leaned forward.

"What about the Novosti people? What have they said?"

"We talked on Monday. They wanted too much—a ridiculous amount." I caught a flicker of faint smiles around the table. "I'm to meet with them again, but I will have to tell them no. I can't afford the sum they ask."

"Who did you see there?"

I read the the names of Pushkov and Likutov from my note-book. Oskin wrote them on a scrap of paper.

"There were some others at the meeting."

"What is the telephone number?" He wrote it beside the names.

Why would he want to call them? I wondered. And how would they react? I remembered what Natasha Alova had said, that there were no monopolies left. But Novosti was an organ of the official apparatus, in which connections still mattered. Could Pushkov, if angered, use his connections to kill the project altogether? What was clear, in any case, was that Oskin meant to check me out. He would deal above-board or not at all, and in spite of the risks I liked that.

"We will study this," the assistant director said, holding his copy of the proposal. "And we will need to meet again. You go on Saturday? So you should come—"

"On Friday," said Oskin. "In my office."

"On Friday," said the assistant director. And we shook hands around.

Moscow's rush hour was starting to build along the street in the bright late afternoon.

"It isn't done yet," Andy said as he swung onto the drive of the hotel.

"But now, at least, you have a chance."

FIVE

FOUND A NOTE IN English on the coffee table yesterday evening, asking if I would please appear at my convenience in a second-floor hotel office to discuss "a question about the style of your room." Well, the style was, I'd say, bravely tacky. But that time being convenient as any other, I went to talk about it with a pretty young woman who explained, with much regret, that I'd been put by mistake in a "suite" costing the ruble equivalent of $220 a night, instead of the $130 minimum single I'd reserved. We both had copies of the reservation voucher testifying to the error.

I told her I'd presented myself at the reception window the previous Saturday, displayed my voucher with the rate shown clearly on it, and taken the room they'd shown me to. I was blameless.

"Have you paid for the room?" she asked.

"Yes, with an American Express card, when I checked in."

"But you can't do that."

"But I did."

"But you see, you can't!"

(After the earlier desperations of lost suitcase and the calamity at Novosti, this was only an amusement.) In that case, I told her, it looked like I would have to wash dishes in the hotel restaurant and sleep in the Metro.

"How are the Metro benches? They look hard."

She was taken aback, I think, by my composure and good humor. I wouldn't have to do that, she said. But why would the hotel have gotten a cable from its office in New York that I was to be in a suite?

Evidently the New York office erred, I said, because she had in her hand the document saying plainly that I had reserved a room at $130. If New York made the mistake, then New York would have to pay. (Don't believe, if you ever were tempted to, that American Express protects its clients from overcharges. For six months afterward they dunned me like mob collectors on the hotel's behalf until finally I paid them off and cut up my corporate card.)

So the maid was sent for my things and I was moved down the hall from Room 1218 to Room 1207 with no pain at all. My new chamber is tiny as a ship's cabin and looks out across another view of the river toward smoking or steaming factory chimneys. The bed is small, pillow hard as a butcher's block, but otherwise I have no complaint. And I don't even have to wash dishes.

Ability to sleep depends on the extremity of crisis. Last night, after writing a long, cautiously encouraged installment of the unmailed Katie letter, I rested like a babe and have risen energetic for whatever wars this day might bring. Before going out, I make one more try to reach my old friend, George Isachenko. He has left Novosti to become head of the All-Union Copyright Agency and to operate a small publishing and filmmaking enterprise. The number I have is wrong—fatal in a great world capital without a telephone book. But this morning the woman at the service desk has a friend who knows someone who knows the number, and I get through.

George proposes lunch together. He will send a car to bring me to his office on the outskirts of the city. But before that I have to telephone Pushkov at Novosti Publishing House, to call off the Friday meeting. Oskin at the Institute will have spoken to them by now, and they will know I'm working the field. Pushkov isn't in, but Likutov takes the call and says the discussion tomorrow is set for 11 a.m. Without explaining, I tell him a conflict has come up and if I'm to meet with them it will have to be late this afternoon. He leaves the phone, then comes back and we set it for 4 o'clock.

❧

"So, it's still the river, is it?" George said.

He had aged handsomely, and still had all his hair, although it was white now. His office was elaborate and large, with a vast desk, couches, and shelves crowded with books. He took down a copy of one of them for me to keep.

"I was involved in this," he said. The book was *Perestroika* by Mikhail Gorbachev. "In fact, I made the suggestion for such a book, and then negotiated all the contracts with foreign publishers."

"Who actually wrote it?"

"He did."

"Really?"

"Yes, really. So tell me what you have been doing."

I recounted the week—the meeting with Pushkov, the absurd price they'd asked, the new prospect of the Institute of Ethnography.

"I know Pushkov," he said noncommittally. "We were colleagues. But why this Institute?"

"Because I have to have a Soviet partner. And they seem to like the idea."

He laughed a thin little rumble in his nose.

"Maybe they like it. But can they do it? What experience do they have?"

"They make expeditions," I said. "I've met with some of their people."

"They make *little* expeditions. For a thing like this, you must have someone very reliable. Someone who can make arrangements, get permission from the authorities. Maybe I should be your partner. I could send one of my filming crews. Think about it. When do you go home?"

"Saturday. I'm talking with the Institute again tomorrow. And I feel some obligation to them. I went there yesterday when I was desperate, and they listened."

"Yes, I understand. But the question is if they really can do it. How many books have you written? Four? What if I were to take one or two of them and publish them in Russian translation to sell in this country? We could put the royalties into a ruble account, which could then be used to pay some of the expenses of the Lena trip. Think about it."

George would be going to the U.S. for several days the next week, and would call me from Washington or New York to let me know where he was staying. He asked me to send a copy of the proposal and also copies of my books.

"We will see what comes of it."

☙❧

I'M SUDDENLY UNEASY WITH prosperity. More uncomfortable because Isachenko is a friend. At this time yesterday I had no partner for the river project. Now I have two in prospect, and Novosti still to deal with. There are issues of tact and of tactics, and I don't want to play any furtive games. I want to be honest with them all.

We ride with his car and driver back into central Moscow, to lunch at a splendid restaurant on the second floor of a small and shabby hotel. The food is wonderful, and includes smoked sturgeon, slices of cold, pink salmon and a passable beefsteak with a poached egg on the top. His manner with the waitress as he orders is gentle, courtly, almost fatherly.

At lunch he remembers aloud each of his visits to Kansas City—which rooms of our house he slept in, the parties we gave and friends of ours he met. He looks very much the powerful Soviet bureaucrat, except that his eyes still are warm and he is as sentimental as ever. His daughter is now 33 years old, and happy. George likes his son-in-law. The grandson is 7, enrolled in a special fast-track English program at school, and appears to be a piano prodigy. He is playing at the level of youngsters 12. The boy's parents have suggested he give up studying piano, at least temporarily, so he will have more time for school. But he won't, and George thinks he may have a career in music. He says it with satisfaction. He is looking forward now to when his grandson is old enough that he can teach him to hunt and fish.

George would be happy, he says, except for one great worry.

His wife, Musa, has not been well. She has had chest pains, and doctors have discovered some kind of growth on her heart that was not there when she was examined a year ago. He has never heard—nor, say the doctors, have they—of cancer of the heart. But what sort of abnormality is it? He will carry X-rays with him to the States next week to be looked at by U.S. doctors, and while he is away Musa will go into the hospital for more tests. His devotion to her, and his concern, are plain.

"She tells me that she doesn't think of it, doesn't worry," he says softly. "But I know it can't be so."

George tells his driver to take us past the Ukraine Hotel on the way to his office.

"You go back to Novosti this afternoon. What will you say to them?"

"The only thing I can say. That their price is too high."

I plod through the last of another rainy day to the Metro, then, and to the Novosti Publishing office. Pushkov isn't at this second meeting, either because he's occupied or possibly out of pique. Likutov says he has spent the week trying to get more accurate information. He reads from his notes. It's obvious that the presence of a little competition has done wonders for their math.

The new numbers are down by nearly half, and the boat by a good deal more than half—from $240,000 on Monday to $108,000 today. Even so, with the equipment, food and other costs I'll have to bear, it will mean an expedition of $270,000 in all.

"It's still more than twice what I have to spend," I tell him. (The truth is, I haven't *any* of it yet!)

Likutov says he will work on the problem some more. Maybe it will be possible to find a different boat for less. But it must be large enough for all the members of the expedition to live and sleep on board. Camping on the river's bank will be fine in some areas, but not for the whole way. The Lena in part of its course passes near the gold workings, "and gold, here as anywhere," he says, "can attract the best people or the worst, including violent criminals." In other parts, the river passes by prison colonies from which dangerous people sometimes escape.

His calculations, though no doubt still inflated, strike me now as more serious and careful. I thank him for his work, but have to say the sum remains too great.

He will continue his research, he says, and send me the results by cable. Good, I tell him, and I will reply. On Monday, the Lena River was a seller's market. On Thursday, with a second player in the game and a third they don't know about, the Novosti people are trying to bid back in.

Going back to the Ukraine, I'm in the heart of the end-of-day Metro rush—a crush of rain-damp humanity pouring along the tunnel in eerie silence, but so immense that at one of the stations I'm actually lifted in the press of bodies and carried for several yards with my feet above the ground. By act of will I prevent myself from screaming. But anyone with a phobia for crowds would have lost his sanity long before he found his train.

SIX

IN HIS DARKENED WORK room on the lower floor of the Institute, Oskin's editing machine ratchets the film jerkily from one spool to the other, projecting the images on a small screen. The machine is old, he says. It was given to him by some Japanese. His only camera also was a gift—an antique 16-millimeter gotten by a friend from a photographic museum in Boston. But the greatest problem is film, which is all but impossible to find in the Soviet Union and unaffordable anywhere else. Sometimes he is able to get from foreign colleagues film that they are discarding because it has gone out of date—so far out of date, in the segment he is showing now, that the images, instead of being in color, vary from sepia to orange.

Never mind the color. It's the content that excites him. The pictures are of a family of reindeer people in the Siberian far north, moving their lodging to follow their herd as it grazes the tundra.

Into the frame comes a travois drawn by two deer, followed by a man, his wife and two children. They unload from the sledge a bundle of hides, some boards, a great many long poles and a kettle.

The man and small boy set about hunting for scarce firewood, making a fire and carrying water for the kettle which they set over the blaze. The woman and daughter, who might be 9 or 10 years old, put up the house, first laying the boards to make a circular floor, then erecting the conical framework of poles 15 feet or more high and finally stretching over them the outer covering of hides. Before the water in the kettle has boiled, the house is complete.

Oskin is proud of what he has recorded on his orange film.

"Except for the skins, which are from reindeer instead of bison, it is identical—even in the technology of the door flap—to the lodges of the plains Indians in North America. The connection is very clear."

The rest of the film shows the children at play, building miniature tepees, sewing tiny hide garments for crude wooden dolls. All their play is in some way a practice for adulthood in a region so severe that the skills of survival are the only ones worth learning.

Oskin stops the projector and switches on the light in the room.

"It's all being lost," he says. "Three centuries of Russian presence, and seventy years of Soviet rule, already have swept much away. What I need is a good camera. A camera and forty thousand feet of usable film. Perhaps you can help me find them in the U.S. Do you think it's possible?"

I tell him I don't know, but I will try.

"Please," Oskin says. "You see what we work with. Soon there could be nothing left to record, nothing to save."

◈

"HELLO, OSKIN," SIMCHENKO SAID as he joined us in the cluttered room. "And hello to the man who loves the wrong woman." We sat in a tight circle on metal folding chairs, with Andy Ostroukh passing the words among us.

"We have studied your proposal," Simchenko said. "It interests us very much. It will have to be approved finally by the director of our Institute, Professor Tishkov. But we find it interesting. There are two big problems."

"More than two," said Oskin.

"Yes, but two to begin with. The first is to get the permission from the KGB. Some of the river, as you know, has been closed a long time. We will have to persuade them to open it. The other problem is bigger. It is the problem of whether, physically, it is possible to do this thing at all, from the very beginning of the river."

"And the budget?" I asked.

"The budget seems all right," Oskin said. "We can do this as an official expedition of the Institute of Ethnography, so all of the expenses can be paid in soft rubles. The money is enough. You say in the proposal there will be six Americans and three or four Russians."

"Including some women in our group."

I'd decided at the outset that my wife and two grown daughters would be part of the expedition. Katie would handle the accounting and much of the provisioning of the enterprise. They would share equally in the work on the river, and all three would keep independent journals. I knew from past projects how their perspectives would richen the experience.

"That could be difficult," Oskin said. "Conditions will be very hard. But the biggest trouble is the number. You must try to reduce the size of your party."

"I don't think that's possible."

"Well," he said, "you have to try." And Simchenko nodded agreement. "The greater the number on expedition, the harder everything becomes. Equipment, transport, everything. I only say to try. But before anything else, before even asking the permission, we must examine the possibility."

He and Simchenko talked several minutes between themselves.

"They're trying to make some strategy," Andy told me. Then Oskin spoke for them both.

"The best thing will be to send two people from our Institute this summer to Irkutsk, near to the beginning of the river. They will talk to the local authorities, and to some experts in that region. Then, if it seems this can be done, they will make a preliminary plan for an expedition next summer. And you will come back, maybe in September or October when the weather is fine and the mosquitoes are not so bad, to make your own reconnaissance and approve the plan."

"To find it impossible now would not be the worst thing," said Simchenko. "The worst would be to come with your people next year and *then* find it impossible."

I agreed.

"The trouble," said Oskin, "is that we have no money for such an investigation. It should not cost too much."

"How much?"

"Possibly three thousand dollars, at the most. We would be careful with the money and give an accounting for every expense. But there is no such provision in the Institute's budget." And he asked the all-too-familiar question: "Could you leave that amount with us now?"

The issue was not trust. But I simply hadn't carried such an extra sum with me for the week's meetings in Moscow. I had to tell him I was not in a position to do it.

"It's impossible?" Oskin said.

"I'm sorry."

His next words would have surprised anyone who has tried to do business in that corrupted town.

"It's all right then. Somewhere we will manage to find the rubles. Our people will go to the area of the river and make their research. If it seems feasible to do, we will say so. Then when you come back in the autumn you will reimburse what we have spent."

At the door, Oskin's massive hand closed around mine with such force it actually hurt.

"Gentlemen's agreement," he said.

And on that basis we went forward.

II

The Matryoshka (Fall 1990)

SEVEN

Moscow, 15 June 1990 (by fax to Soviet embassy, Washington; relayed by fax to Kansas City), from Novosti Publishing House:

Dear Mr. Gusewelle:
    We have checked thoroughly all the prices and we have come to a conclusion that we could have arranged the trip along the Lena River for $110,000 as a minimum. But considering that the trip will take place in the next year and the tendency of prices to become higher, we think the project will cost about $150,000.
    We hope you will inform us about your opinion.

Best regards.
Alexei Pushkov
Director of Novosti Press Agency Publishing House

Kansas City, 24 June (by fax to Vladimir Zaregsky, Soviet Embassy, Washington, to be passed to Moscow):

Dear Mr. Pushkov:
    Many thanks for your further research. Let me be frank in clarifying the situation to this moment. When it appeared from our discussion that the cost would greatly exceed my available budget, contact was made with the Institute of Ethnography in the hope of finding a way to arrange the expedition on a more economical basis. The Institute indicated interest in the project. I now await their comment on the possibilities.
    In the coming week, if necessary, I will telephone Moscow to learn the Institute's views. I will then know best how to proceed. I will be in touch in greater detail no later than July 15.

With best regards.

Moscow, 28 June (by cable), from Institute of Ethnography:

>Agree with your proposals and budget. Doing preliminary preparations. Expect official approval in August. Will be ready to meet you in Moscow in September. You will be informed about details as soon as possible.

>Professor V Tishkov

Kansas City, 29 June (by cable), to Professor Tishkov:

>Excellent news. Looking forward to this cooperation as source of pride for all concerned. Arrangements proceeding this end. Can come for two-week reconnaissance anytime August 27 to September 18, but first half September best. Advise when details in order.

>Best regards.

Moscow, 10 July (by letter), from Institute of Ethnography:

Dear professor Gusewelle:

We have already held the consultations with our colleagues from Siberia and have also sent the papers necessary to receive the permission for your trip along the whole Lena.

We are happy to inform you that you may realize your project in June-August of 1991 as you preferred and in the limits of your budget. Official permission should be received until the end of August, 1990, but we are doing our best to have it sooner.

At the same time our colleagues O. Zaichenko and known to you A. Polevoy and M. Chumalov are working out the route and holding negotiations with local authorities in Siberia.

To receive the official permission for the expedition we have drawn up the preliminary program of your visit to the USSR. This program may be changed according to your preferences.

The quantity of your group (6 persons) is convenient to us. However the quantity may be defined only after official permission is received.

Could you please confirm your participation in the project and your readiness to visit Moscow and Irkutsk in September, 1990. We shall inform you regularly about the project preparing.

Yours respectfully,
The director of the Institute of Ethnography
of the Academy of Sciences of the USSR
Professor V.A. Tishkov (Russian text signed)

Kansas City, 14 July (fax to Vladimir Zaregsky, Soviet embassy, Washington, with message attached for Pushkov):

Dear Vladimir:

Please pass the accompanying message to Mr. Alexei Pushkov in Moscow. I regret that the discussions with Novosti did not come to a successful end. The budget was the limiting factor, as so often is true in the affairs and dreams of men.

But the important thing, from my viewpoint and I hope from yours also, is that this fine and unique project be accomplished— and in a way that will make us all proud.

Warm regards.

(Enclosure for Pushkov)

I have taken into account the revised estimates which you kindly provided. Using $150,000 as a basis for expenses in the Soviet Union, and adding to that the very considerable costs at this end, it appears the project would exceed the budget by an amount I am unable to secure.

The decision, therefore, is to proceed in collaboration with the Institute of Ethnography, whose director, Prof. V. Tishkov, has notified me of the Institute's approval of the project and its belief that the expedition can be carried out within my available budget.

I am grateful for the time and thought you and your colleagues have given to this matter.

Sincere thanks and best regards.

Kansas City, 6 August (by cable), to Professor Tishkov:

Many thanks for excellent preliminary schedule. Will arrive Moscow 5:30 p.m. September 4 from Frankfurt. Accompanied by photographer. Depart Moscow September 18. Please arrange least costly hotels (two persons, one room) Moscow and Irkutsk. Soviet visa office in Washington will need visa authority from Institute. Also please advise when official permission for expedition is received. I look forward to our meeting.

Warm regards.

Moscow, 19 August (by cable):

Confirm receiving your telegram. Glad cooperate with you. Ready receive you in USSR for reconnaissance September 4-18.

Professor V Tishkov

MOSCOW ON A SEPTEMBER evening is bleak as April was, with slanting rain and a low scud of sooty clouds, but at least no spit of snow. M. Chumalov and O. Zaichenko meet the flight. Those initials attach to Mikhail, or Misha, a saturninely handsome young man with a black beard, the physique of an athlete and the eyes of a spaniel, full of amiability and regret, and to Olga, pouty and exotic in red spike heels, designer jeans and a jean jacket with a surplus of oddly placed pockets and loops. Both are in their early 30s, junior members of the Institute's professional staff.

The Academy of Sciences operates two hotels in the city for use of its guests. They are perpetually filled, or nearly filled, with visitors from England, Japan, South Africa, India, Korea, the U.S.—from everywhere, in fact. Most are professors, arrived for conferences or research projects financed either by grants or by the Academy itself. A few are connected with some international agency. Then there is the odd banker or entrepreneur, invited to discuss a contract for some science-related project. Unlike journalists, they are not paying their own way.

One of the hotels is in the heart of town, convenient but old, drab and in disrepair. All that one's rooms are occupied, so we've been put in the newer hotel, comfortable enough but an hour's ride from the airport across Moscow in a suburb on the southern edge of the city, the very soul of inconvenience. Scaffolds are erected beside the portico at the front so that workmen can replace the plaster that must have begun falling the same day the building was declared finished.

The hotel is at the end of a street, through a gate and down a long drive, inside a tall iron fence that encloses spacious weed-grown grounds. In subsequent days, we'll find the weeds beaten down in paths where families from the rectangular apartment blocks crowded along the hillside on the street's far side come to push babies in coaches and exercise their dogs. One of the paths leads to another gate, broken and hanging open, in the far side of the enclosing fence. Beyond it looms a dark wood, and if you follow the path on into the shadow of the ancient trees you come upon something astonishing—a great, lovely *chateau*, also in some disrepair but still handsome, painted pale yellow and white, with a large greenhouse and garden at one side, what must once have been servants' quarters, a small golden-domed chapel fallen into disuse, and a long, grassy mown prospect running from a fountain-grotto at the front of the chateau down a hill between the pressing forest to a lake below.

The great house, with its lands and outbuildings and several lakes, was the estate of a wealthy Moscow merchant before the revolution. It is told that Napoleon made the chateau his personal headquarters during his month-long occupation of the city in the autumn of 1812, before the coming winter and Russian resistance forced his army's catastrophic retreat from Moscow. Chekhov would have set a story in that place if he'd known about it, or possibly he did. The greenhouse is not in use, though there is a family living in it and tending the vegetable garden. Through a window looking down into the basement of the house several women in white smocks can be seen working at stoves, preparing a meal in great iron vessels. The place is now a rest home for professors pensioned off from Moscow State University. Several of them are sitting on the upper porch, reading newspapers or just looking off at the trees, or at nothing. They seem not to notice a visitor going by on the path.

The hotel's name is the *Uzkoe*, after the name of the neighboring estate. Misha insists on carrying our two heavy suitcases inside and delivering them personally to the porter, an old man with a wheeled cart. The first meeting is set for 10 o'clock tomorrow. Director Tishkov himself will come with his driver and car to take us to the Institute, Misha says. Then he and Olga go off with the driver through the rain at the end of their long day.

⚜

"I KNOW THAT TOBACCO is hard to get now," I said, riding with him in the back seat of the car.

Opening my briefcase I took out the carton of American cigarettes, but suddenly was embarrassed to present them. It seemed an awkward gift for the head of an institute of the Academy of Sciences. Tishkov was reluctant to take them.

"It is the brand my wife prefers," he said. "But it's too much."

If you could find them, and had to pay for them in rubles, one package—a package, not a carton—of American cigarettes cost the equivalent of twenty dollars in Moscow. He opened the end of the carton, took out two packs and gave one to the driver, sharing the prosperity, and kept the other for himself, then shoved the box deep into his leather satchel.

Tishkov was younger than I had expected, just 48, with a friendly but somewhat hesitant manner, tousled sandy hair beginning to go gray at the temples, a good face, and an informal, thoroughly Western manner. But that was only in the car. At the Institute, his authority was clear from the homage he was paid in the hallways, and by the way petitioners already waiting in his anteroom stepped wordlessly against the walls to let him stride past and on into his inner office without them. It was a large office but not elaborate, with his desk, some bookshelves, a conference table. Misha and Olga were waiting for us there.

"You go when to Irkutsk?" Tishkov asked Misha. Olga answered.

"On the night plane Sunday."

"Sunday," Misha echoed.

"And today is what?"

"Wednesday," said Olga.

"Yes," said Misha. "It's Wednesday."

"So what must we do before then?" asked the director.

There did not seem to be any plan for our time in Moscow.

"We could start," I said, "by discussing some of the details of the schedule."

"Bychkov will know everything about that. You can ask him when you're in Irkutsk."

I had no idea who Bychkov was. The name was new.

"Where do they stay there?" Tishkov asked Misha.

"Bychkov has reserved rooms."

"So, there is really nothing to be settled."

And that, it seemed, was the whole substance of the meeting.

"Is Dr. Oskin here today?" I asked. "I have something to give him."

"What is it?"

"A camera," I said. "I promised to try to find one." It was an old Bolex, used but in excellent condition, with carrying case and extra lenses.

"Do you mean the camera is for Oskin himself?"

"No, it's for the Institute. For him to use in his work."

"Come back tomorrow, in the afternoon, and we will have the presentation. How much did it cost, this camera?"

"Seven hundred dollars."

"In actual dollars?"

"Yes, seven hundred U.S."

Tishkov nodded approvingly. "Come at two o'clock tomorrow and I will be sure Oskin is here. In the meantime, you are free to see Moscow. Misha will take you where you want to go, and he can practice his English. Maybe it will become good enough that he can be the interpreter for the expedition."

ﾟ｡⋆｡ﾟ

AFTER THIS FIRST PERFUNCTORY meeting the photographer and I go for a late lunch with Misha and his girlfriend, Kristina, to a small restaurant through an unmarked door and up a stair over some offices. Misha's English is limited and halting—not as limited as my 20 words of Russian, but nothing close to what we'll need in an expedition interpreter. Actually, the girlfriend has to interpret for Misha. She will take time from her work to be with us tomorrow morning. Then on Friday she leaves for vacation to the Black Sea.

We take leave of them in late afternoon. I want to spend the evening at the circus, having seen it in Moscow in 1973 and found it a wonder. Especially the acrobats, the lady contortionist who tied herself in knots so complex the mind could not interpret them, the aerialists, and the bears who were equal partners in the tumbling act—men and bears together carrying the equipment into the single ring, doing the act, then all carrying the stuff out together at the end.

But the circus is a disappointment. The bears have no enthusiasm, and seem as terror-driven as trained beasts anywhere. The rubber lady isn't even on the program. The human pyramid of twelve acrobats leans, begins to flex, and in spite of a dozen simultaneous frantic little adjustments finally collapses its whole weight down upon the head of one small woman, who stumbles from the arena with her hands covering her face and blood coming out between her fingers. And in the night's finale, the trapeze artists fail at every stunt, doing one pratfall after another into the net until the crowd gets bored and starts to leave and the whole affair ends with a whimper.

That's how it is with everything now, a man explains. Gorbachev travels from one foreign capital to another, basking in the applause he does not hear at home. And all the best performing troupes, including the best ballet and circus companies, are kept on the road in the West to earn hard currency. What you see here now are the second-raters.

THE GIVING OF THE camera was elevated to a formal occasion. Several of the senior scholars of the Institute were on hand, and I made a little speech about how a colleague of theirs had helped to rescue our expedition when it was in danger of falling through. And how his work was important and required good equipment. Then I took the camera from its carrying case and handed it to Oskin, who seemed astonished the promise had been kept.

He turned it in his big hands with the respect of someone who appreciates a fine machine.

"How much did it cost?" he wanted to know.

The others in the room seemed impressed by the number of dollars.

One of the men there was introduced to me as the oldest scientist on the staff of the Institute, one of the foremost Arctic ethnographers of his day, who had written several important books and who in past years had made many long and arduous expeditions to regions of the Siberian far north. He appeared to be in his late 80s or maybe even his 90s—an elegant little man, fine as a bird, the skin of his face and hands drawn tight as parchment and so transluscent you could see almost to the bone.

They had brought him to the meeting in a wheeled chair. I had the feeling he'd been drawn into this absurd ceremony out of some far province of recollection where he preferred to live, and that he suffered us with the bemusement of a man who had seen many strangers come and go with their bright schemes.

"We're going to travel your country's great Lena River, from its beginning to its very end," I told him. "Is it worth doing?"

His voice was like a faint, dry wind that seemed to come from far away and whisper in the room.

"Anything is worth doing," he said. "It all depends on who is going, and what he is going there to find."

Then Oskin took the camera and the others returned to their scholarship and I went back with Valery Tishkov to his office.

"How are you carrying your money?" he asked.

"In cash, all of it."

"How much?"

"Several thousand dollars. The reimbursement for the Institute, and my money for this trip."

"You must leave it all here. I will put it in my office safe, and nothing will be touched until you come back from Irkutsk."

We counted the bills together, and he wrote out and signed a receipt for the whole amount.

"It's too dangerous to carry a great sum in Siberia," Valery said. "Take only what you might want for small expenses. Siberia is the frontier, a rough place and with a lot of crime. There is danger everywhere, of course. Even in Moscow. The need in this country now is very great."

EIGHT

Notes on Moscow and Muscovites...
The need may be great, and the hardships of daily life worse even

than last spring. But the people, though they complain a lot, bear it with a good measure of grace. One is taken by their bravery—especially of the women, and the way they contrive to make a bit of style from nothing. There is so little to work with, of clothing, cosmetics, anything. Yet a surprising number of them will look at first glance as if they just stepped out of a boutique on the rue Faubourg-St.-Honoré in Paris. The second look shows that it is all improvised. Costumes assembled from bits of this and that—a man's jacket, with a bright scarf for a sash. It's what they seem to hunger for more than anything, to snatch a bit of flash and color from the tedious, gray sameness of their lives. They may not be eating better, but they must be eating differently, the younger generation of women especially. You see them checking their weight on public scales. Many of them are long, hound-lean and lovely—far from the great ships in sack dresses that cruised the streets 20 years ago.

Oh, there still is a lumpish underclass, relentlessly peasant. And there are all the ethnic mixes that flow in from the outer reaches of so vast an empire. But there seem to be more of the others, the wholly Europeanized, one is tempted to say *Westernized*. The odor of tired bodies in crowds is less pronounced and only occasional. Visually, the people simply are not the leaden, defeated masses one remembers from past times. There is a lightness now. And laughter. And a frank interest in—and no fear at all about meeting—foreigners. I remember how fixedly, how enviously, they used to stare at a visitor's shoes. Theirs were all of a kind, so the shoes of a foreigner gave him away as having come from some far and fabulous place. They don't do that any more. They look in a stranger's eyes, to see what they might discover there.

With their books, their parcels, their loaves under their arms, the riders in the Metro car could, taken all in all, be people anywhere, in any great city—maybe Parisians homebound at the end of their day.

Ismailovo Park, uncrowded and inviting on a brilliant autumn weekend morning, might be the Tuileries. Families with children pass in and out of the dapple of sunlight along walkways arched over by birches and plane trees, the little girls with great chiffon hair bows, all eating ice cream. Old men, pensioners wearing medals on their coats, play chess at a table with benches. Somewhere at the edge of hearing a band strikes up a lilting march.

Why these repeated comparisons to the city on the Seine? No, *of course Moscow isn't Paris*. And Muscovites are not Parisians. But they can be stylish and surprisingly light-hearted, and except for the awful daily nuisance of their country's impoverishment they may, in certain personal ways, already be freer than the French. And that, in spite of the crisis of the economy, is the great and astonishing change that Gorbachev has wrought.

Arbat Street, Sunday, with hours to pass before the evening flight...

Artists at their easels—some caricaturists, some classical portrait artists, bringing faces alive in charcoal on their pads. An orator with an electric megaphone, ridiculing the government and the failures of the party, soldiers laughing with the others in the crowd. Poets shouting their verses to circles of listeners. Folk dancers performing for kopecks in a passed hat. Alone, ignored, a solemn baritone belting out some lugubrious theme. Crafts from the whole of the Union are here, lacquerware and jewelry, and religious icons—some possibly genuine, more certainly counterfeit—arranged on tables and street-front window ledges all along the whole several-block-long festival of merriment and commerce that is the Arbat. And all for sale, hard currency preferred.

Matryoshkas dominate. You know them—the Russian wooden dolls that come apart at the middle to reveal another, smaller doll inside, and then another, and another. Usually six or eight to a set, but sometimes much greater and more expensive ones in which as many as thirteen may be nested. The traditional matryoshka is painted as a beautiful young girl's face, brightly rouged, inside a flowered shawl. Every few steps along the street there is another display of them—rank upon rank of charming little dolls, all just a bit different in pattern or color, depending on the taste and skill of the painter.

The most popular matryoshka now has seven figures. The largest is Mikhail Gorbachev. Open Gorbachev, and Konstantin Chernenko is inside. Inside Chernenko is Yuri Andropov. Then

Leonid Brezhnev. Then Nikita Khrushchev. Then Joseph Stalin, mustaches drooping. The last figure is of the founder of the calamity, Valdimir Ilyich Lenin. And he is very, very small indeed. Sometimes, inside Lenin, there is a final object—a tiny bottle, painted black, with a skull and crossed bones to indicate poison. It's the poison bottle of the Bolshevik revolution. The even newer political model has Boris Yeltsin as the outer, largest figure, with Gorbachev the next one inside, already supplanted at the top.

The matryoshka is more than just a souvenir for tourists to carry home as a gift for friends to prove they have been to Moscow. It also is a marvelous metaphor for a country where things are not always as they seem, where the obvious is not always true, where wheels turn within wheels and the way to power—or even to a river—can lead across minefields of scheming and betrayal.

⚜

NEW VALUES ALWAYS THREATEN the old. And as one might expect in a society whose assumptions have been shaken to the root, some people show the strain.

That Sunday midday in the Arbat, with life and protest and humor churning at every hand, a crowd gathered around a street combo that played a jazz anthem of the capitalist West. The musicians, and most of the listeners, could have been young people anywhere.

An older woman, brow clenched in fierce disapproval, glared down at them from the window of her third-floor flat above the teeming street.

Maybe the noise offended her. Or maybe the jazz tune somehow provoked her resentment of too much change too fast. Or maybe she'd just stood in too many lines that day trying to find butter or bread.

Whatever the reason, she flung open the window finally with a howl of rage. And in a gesture as medieval as it was eloquent, she emptied her kitchen slop pail onto the heads of the startled crowd.

❧

I HAVE BROUGHT TOO enormous a duffel, and Misha refuses to let me carry it. Burdened with mine and his, he labors through back halls of the airport, the fashion-star Olga prancing in her jeans outfit behind, then out across acres of tarmac to the waiting-hall for foreign travelers.

In the hall there's a large number of African students. They are an uncomfortable, disillusioned-looking crowd, sitting and squatting on the floor among their baggages. They have come to study in the U.S.S.R., and though what they left was miserable, what they've come to is hardly better.

The Russians seem to have—or to want—nothing to do with them.

At last to the plane for Irkutsk. Inside the cabin there is an argument between some of the Russian passengers about their seats. Then, finally, all are settled and we are airborne, the sun low at our backs, losing hours as we hurtle eastward so that evening comes on with a rush.

❧

THE GREAT DARKNESS—THE darkness of the oceanic vastness of Russia—long ago fell down across the sky. The Tulpolev jet hummed steadily onward, cramped and minimal. Looking out my window, I searched many minutes for any sign of habitation. For the longest time there was none—not one spark of illumination, no hint of city or town. We could have been passing over an utter desolation.

Then, at last, one light! It pierced the black like the very proof of living. I bent closer to the window, shading my eyes against the cabin glow.

It was only one lonely star.

NINE

IRKUTSK ON A RAINY, chilly morning.

To the hotel, which is just across a square and a little park from the airport. It's a spartan lodging, with rough looking men smoking in the foyer next to the cubbyhole of a reception and, upstairs, metal cots in the hallway with more men wrapped in blankets, still asleep.

The photographer and I get separate, small rooms, but space is short and Misha and Olga will have to share. There's some tension about this, but we help carry one bed from their sleeping alcove and put it in the sitting room and hang a blanket to give Olga privacy for her rituals of grooming and beautification, which must be elaborate.

No food in the hotel, so we cross to airport cafe for *pilmini*—minced meat, possibly lamb, in pastry pillows, served in a pale broth—and coming back are intercepted outside the hotel by Oleg Bychkov. He's a small man with a smooth little face, a little exquisitely-manicured mustache and balding head. By title he is Dr. Bychkov, and he's director of the anthropological museum in Irkutsk. He welcomes me as "Professor" Gusewelle.

Not professor, I correct him. My name is Charles, and no honorific attaches to it. I'm a writer. Nevertheless he persists in the "professor" business, although he speaks it henceforth with what I detect as a note of faint mockery. He is not a likeable man, which is disappointing since evidently he is the Institute's chosen organizer and we may spend much time together on the river. I can't say exactly what about him puts me off. He projects a queer combination of superciliousness, nervousness and false congeniality that reminds me somehow of a fancy women's hairdresser—someone who would insist on being called Mister Pierre, Mister Ralph, or, in his case, Mister Oleg. His familial name, Bychkov, fits perfectly.

Tomorrow we are to meet at his office for discussion. I'm eager for talk of the river, but evidently today must be spent touring the town—unchanged in any noticeable way from when I saw it nearly 20 years ago. Bychkov has with him another disagreeable man, a fellow named Valentin. They are friends, or maybe Valentin is an employee of Bychkov. The plan, I'm informed, is that this Valentin, whose manner also is imperious and whose voice is a nail on slate, will be the interpreter for our meetings here and also for next year's expedition. That is not good news.

❧

T HE ONLY RELIEF IN the tedious afternoon came shortly before closing at the natural history museum, quartered in what used to be a church. Having seen a sufficiency of stuffed deer, bear, wolves, foxes and rodents of assorted sizes and habits, I left the others to step outside for a cigarette, and met there a tall, concave young man who asked if I might give him a smoke.

His name was Sergei Orlov, and he welcomed the chance to practice his English, for which he apologized. Though somewhat halting from having little occasion to speak it aloud, his English in fact was rich, complex, even elegant. His current project, he said, in which he'd now invested most of two years, was to translate *Zen and the Art of Motorcycle Maintenance* into Russian.

"Is that what you do?" I asked him. "You're a translator?"

"No, I do it for my own pleasure," he replied. "And because I think it is an important book."

Actually, this Sergei was the night door guard at the museum and had just come on duty. He said he'd attended the language institute in Irkutsk, but decided there was no place for him in the society as it was constituted and governed, so he had renounced it.

"There are a lot of others like me. Mine is the generation of night guards. I wish only to have my life and to be—how should I say it? To be *invisible*."

That would be a trick, since he was a good deal more than six feet tall, about 30 years old, with wiry black hair brushed back to reveal a large welt or scar over his left eye, cutting partly through the eyebrow, as if from some terrible wound long ago healed. His husky voice trembled as he spoke, either from nervousness or from intensity.

"So I come here at night. I go back to my room. I work at my translation. I require very little. My principal purpose is not to be noticed. I want nothing to do with the world. I am outside the pale. Is it correct? *Outside the pale?*"

He looked uneasily past me at Bychkov, the unpleasant Valentin and the photographer coming down the museum stair toward the door.

"I was happy to speak with you," he said. "And I thank you for the cigarette."

He took a step backward as the others approached, and his features resolved into an expression that was inscrutable as a mask.

⌘

THE ANGARA RIVER, THE outlet of Lake Baikal, flows broad and smooth, its surface creased by the power of a mighty current where it passes Irkutsk running west and north toward its impoundment at the Bratsk reservoir and hydroelectric station.

We've come early to an anchorage by the river for a look at a boat of the type being considered for use as the expedition's main base ship. It is a craft of what's called the Zaria (or Sunrise) class— 66 feet long, driven by a 900-horsepower diesel water-jet engine originally designed to power Soviet torpedo boats. It is operated by a crew of three, and seems ideal for our purpose since it can be floated in as little as one meter's depth of water and we will be able to run it up like a canoe on sand or gravel banks when we stop at night at the river's edge.

The large engine room occupies the back one-third of the craft, the control deck and crew's quarters the front one-third. We measure the area amidship that will have to serve as living, sleeping and working space for at least eight, perhaps nine or 10 people. It will be cramped, but possible. The man showing us the boat says the Zaria can be converted for hospital use, with bunks installed along one or both sides of the central compartment. It's a possibility to consider.

We also look briefly at a second type of boat, Yaroslavits class, a sturdy, deep-draft vessel that we'll have to use at the start of the journey to travel up Baikal, which is subject to capricious and violent windstorms, to the place where we'll begin our climb to the river's source. And also possibly near the expedition's end, the last several hundred miles above the Arctic Circle to the polar coast, where the northern autumn will be turning and the Lena, swollen to a giant, can swamp a lesser craft. Space on the Yaroslavits will be more cramped even than on the Zaria, but comfort is not the point.

To actually *see* these boats of the type we may use gives a sense of palpable reality to the venture.

⚜

B YCHKOV HAD COME TO the meeting already in a rage, and his thin pretense of civility quickly evaporated.

The budget, he said, was insufficient. He could find no money in it for himself—and it was clear he planned to profit richly from this expedition.

"What about this item, '*Development Expense*'? That should be for me."

"Those are costs of the American side," I explained carefully. "For the trip to Moscow last April. And for this reconnaissance. The development money has already been spent. Look under '*Scientific Consultant.*'"

He refused to turn to the proper page. His fury deepened. He was not interested, he said, in any arrangements I may have made with these Muscovites. (He no longer could bear even to call Misha and Olga by their names. He referred to them, with contempt, only as *these Muscovites.*) Either he would be the organizer of the expedition, or he would not. But without him, he promised, we could do nothing.

"What do these Muscovites know about Siberia or about the conditions?"

To begin with, he said hotly, it was foolish—entirely foolish— to propose going to the very headwaters of the Lena. The first part of the river was impassable. It would mean weeks spent trying to traverse swamps, in the worst season of mosquitoes.

"The native people pass that part sometimes with horses," Bychkov said. "Even with horses it is difficult. And for you, impossible. If you are determined to try to do it, then I will have no part in this."

He and the Muscovites then fell to arguing. Rather, Olga and Misha were attempting to discuss, but Bychkov's voice rose in volume and shrillness.

"What's being said?" I asked the unpleasant interpreter, Valentin.

"It's unimportant."

"*I want to know.*" The fellow aggravated me intensely.

"I will tell you later."

"No, damn it. Tell me now!"

"They are discussing a helicopter."

The dispute raged on for several minutes. Then Misha, through Valentin, explained.

"Oleg is saying that it could be possible to go by a helicopter from the shore of Baikal into the mountains where the Lena begins. Or maybe from the town of Kachug. And to land for some time to make photographs."

"But that's not what we want to do."

"I know," said Misha. "But it is what Oleg is saying."

⚜

THE WHOLE MORNING IS thus occupied with argument and Bychkov's sullen obstructionism. At the end of it we go all together for lunch at a hotel near his office, where the interpreter, Valentin, sitting next to me at the far end of the table, finally is of some use.

There are two reasons for Bychkov's anger, he says.

First, in the letter from the Institute enlisting him in the expedition—a letter he will show us another time—I was described not as a journalist and writer but as a foremost American anthropologist on the faculty of the University of Texas. Bychkov had then spoken by telephone with professional colleagues in the U.S., who'd said they knew of no such person and warned him to be on his guard. He must be dealing with an imposter.

So he suspects Moscow may have passed me off to him under false colors, considering him just a Siberian bumpkin. This is compounded by his normal dislike of Muscovites, whom he considers arrogant and condescending. "They even speak differently than people speak in Irkutsk," says Valentin. So I have been caught, without knowing it, in this web of confusion and deception and animus.

I have hoped the discussions can be gotten back on a more civil track in the afternoon, but instead Bychkov goes off with a film crew from Moscow, sending us with Valentin to visit another church—it is lovely, and one of the few actually in use, but we are not much interested; we've come on business, not as tourists—and afterward to wait for him at his house which is nearby.

His house is more than 150 years old and charming to look at, in the traditional Siberian wooden architecture. But it is without plumbing. Water has to be carried from somewhere in a large galvanized can. The sanitary provision is a leaning, ramshackle privy reached by a beaten path through waist-high weeds, with several pages torn from a slick-paper magazine and spiked on a nail for the expected use. It is surprising and sad that a man of some stature in the town must face such a daily humiliation.

Afternoon draws on, deepens into evening. Bychkov still has not appeared. Misha and Olga have managed to light the gasoline burner, gotten water from the can and are making tea, chatting and laughing, seeming undisturbed by the catastrophe. Valentin draws me aside, to the little porch at the back of the house, and opens the matryoshka.

"It is finished now," he says, "between Oleg and the Muscovites. Everything is finished. He will not cooperate any more. You will see."

The announcement leaves me breathless. We are supposed to travel more than 100 miles on a bad road the day after tomorrow, on Thursday, to the town of Kachug, the highest settlement on the river that can be reached overland, to set eyes on the Lena for the first time, visit an archaeological site, and have a talk with the local authorities.

"Probably Oleg will not even go with you to Kachug."

Valentin bends close in the dusk, to be sure I have fully understood and to gauge the impact of his revelation.

"But there is another option," he says. "The option of Oleg himself. Tomorrow you go to Baikal. When you come back from there, Oleg says that you must come to his office without the Muscovites. You must find some excuse to leave them at the hotel."

Misha comes out onto the porch, then, carrying his tea and a cup for me. He looks quizzically at Valentin.

"Is there some problem?"

"Many," the interpreter says. "But possibly they will be clarified."

TEN

E AST ALONG THE ANGARA in the morning on the good paved road from Irkutsk toward the great lake. We stop in a village on the way to visit with a man named Yuri Panov, who tried to enlist in the Ukraine to fight the Germans in World War II. But someone remembered a wisecrack he'd once made about Stalin, so the authorities told Panov, *We can't trust your gun.* Instead of sending him to the army they sent him for seven years into Siberian exile. He was assigned to a camp of woodcutters. But he'd learned some slight artistic skills in school, so rather than working in the forest he was given the job of making signs and posters for the camp. It saved his life, he says, because few of the woodcutters could survive the winters and the short rations.

When his term of exile ended, Panov did not go home. He'd grown used to the climate, so he stayed, married, raised a family. Now he grows potatoes in his garden, and fishes in the Angara, and does a bit of carpentry for hire. In his own time he carves from the larch and pine logs of the forest tall statues that are like totem poles. The faces on the totems are the faces of his tormentors, Stalin and Lavrenty Beria, chief of the secret police. Lower down on the poles are other unnamed faces, open mouths screaming in torment. They are the victims of the terror. Yuri Panov has erected these amazing sculptures in his little yard, directly in front of his house, for anyone to see. And in these changed times they have attracted some interest. *Pravda* even sent a photographer all the way from Moscow to make pictures. When the pictures were published he began receiving letters from all over the Soviet Union. A few were critical, he said, but most of the letter-writers approved of his work.

The road toward the lake is hilly, and on one of the hills the old van we're riding in begins to smoke from under its hood, then lurches to a halt. The driver has on the floor beside him a can for extra water, but the can is empty. He finds a house, carries water from the well to fill the radiator, then drives on, the can empty again. His notion of providence is to double his speed on the downgrades so that the vehicle can coast part of the way up.

Baikal sparkles in the clarity of September light. And the vast lake itself is so transparent that it seems to merge in an unbroken continuation of air and sky. Far across, the mountain range that forms the eastern rim of the enormous cup shows as a faint, low shadow. The interpreter, Valentin, has brought with him a friend, who speaks a little English—a slight, beaten-looking lad named Ivan, who once passed a winter in a borrowed house in the village here on Baikal's shore. Winter is much the best season, Ivan says. There are no insects. Of course the cold is very great, but you do not feel it because the winter months here are windless. When the lake freezes, it is possible to walk on the ice to visit villages that can be reached no other time of year.

Leaving Valentin, Misha and Olga in the settlement below, the photographer and I climb with Ivan on an animal trail that threads up the hill face to a promontory several hundred feet above the lake. From that vantage, the gradations of blue reveal Baikal's depths—pale near the shoreline, shading darker, then changing abruptly to a fathomless ultramarine where the water ledges away suddenly into the mile-deep abyss. A hydrofoil excursion boat comes up from the direction of the Angara, carrying a load of picnickers and berry-pickers to their day-outings. Riding high on its planes, the machine is like some aquatic insect striding over the polished surface, spreading its V behind.

To the north, in the direction it is headed—but farther than such boats go—in a high valley of the western mountains on whose lower shoulder we now are perched, is the very beginning of a river I hope soon to see, but the traveling of which seems to become more complicated every day.

⚜

Bychkov's manner was congenial, almost unctuous now, as he handed me the sheet of paper to examine.

He had drawn up a budget of his own—a variant of mine, but with no mention anywhere in it of the Institute in Moscow. By elminating any share for Tishkov's organization, and reallocating all that for himself, he had kept the final total the same.

"You notice that the travel to the source is omitted," he said through Valentin. "It's possible only by helicopter. That is definite. All the rest is possible. But not with the Muscovites."

"How do you mean?" I asked him. His meaning was plain enough, but I was startled by his brazenness.

"The Muscovites want for me to organize this expedition, but for themselves to control it. And I will not do that. I do the work, and they take the money? When all the knowledge and all of the contacts are mine? Do you see?"

"Then you're saying—"

"I'm saying you have to *leave* the Muscovites. It's impossible with them. But I can make this expedition. I can arrange all of the necessary contracts. And I will travel with you on the Lena from a place called Chanchur or from Kachug as far as Yakutsk, which is more than halfway. And a colleague from Leningrad who is an expert on the lower river, the northern part, will go the rest of the way to the end."

"I'll have to think about this," I told him.

"I promise you. It's the only way. I will go to the U.S. next month to give some lectures. You may give me your answer then. Here is the telephone of my friend in Eugene, Oregon." He wrote it on the back of his business card.

"May I take this paper with me?"

"I have no other copy," Bychkov said. "But you can see the

amount is the same. For all the arrangements. For my services as organizer. For my colleague from Leningrad and for my friend, Valentin, who will be the interpreter for the expedition."

"That hasn't been decided."

"What hasn't?"

"About the interpreter," I said.

"But what question is there? You can see that Valentin is very competent."

"The issue isn't competence." It was delicate to speak about, since this whole dialogue had to be passed back and forth from the mouth of the very individual being discussed.

"The point," I said, "is that we will be together on that river a long time—for many weeks. In close quarters. It's a matter of the personal chemistry of the people involved, which has nothing to do with competence."

Both of them, I could see, were taken aback.

"We can talk about it on the trip to Kachug," Bychkov said. Evidently he meant to go with us, after all.

"Valentin won't be needed for Kachug," I said.

"Oh?" said Bychkov. "But you will need an interpreter there."

"I have someone else in mind."

Bychkov raised his eyebrows and twitched his little mustache.

"As you prefer," he said.

"As you prefer," repeated Valentin in English, dismayed to find himself abandoned so easily by his friend for the friend's own convenience.

ELEVEN

W E'RE NORTHBOUND OVER A road that becomes more broken hour by hour, our cargo of people and bags lurching and colliding in the back of the ancient minibus. Stop at noon in a town that is the administrative center for the Buryat tribespeople of the region. Bland food in a dismal cafeteria, flies humming in swarms through the open window and collecting on the broad Mongoloid faces that fix upon our group with a somnolent curiosity.

As we cross a lobe of the steppe—tawny grass and few trees—Sergei Orlov, the museum door guard, points through the window to a distant cluster of low mounds or hills.

"It was a sacred place for the Buryat people," he says, "ceremonial stones and ancient petroglyphs. Then, in the time of Brezhnev, there began to be a cultural revival which the regime feared. So they came with dynamite and blew up that place." He falls silent, rocking with the movement of the bus. "It was shameful to do. It is shameful even to speak about. But I think we must speak about it. We have learned much about our history in these last years."

Then out of the grassland and into a mixed region of forest and small farming. On the left, nearby as we pass, a dozen cows are grazing in a field of ripening grain, perhaps barley—trampling down what they do not eat. The field is unfenced, and no herdsman is in sight.

"What does it mean?" I ask Sergei.

"It means simply that the grain will be lost. And no one cares. That is the trouble with this country. No one cares."

It is almost evening before we crest a last rise in the land and start down, with forest on the left-hand side, some little plots of cultivated land on the right, and a broad valley opening ahead. In the center of the valley are the roofs of a town, on the far bank of a watercourse that is crossed by a plank bridge laid over pontoons.

"It's Kachug," says Bychkov, turning to speak over the clatter of the bus.

"And the river?" I ask him.

"It's the Lena."

We leave our bags upstairs in Kachug's one small hotel, a primitive lodging which, like the one in Irkutsk, has metal cots in the hallway to bed the overflow—though one cannot imagine many casual travelers coming to such a place. Then we go outside and follow the descending street to the bridge.

Past the last wooden building the river can be seen coiling down out of the dark-furred Baikal Mountains. Burnished gold by the late sun, it curves onto the flat of the valley, approaches the town, then flows with audible force—running clear as vodka over an unsilted pebble bed—under the pontoon bridge and on between the flanking hills toward its distant Arctic destination. It's a powerful moment, to see for the first time a river you have dreamed for so long and to find that it does not just satisfy but surpasses your expectations.

If the Lena is this splendid here, where it has hardly more than begun, what must it become after traveling another thousand miles? Another two thousand, and more?

My feet, quickening, carry me down the steep bank, tripping and sliding on stones that are rounded by millenia of tumbling. Crouching at the edge, I plunge my cupped hands into a current cold as the memory of winter, or the expectation of winter to come, and fling the water over myself, wetting my head and jacket. I do this with powerful emotion. The others are watching, and of course I know they are watching. So I cannot be sure afterward how much of this little performance is genuine, and how much calculated theater. Surely it's some of both.

I am with Sergei, now, and the young woman he lives with and means to marry, whose name is Victoria. Vicka, he calls her. We are walking along the river's edge outside Kachug, through the blueness that soon will be night. Vicka is a small, blonde girl, so slender as almost to be frail. When they met, she was a child of a tiny village in the *taiga* somewhere near Bratsk, so timid that she scarcely could speak. He brought her to the "great" city, Irkutsk, and he has begun to teach her English. She understands some, he says, but is afraid to say the words aloud. They are both souls out of place and time, Sergei told me on the bus while she slept. And she has agreed to share his life beyond the pale. Already he speaks of her as his wife.

I REMEMBERED HOW GENTLY he'd held her as we lurched through the dusty afternoon on the awful road. And the idea came to me in that moment, fully formed.

"There's something I want you to consider," I told him.
"Yes?"
"I would like you to be the interpreter for our expedition."
He halted, shoulders slumped, as if I'd struck him a blow.
"I couldn't!" he gasped.
"Why not? Your English is good enough."
"But I speak slowly. I am not professional."
"It isn't speed that's important. You understand the complexity of language. You know the weight of ideas."
He strode on, much agitated, his ungainly long legs devouring the river bank as though to put distance between himself and my threatening proposal.
"I would have to leave Vicka. And it would put me in contact again with the world, of which I'm afraid. Then perhaps you would give me some money, of which I'm also afraid. Money ruins everything."
"Yes, I understand what you're saying," I told him. "But it's not just yourself to consider. There is Vicka, and the things she might need—things you would want her to have. I agree, money can be a problem. But it also can be a means of safety."
"It could be. But it makes me feel strange, even to talk about it. If I were to do this thing at all, it would not be for the money. It would be for the thing itself, and for what I might learn about my own nature. Anyone who makes such a journey must come back changed."
"You'll think about it, then?"
"How can I *not* think about it?"
The girl, Vicka, was looking first at one then the other of us as we spoke. Some of it, I think, she understood.
"I need someone I can trust absolutely," I told Sergei. "Someone who will be my eyes and my ears in this strange place."
"I'm frightened by it," he said. "But, yes, I will consider."

⌘

OLGA AND VICKA ARE in a room together. Four of the men—Bychkov, Misha, Sergei and I—are on cots in a kind of chilly dormitory. The driver sleeps on a seat of the bus. And the photographer, who has taken a cold and wants privacy, is installed alone in the only room with a toilet. The facility for the rest of us is a crusted horror at the end of the hall.

On Thursday morning we go to talk with an official at the Lena Boat Company, a river man with whom the expedition must eventually deal if it is to get a boat of the Zaria type, or any other type. He is busy, and not especially friendly. Kachug used to be a thriving river port, full of shipping enterprises and the racket of river men carousing through its streets. But timbering in the mountains has changed the snowmelt patterns, so that the spring run-off, instead of being released gradually, comes through in a brief, violent flood, often taking out the floating bridge that is the town's one link with the world, then rushing on so that the river quickly falls. The uppermost point of Lena navigation has receded a hundred miles or more downstream, and Kachug is a sad backwater. If we hope to travel this upper river, we must plan to pass Kachug between the 20th day of June and the 10th day of July, the boat company man says. After that, the water will be gone.

In the afternoon we drive several miles out of town to where Bychkov wants to show us some petroglyphs on a cliff beside the Lena, in a place where he claims excavations have yielded evidence of continuous human habitation for 140,000 years. The cliff markings are so faint that we are able to discern them only by the outlines drawn in pencil by a team of Russian archaeologists who came here a year ago to make photographs. While we scramble along the ledge, Bychkov, Vicka and the driver are busy with a great harvest of fat yellow mushrooms—a prized variety found only in the autumn. They have gathered several large plastic sacks full.

The mushrooms provide the only real comradeship of the Kachug trip. Bychkov takes charge with enthusiasm, and makes a collective project of cleaning and cooking them. We work in the chambermaid's room downstairs, using her faucet and hotplate. The people of the hotel are amused, and a little Gypsy boy watches. The mushrooms boil a long time in two great kettles, cooking down to make a thick, dark gravy. We carry the kettles upstairs and all gather in the dormitory room to eat mushrooms and tear off chunks of coarse bread to dip up the sauce.

The water in the whole hotel has gone out, so there is no way to use the common bathroom which is broken, seatless, and may be unusable anyway. Lack of drinking water is a problem. For periods the lights, too, have gone off, then flickered on again, but the water will be out for the whole night. It is very late, now, and the others are asleep. I am talking at the end of the dark hall, by the window, with Sergei and the little Gypsy boy, who is 15 years old and travels with his parents all over the country to sell *babushkas*, or head scarves, and cheap sweaters. The Romany people used to travel by caravan, but now in most places it's forbidden, he says, and in Siberia impossible. So they carry their wares by plane, train and bus. They will stay in Kachug for a few days, then move on to somewhere.

I ask him about his life. Is it hard? No, he says, it is *normal*, which in Russian means okay. He has never been to school. He likes winter best. "You come home at night, and there is a fire. Or you can go to ski. In summer it is too hot, and what is there to do? You might have a chance to go to the movie, or perhaps eat an ice cream. But winter is much the best."

The boy asks what I know about the lives of Romany people in other parts of the world. I tell him about how the Gypsies come in the fall to Paris and gather with their caravans in a great encampment in the Bois de Boulogne. He whistles softly between his teeth. I tell him how the Gypsies in the United States make a convention each year to elect their king. *A king?* he says. *For Gypsies?* He cannot imagine it. He presses his eyes closed, trying to deal with this multiplicity of wonders.

The sky outside the window is dusted bright with the numberless suns of the universe that contains us all, as we talk a long time into the night—a man far from home and full of worries, and a child whose tribespeople are citizens of nowhere, the notions of both of them filtered through an embittered mystic who is determined to live apart. No history connects us and yet, by the accident of being awake together in that strange place and solemn hour, we seem very close.

TWELVE

A ND STILL THE MATRYOSHKA had one more face to show.

༄

W E ARE BACK IN Irkutsk, with the road dust scrubbed off and installed again in our hotel across the square from the airport, from where we leave early tomorrow morning back to Moscow. Misha and Olga have gone off into the town to talk with some geological group about the possibility of hiring one of their helicopters at a more favorable price.

Now the deplorable Valentin resurfaces, with his little friend, Ivan, in tow. There is something more he would like to say about the Oleg question, and I go with him to an apartment he and Ivan are caretaking for a professor acquaintance—a small, crowded, bookish flat. Ivan withdraws to the kitchen to cook a pan of sour, fried biscuits and make a pot of tea.

༄

T HE PERSPIRATION STOOD OUT like beads of oil on his heavy, unpleasant face and among the hairs of his beard. His eyes were wide with astonishment at the thing he was about to do.

"You can see for yourself," began Valentin, "that it is finished between Oleg and the Muscovites. That must be obvious, even to you."

I disliked him more than I had before.

"There is the possibility to do it with Oleg. But Oleg will not consider the upper river. He says it is impossible."

Ivan brought the biscuits on a plate, and the tea, and sat in a chair with his hands folded. Valentin took the long breath of a swimmer before a dangerous dive.

"*But Oleg is wrong. That part of the river is possible,*" Valentin said, his voice whiny and breathless, the words starting to tumble over one another in haste.

"I have talked to a friend who knows that place. He said it can be done—he has done it before. It can be arranged."

"Can it?"

"Yes, certainly. If Oleg refuses."

"And who does the arranging?"

"My friend. He and I. We have the possibility to make every-thing for you." He sat back then and mopped his face, relieved to have gotten it out. "What do you think?"

What I was thinking was how strange this country was, and how disfigured some of its people had become through so long a history of deceit.

✥

UP AT 4:30 A.M. Breakfast of saved bread, cookies, tea made in the cups with an immersion coil in Misha and Olga's room. Their beds are side by side now in the sleeping alcove, and the privacy blanket is down. Those two clearly have found a happy accommodation. Misha's eyes are even more spaniel-like.

One of the endearing virtues of the Russians is the way they carry their little comforts with them. A bit of black tea. A few cubes of sugar. Something edible wrapped in a scrap of paper. If they have water and an electrical outlet, they can make a party. And no one shares more willingly. (Nothing more will be heard, this trip or ever, about the girlfriend, poor Kristina, whose vacation to the Black Sea enabled her to share more than she knew.)

The plane lifts out of Irkutsk in darkness and races the sunrise westward. It is a long flight, with time to sort out the confusion of this week.

I know, even if the Institute in Moscow doesn't yet, that there is no hope of Oleg Bychkov's cooperation, and that's probably to the good. It will be necessary in some tactful way to make this clear to Valery Tishkov. The problem will be his, not mine, to solve. I had hoped to leave Moscow with everything known, with all the details settled. But that's not how it will be. If anything, the uncertainties have multiplied. The plane makes its turn over Moscow and the bend of the river spread out below. After the road to Kachug, Misha says, he thinks he is coming into Paris. And the Uzkoe Hotel, a further long step up from the one in Irkutsk, could be the Ritz.

Monday, to a meeting with my old friend, George Isachenko, whose secretary serves sandwiches on the coffee table in his office. He is disappointed that I'm going forward in this partnership with the Institute, and remains doubtful that they can do what they promise. "Be careful," he says. "About everything, you must be very careful. But especially about any contracts. Sign nothing unless you are sure."

He will be in the U.S. again in November, and if the collaboration with the Institute is not working out as I hope, we will talk again. I ask how things are with Musa. He remains worried. After months, the problem of her heart still has not been clarified.

Valery Tishkov comes with Misha and Olga to the hotel in early evening. Sitting on the bed and on chairs in my room, we go over in detail the understandings reached in hours of night discussions in Irkutsk and Kachug: the costs of all we will require, the timetable for the expedition written out day-by-day on a yellow pad, the question of doing, or not doing, the uppermost river. My selection of Sergei Orlov as the interpreter, and the difficulty of dealing with Bychkov.

Tishkov takes from his coat pocket the envelope with all my money still in it. He asks if I will carry it back with me and open a U.S. bank account for the Institute. "We will use it to buy equipment we need," he says, "and for expenses of our scholars when they travel to meetings." Then we go to a dinner he has arranged in a private alcove above the hotel dining room. Tishkov talks frankly, openly, about the political situation. He believes that Gorbachev's usefulness is finished—that he has made his contribution, and now it is time for someone else. Conditions in the country are difficult, but not so difficult—not yet, anyway—that we cannot make this expedition work.

On the next afternoon's Air France plane my thoughts all race ahead to Jennie, my younger daughter. She is 20, and has taken time out from college to go back to Paris for a year to study drawing and painting. Settling in has been an ordeal for her. Apartments are hard to find, and fiercely expensive—most of them beyond her frugal budget. One morning she got up before dawn to get the newspaper listings and went at 6 o'clock to answer an ad that sounded reasonable. There were 60 people already ahead of her in the line.

After three months, she still has not gotten a place of her own. Mr. George Whitman at Shakespeare and Co. bookstore, where she worked part-time before her painting class began told her that in an emergency she could use a room above the store. But for now she is living in a borrowed flat—one tiny room and bath. After four months, I'm eager to see her and buoy her spirits if I can. We have one night in Paris before flying on to New York and home.

⚜

"YOU'LL PROBABLY BE MORE comfortable staying in a hotel," I said. "Jennie's place is awfully small."

"That's all right," the photographer replied.

"No, I mean *really* small. It's just one little room."

"I don't mind." He didn't know Paris, and may have been afraid about finding his way.

We went that night to a Greek restaurant off the Place Saint-Michel, one we used to visit when we lived there—merry and cheap. That is, it *was* cheap. With the dollar gotten anemic, even a cup of coffee at a table on the street had come to cost as much as we used to pay for a meal. Three is an awkward number. There was no time to really talk. We walked back to her place through the night crowd of the Quarter and took the cage elevator up.

The photographer, still suffering a cold, was given the room's one cot. Jennie and I wrapped ourselves in blankets on the floor, which was chilly and incredibly hard. Maybe I slept a little. Mostly I remember sitting on the window ledge, smoking, looking down into the empty street, the problems of the expedition turning in mind while I prayed for light to come.

The two of us went in the morning to the *brasserie* she frequented.

"I'm sorry about the bed," she said.

"It doesn't matter."

"Once, when you'd finally gotten to sleep for a few minutes, you began to snore a little. He reached down from the bed with his arm and shook you awake."

I didn't remember.

We finished our coffees and croissants, then walked together along the known streets, talking in the little time we had. The photographer had gone off alone with his camera on the chance of finding some worthwhile subject.

"How did it go in Russia?" she asked.

"I don't know yet," I told her truthfully. "I won't until I've had a chance to think it through."

"But do you believe the expedition will really happen?"

"Right now, if I had to bet, I guess I'd say it was even money either way."

III

Acts of Faith

(Winter-Spring 1991)

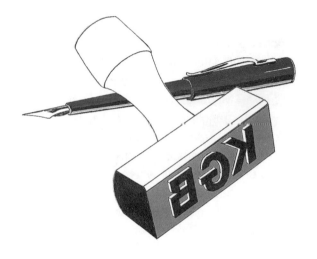

THIRTEEN

TISHKOV HAD HOPED TO have the KGB's permission for the expedition by summer's end. But the KGB was silent. He was not so concerned, he'd said as I was leaving Moscow, because the Academy of Sciences wasn't without influence. Certainly, he believed, official approval would be received by sometime in the fall.

From early autumn through middle January, Tishkov will be at the Huntington Library in San Marino, California, doing research on the early Russian commercial and colonial presence in North America, and also U.S. involvement in gold mining ventures in Siberia which began under the Czars and continued for several years into the Soviet era.

For a month, late September to late October, I'm away from the paper, leading a seminar for young writers at Baylor University in Waco, Texas. Mornings, before class, and again for three hours each evening, I struggle with the language tapes, trying to get some rudimentary grasp of Russian. I also write a report of the reconnaissance, and prepare for Tishkov a document summarizing in detail my understanding of where we stand after the visit to Irkutsk, and the basis on which we'll proceed. Copies are posted both to him in California and to the Institute in Moscow.

There's a conversation about the project in early November with the publisher of *The Star*. What will it cost? he asks. I tell him. The newspaper will cover part of it, he says, but only part. There'll have to be other backing as well. And that's reasonable. Newspapers are not in the habit of mounting major foreign expeditions. I have spoken already with an acquaintance in a large Kansas City-based company about the possibility of corporate sponsorship. He seemed receptive, but with the economy turning sour it is a poor time to be knocking on doors.

What about ABC? the publisher asks. The network is owned by the same company that owns *The Star*, but I have no idea where even to start there. He picks up his phone and speaks to his friend in New York, head of the company's broadcasting division, and gets the name of a producer in Washington, Dennis Kane, who makes documentaries on contract for the network. It's agreed I should go to Washington to explore possibilities of financing from that or some other broadcast or publishing source. But Kane is traveling outside the country. What's more, we're getting on now toward the holiday season, and it turns out appointments can't be arranged until sometime in January.

January 14.

Morning meeting with Dennis Kane. He's cordial, and thinks the project is interesting, but seems a little unclear about why I've turned up in his office. I'm not a filmmaker, and he's therefore skeptical that we'd get anything usable for broadcast. Of course he'd be willing to look at what we bring back from the river, he says, but it's nothing he'll put any money into.

Lunch with Bill Dickinson, Washington Post Writers Group, an old acquaintance, to try the idea of sending out a series of journal-type pieces through the summer as the expedition proceeds. That could be wonderful reading, he agrees. But it's a one-time thing, out of the syndicate's normal run of ongoing features. And it could conflict with a new regular column they're planning to start from Moscow.

Calls in afternoon to a contact in New York, who has sounded out a couple of book publishers. They are interested, but the kind of advances they might be willing to make won't begin to dent the cost.

January 15.

To National Geographic Television. Again, coffee and cookies but no encouragement. Their current format is inflexible: three 20-minute segments in the hour program, with each segment on a different subject and built around one central character. In what I'm proposing, *the river* is the main character—and it can't be traveled in 20 minutes.

Then to the last and most humbling failure of all, at National Public Radio, for an 11 o'clock appointment with one of the NPR producers. I have sent her two weeks before a detailed proposal for a series of short, firsthand reports—interviews, description and the like—following the adventure from its spring beginning in the mountains to its autumn end on the Arctic coast, catching the sense of the place, the turning seasons, and the people met along the way. The tapes will have to be gotten out from the river at intervals by helicopter and hand-delivered by courier to Moscow for relay to the U.S. But in talking about this with the Russians, it seems it could be possible.

⚜

"GOD, IT'S A GOOD thing you came early," she said, looking at her watch. "Because I have another 11 o'clock." It was seven minutes before the hour.

Her breathless tone was meant to convey her incredible busyness, and also to suggest how very lucky I was to be even her *spare* 11 o'clock.

"You'll recall I sent you a—"

"Yes, I know you did. You sent some kind of paper." The heavy, round-faced young woman made a desultory gesture toward the mounded clutter of her desk. "It's here somewhere."

"What I'm proposing is a series of river journals from Siberia."

"That just wouldn't interest us," she said. "We're a news program."

"But I thought—"

"It's just not the kind of thing we'd do."

Fine, I wanted to tell her. But where I come from, people would have the manners to say that in a telephone call, instead of letting someone travel halfway across the country to get the news. But then, no one I know is a 30-year-old broadcasting whiz with her finger on the pulse of the world and her jaws clamped on the public tit.

It was plain she'd already moved on in her mind to other, bigger things.

"It's kind of crazy around here," she said, "with everything that's happening in the Gulf." President Bush's deadline for

Saddam Hussein to begin a withdrawal from Kuwait was only hours from expiring.

"I'm pretty involved in that." Her confidential tone implied that, if war came, she would be personally dive-bombing Baghdad. "So if you'll excuse me." She dismissed me by standing.

It was plain that her *real* 11 o'clock had to do with something that mattered, and she didn't want me in the way.

⚜

I FLY HOME THIS evening with nothing accomplished, nothing in hand. Waiting in the mail is an envelope posted by Tishkov on his last day before returning to Moscow. In it is the memorandum of understanding I'd sent him, with notations of a few small changes he wants made. They have mostly to do with finances—not the total sum, but shifting some of the amounts to give greater incentive to the people in Irkutsk.

What people? I wonder. Not, surely, Bychkov.

In his accompanying letter, Tishkov tells that Misha and Olga have been back again to Irkutsk in December, and have already written a subcontract with an organization there that will help prepare the expedition at its start. "With all our unrest and crisis," he writes, "I am really concerned to be completely sure that the Institute will provide all possible service and assistance, and at this moment I believe we can do it." He asks that I make a final version of the "contract" and send it to him in Moscow by fax.

The next night, on January 16, American warplanes launch an attack on Baghdad, and the Persian Gulf conflict has begun. In the excitement of the days to follow, it is unlikely anyone in Washington will give further thought to a newspaperman from Kansas City who came to bother them with some harebrained proposition about traveling a Siberian river.

FOURTEEN

I REALIZE THAT IN conversations with friends, with colleagues at the office, and in the talks I give to various public groups, I have begun to speak of the expedition as something that is going to happen. It's as if these declarations will make the fiction true. I can't explain it otherwise. But I know it is foolhardy, and each time afterwards I feel ashamed and a little frightened.

In late January I have to go to Wichita to talk to a state meeting of Kansas newspaper editors. The Coleman Company—maker of the lanterns several generations of Americans have lit their camps by and the stoves we've turned our flapjacks over—is based in Wichita. I have made an appointment with Jim Reid, an official of the company.

The highway south is treacherous from a blizzard that has blown in off the plains, and I am late to the meeting at Coleman. Reid is an outdoorsman, a quail hunter devoted to good dogs, so we have that in common. He's also a careful man, whose face is unreadable as I spread out the map and speak of the great river and my reasons for wanting to travel it. I'm afraid I have talked too fervidly and too long. Reid sits silently for several moments, looking at the map and then finally at me.

❧

"YES," HE SAID THEN. "It sounds like something we'd want to be involved in."

That decisively! The defeats 10 days before in Washington made his words all the more remarkable.

"Whatever we have, you're welcome to take in whatever quantity you need. If it's not in the warehouse here, we can send it directly to Moscow from our inventory in Germany."

"Understand," I said, "I'll be leaving it all behind at the end, for the Russians to use. Nothing will come back."

"That's even better." He led the way from his office down a corridor to the factory display area. Tents, canoes, lanterns, stoves, cooking and mess gear, coolers and storage chests, sleeping bags—

everything we could need was there.

"You're loose in the toy store. Have a look around. I'll give you some catalogs to take with you, and when you've made your decisions you can send me a list. Maybe I'll have some suggestions. The only thing I'd ask," Reid said, "is that you take ours if we make it. If we don't, I'll see if I can help."

Still stunned, I looked around the large display room.

"Except for food—"

"We don't do food."

"—I can't imagine anything except a water filter—"

"I can give you a name."

"—and outboard motors."

"I have a friend at Yamaha," Reid said. "I'll put in a call."

❧

(WITHIN A FORTNIGHT, THE first cartons will arrive from Wichita, and there will begin accumulating in the warehouse across the street from the newspaper what will grow finally into a mountain of 3,400 pounds of equipment and supplies—*for an expedition that I have neither the permission nor the money to undertake.*)

From Reid I go to the luncheon with the editors, then back to the motel to lie down a while before trying the icy five-hour drive home.

The chest pains come more often now, and at unexpected times. Several hours or sometimes a whole day will pass and I am able almost to forget them. Then they come again with a sharpness that breaks a sudden sweat. Lying on the motel bed doesn't help this time. So I resort to the one crazy method of relief I have found—doing situps and pushups on the floor of the room. It may not be explainable or even sensible, but after I have done that the discomfort usually is less.

FIFTEEN

I HAVE BEGUN READING THE journal of the DeLong expedition. The main city library cannot locate its only circulating copy, either on the shelves or in the basement where old and seldom-called-for books are stored. Evidently it has been stolen—although it's a mystery what would have led anyone to pilfer so arcane a document.

It's no matter. I have persuaded the librarians to let me borrow the copy from the noncirculating collection. It was published in Boston in 1883 by Houghton, Mifflin and Company, and consists of two heavy volumes totaling 911 pages, with maps, prints from wood, stone and steel engravings, and is handsomely bound with a dramatic illustration of the ship on the books' embossed leather covers.

"At 10 a.m. inspected the ship and crew, and found everything neat and tidy," Lt. George Washington DeLong writes in his log for Sunday, July 13, 1879. *"Clear and pleasant weather; smooth sea."* But his ship, the Arctic steamer *Jeannette* is only in its sixth day out of San Francisco, bearing north. And the nightmare has not yet begun.

⁂

THE CARDIOLOGISTS' OFFICE WAS spacious, sunny, and richly appointed as you would expect for a specialty that generates such a stupendous flow of fees. People whose pumps have gone bad will pay almost anything for a reprieve—or their insurers will.

The couches and lounge chairs were full of such folks, all with a frightened look. I sat there turning the pages of a travel magazine, feeling out of place among them. The pains, my own doctor had assured me, were from acute indigestion brought on by stress. All the same, he'd said, considering my plans for summer, it might be well to do a treadmill test. So I'd just run on the machine— longer and faster and steeper than a man of my age and sedentary habits had any right to do. And I was waiting now for the specialist to inspect the chart and offer his congratulations.

Time passed. I read a second magazine. The invalids came

and went. My name was called.

"We have an abnormality," the doctor said.

He was a young, humorous-looking fellow with a red mustache and an easy manner.

"What do you mean, *an abnormality?*"

"Major blockage of one or more arteries," he said, measuring the effect of his words. And the effect was dazzling. I had the queer sensation that I was observing this conversation from outside my body, somewhere in a far corner of the room.

"How serious is that?"

"How serious? Well, there's no way of knowing until we get a better look. But I'd rate the chances of a fatal heart attack at somewhere between ten and fifteen percent within a year."

Perhaps you wonder—I had—about the grace with which one reacts to such an announcement. I can say from experience that you don't react at all. You just sit woodenly, speechless, like someone who's taken a blow to the head.

"It's possible we can get by with balloon angioplasty. Or it might require bypass surgery."

"But I don't have time for that!" I croaked, trying to collect myself. "I have a major project planned for summer."

He smiled under his mustache.

"People never think they have time. But after we've taken a look their feelings about it usually change."

I asked what he meant by *taking a look.*

"We'll do an angiogram—run a catheter directly up into the coronary arteries to see exactly what the problem is. You're in the hospital one day and out the next."

"And that's the definitive test?"

"Absolutely."

"How soon can we do it?"

"Check with the secretary out front. She ought to be able to schedule you for sometime next week."

The heart cases out in the waiting room seemed less feeble and pathetic, now that I'd learned I was one of them.

JAMES GORDON BENNETT, FLAMBOYANT publisher of the *New York Herald*, wanted an encore for the international splash he'd made when his reporter, Stanley, found Livingstone in the Congo. Young Lt. DeLong, had an abiding passion to explore the Arctic. Their ambitions met in fatal combination. Bennett provided the ship and financed the expedition. The U.S. Navy, not without some misgivings, supplied most of the thirty-three men aboard, the 35-year-old DeLong commanding.

Their mission was to pass northward through the Bering Straits and on into the Arctic Ocean in an attempt to reach a goal that had eluded men to that day, the North Pole. Of crew members who set forth up the California coast on the *Jeannette* that sunny afternoon in July, only twelve would live to see their homes again.

By the first of September, the ship was progressing cautiously through gathering ice. By September 6, she was locked in the drifting pack, where she would remain imprisoned for the next 22 months—through the agony of two whole Arctic winters—while provisions dwindled and sickness and bitter enmities broke out among her crew. On June 12, 1881, a month short of two years since she'd left San Francisco, the *Jeannette* was crushed and sunk. Stranded with his ragged company, three small boats, sleds and sled dogs and provisions salvaged from the broken ship, DeLong determined to strike southwestward across the ice and occasional leads of open water and try to reach land in the delta of the Lena River. The expedition was a failure. But if they could reach a native settlement there before another winter caught them, they could survive.

⚜

THE MAN IN THE next bed was only 42, but he'd already had one heart attack and was afraid of what they'd find.

"I get quite a bit of pain," he said. "But I can live with that. They want to do a bypass, but I just don't want them cutting on me, no matter what this shows."

They wheeled us down together to the prep room. Getting a catheter stuck in your heart is a lot like going in for an oil change and lube. It runs right on schedule. His test was 10 minutes before mine, and we were all lined up on rolling carts, some waiting to go in, others just coming out.

I thought of the *Jeannette,* and how there were a lot worse places to be than in a hospital. I also was thinking about the river project, and how many problems there were to solve—above all the problem of financing. If I'd gotten myself into something I couldn't finish, being certifiably sick would at least be a way to back out without too much humiliation.

⁂

H E MUST HAVE BEEN a young man of great inner resources, DeLong, though perhaps too inflexible, as some later charged. With 500 miles to cross to the Siberian mainland, he determined his men must travel by night—such "night" as there is at the 77th north latitude in summer—and sleep by day to avoid snow blindness.

The hours for rising, meals, rest breaks and sleeping were rigidly fixed and enforced. Each day he held a kind of inspection, at which the physical condition of each man was noted, and the remaining provisions inventoried. At the end of July the bedraggled party made brief landfall at a stony, mountainous island. Although it was barren, occupied mainly by gulls and unable to sustain life, DeLong claimed it for the United States and named the place Bennett island, after the man who'd bankrolled their catastrophe. The gravel spit on which they'd first stepped he called Cape Emma, for his wife.

⁂

T HE CARDIOLOGIST AND NURSE assistants are specialists in the procedure. They perform it many times a day, hundreds of times in a year. Their relationship with the patient wheeled under the light of the surgical theater is as impersonal as the relationship between the mortician and a corpse—except that, in this case, the corpse has a pulse, and looks up at them with some alarm.

The catheter itself is most of a yard long. It is introduced through an artery at the groin, and run up through the vessel to the heart itself. Because the interior walls of arteries are without nerves, no sensation could be felt. All I noticed was the movement of the surgeon's arm as he inserted the rod—the same motion, and as casual, as a mechanic using a dip stick to check the oil in a bull-dozer.

❦

ON SEPTEMBER 12, CAUGHT in a violent gale as they approached the Lena's mouth, the three boats were separated. What happened to one of them will never certainly be known. The second was blown far to eastward, gained the shore near a huddle of native huts, and those it carried were saved. The third, with DeLong and 13 of his men, also reached land, grounding finally in the muck of the delta, but nowhere near any habitation.

With winter bearing down and the temperature plummeting, two men, the strongest, were dispatched ahead, eventually made contact with a native hunter, and survived. The other 12 struggled on to the south, weakening by the day, looking for the village they never found. Before that ghastly march ended, they had killed and eaten their one remaining sled dog. Some of them had eaten their boots, stumbling through the snow on feet frozen blue.

❦

"IT WASN'T ANYTHING!" THE man in the next bed said. "I didn't feel a thing. How'd yours go?" We were like new mothers comparing notes on childbirth, and I could hear the nervousness in his voice. His wife was with him, and he was waiting for the cardiologist to come in with the report.

They pulled the curtain divider between the beds for privacy, but I could hear the doctor telling him.

"Here's a diagram of the heart and arteries," he said. "And I've marked where the problems are. In four major arteries you have blockages of one hundred percent, eighty percent, sixty percent and fifty percent."

I could hear my roommate groan. His wife didn't say any-thing.

"We'll need to schedule you for bypass surgery."

"Aw, Christ!"

"I know," the doctor said. "But you really don't have any choice."

⋙⋘

"**O**CTOBER 23RD, SUNDAY," READS an entry in DeLong's journal. *"One hundred and thirty-third day. Everybody pretty weak. Slept or rest-ed all day, and then managed to get enough wood in before dark. Read part of divine service. Suffering in our feet. No foot gear."*

Every day he wrote, in a careful hand made steady by his stub-born will. The entries record the deaths by ones and twos.

October 30 is the last. *"140th day,"* it says. *"Boyd and Gortz died during night. Mr. Collins dying."* A rescue party reached that place in March. DeLong was lying on his side, partly buried in snow, his journal beside him and one arm and hand upraised. It was said that even after five months they did not look like dead men. The Siberian cold had preserved the color in their faces.

⋙⋘

A FEW MINUTES LATER MY doctor, a different one, came in the room. Katie squeezed my hand. He was carrying the same heart diagram, and I remember that it was printed on yellow paper. I craned my neck to see it, so I could at least have a preview of the news.

There weren't any marks at all on the diagram.

"It's fairly unusual with men," the doctor said. "More often it happens with women." I knew they were listening on the other side of the curtain.

"But sometimes we get a false reading on the treadmill."

That was the good news. The other part of it was that now there was no graceful way out of what I'd gotten into.

SIXTEEN

TIME RUNS THROUGH MY fingers now like water. And the problem of money haunts every waking thought. I speak again with the possible corporate sponsor, but the conversation is inconclusive. The economy has worsened; profits have taken a dive. Anyway, the venture remains uncertain, since official permission from the KGB still has not been received. He says to let him know when that is in hand. Without it, I know perfectly well, my case for support is weak.

A friend arranges a luncheon with two business/social contacts who might be of help. One heads a major foundation and the other is wealthy from the recent sale of a business enterprise. It is a pretty luncheon at a pretty club, and I feel shabby and desperate in their company, but I spread my map and give my peroration.

Siberian expeditions don't fit in his foundation's concerns, says the first man. But he has an idea. Why not get American Express to underwrite it? I could charge the whole affair on my gold card, and they could use the pictures in their ads. The president of American Express is a friend of his, he says, and he'll call him about it— although I know absolutely that he won't.

The second man has a different inspiration. What I should do, he says, is invite a bunch of well-heeled men—fellows like himself, presumably—to go along on the river and split the cost between them. It ought to be a cinch, he says, since a hundred thousand bucks really isn't much money. (Evidently I have failed to make clear the rigors of the journey.)

The friend who arranged the luncheon is someone I have known for years, and means well. A further thought occurs to her. Her organization has as one of its clients a major brewery. They sponsor sporting events. Why not this expedition? I should understand, though, that advertisers want their money's worth. It would mean, at a minimum, painting the main ship the brewery's colors, with the company logo and possibly a mural-sized beer can on the side.

This struggle has taken on a goofy, dreamlike quality. Meantime, another page falls from the calendar. We are into

March. On the month's 12th day, the fax machine at my newspaper office hums to life and scrolls out the first page of a lengthy document from Moscow.

> *Dear Charles,*
> *I would like to inform you that we have received the agreement which you prepared. It is quite satisfactory excluding some details that are not significant and can be discussed in letters.*
> *All main points of your reading of the agreement remain valid. But we have to change only the form of the agreement in order to bring it in conformity with the demands of our legislation and of our official bodies.*
> *I send for you our reading of the agreement. As for concrete details of the trip, they are described minutely in the letter I'll send you with one of my acquaintances who is going to post it from the U.S. on March 13-15...*

Valery Tishkov's cover letter goes on to say that, because of the breakdown of order and the worsening need in the U.S.S.R., he fears much of the expedition equipment could simply disappear if we trust it to internal airline baggage handling. He now thinks it safer to plan on traveling from Moscow to Siberia by rail, carrying as much as we can in the train compartments and sending the rest on a sealed car after us.

He asks that I read his rendering of the agreement, sign both the English and Russian versions, and return them as quickly as possible. Then the machine begins issuing the final document. My draft to him had been headed, "Memorandum of Understanding," which I'd imagined less binding. His, although it contains essentially the same matter, is framed as a formal contract. The Russian text ends with the seal of the Institute, his signature and a place for mine. Then the English text begins coming through. After one page and part of a second the machine hesitates. The connection to Moscow is broken.

It's after midnight there. His fax machine can't be raised in a dozen tries. I dictate a short cable, saying I'll have to wait for the copy his friend is carrying to mail. The English text stopped in the section titled "Obligations of the Parties"—obligations I still have no means to meet. I'm glad for even a few days' delay, but the reprieve is short. A week later a large envelope comes postmarked from New York. I open it, and turn to the last page of the English translation.

Should one of the parties break their obligations, the final paragraph reads, *it must recover to the other party the losses caused by this breaking.*

Tishkov is a careful man. I know that he already has entered into several smaller contracts in Irkutsk. Now, before he signs the big ones, he wants to be sure he's covered. I don't blame him. He can't know that his American partner is operating mostly on hope. But he is taking no chances. I lay the dangerous papers aside, unsigned.

And the sleepless nights begin.

I'm afraid to lie on the bed, because the nightmares only amplify the facts, which are themselves unbearable enough. I am learning, if I didn't already know it, the importance of passing through life with a partner—someone you can turn to and touch when the darkness and the alarms come crowding, and who will say, against all reason, "You've gotten this far. Surely it will work out—somehow." Katie, for me, has been that partner.

Mostly I sit, smoking, in a chair in the dark bedroom and turn it endlessly in mind. What binding force could such a contract have? That isn't really the point, though, is it? What would be the cost, in humiliation and dishonor, of having to confess to Tishkov, in the last hour, that I'd failed miserably at my end? *Insupportable,* is what that would be. It's still possible the KGB's permission will not be gotten. But if it is, I haven't any choice.

In the darkness of the silent room I do the mental addition: the equity in our house, and in a piece of country land I care a lot about. Even, in desperate humor, the value of my bird dog, Rufus. But would I do that? Have I any right to do it? The idea frightens me, and I push it aside.

⊱❦⊰

TWO-THIRTY A.M. IN Kansas City was already the middle of the working morning, Moscow time. A faint hissing and crackling sounded in the earpiece, then a voice came on the line. It was Tishkov, from his office in the new building of the Institute on Leninsky Prospekt. He was sorry for the hour, but the international circuit was busy until now.

Had I received the contract?

"Not all of it," I said. "The transmission was—"

"What?"

"—it was broken. I didn't get—"

He was talking, too. And our shouts collided in a garble somewhere over, or under, the Atlantic.

"I got the Russian version all right. But the English one stopped after the first page."

"So you don't have it?"

"No." It was a lie. "I'm waiting for the copy you mailed."

"I see. All right. But it's necessary to have it as soon as possible."

"I tried to tell you by fax, Valery. We couldn't get through."

"The machine should work. It works every day from Canada, from Sweden, from other places."

"Well, it doesn't work from here." That much was the truth.

"There is one other important news," Tishkov said.

"What's that?"

"About the official permission from State Security. It is final now."

"You have it?"

"Yes, I have it here. The whole schedule is approved. From the beginning of the Lena to the end, without problem."

That was the end of March. Only eight weeks remained, and the knot was drawn tight.

SEVENTEEN

PATRICK DOLAN HAS BEEN the principal friend of my middle life. The autumn of the year I lived with my family in France, he came to hunt ducks with me in the great reed marsh of Brittany, *La Grand Briere*. And when we were in Africa, he came for the sailfish that rise in August and September in the rich current that runs down from the Canaries and bends in near the coast of Senegal—fishing them with light line, from a 20-foot native canoe hewn from a log, four miles out in the Atlantic with the African coast just a low, dark brush stroke on the horizon. We have seen a lot of sunrises and sunsets together in some fine places.

I try to dismiss the terror for a couple of days with Pat at the rough cabin at the farm. We fish the pond, just coming alive to spring. And prowl the woods, following deer trails, looking for turkey sign. I can't leave it, though. Sleep comes no easier in that place of good memories. In the chilly middle of night, I sit on the screened porch with the volume turned low and try to concentrate on the Russian language tapes.

"How's it going?" he asks, as we drive the hundred miles back to the city across the waking countryside.

"The KGB approved it."

"That's wonderful. How's the money going?"

"I have part of it. Not much, but part. Don't look at my hands or you'll see how badly they shake."

"It's going to happen," he says, and we ride on silently for several minutes. Then he turns from the passenger seat. "I want mine to be the next in the bank."

In more than 35 years as a journalist I have never done anything I could not either afford myself or persuade an editor to finance. Now I'm a beggar. It is the first week of April, and I'm having breakfast with another friend, unnameable here. He is the head of a major international company, but a most uncommon man, able to separate the responsibilities and pressures of that life from his other one—a life of ideas and words and imagination. It's a friendship whose account I do not want to overdraw.

I have a big problem, I tell him, and lay out briefly the expedition's plan and purposes.

"I have to ask you to believe, as a friend, that what I'm asking for is advice. Not money." And I mean that. Or I believe that I mean it. He has been involved in many projects and he should be able to tell me how such things work, or don't work.

"All right. I believe you."

"The Russians are waiting for me to sign a contract. I don't know if it's enforceable. But it's at least morally binding. I have eight weeks—a little less now—to raise a lot of money."

"How much?" he asks, and I tell him.

"What I'm asking, I guess, is whether you think it's possible."

"What's your nut?"

"My what?"

"How much are you short?"

I add up the numbers on a napkin, and he looks at the figure.

Just offhand, he says, it ought to be possible. "What happens if you don't sign that contract?"

"It's finished."

"Let me think about this a little bit and get back to you. But I believe I'd sign."

His call comes early the next afternoon.

"It's the kind of thing a company like ours should be part of," he says. "We'll do half of what you still need." I'm dizzy at the words. And I'm remembering what I'd asked him to believe.

"I told you all I wanted was advice."

"I know you did, and I appreciate that. But this is what I think we ought to do. My advice is to take it, and go do your river."

The encouragement is huge, and the beggar is filled with new hope. But there are difficulties besides money. That same week a letter comes from Sergei Orlov in Irkutsk, the museum guard I'd persuaded to interpret for the expedition. It's obvious the malicious Bychkov has been working on him, and has poisoned him with the idea that anything done in collaboration with Moscow can only result in his being cheated and misused. Sergei's letter has an undernote of regret, but he has decided not to go with us after all.

I post a letter back to him the same day, telling him my distress and asking him to reconsider.

⚜

IN THE STATE BETWEEN napping and waking, the sound of the telephone—always at that same awful hour—came like a blow to the solar plexus. The inevitable hissing and crackling preceded the voice.

"I think you were sleeping. This is Valery Tishkov in Moscow."

"Yes, I can hear you."

"Well, Charles—I have sitting with me here in my office the people from Irkutsk with whom we have made some arrangements. We are talking about the main ship."

"Is there a problem."

"With the ship, no. There are two variants. One is a military ship, and the other a regular ship. If the regular ship is not ready in time, we will take the other one. Either way it will be okay. The problem is something else. We have made an agreement with these people, and already we have paid them a big sum of rubles. And I am still waiting from you the contract."

"It's in the mail," I told him. This time the truth. "I signed them on April 19, and sent them by express mail."

"By mail? It would be better to send by fax."

"It doesn't work."

"But it *must* work."

"It doesn't." Also the truth. "With the contracts there's a letter," I shouted into the phone. "It's a long letter, with many points covered. But there are three I'll tell you now. First, I think Bychkov is making problems in Irkutsk. If he goes at all, he has to understand he's a consultant. Nothing more. It's not his expedition."

"Bychkov...yes." Valery sounded as tired of the name as I was.

"Second, Orlov, the interpreter, has decided against it. Have the Irkutsk people try to convince him. However it turns out, we're not going to take Bychkov's friend, whose name is Valentin. If I have to, I'll find someone else when I get there. Now, the last point, which is the biggest. The size of the American party may have to be increased."

"How much increased?"

"From six to eight. There's a possibility two video people may come with us."

"It will be hard to do," Tishkov said. I could hear him break the news in Russian to the people in his office. "It will be very hard."

"We have to try. It's important."

"You have seen the type of boat yourself. Conditions will be very bad, very uncomfortable."

"Comfort doesn't matter. We may have to do it."

"In any case," Tishkov said, "we will discuss. You sent the contracts when?"

"On the 19th, express."

"It's already ten days. Very slow. You should have used fax."

✂︎

B ESIDES THE NEWSPAPER, WHICH is the largest sponsor, the other supporters are three companies and three individuals. The money is not all in hand, but the end of the begging is close—or at least in sight. It came from people I know, and was given graciously. But I feel like a bankrupt with no credit left to spend.

Meantime, there are endless details. More dry food and other provisions to assemble. A morning spent with people who come from Coleman to show us about repairing equipment in the field. In a few days the air container will be delivered to be packed, and its shipment to Moscow will have to be coordinated with the arrival there of the canoes and fuel Coleman is sending from Frankfurt.

Time accelerates. Each frantic day, the list of things undone is carried over to the next day's list. The lists become absurd. But everything on them is essential. Bug suits. Water filter. Negotiations by phone with the videographer who lives in Santa Fe. As many innoculations as one would need for a foot crossing of the Congo.

Special dietary requirements must be considered. The photographer suggests consulting the videographer again to see if he might have a preference for any particular kind of bulk granola. Our eyes widen with hysteria. We erupt! There already are a couple of hundred pounds of the stuff in the stack at the warehouse. And while there may be subtle granola nuances, that does not rank high on our list of desperate concerns.

The days just fall away like leaves, and, under the best of circumstances, we will not have time for everything.

And then comes the firestorm.

EIGHTEEN

MAY 2, THURSDAY MORNING, at the newspaper office. A call from a secretary, asking if I can meet with the executive editor, the editor in chief and the publisher in the publisher's office. "When?" I ask. And she says, "Now. They're waiting for you upstairs."

The faces arranged at the long table in the publisher's conference room are stern. Jim Hale, the publisher, speaks first from his place at the head. It seems that an executive of one of the sponsor companies, a man the publisher sees socially, has startled Hale at a party by saying something to the effect of, "What's the matter, can't you afford to send your man to Siberia? Rich as the paper is, I'm surprised we have to help you out."

Maybe it was only a graceless attempt at humor. Or maybe more than that. In any case, the publisher was embarrassed. And now he can imagine the possibility of other such gibes from those who have supported the venture. He is not so much angry as just uneasy about the awkwardness the Lena project may have created.

The editor-in-chief also raises the question of whether it presents an ethical problem for the newspaper to join other local companies in financing the expedition. It takes my breath to hear these reservations voiced at so late a date. At every step, I have kept them informed in detail—the sums of money raised, and the sources of it, and the amount of the remaining shortfall. As early as January, before any support was received, I'd had a conversation with the editor on the specific subject of ethics. Going outside the paper for funds was something I'd never before done, I told him then. And I wanted to be sure he was not uncomfortable with it. He wasn't, he said, considering the size and special nature of the project.

The issue of corporate sponsorship had seemed settled. But now, one clumsy remark to the publisher has wiped that January conversation from memory.

The executive editor considers the problem aloud. One solution, he says, could be for the paper not to publish installments of the journal sent out from the river as planned. That would avoid any implication that sponsors had underwritten work in the paper.

"I don't know," the editor says, his manner grave. "I still have problems with it."

The thing hangs in the balance in that room. What I feel in the moment is despair at all it would mean—in shame as well as money—to try to undo this now. Also real regret at the publisher's discomfiture, since he is a man I respect and like. And, finally, amazement that there should suddenly be so little recollection of all that has been considered and discussed in these preceding months. Drained and dizzy, I slump in the chair and stare at my hands, turning it all in mind.

It is one word—just one—from being ended. Because I know that if any one of them speaks the word *"No,"* the other two will have no choice but to come together in support of the decision. Fortunately, the publisher understands that, too. He is leaving in an hour, he says, to travel to Texas for his sister's funeral. The two editors and I should think the situation through and come to some recommendation among ourselves. We will meet again on Monday or Tuesday, after he returns. For the moment, the danger is circumvented.

The next two days I spend drafting and revising a detailed history of the project and argument for its continuation which, though long—several single-spaced pages—I hope they will read. I close with a summation of the situation as it now stands:

> *The departure for Moscow is scheduled for June 4. Interpreter, guides and crew have been hired on the Soviet side. The Russians even now are finishing the fitting of the main boat in Irkutsk, and very shortly it will begin its journey by rail to a point on the river some 300 miles north where it can be floated.*

Each day is critical. Airline space is reserved, cancel-
able without penalty only in the event of civil unrest.
Tonight I'm to notify the video cameraman and sound
engineer with a definite yes or no on blocking out their
summer for the project. This week the visa applications
must go out. There's a mountain of equipment in the
warehouse, with more arriving daily. Medical supplies
must be assembled. The air container has to be trucked
down from Chicago so it can be loaded out of here on
May 20.

I've lived this thing for 15 months. It has been
complex beyond my wildest imagining. My digestion is
giving me hell, and it's been a long time since I slept
through the night. Every deadline is urgent now. And I
still have the last of the money to raise.

So time is precious. If I stand still, I fall.

THE EXPRESSION OF THE editor-in-chief was even more somber than the last time we met around that table.

"I have given this a great deal of thought over the weekend," he began slowly, and paused to let his words gather weight. "I've really agonized over it. And I have to tell you that I am still—"

Well, here it comes, I thought. When you stand against the wall and hear the rifles cocked, a kind of numb resignation takes over.

But the publisher had gotten up and walked around to the far end of the table.

"*We're in this,*" he said. "And we're not going to kill it!"

The bullet was caught in mid-flight.

"We're going to do it. The only question is how." His intuition was exact, elegant. He knew how close it had been. "We have a problem, and what we have to decide is how to solve it. We've got a couple of options. One is for the paper to cover it all. How much, exactly, is involved?"

I told him again.

"That's not such a big problem," he said. "Hell, I sometimes have ten-million-dollar problems."

But it was a problem for me. I'd never intended for the newspaper to finance the whole expedition, and that had been understood from the start. There was just no way the paper could publish enough words and photographs from Siberia to justify so great an investment. And I told him so.

"I couldn't be comfortable with that. I couldn't look you in the face afterward. And I don't think I'd have any choice but to—"

"Don't say it," he said. "Don't say something you'd be sorry for. I have a long memory."

⚜

I N THE END, THE decision is to leave the financing as it stands. The paper will not publish a series from the river, and will receive only the same credit for sponsorship as the other supporters of the expedition. I will be on a leave of absence during the months of the expedition. Also, a corporation—Northbound: The Lena River Expedition, Ltd.—will be formed to handle the financial transactions, so a meeting with lawyers is added to the list of things that must be accomplished in the fleeting days.

In that afternoon's mail, there's a letter from Valery Tishkov, covering some last details. The Institute has talked further with its contacts in Siberia. They now believe the uppermost river can be negotiated on foot and by rafts, and he describes the equipment we will use. The loads to be carried over the Baikal ridge to the source should not exceed 25 or 30 kilograms—55 to 66 pounds— for each member of the six-man raft party. If necessary, porters will be found to help.

"We inform you," Tishkov writes, "that Oleg Bychkov has refused to be involved in the project." (And that's good news.) "The consulting has been taken over by researchers from the Institute of Geography in Irkutsk, having expert knowledge of the river." Finally, Tishkov advises that the raft party be vaccinated against insect encephalitis. (U.S. health authorities, however, are aware of no encephalitis prevalent in the Lena headwaters area. And, in any case, no vaccine is available in this country.)

That same night, as we are at dinner with friends, there's a call from Tishkov in Ann Arbor, Michigan, where he is taking part in a symposium. First, he says that Sergei Orlov, the interpreter, has reconsidered and will go with us after all. What's more, Tishkov has decided he would like to travel part of the river with the expedition himself, provided his wife will permit it. I'm elated, since his knowledge of the region's history will be a valuable resource.

Time accelerates even more, now, if that's possible. The video team is contracted, and equipment bought for their use. The air container arrives, is packed, and disappears on a truck. The water filter and outboard motors have not yet come, but it will be possible to get everything transported if we can manage to carry nearly 1,200 pounds among the eight of us in checked baggage. The airline grants an exception.

In the haste of all this, I've done a foolish thing. Foolish and thoughtless. Imagining that this expedition will be of interest to other news organizations in our town and possibly elsewhere, I have written and mailed out a brief description of the venture, listing a colleague in *The Star*'s special projects department as the contact while we are away. In writing it, I reached for the materials at hand, my office stationery. That was a mistake.

The rebuke from the executive editor is swift. He is a friend, and has been supportive of the expedition, but he feels betrayed by my misjudgment. The whole point of our discussions, he reminds me, has been to separate the paper from the project. "I cannot imagine," he says in his stinging letter, "that you are in any way willfully flouting the spirit of our policy. But I must say… your actions lead me to believe that you have become so single-minded about completing this expedition that you have lost sight of how any of this might reflect upon the newspaper or influence the course of your career."

Words committed to paper sometimes have a militance not altogether intended. But his central point is beyond dispute. I'm a man who's become prisoner of an obsession—a bird powerless before the snake.

Our older daughter, Anne, graduates from college in New York in late May. On the way, we stop in the town of Rochester in central Indiana for an evening with friends, Bill Wilson, the editor of the Rochester paper, and Ken Hoff, a physician. Ken has put together a comprehensive medicine chest, anticipating every illness or injury the expedition is likely to suffer.

Pushing on east, then, we meet Jennie at La Guardia Airport, burdened like a mule on her inbound flight from Paris, and drive up together to Poughkeepsie for the ceremony. There's a procession of graduates on a sunny lawn, with programs folded as fans to stir the surprising heat, followed by champagne in plastic glasses under the shade of ancient trees, and tears of young friends parting. Then a frantic rush back cross-country in two loaded cars. When we are home, only six days will remain before the expedition's departure for Moscow, by way of Minneapolis and Amsterdam. The Russian embassy in Washington still has not issued our visas.

⚜

THE CABLEGRAM, DATED MAY 23, was waiting at the office.

> *After trip to Irkutsk inform impossibility to increase American group more than six persons. Otherwise it will take considerable financial spends including renting second ship.*
>
> *Regards Tishkov.*

Exactly as I finished reading that, the phone on my desk rang. After the usual noise, I heard Misha's slow voice, grappling with the language. But a moment later the connection was broken.

The Institute's damned fax still wouldn't work. And the international phone circuits were loaded. It was nearly 3 o'clock the next morning before I finally got Tishkov on the line in Moscow.

"I have your cable," I told him. "It's too late to change."

"But it makes many difficulties."

"I don't care. We have to do it, and on one boat."

"The discomfort will be great."

"It's too late, Valery. I'm bringing eight people."

"Bring them, then. We will find a way."

IV

Divisions (early June, 1991)

NINETEEN

MOSCOW, FRIDAY, JUNE 7.

We made connections at the airport in Minneapolis with the final two members of our expedition, and also with our Russian visas, which had to be hand-carried by the flight crew on a plane from Washington. From there our journey was uneventful—or as routine as could be expected with more than a half-ton of checked baggage.

Now it's the Uzkoe hotel again, and of course raining again. And lying awake at night again, watching the clock mark off the hours—1:50 in the morning, then 2:30, then 4:05.

Katie and I are in one room, Anne and Jennie in another, the photographer in a third with his wife. She is an artist, and was included not only to help with his equipment but also with the thought that her sketches might later serve as book or article illustrations. The videographer and soundperson are in the Academy's other hotel, the old one in the middle of the city. The night is warm and windows have to be left open. There's a hum of mosquitoes above the beds.

My mind is spinning. I am thinking about the upper river. And about encephalitis, and what I may have gotten my family and the others into. But those are only night thoughts. There is a more tangible problem.

Yesterday morning in Amsterdam, just before the flight to Moscow, the videographer announced that one of the two cameras had stopped working. At first he thought it might be batteries. He tried new ones, but the camera was dead. Then he powered the second camera with the first batteries, and it worked fine. There is no explaining it. The equipment all is new. Repair is impossible, and the best hope is to have a replacement flown from the U.S. and hand-carried from Moscow, praying that it will reach us in Siberia before we actually leave for the river.

I regret snapping at the photographer when we were eating in the hotel dining room last night.

I was speaking my worry about the camera, and he declared

the obvious: that the expedition could not be stopped for lack of a backup. I *knew that*, I said. But I was worried all the same. I didn't see how we could risk our only camera in the white water of the upper river. If something happened to it there, and if the replacement didn't come, the filming would be finished.

But the videographer had a box that was supposed to be waterproof, the photographer said. "I guess we'll just have to leave the decision to him."

"No. We *won't* leave it to him. I'll take into account what he says. But I'll make the call." I was touchier than I needed to have been. But the point is correct. In the end, responsibility for the expedition's outcome falls to me.

It's morning, now, and our group from the Uzkoe has ridden the Metro in to the other hotel. There's to be a session today in Tishkov's office at the Institute, where I will meet for the first time our expedition partners from Irkutsk. Misha will call with the hour of the meeting.

Shortly before 11 o'clock the room phone buzzes, but it isn't Misha. I recogize the husky, high-pitched voice on the line.

"Sergei!"

"I must speak with you," he says. "Now. Privately."

"Where are you?"

"In the reception of this hotel. It's something important."

⚜

HE WAITED IN THE small lobby, which was cluttered with the bags of groups of foreigners just arriving or leaving. We stepped together against a wall, out of the traffic.

"I remember that you wanted me to be your eyes and your ears," Sergei began. His face was drawn, and his lips trembled as he spoke. "Well, I have come to tell you what I have seen and heard."

"Yes?" I couldn't imagine what had agitated him so.

"You should know that the Irkutsk people have come to Moscow to refuse."

"To *what?*"

It was inconceivable that I'd heard him right.

"To refuse to take part. They are worried about two things. First, that the Institute will not be fair with them about money. And also they do not want any Moscow people—Tishkov included—with them on the journey. Especially Victor, who is the leader of the Irkutsk team. You have to meet with them."

"When?"

"Now, before you go to your meeting with Tishkov."

E XCEPT FOR MISHA AND Sergei, the small room on an upper floor of the Institute's new building on Leninsky Prospekt is a room of strangers.

Does the expedition really hang in the balance here? Clearly the suspicions and regional resentments run bitter and deep in the disintegrating state. But I can't know—will never know—if the crisis is as dire as Sergei has painted it. I try to conceal my panic by getting straight to the issue.

"I understand we have a problem."

A stout, bearded man named Stanislav Goldfarb speaks first. He is head of the organization in Irkutsk to which the Institute has delegated responsibility for all the logistical arrangements—hiring of the boats, movement of cargo, contracting for planes and helicopters. It's the money that most concerns Goldfarb. What guarantee is there that he will be paid? In what form will payment be made?

There is a tall man in the room, also bearded, who I learn is on the staff of the Moscow Institute, but evidently in sympathy with the Irkutsk people. Or why else would he be there? The Siberian delegation also includes a slight, stiff fellow in business suit, with Asian features. He turns out to be a banker from Irkutsk—brought along by Goldfarb as insurance against trickery either by the Americans or the Muscovites.

Then it is the turn of Victor Paolovich Gulevich, and as he begins to speak it is clear from the attention he commands from the others that his views carry much weight.

He is 37 years old, from the Geographical Institute of the

Siberian branch of the Academy of Sciences. Gulevich, two of his colleagues and the interpreter, Orlov, are to be the Russian members of the expedition—if there is an expedition.

Victor is of medium height, and wears a gray suit, black shirt and white necktie. He looks for all the world like a hit man from the Chicago mob. The suit seems tight in the shoulders, and I get the impression he feels as uncomfortable in it as he does in this elaborate office setting. His eyes are a startling blue. He is instantly likeable and powerfully impressive. Standing with his back to the window, the panorama of the city spread out behind and below, he opens a small notebook. With confidence and clarity he lays out his thoughts and the preparations he has made.

One thing troubles him—the talk of Moscow people going on the journey. He has led several expeditions, and taken part in others. He has trekked, often alone in winter, in remote Siberian areas.

"The expedition leader is the one with the vodka, the money and the gun," he says. He is smiling now, but his eyes are serious. "You have the money. I will have the vodka and the gun. So we lead. *But no Muscovites.* It's absolute."

"They want you to speak to Tishkov," says Sergei. "To tell him."

But how can I do that? Except for Tishkov and his Institute, we would not be here at all. "It's not my business to tell him he can't go. Let Victor tell him."

"They say you must do it."

The talk turns back to money again. There is only one contract, says Goldfarb, between me and the Moscow Institute. I will pay Moscow, but what if Moscow does not pay Goldfarb? Well, why not *two* contracts—one with Moscow and another with him? Both could be paid by me directly. Then what about the interpreter? How would Orlov be paid, and by whom? And also Victor's team? Each point provokes an eruption of voices, all talking at once. What takes a minute to tell here takes more than three hours in the doing.

Victor has no part in the rest of that. He has closed his notebook and looks from the window as the voices of the others clamor endlessly on.

"Too much talk," he says afterward, at lunch in the Institute cafeteria. "But after the talking, we will have a river."

And I take it from that he has made his decision.

He will fly back to Irkutsk on tomorrow night's plane. It will take me another week here to handle last details: the financial arrangements, clearance and on-shipment of part of our cargo and provisions. Then the Trans-Siberian Railway will carry the Americans and our goods eastward five time zones to meet the other Russian members of the team. They all are Victor's chosen men. And with him, clearly, we are in huge luck.

But first, before this afternoon ends, there is the meeting with Valery Tishkov. He had planned only to welcome our American party, and seems surprised that the people from Irkutsk have joined us in his office. I lay out the issues the Siberians have raised, concentrating mainly on the financial ones. A whole new set of contracts will have to be written.

"It means you will miss Leningrad," Tishkov says. I'd planned for the American party to spend three days there, and Tishkov had made arrangements for briefings on Siberia and its peoples at the Leningrad ethnographic museum. It would be helpful background.

"The others will go. Katie can make notes for me there. It can't be helped."

The more delicate issue I touch on obliquely, cautiously.

"We have another problem, Valery," I tell him, and I can sense the others watching, listening intently.

"What problem?"

"Of numbers. The expedition cannot be more than twelve. Eight Americans, four Russians."

A shadow of surprise flickers across Tishkov's face. He knows that Victor's team and the interpreter make four, and that he would be the thirteenth in the party.

"The fault is mine," I tell him, though I don't really mean that. "We talked at first about my bringing six from the U.S., and now we're eight. We discussed it this morning. Victor feels very strongly it is impossible to increase the number. I'm sorry."

"I see." Tishkov toys with some papers on his desk. His face is expressionless, but I know he is stunned. The question is how he will react. It could go either way, to anger or regret. He could say simply, *The hell with you all*. And we would get on a plane to New York. The Institute, after all, is the expedition's official sponsor.

Tishkov looks up from his desk, and down the long table to Victor who is sitting at the far end. The eyes of the two men, the Muscovite and the Siberian, meet in perfect understanding.

"I'm sorry, too," Tishkov says. A little sigh escapes him. "I would have liked to do it. But it's true, even with twelve the difficulties will be great enough. Probably it's better." And with this further graciousness on his part, the crisis is disposed of.

⚜

HIS FLAT WAS NOT far from the Hotel Uzkoe, in a block of rectangular cement apartment buildings. Tishkov apologized for its modesty, but it seemed spacious by Russian standards—a bedroom for Valery and his wife, who is an art museum curator; another small room for their son, who was studying for his second-year examinations in history at Moscow State University; also an entry hall, small kitchen and study. They lived well, if not extravagantly.

He excused himself and left me in his study. Shelves of books lined the walls. There was his writing desk, covered with papers, and more papers stacked on shelves and chairs, and good art on the walls, some of it original. It was a room of taste—and of ideas.

A fluffy black cat appeared. And briefly the son, Vasily, a bright boy with good English and the final-week terror in his eyes. Then Valery came back, without coat or necktie, collar open, having traded his shoes for slippers. He seemed younger and not so formidable, a scholar now instead of an administrator. He brought a tray with little slices of sausage and bread, glasses of fruit juice and a bottle of slivovitz gotten on one of his trips to Yugoslavia, and set it on the small table between us.

"So," he said. "It would have been nice to go with you to the Lena." His regret was genuine.

If he could have traveled part of the river with the expedition, he said, he had planned to take no summer holiday and save his vacation for a project next year. But he was philosophical about it.

"I will stay here and work on my monograph instead." He indicated one of the piles of manuscript on the desk. "So you see, there is some good, too."

I liked Tishkov. He was a decent and congenial man, and would have been good company on the journey, besides being knowledgeable about the region's history. What was it about him the Irkutsk people resented so? His position, I supposed. Or maybe his Moscow comforts. Clearly they distrusted him, and that seemed to me a mistake. They'd been fairly dealt with.

"I wish you were going, too," I told him. "I feel bad it turned out this way."

"Never mind. It's all right."

"Victor's a good man, and I have confidence in him. But you know how grateful I am to you. For an outsider, the politics here can be difficult."

He waved my apology aside.

"I know very well the feelings of these Siberians. They feel they have been controlled and exploited by Moscow, and that all decisions have been made for them by people far away. It's a matter of long history."

He bent to pour another small glass of slivovitz, then raised his face to look straight at me.

"And about these things," he said, "they are of course mostly right."

꧁ ❧ ꧂

THE WALK FROM THE Metro exit to the hotel is the better part of a mile, most of it uphill. I had meant in this last year to give up tobacco and get myself fit again. But with the worry about money and the press of so many things to do, nothing came of those intentions.

The pull up the hill is painful. How desperately out of shape am I, really?

In light of what lies ahead, the question haunts.

TWENTY

H OT IN THE ROOM. Outside probably cool, or even chilly, but I don't dare open the window or the hungry mosquitoes will come swarming in. Have killed several already, and others can be heard humming.

How many more days and nights must be spent poring over papers and working the calculator? Everything the Institute and I had put into one contract now must be subdivided into several separate ones. A contract with Goldfarb and his organization in Irkutsk. Another agreement with the Russian expedition team. Another for direct payment of Misha and Olga for their work with the Irkutsk faction. Another for the interpreters—Sergei, the mystic, and also the interpreters in Moscow and Leningrad.

Typewriters at the Institute don't work. Paper can't be found. Carbon paper is out of the question. And everything must be written out in duplicate, both in English and Russian translation. Bread and dry little cookies are brought in to gnaw on at what ought to be the meal hour. Misha boils tea. Strangers pass through and there are unrelated conversations. I spoil the page. Spoil another. Olga clicks her heels in the room and the hall outside. Misha reads over my shoulder, murmuring things I don't understand. The sums don't add up right. It has to be done again.

After that are the first of the payments. Going to hotel exchange windows—not banks, but hotels—trading money for rubles, and then like Mafioso in the back seats of moving automobiles passing the rubles to those owed them. Not sheaves of them, or even bundles of them. But whole satchels full of rubles. ("Maybe someday," Goldfarb has said, "we will be able to conduct affairs as it is done in other places." That time seems very distant.)

Those are the days. Nights, I worry, not so much for myself, really, as for the others. If we can manage to hold in mind the sense of adventure, the great luck of being here, then we can get through. But I do worry for them and for the discomfort that may be ahead. I hope no great dangers. Have I been a fool to bring them? I ask myself that, and can't yet know the answer. When I asked Victor to what hazard they would be exposed, he said, "No more danger for being women." That is something, but not quite a whole answer. I must do anything to keep them safe—including, if necessary, turning back before the end—because I could not live with risking them in some serious way. I'm not thinking of the discomfort of bugs and hard living and such. They are strong-natured and can bear that with humor. I'm thinking of the *worse*, although I can't know what it is. I must watch everything: their health, their safety, their happiness. The work will be done if all the rest can be kept well. If it can't be, the work is meaningless. We will take readings of all of us as this proceeds. And above all the other, smaller worries, we will worry about, and inspect for, the ticks. Tishkov keeps insisting the ailment is encephalitis. Could they be speaking of Lyme disease? They also say only one tick in three million carries the virus.

When worry is unbearable, I power up the short-wave radio we've brought, and in the dark room turn the dial trying to get the BBC or Australia or even a French station—any congenial voice. Gorbachev and Bush have agreed on a date for their summit meeting the end of this month. Wednesday, June 12, is the first round of the Russian presidential election—in which, as it turns out, Boris Yeltsin will win without need for a runoff, and the people of Leningrad will vote to again call their city St. Petersburg. But for now, Leningrad is still the name. And I'm lonely with all the others gone off to there.

Breakfast in the hotel buffet with a Chinese physicist from the University of Georgia and an English chemist from Yale. This place churns with people on fellowships, junkets and deals. The physicist says he met a man who was going to, or had just come back from, *an international jew's-harp convention* in Yakutsk, a great town on the middle Lena, reachable only by plane. The strangeness is without end.

Supper in the same buffet another day with a lady astronomer from Jet Propulsion Laboratory in Pasadena. She is a lovely young woman whose father is a Lapp reindeer herder in Finland. Or used to be. The fallout from Chernobyl has poisoned the moss the reindeer eat, she says, and destroyed a centuries-old way of life. She wishes someone would write about the Lapps and their culture before everything is forgotten.

Each morning to the Institute, and the contracts again. Or to an exchange window to get someone paid. And errands between times. And lines everywhere.

To the U.S. embassy, to register our presence and intentions in the country, just in case anything goes wrong. I'm directed to some bureau in the building called "U.S. Citizen Services"—but there is damned little inclination to serve. Petty American clerks also have fallen into the Moscow slow-step. Two of them stand chattering, far from the service windows, and when finally one does come forward it is with leaden reluctance. What they were talking about were tricks for steering groups of U.S. students to some other office. Otherwise they'd be overrun with kids, one says—and might be required to work. Outside the embassy, Russians stand in a crowd, hoping to get visas. At the service window next to mine, an American is trying to unravel the procedure of getting a relative to the States. He's told to come with the relative tomorrow, and show his passport. It could help.

"Is there any chance he could get to the front of the line by the end of tomorrow?" the petitioner asks.

"Who knows?" comes the laconic answer. "He might."

One free weekend day, on Sunday, to revisit Arbat street and see if the surprising spirit of last fall has survived the worsening economic crisis. It has—in astonishing measure. The public orations, reminiscent of Speakers' Corner in London, have become more strident. The denunciations flung at the government are now not merely critical but openly ridiculing.

Everywhere there is music. One moment is especially fine. Three middle-aged ladies with guitars and banjos have stationed themselves against a building front, whanging out a boisterous song. They look nothing like musicians; more like housewives from Bemidji, Minnesota, on a tipsy romp. A crowd has gathered, and in it is a small, older woman with a blue *babushka* wrapped round her head. As she listens, her shoulders move in time with the beat, her feet begin to shuffle. She puts down the plastic bag she is carrying. And finally, unable to contain herself, she steps out of the crowd and into the open circle and begins a wonderful, complicated dance of some traditional kind. The crowd laughs and cheers her on, clapping in time with the music. Then a young man comes out and joins the little woman. Then another.

What these Muscovites can't know—what no one could know, then—is that before this summer is over their laughter will end, their courage will be tested. History will take a lurch, and the world will change in a way that on this Sunday is utterly unimaginable.

But so much time just wasted! So many futile days! The others are to arrive back on Thursday morning on the all-night train from Leningrad. That same evening, we're to haul ourselves and all our detritus aboard the Trans-Siberian to begin the journey east. But which train, exactly, are my people coming on? Wednesday is the election day, and Misha has neglected to call. So I go myself to the Komsomolskaya station to look on the board and write down the times. Three likely arrivals from Leningrad are listed. To meet the first one will mean rising at 5 a.m. to catch the Metro.

I do. They aren't on it. Or on the second train. Or the third one at half past 8. The passengers stream along the platform, porters following with wagons of luggage, and finally I'm alone there in a rage.

⚶

THE INSTITUTE'S HANDSOME NEW building can't be entered by anyone off the street, as the old one could. There's a security guard at a desk inside the entrance, and a signed access slip is required.

People were just coming to their offices, and I waited in the courtyard outside until I saw someone I knew. It was the tall, bearded man named Lev, who had been at the first meeting with the Siberians. He promised to get me a "device"—a pass—for the building. But no one could be found upstairs, so he came back without it and talked me past the guard on the promise of getting the device later.

It was Tishkov I wanted to see, but he hadn't yet arrived. So we waited in Lev's small office just across the hall. Then Misha appeared, in his usual aimless confusion.

"Where were you?" he wanted to know.

Frustration can bring you finally to the exploding point.

"Where *was* I? Standing around the damned railroad station, waiting for my people. Where were *you*?"

He said that he and Olga had come to my hotel at 6 a.m., found me gone, then met the train and taken the others to the Academy's hotel in central Moscow. Then they'd gone again to the Uzkoe, hoping to find me.

But why hadn't he called yesterday to tell me the plan.

Misha gave his baffled shrug. "Because we didn't want to disturb you."

I erupted.

"I'm fed up," I shouted at him. "I've been in this town for a week. The whole time has been spent dealing with other people's needs. For papers. For money. From now on—" I tell Misha, "—from this moment, we're going to be dealing with *my* needs."

The show of impatience saddened him. His brown eyes became more spaniel-like.

"My first concern is the cargo. It's been in Moscow for days. It is thousands of dollars worth of material. We have spent more thousands to get it here. *And it's still here.* I'm not getting on tonight's train without knowing exactly the plan for it—when it leaves, how, and when it arrives in Irkutsk."

"You should trust me more," Misha said.

"It's not a matter of trust. It's a question of doing just a few things right!"

⚜

WHILE MISHA GOES TO clarify the cargo problem, all the personal baggage from the rooms and the held-baggage locker at the Uzkoe must be transferred to the downtown hotel in readiness for the evening train. It takes until nearly 2 o'clock, when our group is scheduled for the last meeting with Tishkov.

"There was a call for you at the hotel," my wife says in the

car. "It was from a woman who said you knew her son. She wanted me to tell you he is a fine boy and has been working very hard
for you in Irkutsk."

I couldn't guess who it might be.

"I think she said his name was Ivan something-or-other."

Ivan? I sift memory for a clue. Ivan? Then I remember. That
was the name of the slight lad who was a friend of Bychkov's disagreeable interpreter, Valentin. It was a mystery how the mother
had even known we were in Moscow, much less tracked us down
by phone. The news here travels by means unknown. But never
mind, there was no further trouble Bychkov or Valentin or any of
them could make now.

"She left a number, in case you wanted to call her back."

"It's unimportant. They're just trying to work us for some
crumbs."

❦

W E HAD TO WAIT again for the "device" that would let us get up
to Tishkov. Evidently there was some confusion, because the
wait was 30 minutes. Standing under a building eave in the cold
drizzle outside the Institute, the photographer was concerned
about money.

Specifically, he was worried about how much cash I was going
to be carrying on the river.

"I'm paying the Irkutsk people part when we get there, and
part at the end. That's how we wrote the contract. The rest I'm
leaving with Tishkov in his safe, including what we owe the
Institute. And I'm carrying with me about eight hundred dollars in
personal money."

"The thing is," he said, "in this country anything you count on
is going to be wrong. Something's going to happen, so why not be
prepared for it?"

"We have plenty of money."

"What happens if the boat breaks down and they need a thousand dollars to get it going?"

"They have it," I told him.

"Yes, but is it going along with them?" His voice slid up in pitch. "I'm saying if we're sitting in some town and they need money for us to get going or we sit there a week, I say we pay it and get it back later. So I think we need money. That's all I'm saying. If you have eight hundred, I think we're covered."

The cold and the drizzle had chilled us all.

"I mean, this is a perfect example of things not working," he said. "Here we are to see the head of the Institute. All he has to do is send some lackey down with a pass, and we stand cooling our heels. If they can't accomplish something like this here, think what the situation's going to be out there. You know?"

Mercifully, then, a secretary came to fetch us, bearing the device.

I didn't quite know what to make of it at the time. But thinking about it afterward, I believe the photographer only wanted everything to be certain. I had to agree that certainty would be comforting. But in an enterprise like this one, absolute control was an impossibility. Many things were bound to be unknown.

Tishkov wore his official manner for this last meeting. A member of his scientific staff gave a map briefing, then Valery himself had some final thoughts.

With its colleagues from Irkutsk, the Institute meant to do everything possible to make the expedition interesting and fruitful. To undertake such a journey would have been much easier four years ago, he said, before the situation in the country became so unsettled.

"The economic crisis now is very strong. It was bad before, but now it is terrible. The country is in a state of transition and transformation whose end we cannot know. So it would have been easier before.

"But, on the other side, you are lucky because you are the first to go at a time when you can ask any question to any person on any subject and get answers without any reservations. You will get real information." For many of the people along the river, he said, the contact with us would be their first ever with foreigners.

The others were taking in the panoramic view of Moscow from the large windows of the director's 18th-floor office—the river, the Lenin Hills, the University, a great sports stadium, and, wrapped by a forested park, a small domed building that was rumored to be Gorbachev's house. Valery and I were looking at the wall map of the sprawling Union, with the great river curving south to north across its eastern part. I asked him: "What will this map look like in five or ten years?"

"Well, the map will be about the same. But the political and administrative divisions based on ethnicity could be very different. For instance, I believe the process of secession of the Baltic republics from the Soviet Union is inevitable."

He spoke also of the separatist movements gathering force in other parts of the country—in the Caucasian republics, and in Georgia—and of the trouble that secession could set loose among peoples whose old enmities had been held in check by the umbrella of Soviet power.

"But who knows?" He shrugged. "The dissatisfaction with the present status—economic and political and cultural—is so great that it does not always reflect objectively the real situation, but only the emotional psychology of people." He swept his arm across the map. "For such a huge country and variety of cultures and economic activities," he said, "you cannot keep everything together just with an iron hand."

I looked at my watch. While we'd been at this meeting, Misha should have been putting our canoes and other bulky items on a mail car bound for Irkutsk, and it was time now to begin moving the rest of our cargo from the hotel to the rail station for the 9:30 p.m. train.

"So take care," Valery said. "Be careful of the forest, the wild animals—and the people. Some of them are a little bit angry. And remember that the summer on the Lena is short. If an expedition arrives at the northern edge of Asia too late, it must stay there through winter and wait for another spring. That's all. It's a small problem."

It was only a joke, of course. But I could not help thinking of the expeditions of DeLong and others, in a time when such a warning had weight.

"I will come tonight to see you at the train," Valery said. "To be sure you are moving in the direction of Irkutsk."

TWENTY-ONE

THE RAIL PLATFORM AT dusk is like some spectacle of wartime evacuation, combined perhaps with a Middle Eastern bazaar. A crowd of thousands, milling, pressing—wearing the faces of all the Soviet nationalities. Vendors shout. Children scream. Loudspeakers blare unintelligibly into the gathering dark.

Misha is there, with Olga, carrying their valises for Irkutsk. They will see the expedition begun, Tishkov has said, and will remain there—reachable by telephone or radio or courier—to help deal with any logistical or bureaucratic obstacles we might meet on the river, and then will fly to meet us at the Arctic coast. The canoes and other goods put on the mail car should reach Irkutsk one or two days after our faster train.

Lev, the tall man from the Institute, says he has a friend who is an Aeroflot pilot on the Moscow-to-Irkutsk route. He will arrange for the friend to carry the replacement video camera to us when it arrives in Moscow. If we have left Irkutsk before it comes, someone will try to bring it to us on the river.

Our remaining baggage and equipment fills four large porters' wagons—a mountain to be moved. The photographer is certain it cannot all be made to fit in our five compartments, and that some must be left behind. The train slides in beside the platform for loading, and porters and all of us labor in fire-brigade fashion to heave the cargo on board. I climb inside to check, and find the photographer has commanded the porters to put *everything* in Misha and Olga's compartment, stacking it full from floor to ceiling, all the way to the sliding door. "That's *their* room," he says. "I hope they're comfortable."

Anne and Jennie work with Misha to redistribute the goods. Stowage is found under the berths in each compartment, and more on the overhead racks and in a space over the door. Then Misha and the woman car steward roll back the carpet in the corridor and remove panels to reveal more cargo space under the floor. In the end, everything fits, with hardly any inconvenience for anyone.

As promised, Valery has come late from his office to see us off. But there is little time to talk. He says he hopes that we will not

find too many difficulties on our route, or too much discomfort. I
tell him we expect some of both, but not to worry about us. It's
because of him we have managed to come to this moment.

❧

THE WHISTLE PIPED, AND porters fled the car. All was stowed, and
everyone had room enough. Finally we could look from the
windows as our train, the "Baikal," glided through the Moscow
evening, past great lighted blocks of apartments and out toward
open country.

The vexations of the week had given way at last to vaulting
excitement. The feeling was more of an ocean voyage than a land
trip. Our compartments were cozy. The woman steward came with
tea, and we had brought a sack of pastries from the hotel buffet.

Beyond the apartments, there were only isolated small houses
at trackside, lamps showing yellow in the windows. Night had deepened, but sky still could be seen lighter above the trees. Beds were
made up.

Then all were tucked in, all congenial again. And sleep came
very soon—the first absolutely untroubled sleep in longer than I
could recall—with the rocking of our schooner train upon the
Russian sea.

❧

FRIDAY, JUNE 14.
Awake to an explosion of green. Mixed birch and poplar and
pine forest, with fields opening, wooden cottages and garden huts,
and paths leading away through forest to other places. Mountains
of lilacs in the last of their bloom. Banks and clumpets of wild rose.
Purple larkspurs, and other small white and yellow flowers—all
flashing past the window.

Morning tea. Then the ordeal of the bathroom—only one at
the end, for the whole car. After experience in many countries I
have decided all the Europeans at some past time must have held a
conference and, agreeing that bodily functions were a shame and a

disgrace, resolved to make sanitary facilities as degrading and primitive as possible. The virtuosity of the Russians surpasses even that of the Italians. The seat of the toilet in our car is elevated only six inches, at most, from the fetid, puddled floor.

We buy some excellent candies from a girl pushing a cart along the corridor. On the chilly platform at Kirov, just before noon, Misha finds bottled mineral water and comes back with enough for all. Then on to the east; sense of the country slowly rising toward the Urals; some blue shadows that look like foothills at great distance ahead. Long stretches where the forest seems more predominantly pine, but even here the trees open onto prospects of vast fields—oats, possibly, or some other early-summer grain crop full in the head. Also incredibly lush pastures with only a few sheep and cattle in them, all unfenced, watched by herders.

Rickety hamlets with a patched-together look are connected to other fields and perhaps other hamlets by mud paths. A flock of goats. Chickens in the stick-fenced house yards. Ducks and geese in the sloughs and canals that thread through the low fields at track side. Old couples bend to work in their little rectangles of potato plants and onions. There is rain intermittently today and everything has a gumbo-ish, murky look. The houses and their frail fences seem transient, built without any intention or hope or even thought of permanence.

Only the land itself looks eternal. It is vast and fat and green. Released to its destiny, it would seem that such an abundance of land might feed not just Russia but half the world.

Lunch in the dining car: cold meats, sturgeon soup, beef Stroganoff, bread and tea. A surfeit, for 50 cents apiece. I have carried my briefcase with me, heavy with what we've come to call the *loaf*. The loaf is a bundle of travelers' checks and currency—nearly $40,000 in U.S. dollars—with which to pay all the expenses in Siberia, for people, boats, planes. Two hundred rubles, about eight dollars, is considered by Russians a poor but living monthly wage, so the loaf represents an inconceivable fortune. I can't safely leave it anywhere, even in the locked compartment.

We finish lunch and go back to our car.

"Where's the loaf?" asks Katie.

"Christ!" I break the land speed record half the length of the train to the dining car. The briefcase and loaf still are there, against the wall under the table. I'm relieved but also ashamed. Stupidity like that our enterprise can't afford.

Much afternoon traffic met coming the other direction—coal cars, and others stacked high with corded pulpwood from the Urals. By middle afternoon the climb has steepened, the train slowed. At a stop in some dismal place, Misha, in his slicker with the hood drawn up, goes out to exercise on the platform in a pelting rain.

Saturday, June 15.

The last of yesterday was spent in slow pulls upward and rushes down as our long train traversed the heaves of the mounting land.

Missed dinner. Passing eastward, we have reset our watches as we progressed from one time zone to another. But it turns out all trains and planes in the Soviet Union operate on Moscow time, and that is the time displayed on the station clocks.

The videographer set up his "theater" in our compartment, for viewing the Moscow footage on a two-inch monitor. Much of it looked splendid. Then the batteries ran down and the show was finished. It was midnight, but the sky on the left-hand side of the train—to the north—still was pale as afternoon. A mountain river ran silver below us in the valley up which we climbed. "These are the white nights," said Misha.

This morning we wake late, halted at the station in Sverdlovsk, and must wait until the train rolls again before using the hateful bathroom to which, sad to report, we're becoming accustomed. Sometime in the night, just beyond the crest of the Urals, we passed the monument that marks Europe's end and the beginning of Asia. We're in Siberia at last, and now the oncoming trains are more frequent. On the flatcars of one are automobiles and vans *with the people riding in them.*

Through Tiumen—an ugly, rusted looking place. Past three cooling towers of what might be a nuclear generating plant, though I can't be sure. Then great depots of stacked wood, and sawmills, and acres of sawn lumber. Then out onto an immense tableland, level to the end of seeing. Stop again at midday at Ishim. The latitude here is slightly north of Moscow, but the heat is fierce, hammering down on the platform where little women in head-scarves at umbrella-shaded stands sell cucumber pickles, strawber-ries and some things we can't identify.

Of our 10, including Misha and Olga, only five can face the dining car again and the inevitable Stroganoff, which today is called "goulash" and comes with cabbage soup and a dollop of sour cream floating. Tomorrow, we joke, the Stroganoff may be called "turkey and dressing," or, at breakfast, "pancakes and sausage." The taste of the *mineralnya*, the bottled mineral water, changes depending on where it was taken aboard. Here it is salty, with a sulphurous smell of rotten eggs so powerful the stuff scarcely can be brought to mouth. After lunch we run tap water through our fil-ter, and fill all the canteens.

The afternoon stop, Nasvayevskaya, is a hamlet so small it has no platform, only a place to stand on the ground between the trains. A *babushka* comes with a tin pail of potatoes boiled with dill, her pail covered with a cloth. She sells them in paper cones, a frac-tion of one ruble for a cone, and they're delicious!

Then on toward Omsk, across the western Siberian plain which lies between the steppe to the south and the *taiga* forest region to the north, with the great Siberian plateau ahead to the northeast. The first of the great rivers, the Ob, flows broad and tur-bid under the iron bridge at Novosibirsk just at sundown, a vast, polluted industrial river, but painted golden in that hour.

Sunday, June 16.

Full daylight at 2:30 a.m. I stand in the vestibule between the cars, awake, alone and smoking. And still the land is of such end-less flatness as almost to take the breath. The level landscape must be poorly drained, because the green is broken here and there by groves of dead poplars, their roots drowned, bleached to white sticks and spectral in the mist of morning.

Then I try to sleep. And wake again. And still the same view from the window. So vast is the country, so immense the distances, that you can ride an afternoon and a night, and the next day find the topography utterly unchanged.

We have our first small health problem. Jennie is bothered today by a miserably sore throat, likely from all the wettings in rain showers on the streets of Moscow. We excavate the medical kit from under a berth, read the instructions on the bottles, and give her the antibiotic Ken Hoff has sent for such ailments. If that's the worst of our maladies, we'll be in luck.

The stop at Achinsk is not a disembarkment, only a momentary hesitation in the eastward plunge. What can be seen of the place from the car is hideous, as so much of the settlement in this part of Siberia seems to be. All broken concrete and rust.

After Achinsk, though, the country tips first gradually then sharply up toward what the map shows as the Krasnoyarsk range. Soon we're in glorious folded country, pines reappearing with the birches and poplars. Steep alpine meadows. Families of Sunday picnickers out. The *dachas* and little gardens neater, brighter. Flowers again. Mostly the trains we meet now carry logs and sawn lumber. The land seems little and gently used.

The second great Siberian river, the one Yuri Simchenko wished I'd loved instead, the Yenisey, is met at the city of Krasnoyarsk. Farther north, it must be wonderful as he says. But here, like the Ob, it is only large. Parked on its bank are what look to be three or four *hundred* orange combines, manufactured in Krasnoyarsk and waiting to be shipped off to cut the summer's harvest. The city, according to Misha, is the principal center of a large region and may be one of the richest towns in the Union. It has a solemn, industrial feel about it. Just on beyond, though, is a little vision of Switzerland—clusters of weekend houses, many quite charming and elaborate, enough of them to make a substantial village flung out across a hillside, and lakes with people swimming. Then another such settlement, where tidy garden plots are arranged along the bank of a bright, trouty-looking stream.

The towns come faster now. More boiled potatoes and some good *pirozhki* at the Ilyanskaya station, then across the Biryussa River and another stop at Taishet. The watercourses smaller, but clarifying. You see the force of them rushing under the bridges. The larger places are announced by the sooty brown fans of smoke their factory chimneys spew out across the breadth of the horizon. But between them is good country.

⚜

A PALE CRESCENT MOON climbed up the afternoon-bright sky outside the train window. It was twenty minutes before midnight of our last night aboard. Time lost in the first two days had been regained, so we would reach Irkutsk on schedule at 9:40 tomorrow morning.

The journey, which we'd rather dreaded, now seemed far too short in retrospect. We would regret its coming to an end.

Two powerful impressions dominated: of space and wealth. Yes, *wealth*. With resources in plenty, especially of land, only the monstrous failure of the system could account for the country's inability to feed itself and to prosper. The railroad on which we'd ridden was a marvel of achievement. Some Soviet science is splendid—and some, of course, disreputable. There are isolated wonders.

But until the country could manage somehow to harness all its wasted potential and allow expression to the thwarted enterprise of its people, it would be fatally crippled. The image that suggested itself was of a truck driven too long, too hard, with no maintenance at all, and operated the whole time on the wrong fuel.

If you ask what's broken about it, the answer is that *everything* is. Repairs are not feasible. Parts aren't made to fit. The only answer is to junk it, and build a machine that runs.

TWENTY-TWO

IRKUTSK, MONDAY, JUNE 17.

On the station platform, upturned faces. Most of them still unknown. Women with bunches of roses in their arms—the Russian greeting. One of them I recognize as Sergei Orlov's Vicka, the *taiga* waif, looking quite lovely and sophisticated in a pale spring dress. Victor is there, and Goldfarb, and other men I take to be some of Victor's crew. Our goods are unearthed from the various burial places in the train car, passed down and loaded aboard an ancient red bus. All crowd in after, and we are transported to the Angara Hotel in the center of the town. Equipment is left on the bus, to be taken for safe storage in locked rooms of Goldfarb's offices.

We're on the seventh floor of the hotel, and Victor's first advice, earnestly delivered, is to be careful of theft. Door casings are splintered, and every lock on every room looks at one time or other to have been forced.

Then to Goldfarb's office in afternoon for a meeting. Victor conducts it, trying to make known the plan for the days before leaving. But all is chaotic—all speaking at once, and the plan indecipherable. Then an argument flares between Goldfarb and Sergei, who flies into a shaking rage and denounces Goldfarb as a former Komsomol (young Communist) toady who's only become a capitalist to suit the times.

The photographer, with good reason, has no interest in going to the several meetings Victor has arranged at institutions in Irkutsk. He wants to spend the days here working independently, and he speaks of his need to use the early morning and late afternoon light. Many people are in the room, including some of the Russian women. It's a crazy affair, and Victor seems disheartened. Then it's necessary—why just at that moment I can't know—to rush to a bank to change thousands of dollars to rubles to be deposited to the account of Goldfarb's organization. Then back to the meeting, which has droned on in evident uselessness.

After the long train journey, the hotel has no hot water. And none is expected until tomorrow. But Goldfarb has arranged for the men to go to a sauna. One of the Russian women, Ludmilla, will take the women members of our party to bathe at her flat.

The venerable red bus stops on a gravel drive outside what looks like an abandoned warehouse. Through an unmarked door, down a dark stair, around a corner and into a perfect marvel of cleanliness. It must be some kind of bathing club. A woman attendant meets us with towels and muslin wraps. The purging heat of the steam room is followed by a plunge in a cold pool, then the hot room again—all of us flushed bright red and sweat-beaded—then the cold pool again, and finally a shower. Wrapped in the loose covers, we pass into another small room where the attendant has laid a table with cookies and a pot of black tea. All this is done with the flawless elegance of some fancy men's club in Boston or San Francisco. It's altogether unexpected and unexplainable here. But with the crust of travel sweated off us, Irkutsk seems eminently possible.

◦⁓⊰⊱⁓◦

WAITING IN THE ANGARA'S lobby when we came from the sauna was someone I'd hoped never to see again—the rejected interpreter, Valentin. His little friend, Ivan, was with him, and a large, flat-faced man he introduced as Vladimir Yevmenenko from Yakutsk.

"I want to discuss with you your program," Valentin said.

"What program?"

"I have been working all winter to plan for your arrival."

"That was a mistake," I told him.

"No mistake," he said, smiling his disagreeable little smile. He still imagined that he somehow could fasten himself to the enterprise. "I have arranged many things. According to our agreement."

"We don't have an agreement," I said to him.

It was as if I hadn't spoken.

"At the museum of Siberian wooden architecture, I have arranged for some dancers to perform in their traditional costumes. You may film and make photographs."

"We wouldn't be interested."

Perspiration stood out on his heavy face, and his words came faster in panic.

"This man—" He looked desperately at the big, flat-featured fellow. "—has concluded a contract with Goldfarb for the boat from Yakutsk to Tiksi."

"Has he? That's fine. But the boat is Goldfarb's business."

The big man stood with his hands in his coat pockets, and seemed not to understand a word of any of it. Little Ivan looked on, smiling sadly.

"Listen," I told Valentin. "If you want to talk with anyone, it should be Victor Gulevich. He is the leader of the Russian team."

The big man went off to make a call from a telephone in the lobby.

"How did you find Moscow?" Ivan asked.

"Fine."

"My mother said she spoke to you there."

"No, she spoke to one of the others."

Valentin looked silently at his feet, understanding at last that he'd failed completely. Then the big man came back and the two of them whispered together.

"It will be better," Valentin said, "if you do not mention to Goldfarb or Gulevich that we have had this conversation."

"Sorry," I told him. "I don't do business that way. I'll speak to Victor tomorrow. Then you can talk with him if you want to."

He wouldn't, though. The three of them went off forlornly together. The rascal had tried, and in such times I suppose he couldn't be blamed. But he knew now it was finished.

⚜

T UESDAY IS A GIFT of a day—by hydrofoil up the Angara River to Baikal, then an excursion on the track of the abandoned spur of the Trans-Siberian Railway that used to circle the southern end of the great lake. The morning is splendid and bright, freshened by Baikal's cool exhalations, and the passenger boat strides up the river on its wings, making the 36 miles in 50 minutes, green-forested bluffs flashing past and behind.

At the tiny settlement of Port Baikal, on the shoulder of land where Baikal empties into the Angara, cows roam the one track. Our "train" is a single antique car, powered by a truck motor and operated by a white-haired driver.

This outing is an indulgence, but one I've asked for especially. The other expeditioners should get a bit of a sense of the country— something more than cities and meeting rooms—before going to the river. The videographer and soundperson woke up with bad stomachs at the hotel. The photographer preferred to prowl Irkutsk instead. So our American party is reduced to Katie and me, Anne and Jennie, and the photographer's wife. Some of the Russians we're beginning to know. Besides Misha and Olga, and Sergei and his Vicka, there is pretty, generous Ludmilla, and one of her friends.

The spare little man with a comical squeak of a voice is Alexander Dimitrivich Abalakov, called Sasha by the others. He's a geomorphologist by profession, and we will learn that his maternal grandfather, Benedict Feldman, was an American citizen who emigrated to Russia in 1917 or 1918 to fight in the Revolution, then lost his life in the late 1930s in Stalin's terror. Also there's Vladimir Alexandrovich Donskoi, called Volodya, the youngest of Victor's team of three. We don't know yet how dear a friend Volodya will come to be, with his quiet, humorous manner hiding iron loyalty and great strength.

Finally, we are joined by a lady journalist and rock-hound from Irkutsk, an older woman with a sweet face and a smile of golden teeth. As our little car rattles along the track, our eyes are on the lake, but hers are fixed on the stones exposed in the bluff on the inland side.

The railroad from Moscow to Vladivostok, linking Europe with Asia's Pacific coast, was known as *"The Iron Belt"* of Russia, Sergei explains. And this one short piece of it around Baikal's tip was its *"Golden Buckle"*—so called because, at nearly one-quarter million dollars a mile in 1904 dollars, it cost one-fifteenth of the whole amount expended from the Czar's treasury.

Along the most difficult 50-mile stretch, half of which we'll travel today, the flank of the mountains plunges to the lake's shore in a succession of sharp-spined buttresses, creating a formidable barrier of bays and vertical clefts. Ten thousand laborers had to move more than five million cubic yards of earth and stone, build 200 bridges and bore, with hand tools, 33 tunnels through the obstructing rock. Most of the tunnels are short. One, the longest, was dug through from both sides at once, Sergei says. And when the ends failed to meet, the engineer responsible shot himself. It's told now that, at night, his spirit still walks the tunnel—perhaps endlessly redoing his calculations. We stop there, and some of us walk into that dripping vault of moist stone until the light vanishes at both ends. But the engineer is nowhere to be seen.

A bit later all climb down, and descend together to a shelf of grass and wildflowers just above Baikal's pebbled beach. There's a little roofed shelter there, and a rough plank table. The men set to work gathering firewood. Sasha and Volodya find two forked sticks and a metal bar from an old camp farther down, and soon a fire is blazing. They have brought everything—a hatchet to chip logs for firewood, two aluminum pans for tea water hung from the rod. Victor had suggested we take food along for lunch, and we have. But only for ourselves, and only scrappy stuff left from traveling: some bread, part of a cheese bought in Amsterdam, airline packets of jam and peanut butter. Now we feel ashamed, because from satchels and packs the Russians all begin producing roasted chicken, tinned fish, pieces of meat to be skewered over the fire, tomatoes to be cut for salad with wild onions gathered from the hillside.

Everything they get is rationed now. In some places, coupons are necessary even to buy matches. How long they have planned and saved for this we can't guess, but it's understood immediately that we must share, or seem ungrateful.

⚜

WE WERE IMAGES TOGETHER in a Monet painting. The time indefinite. Nationalities unknown.

The fresh breeze bending the stems of flowers and grass. Olga sunning in a halter top. Others wading gingerly on tender feet. Men skipping stones. The vast lake still as a glass, with faint shadow

of mountains on the far side. Clouds in sky, and reflected in lake—
no definition between the two.

This produced a curious effect, an impression that one might
be standing at eternity's edge. No perspective by which to measure
anything, so that a resting gull quite near appeared to be a ship at
great distance. Then, suddenly, the ship rose in flight.

The moment was so delicious that I wished it would not end.
And I experienced a revelation that, while commonplace, came
with astonishing force.

For most of my adult life we and the Russians have looked at
one another through bomb sights, the red buttons close at hand.
How could that have been? It was irrational, yes. It was risky to be
sure. But I was struck now that it was something more. The very
idea that our dogmas and the stupidity of our leaders—principally
theirs, but ours as well—and the influence of the generals should
have brought us so near to making war against people like our
companions on this shore was in the most absolute, most moving
sense an *obscenity*.

⚜

O
UR LITTLE TRAIN CAR hesitates coming back, so that the journalist lady
can show us a wonderful wild orchid she's found growing. And in
the labyrinthine way of things, Ivan is waiting on the pier at Port
Baikal. Possibly sent by Valentin? Or how might Bychkov figure in
it? We are courteous to him, but not cordial. He sulks in a seat at
the back of the hydrofoil returning to Irkutsk.

"No matter what your day was, mine was better," the photographer announces at dinner.

He has visited an eye clinic and a children's day school, and
made some wonderful pictures of people in the streets.

"What about laundry?" someone asks.

I don't know, unless perhaps to give it to the floor maid. I
haven't thought about it. It's enough for me that an amazing
sequence of accidents and miracles has brought us to this point.
But the others are concerned with their own needs, and perhaps
startled by the difficulty of the place.

Nor can I answer to their satisfaction the next question of the videographer and soundperson. "What's next," they demand to know. "What's the program."

The *program* is only to learn what we can here in Irkutsk, then go to the river, and try to go down it to its end. The thing cannot be scripted, only surmised. But we will talk, trade views, mediate.

Tomorrow begins with a meeting early at the Institute of Geography. Then another meeting at the faculty of history at Irkutsk University. I will go to those alone. But my immediate worry is for Jennie. The throat infection that began as we were leaving Moscow has worsened. Tonight, after the excursion to Baikal, she had two degrees of fever and was unable to eat.

TWENTY-THREE

THE RUN OF SPARKLING days continues. But now there are two disturbing developments. The train car with the rest of our goods still has not arrived. And Jennie's throat is worse.

The early meeting at the Institute of Geography with several of Victor's senior colleagues is a rather formal affair, in a large conference room with maps on the walls. Victor introduces me, I speak a bit about my first visit in 1973, my reasons for coming back, what we hope to do.

Seated at my left is the one I take to be most senior, Dr. Alexei Belov, head of the biogeography department—gray hair, tinted glasses. He makes the first reply. The two great challenges before Siberia now, he says, are the human problems and preservation of the environment. Linked problems, certainly, and comparable in many ways to the problems of the Amazon, although not yet irreversible here.

The vast space and rich resources, says Belov, hold great potential. But the question is on what terms that potential will be exploited.

Development began in the south, along the Trans-Siberian

Railway, and is proceeding south to north. The northern regions are younger in development, but not in culture or history. Yakutia, the ethnic republic through which the river flows for most of its course, is now trying to chart a management plan for the Lena basin. The Yakuts, the largest indigenous group in the region, are taking charge of their own affairs. "And it will not be for the Siberian people as it has been for the American Indians," Belov says. "Because the Russian Siberians—the ethnic majority—are on the side of the local people."

Historically, he says, the native people—the Yakuts, horse and cattle breeders and herders who came up out of Mongolia in the 12th century, and the Evenks, who from before remembered time have followed the reindeer through Siberia's forests—have had a special reverence for nature.

But the condition of those peoples today is far from good, Belov says—and his colleagues nod their agreement. "Infant mortality is in the range of twenty per one thousand births. The pressures of a harsh environment are compounded in the cities by technological pressure. So life expectancy is short," he says. "*Statistically*, it is made to appear that medical care is increasing—more doctors, clinics and so forth. But the statistics of *actual health* are declining."

The severity of human needs has begun to affect native attitudes toward the environment. The change tends to be generational, with the younger people arguing for faster development, greater exploitation of the region's mineral and other resources. "So the Lena region is in a stage of evolution," says Belov. "Much is said these days about integrating the Soviet economy into the world economy. And to speak of that is also to speak of the integration of the Soviet Union into the world environment, the biosphere.

"Siberia, you might say, is a kind of laboratory," he concludes. "To see if it is possible to *develop*—without *destroying*—the cultures and the land."

Belov's passion about these issues is intense, and obviously genuine. Talk then turns briefly to the Lena itself. It may, the geographers say, be unique among the world's major rivers in having not one dam or power station along its whole length. "Of all the great

rivers in our country," Belov declares, "the Lena is the most isolated, the least changed—preserved in nearly its primal state."

On then to the history faculty at the University. Victor has
other preparations to attend to, so only Sergei Orlov and I will make
this second meeting. I begrudge the time it will take. You know the
feeling, perhaps—when you already have more information than
you think you need about a subject, and do not want to be confused with more. So I keep this appointment only because it has
been arranged for me, and only to be polite.

❧

I HAD FINISHED OUTLINING our intentions in reasonable detail. And
now an extended silence hung strangely in the room, whose
walls displayed photographs, maps and a few paleolithic artifacts. I
waited, looking at the faces around the table.

"Well," I said finally, Sergei interpreting. "What do you think
of it?"

"What do I think?" said Michael Turov. He was a member of
the historical faculty's department of archeology and ethnography.
"I think you are all very brave."

The declaration startled me. I searched his bearded face for
some hint of humor. There was none.

"Ask Professor Turov what he means by that," I told Sergei.
"Tell him we don't think of ourselves as particularly brave."

Sergei repeated it. And Professor German Medbedev, the
head of the department, spoke up from his place at the end of the
table.

"You say that you expect the climb over the Baikal ridge to the
Lena's source, and then to the place where you will put in your
rafts, will be twelve miles," he said. "But it will be more than thirty
kilometers, about *twenty* miles.

"Then there is the problem of bears. The area of the Lena
headwaters has been a natural preserve for a long time, and the
bears have become very numerous in that region. Every year there
are some fatal encounters. It is necessary to have with you a local
man who knows bears and can stop an attack with a gun."

He was listing the problems methodically, ticking them off on his fingers. And he had gotten my complete attention.

"Also," he said, "there is the encephalitis, which is carried by ticks. You have not had the innoculations—I believe there is no vaccine for it in the West. The course of injections is one month, and another month to achieve full immunity. You leave in three or four days. It's useless even to begin.

"The native people of the region have some immunity through cows' milk and mothers' milk. But the only thing you can do is try to stay away from vegetation and travel in areas that have been burned. And you must check yourselves for ticks every two hours. If a tick is on you, and he is taken off before two hours, usually it is no problem. Unless he bites you here—" Medbedev indicated the area of his throat. "Or here." His wrist, under his watch band. "In those places you do not have the margin of time. May I have your notebook?"

He diagrammed the method of removing ticks, by passing a thread around the creature in a series of slip knots to withdraw it intact from the skin.

"You must use sometimes three or four threads for one tick. If an infected tick has been on you more than two hours, it is bad. But five hours is critical, the most dangerous threshold. Then each day for three days you must give yourself a shot of gamma globulin. It can perhaps help—although I do not know if it can be found here now. We will give you the name of a doctor, a specialist who may have some."

"How serious is the disease?" I asked him.

"It begins with symptoms like flu," he said. "Fever and aching—three to twenty days after infection, but an average of seven days. There is no treatment, although one must be gotten to the hospital for palliative support. The damage is neurological. You may die. Or it may cause one's brain to be like the brain of an idiot. The best variant—"

That's how he put it. The *best* variant.

"—is paralysis."

The place we intended to go had begun to sound pestilential. Then it was Turov's turn again.

"Also there is the river itself," he said. "You say you expect water of moderate difficulty. But the upper part is of the hardest degree of difficulty. It is like a slalom, crashing from one wall of the canyon to the other, with boulders larger than a man."

"What is more," Turov continued, "the snow was very heavy in the Baikal Mountains last winter." He took a box of stick matches from his pocket, and emptied the matches in a jumble on the table. "The fallen trees will be like *this* across the river."

"It could take as much as three weeks—" said Medbedev.

"No, four," Turov corrected him. "Maybe even six."

"—to travel the uppermost part of the river, from the head-waters to Kachug."

"Are you saying it can't be done?"

"I'm saying that you will have to carry your boats, everything, around all the impassable places. Believe me, you will find there only pure torture. Of course," he added with a rueful little smile, "torture is itself a form of learning."

"But it's also *time*," I said.

"Exactly. Much, much time."

Bychkov had said last year the upper river was impossible. Now these men were saying the same. What if they were right? Suppose it did take a month or more to travel the first 150 miles of a 2,800-mile river. Our expedition would fail foolishly there in the mountains at the very start, having already lost its race with the short summer to the Arctic coast.

Medbedev was writing on a piece of paper the name and tele-phone number of the woman doctor from whom it could be possi-ble to obtain several capsules of gamma globulin (though, as it turned out, we would be unable to reach her). The professors were talking among themselves—discussing, Sergei said, the possibility that we might rent horses in some village near the shore of Lake Baikal, and attempt the trek on horseback with native guides.

The plan that had seemed so fixed was coming desperately unraveled.

"Ask them if we can meet again tomorrow morning," I told Sergei. "I want Victor to hear what they have to say."

❧

T HE REST OF THIS day is too crowded. The red bus is waiting at the hotel to carry us off to a luncheon at the dacha of Sasha Abalakov's parents. Both his father and mother were university professors. They are hospitable—with no fewer than 16 people pressed round the table in their cottage. Sasha opens a trap door in the floor of the room and brings up fresh raspberries for dessert. The open trap sends up a breath of cold from the root cellar, whose earthen walls still are frozen in June.

Anxiety gnaws, and I hardly can eat. Then there is a visit to a reconstructed log church. After that, a drive to the village farther up the Angara to film Yuri Panov, the sculptor of political totem poles whom we met last September. He is not home, but his wife expects him any time. We wait on the dirt road out front, while the sun slides down the sky. When Panov does come, the filming goes badly because of my distracted amateurism and the failing light.

It is nearly 9 o'clock before we are back in Irkutsk. We have missed a dinner Goldfarb had arranged in a Chinese restaurant. The hotel restaurant is closed as well. The Americans gather in one of the rooms, and I recount in complete detail everything that was said in the morning meeting with the professors. Consensus is immediate. The risks—for the members of the raft party and for the expedition—are simply too great. We have no choice but to use a helicopter to travel to the source, and along that initial stretch of the river. I am bitterly disappointed, even if I know it can't be helped.

The photographer and videographer will go with Victor and me to tomorrow's meeting with the professors. But it is impossible to imagine what could change our feelings about it.

❧

V ICTOR SLOUCHED LOW IN a chair, jaw clenched, listening to the professors recite their litany of difficulties. His agitation was plain to see.

"Victor does not understand the reason for this meeting,"

Sergei whispered. So we stepped away for a moment to the end of the room.

"Who involved these people?" Victor said.

"I thought you arranged yesterday's meeting."

"No, Goldfarb did."

"Well, they have raised some questions about schedule—the time it will take to do it. I thought you should hear them yourself." It was delicate. I didn't want Victor to think I'd lost confidence in him.

"All right," he said. "I will listen." And he sat again at the table.

The professors had brought with them another colleague, a wizened, bearded little man they described as the foremost explorer of the upper Lena. He spoke very slowly, very certainly, through his dark whiskers.

"With a helicopter," he said, "anything is possible. It is the only way."

"If this expedition had been planned correctly," said Turov, "we would have been asked to give our advice, and we could have told you this at the beginning."

The expert nodded.

"By helicopter, yes," he said. "By water, no. You cannot even dream of traveling the upper part of the river with rafts."

Victor's voice was very soft as he leaned toward him across the table—the voice of fury just barely contained.

"Tell me. Have you, yourself, ever actually traveled that part of the river?"

The little man smiled derisively.

"No," he said. "And what is more, I would *never* do it."

"Then you speak of something you haven't seen!"

Argument erupted, then. A little of it I got, from the hours spent with the tapes. Some Sergei interpreted. Most I missed. At one point, Turov slammed his palm flat on the table, pushed back his chair with a clatter and stood.

"*Let* them go," he said. "Just let them go!" He stalked to an open window, lit a cigarette and stood with his back to the rest of us, smoking, wanting no further part of it.

It wasn't settled in that room. It couldn't be.

We walked down afterward, the three of us with Sergei and Victor, to the embankment of the Angara where it ran dark and powerful past the city. We spread the map in the brilliance of the late-morning sun and reviewed it all again.

"The problem," said the photographer, "is that we won't be able to travel fast. We may have to stop someplace and wait for a day, two days, until the light is right for making pictures."

And about this he was perfectly right.

"Look, we came to do the whole river," I told Victor. "We *want* to do the whole river. It isn't a question of what we prefer."

It sickened me to think of missing that first wilderness part— of giving it up before we even started. But it depended on so many things I didn't know—that none of us could know until we got there and found the truth for ourselves, when knowing might be too late. And did I have any right to put the whole enterprise at risk for the sake of that first 150 miles?

"It's a question of time," I said. "If we use a helicopter, then time isn't an issue."

"The helicopter is one variant," Victor said. "It can be arranged." But it was clear the very idea of it disheartened him.

We stared together at the map, spread out at the base of the stone stairway that came down from the street to the river. Some young people paused on the walkway above, peered down curiously for a moment, then passed on.

"I have checked it all," Victor said. "I have talked with a man at a forest station not far from the place where we begin. The ticks are not so bad. We will check ourselves carefully. But the forest guard says that, for some reason, there are only a few of them this year. I will carry a gun for bears, and I am able to use it."

"Those aren't the biggest problems. If it takes us a month—"

"It won't," he insisted. "It will take one week. Maybe nine days—no more. And the river *can* be passed. It's true there was much snow, and there were many fallen trees. But the melting in spring also was heavy, and it must have carried a lot of them away."

He looked at me, and his eyes begged for belief.

"It is your expedition," he said. "So, in the end, I will do as you say we must. But understand that I have been planning for half a year now to travel the Lena from its beginning to the very end. When a thing is planned, it should be done."

You could hear his enthusiasm begin to rise again, with a force that was hard not to share.

"In my opinion, the upper river will be the most delicious part. It is the part where we will have the chance to prove ourselves against real things. Not against bureaucrats. Not against this crazy system. But against real things—perhaps bears, and the river itself."

His fist was clenched, now, not in anger but in utter resolve.

"Not to do that part of the river," he said, "would be like *taking the raisin out of the bun!*"

I had begun to understand better how many uncertainties lay ahead. If we were to trust this man with critical judgments for the next two months on the river, how could we not trust him at the start? We looked at him—at his fierce smile of absolute conviction—and then at one another. And I believe we suspected then, reckless as it might be, that we would leave the raisin in the bun.

"Let us sleep on it," I told Victor. "And I'll give you the decision in the morning."

"It must be tomorrow," he said. "Already many things are in motion."

⚜

ANOTHER MEETING IN GOLDFARB'S office runs deep into evening. The car with our cargo did not come on today's train, either, and now time has gotten critical. Unless it arrives tomorrow, on Friday, Sunday's departure is sure to be delayed.

All there, except Jennie who is sleeping at the hotel. Katie, Anne, the soundperson and the photographer's wife have been alarmed to learn that we now are inclined to return to the original plan, in spite of the professors' warnings. And Victor makes his case again for the benefit of the others. Goldfarb also speaks.

Some of those men were his teachers at the university, he says. "When they are in the *taiga*, they are really good men. But there is jealousy, I think." They may resent that he did not organize the venture through them. "Also, with the economic situation now, they no longer have the possibility to make such great expeditions." In other words, if they can't do it themselves, they want no one else to. Human nature is everywhere the same.

Glasses are found, and a small bottle of vodka is produced and poured around. "To your decision," says Victor, and lifts his glass.

We go out into the night, after 11 p.m., the photographer and videographer convinced, with me, that it is feasible, the dismay of the others evident. Afterward, in the hotel room, I try to give Katie a conciliatory kiss on the neck, but she draws furiously away.

"You know I'm completely against it!"

TWENTY-FOUR

FRIDAY BEGINS WELL ENOUGH. Sleep has mended spirits, and Katie awakens if not happy with the decision at least resigned. Victor is in the hotel lobby early. We've decided to do the whole river, I tell him, and he's elated. But it depends on the train coming with the rest of our cargo today, and on getting the gamma globulin for the raft party. (He will try to reach the doctor again—and again will fail. Evidently she's away from Irkutsk.)

Meantime, there's much work to do. The food and equipment stored under lock at Goldfarb's office must be sorted and divided in two rooms. The Russians are awed by the sheer bulk of all we've brought. One room is for the provisions and gear that will have to be carried over the Baikal ridge to the headwaters. The photographer and videographer, because they will be working as we climb, will need to travel light. I will carry a pack of 40 to 50 pounds. Victor, the other two Russian rafters and four men he's hired as porters will have to manage all the rest, including the two inflatable rafts, three tents, their personal gear and the videographer's heavy tripod and camera box. It seems impossible, but Victor is determined they can somehow manage it.

The other room is for the rest of the cargo—the much greater part—which the other members of the expedition will bring around by rough road, using the red bus and possibly a flatbed truck, to Kachug, the first town on the Lena, where the two groups will be reunited when our raft party comes out of the mountains.

We are beginning to know the other main members of Victor's team. Volodya, who was with us the day at Baikal, is a tall, studious looking young man with large brown eyes magnified through thick glasses, a soft voice and gentle, self-effacing manner. His work at the Geographical Institute has to do with Siberian population distribution and causes of mortality.

The other is Valerei Dimitriavich Sherstyanikov—Valera, he's called. Like Victor, he has the look of an athlete. Those two are friends from university days, and have made other, smaller expeditions together. Valera lost most of four fingers on his right hand in some accident so early in childhood that he does not remember the event, but it seems in no way to handicap him. He is a hydrologist, who studies the quality and flow of the region's rivers. Valera speaks no English at all, but smiles quickly and gives the impression of someone you'd be glad to have beside you in any sort of bad situation.

Victor will pass his 38th birthday on the river, Valera his 37th, Volodya his 30th. "All of us are Lions," Volodya says, meaning they all were born under the sign of Leo. On July 22, the last day of Cancer—exactly one month before Valera's—I will mark my own anniversary, the 58th, oldest of them all by 20 years. What might that day bring, and where will we be then?

The division of the equipment goes smoothly at first. Misha comes to announce that the train car with the canoes has just arrived—news that buoys us all. Katie and the photographer's wife are trying to plan rations for the boat journey up Baikal, the climb, and the overland travel to Kachug, and extricate those provisions from boxes in the main, unsorted heap.

Then, unaccountably, there's new contention.

"Why can't the Russians take their own food?" the photographer asks, though lord knows we have enough. The food we brought, I tell him, trying not to bristle, is for the whole party of 12—in fact, enough for 14 people, to give a margin—for the whole length of the river. "That was the deal I made," I say. "Food's short here."

"All right. But I don't see why we have to furnish sleeping bags. They must have something they can use."

"Because that's why I brought the bags." Again, there are 14 sleeping bags for 12 persons.

Now every item becomes an issue. I put one of the small mountain stoves and a container of fuel with the pile for my pack. He thinks that's foolish, and maybe it is. But if dry firewood can't be found in the upper canyon, I want to be sure of a way to boil drinking water. We can't afford illness so far from help.

"The stove goes up," I say. Not so much in logic, now, as stubbornness. "I'm the one carrying it. It goes."

The work is slowed by argument over details. It's plain we won't finish, and that much will have to be left for tomorrow, the last day. The Russians are mystified at the fissures they see opening among the Americans. I can read it in their eyes. What will their relations be with us, they must be wondering, if we're already at odds *among ourselves*? (The dissension has so demoralized Sergei, he will confess the next day, that he has lain awake until dawn, considering whether he should quit the expedition.)

We go back to the hotel for a late supper, with far too little accomplished. Olga has spent the day in her room, recovering from what Misha describes as "food intoxication"—some kind of stomach bug that has smitten her with violent and unrelenting diarrhea. Our medicine chest yields the remedy, but it is left to the soundperson to explain to Olga, woman to woman, the efficacy and application of suppositories.

A sour mood hangs over the night's meeting. Afterward, sleepless in the half-light of the room, I turn the situation in mind and understand, finally, that I have created the problem myself.

When Victor speaks to one of his men, saying what must be done, there is no discussion. The decisions, and the responsibility for them, are entirely his. His relationship with the others—although they are his friends—is unencumbered by any pretense of democracy.

I have tried a more collegial style, imagining we could find our way to the Lena's end through consensus. And I have been wrong. Now everyone imagines himself a leader, and the result is indecision and endless talk. *Like meetings of some American komsomol*, Victor has said. Of course the natures of Russians and Americans are different because of our different histories. But what I should have said, in recruiting the others, was, "You go by invitation, and you go on my terms. And if that doesn't suit you, now's the time to say so. Because that's how it will be."

When I was a young officer in the military, command had seemed an easy thing. The lines of authority were clear. And now I have learned something that will be useful if I ever attempt such a thing as this again, which is that an expedition has more in common with a military operation than a democratic exercise. For now, though, the harm is done. But I can't be concerned with that. We have obligations to the expedition's sponsors, to the Russians, and to this task we've set ourselves. We *will* get down this river if it's humanly possible, and civility is not the issue. What counts is only that we do our work along the way.

These are the night thoughts.

And in the morning Jennie is worse—her throat inflamed, covered with pustules and so swollen she scarcely can swallow, the fever rising. We will begin treating her with a different and stronger antibiotic. It's necessary to consider the possibility she may have to be left behind. But left where? Here? Or sent back to Moscow— with the idea she might rejoin us by plane at some later point? Or be flown back to the States, missing the river altogether?

Katie stays with her, and the rest go to complete the sorting of equipment. A plan is made for the food. One set of provisions will be packed for the overland party. The photographer's wife will supervise the rations for the American and Russian rafters and the porters climbing with them to the headwaters, and also for the days on the upper river until the rafts arrive at Kachug.

Somehow the day is accomplished. The climbers' packs are built. Mine is heavier than expected, and in the end I leave out the stove and fuel that provoked such resentment. The load is well-balanced and feels comfortable as I cross to the hotel, although carrying it 20-some miles, much of that climbing, may be a different matter.

I find Jennie slightly better. And dinner is a more congenial affair. Anticipation has begun to lift us, as I guessed it might. Then there is a final crisis. Olga, recovered from her malady, and Misha have demanded a meeting.

"WE WANT TO SPEAK about going with you the first part of the river," said Misha. "At least to Zhigalovo. Or maybe to Ust'Kut."

I couldn't believe he'd propose it, on the last night before leaving.

"It can't be done," I said. Victor's insistence on having no Moscow people along was absolute. In any case, cramped space would forbid it.

"Why not?"

"You heard the discussion with Tishkov," I told him. "Twelve is the limit."

"But we expected to go."

"That's not what Tishkov said. He said you and Olga would remain in Irkutsk, to handle any problems that came up. And that you'd meet us at the Arctic."

"I don't think he said that."

"Call him, then." The suggestion surprised him. "Call Tishkov, and ask him yourself."

"It's Saturday," Misha said. "He won't be at the Institute."

"Call him at home, then."

Sad-eyed, he shook his head.

"I would not prefer to do that. But we, Olga and I, have worked very hard on this project. We would like to go part of the way."

"I'm sorry," I told him. There was no doubt they'd worked hard. But they had been paid well for doing it.

"You will have many problems on the river. It's sure. Problems with local authorities, which maybe Gulevich and his people cannot solve."

"Then somehow we'll contact you here. That's what Tishkov said to do."

Sergei was with us, interpreting. And Olga spoke up, then.

"I have lost many tears because of this project." *Yes,* I thought, *but you found a man.* Olga was cleverer than Misha, and also tougher.

"Without us, your expedition could not have happened."

"Without the Institute, you mean."

"We arranged the licenses for traveling in closed places. We arranged permission from the KGB to open the river. We made the contracts with the Irkutsk people."

"I know all that. And I'm grateful."

Her face hardened, and her slightly almond eyes narrowed.

"You understand that you are here as official guests of the Institute. It is only by authority of the Institute that you can travel the river at all."

"Is that a threat?" I asked her. If it was, I knew she had neither the right to make it nor the means to back it.

She knew it, too.

"No, it's not a threat."

"You can travel with us on Baikal, to the start," I said. "Then you come back to Irkutsk."

That was the end of it. They went disconsolately back to their room.

⚜

N IGHT—OR WHAT PASSES for night at this latitude. The last one for a long time that we will spend in a regular bed.

The trail is not inclined upward, as a mountain trail should be. It meanders through a spongy lowland, with vines and great-leaved foliage pressing in from either side, exuberant as the verdure in a Rousseau painting. I notice a black insect crawling on the shirt-back of the man ahead of me, and reach to brush it away. Then I see there are more on his neck and in his hair. We stop, all of us, tearing at our clothes. Our bodies are covered with the nasty black bugs—so many of them that our skin seems to move. They cannot be brushed away. They are fastened to us, some only lightly, others attached firmly, swollen to the size of grapes.

I hear myself shout out hoarsely, and sit up in a sweat. "What is it?" Katie asks, alarmed. "Nothing," I tell her. "A dream."

Now the way is impossibly steep, loose stones dislodging underfoot and clattering down. The weight of the pack increases with each upward step gained. The sun arcs across the sky above us, but the summit, instead of coming nearer, recedes. The others pass me and climb on ahead, then they stop, looking back, waiting. It is clear I cannot proceed. They come back then, and in an agony of helplessness and humiliation I watch as they divide up my part of the cargo. Now the pack is empty, but I can neither go ahead nor imagine any way to go back down. The sense of failure is total. I retch, and digestive fluids surge searingly into my throat.

Stumbling to the bathroom, I spit into the sink and rinse my mouth with water from the tap. This time Katie has not wakened. Looking down from the window into the alleyway behind the hotel, I watch a woman in a blue smock shuffle through the stillness of the lonely dawn. It is half past 2 a.m. After her, two drunks come reeling, supporting one another in a crazy embrace. A truck passes. Leaning against a wooden packing case, the two men sit to smoke.

Afraid to sleep again, I get out my journal and bring the entries up to date through yesterday. It helps to put one word after another. Words steady the churning, and give the illusion of order to the ungovernable. Only when writing is a writer ever safe.

Now morning. And Jennie is much improved. She is able to swallow. The thermometer shows her temperature at half a degree below normal. She insists she is fit enough to go. All of our party will travel up Baikal to the cape where the climb will begin. The six rafters and porters will start up, and the others will wait on the boat below for three days, until the porters come back down unburdened. Then they will return to Irkutsk and load the main cargo for the overland journey to Kachug.

Departure is planned for 9 o'clock. Our vessel is at its mooring on the Angara—a squat, 50-foot metal-hulled boat of the Yaroslavits type. With the eight Americans, Victor, two Russian rafters, four porters, the interpreter Sergei, and Olga and Misha who will go with us up the lake, our company is swollen to 18, more than twice as many as the little ship was meant to accommodate. Gear is heaved aboard. But even with much of it lashed top-side, covered with a tarp, the crowding in the two small cabins below, fore and aft, will be extreme. Some people will have to sleep on floors, or atop food boxes. Some of the Russians will pass the nights sitting up.

At 10 o'clock the crew still has not shown. Anne goes with Sergei back into town to find a bakery and buy a large supply of bread. The Russians also have brought loaves. The sky above the town is bright and clear, but a wall of impenetrable fog rises white over the cold water of the river. Maybe there has been some misunderstanding about the time of leaving. Or the problem could be something else. "The crew arrived with the boat not long ago," Victor says. "And it's possible they have gone to drink."

⚜

A PARTY HAD COME to wish us off. Goldfarb we would not see again. Volodya and Valera would be waiting with the others in Kachug.

"Dear Charles," said Volodya—in his shy, formal way of beginning almost every conversation. "I have to pay you."

"Pay for what?"

"For the knife, of course." To Victor and his team I'd made gifts of three of the fine skinning knives sent with us by the Buck Knife company in California. Volodya pressed into my hand a shiny five-kopek piece, worth at that moment about one-fifth of a U.S. penny.

"Two things must always be paid for," he said. "A knife and a dog. Or else the knife will be lost, and the dog will die."

Then the crew appeared, looking only a little disheveled, and Anne and Sergei came back with a dozen dark, crusty loaves in a sack. A bit after 10:30 a light wind rose, the sun burned through the shroud of white, the diesel engine of the Yaroslavits growled to life and hawsers were unwrapped from the pilings.

The figures at the anchorage grew smaller, waving as long as they could be seen.

Fog banks lay against the dark hillsides, and in places flowed down to fill the river, where fishermen in native wooden canoes anchored in the current. Then we had to stop, waiting for the way to clear again. The air, when the fog wrapped the boat, was chilly as autumn. And the delays—although we couldn't know it—were only the first of many longer ones to come.

It was well into afternoon before we were able finally to see the great boulder that thrusts above the water to mark the Angara's beginning. As we neared that place, the river's bottom rose up to meet us, giving an illusion the boat's speed had increased. The bed of rounded stones flashed under and past, seen through water as transparent as air. Huge grayling, some nearly as long as a man's arm, fled away to either side, swift as birds in flight. Everyone was above deck, and our excitement swept any troubles away.

To the right lay the last dark point of land thrusting outward into the immense blue lake, which met us with its breath of greater cold. And then, suddenly as if we'd been launched from a cliff, the shallow bottom fell away into the mile-deeps of Baikal. Victor was beside me at the rail, and at exactly that moment his hand closed powerfully around my wrist.

"It is begun," he said. "May God be with us."

V

A World of Shattered Stone:
The Upper River

TWENTY-FIVE

ALREADY WE HAVE BEEN too long aboard. The place where the climb to the Lena's headwaters will start is called the Pokoyniki Cape, named for *"those who have found peace"*—in blunter translation, the Cape of the Dead. It lies only 250 miles up Baikal, and we'd planned to reach there the second night, but the trip has taken parts of four days instead. So already precious time is lost.

The first afternoon was fine, with panoramas of incredible beauty as the mountains that rim the lake's western side grew higher, fiercer. On that shore, sheer faces plunge to the water, some with grottoes at their bases. In places where roots can find a purchase, forest grows. Above those is the smooth slant of emerald alpine meadows. And higher still, summits capped with snow. That night we passed at an inlet called Bukhta Peschanaya (Sandy Bay). There was a forester's house, a rough plank table, and a place for building fires. Logs were dragged, a stew boiled. In the smoke of the fire, the mosquitoes were not so bad. All sat to eat together, and there was a sense of comradeship and shared adventure binding the group at last. The wild-bearded forester came to visit, smelling powerfully of what he'd drunk. To relieve the crowding, six Russians slept in one of the large tents, and Jennie, Anne and I in another. The rest spent the night on the boat.

On the second day our progress slowed. The great lake can be whipped by terrible winds in this season, but now it lay still and dark as pooled oil. Our enemy again was the fog, which billowed up from the cold water and hung in a curtain through which our Yaroslavits could not pass. Wrapped in heavy coats, we crowded into the tiny cabin or walked the rail above, made tea on one of the gasoline stoves, examined maps. When the fog lifted a bit, the machinist went below to start the engine and we were able to advance for part of an hour, the captain and mate pressing their faces against the glass of the wheelhouse, feeling their way cautiously, studying their charts. Then the whiteness closed, and we stopped again.

By noon we were blocked completely, and had to lie at mooring the rest of the day in another bay, that one named Beautiful (Bukhta Aya). There was a rotting pier with a ship already tethered there, halted for repairs—a research ship, with a bathyscape on its deck. The bay was flanked by high stone cliffs that vanished and reappeared in the drifting fog. Inland could be seen a rising green meadow dotted with sheep and, at a distance, the rough wooden lodgings of the Buryat shepherds. We built a fire ashore and huddled around it for lunch. The Russians approve especially of the tinned tuna, which can't be gotten anymore—at least not in Irkutsk. Volodya says he remembers eating it once when he was a boy, but that was so long ago that he has forgotten the taste.

Then the rain came, driving us back aboard our ship, and worsened all through the day. The Yaroslavits' one small head must serve for the eighteen of us, twenty-one counting the crew, and is best visited at strange hours. As I crept there barefoot on the cold deck at 2 a.m., rain still was pelting and fog hung close. But sometime after that it must have lifted, because we woke as the boat nudged to a mooring at a different and hideous place.

Its name was Khuzhir, or Salt Lick, for the mineral that deer and other wild animals once found there. After the animals came the people, settled by order of the government in the late 1930s to fish for *omul*, the Baikal whitefish. A processing plant was built, but a few years after that, the same government closed the fishery, leaving the people of Khuzhir marooned without industry or occupation. The look of brokenness and defeat was total. Derelict boats subsided in rot on the stony beach, although a couple still appeared to have families living in them. Mud streets ran up into the hamlet, and a man on a motorcycle with side-car churned along one of them, flinging up a gooey spray. Our supply of bread was decreasing, and Victor and two of the porters put on rubber boots to trudge up the hill past the dismal board lodgings, the party headquarters and the sad, weathered little movie house in search of a bakery.

We had passed from the main lake into a large strait, known as the Minor Sea, lying between the shore and Baikal's largest island. Misha pointed out the place on the map. From Czarist days, he said, Olkhon Island had a history as a place of exiles—Poles, Ukrainians, Germans and others sent there after uprisings and wars.

The rain lightened. The weather gave promise of clearing. Even in the most wretched places, Russians bake good bread, so Victor's errand was successful. We were glad to hear the rumble of the engine. Salt Lick is no place to linger. The first sun in more than a day broke through the overcast, and we watched the changing topography of the huge island slip past: at the water's edge, a spire of lichen-crusted stone held sacred by the native Buryat people; then another settlement seen at great distance, huddled at the base of a vast sand dune; then dark hills crested with wind-blown pines; then more looming rock faces.

Victor is a passionate fisherman, and he and his team are amused by the gear we brought. Fishing in these waters is "very specific," he says. No lures of the sort we have will ever fool a grayling. At lunch, with the ship drawn up in a rocky cove, we got the chance to try. Clambering up the cliffside and out onto a shelf of projecting boulders, we could see fish—fine, fat-bodied ones—feeding among the stones. Anne took one on her second cast, and then another. Our comrades were delighted but also a bit amazed, since fishing isn't something Russian women commonly do. In only a quarter-hour we had four—not a meal, but enough for a taste for all.

We have borne on now to northward, the lake's surface showing a light chop. Here hummocks of stone project above the water, limed white by the colonies of gulls that flutter up shrieking at our passage. Baikal is home to the world's only fresh-water seals, called *nerpas*. With luck, we might see some, Victor says. And our luck must be running, because it is not long before a curious little face, large-eyed and bewhiskered, shows itself close beside the boat. It's a good omen, and Victor is encouraged. By evening we will certainly be at the Pokoyniki Cape, he says, ready to begin our climb at an early hour.

We aren't, though. Patches of fog come drifting, and combine to make a wall. And by afternoon we're stopped again. The captain nudges the Yaroslavits ashore. Our whole party goes far down the rocky beach, upon which past storms have tumbled up windrows of rounded pebbles, some as big as melons. We drag driftwood to build a fire for warmth against a wind as cold as December that comes raking off the water and through our coats. A strange, drumming sound is heard, grows louder. From behind a screen of scrub pines, then past us and out across a grassy clearing, comes a herd of horses—Buryat ponies gone wild, Victor says—in full run, uncut manes and tails flying.

Also running, but along the beach, comes the captain, arms waving, hurling silent shouts into the wind. The waves are rising, becoming dangerous for the boat. Together we fling and drag the burning logs into the water's edge, then hurry back aboard the Yaroslavits to spend a night heaving and pitching, but anchored safely out from the rocks.

The videographer and soundperson mean to sleep on deck, out of the crowding, but are driven back inside, dripping and miserable, by yet another spell of driving rain. The wretched weather seems to have no end.

TWENTY-SIX

IT HAD BEEN FOUR hours since waking to the sound of the motor starting, and the shudder under me of the food boxes on which I'd made my bed. The time then was 5 a.m.

Breakfast was taken in haste and nervousness, then packs were dragged topside. Distribution of foodstuffs for the climb had been assigned to Misha—a mistake. His carelessness would be discovered and paid for later.

"*Thick milk,*" said the captain, staring glumly into the fog. Ten minutes short of our destination we were stopped again. Then, by the power of our wishing, it lifted and we ran the last several hundred yards to shore.

A little weather outpost called "Sunny Station" perched just up from the lake's edge. The young meteorologist came down to meet us, and he and Victor went together to the station, a single wooden cottage with instruments on poles at the side, to send a message to Irkutsk, saying we were about to begin the climb.

I wondered if they'd put the outpost there for any reason

besides the haunting beauty of the setting. All around lay a field rank with waving grass and wildflowers. Behind was a forest of larch and pine, with mounds of wild azaleas in flower at its edge. Then the steep, tree-furred hills that were the mountains' beginning. And finally—seeming very near in the sudden clearing of the morning—the mountains themselves, in ascending ranks, their upper parts vanishing into a low bank of clouds. Unseen up there somewhere was the comb of the ridge, and beyond that the Lena.

It was beautiful to look at, if you didn't have to wonder about getting up it.

The days on the boat had let me sort out the people and their duties. Little Sasha, the geomorphologist with the squeaky voice, would be one of the porters. Vladimir Alexandrovich Kuzmin, a cheerful man with red mustache and goatee, would be another. He was, I'd learned, a specialist in cybernetics. Then there were Victor's and Vladimir's sons, Alyosha and Edward. They were boys of only 16 and 15 years, and I worried when I saw the packs they meant to carry. I needn't have.

The rafters, besides Victor and the three Americans, would be Alexander Oktyabrevich Shepotko (Big Sasha) and Andrei Stepanovich Petrash (Andrusha). They, too, would climb with loads.

This Big Sasha, a 40-year-old theoretical chemist, looked like a man from the mountains of Kentucky. Tall, coonhound-thin and a bit withdrawn, he was a minimalist. His only items of personal gear, as far as I could ever see, were a metal spoon and the empty sardine tin he used for both bowl and teacup. Those hung by a cord from his belt.

Andrusha was a slight fellow of 31, still a student in search of some vocation, *any* vocation, who squinted myopically at the world through unconfident eyes. Andrusha was somehow comical, and not very adept, but he was willing—a quality that would count for something where we were going.

We six would travel the upper river together. When rafts and supplies had been gotten to the put-in place, the other four would retrace the way back down to the lakeshore and the waiting boat, and return with the rest of the party to Irkutsk.

Victor came from the weather station, his message sent. The sun's appearance had been brief. A light mist began to settle. "How much are you carrying?" I asked him.

"Is okay."

"How much?"

"Maybe forty kilos. No more."

Forty kilograms was nearly 90 pounds. In his load were the videographer's heavy tripod. A 30-pound metal camera box. God knows what else.

"Let me lift it."

Using both hands, I barely could get it off the ground. It was a hundred pounds at a minimum. The loads of the others also were stupendous, but Victor's was the greatest.

Big Sasha and the meteorologist together hefted it so he could put his arms through the straps. They were making adjustments, trying to get the balance better. Pain and surprise showed for an instant on his face, and I knew Victor couldn't believe it either. Then his expression was only determination.

"Is okay," he said again.

"No, it *isn't* okay."

No man I ever knew would even have tried to carry such a pack 20 miles on level ground, much less climb with it up a rough trail over a crest of mountains. But that was the only way to the river.

The photographer and videographer were saying their good-bys. Katie's anger about the climb was gone, but I could hear her concern—Anne and Jennie's, too—along with their excitement.

"Be very careful."

"I will."

"And check for ticks."

"Remember, every two hours."

"I will. We'll all be careful. And we'll see you in Kachug." I looked at my watch. It was just before 10 o'clock on the morning of June 26. "In something like a week."

Victor had taken the bear gun from its canvas wrap and loaded the magazine, leaving the chamber empty. He held it horizontally across his middle with both hands, leaning forward, as if the gun might somehow help balance the weight behind.

"Yes?" he said.

And, turning, he led us in a single file up past the meteorologist's little house and across the green meadow of flowers.

❧

THE FIRST OF THE way is flat. After the field there's a pine lowland,
scarred and thinned by an old fire, with wild iris and primrose
blooming. My own pack seems possible. Looking at the others, how
can I complain?

The way steepens. Up ahead, through the trees, can be seen
the gorge up which we must climb. Quickly I'm suffering. My wind
is not so bad, but my legs begin to cramp. I damn all the cigarettes
I've ever smoked. And damn all the years it's taken me to get here.
Ahead, the Russians under their awful loads are climbing as steadily
as goats.

The way steepens more. On the worst parts, I try to gain 10
steps before stopping. And I know that the others are slowing on
my account. Ten steps more, and stop. Loose stones roll underfoot,
and rubbery legs struggle to regain balance. Then another 10. Then
the pitch moderates, and I'm able to get 20 steps—once even 50.
At one stop Victor leaves his pack and comes back down, concerned. He takes my pulse and checks my fingers for clubbing. He
knows what to look for. The trouble's not the heart, though, but
the legs.

I make myself think of other things. Of the thickets of rhodo-
dendron we're climbing through, and the columbine and lady's slip-
per and little orange flowers, with petals like poppies, that cling so
stubbornly among the moss and rocks. The rain comes harder now,
and wets us through before we can unshoulder packs and get
waterproof jackets on. Ten steps. Then 10 more.

The afternoon stop is on a level shelf, with a stream running
through a cathedral grove of ancient pines. Little Sasha finds a fall-
en branch and uses his hatchet to cut away the wet outer part and
get shavings of dry, inner wood. This small man with the comical
squeak of a voice is a skilled outdoorsman, builder of a quick fire.

More wood is added. Pots of stream water are hung to boil over the flames.

Soup. Chocolate bars. Hot tea. An hour's rest, and unburdened legs get some feeling back.

Then worse and steeper afterward. "God damn it," I groan to no one. "This is a young man's work!" Big Sasha has heard, although I didn't mean for him to. He doesn't know English, but he knows despair when he hears it and wants to take my pack—indicates how he could hang it on his front. It's absurd! His own towers a good two feet above his head. Then the boy, Edward, asks if he might have it. I call Victor, and through him—with signs, and with the few words we know of one another's languages—make known the importance to me of getting up this mountain and to the river with my own gear. Pride counts for something, I tell them.

It is a powerful argument, Sasha admits. They nod, understanding and accepting it. And we labor on up.

The contours of these mountains are not shaped by the patient processes of time. They are the product of violence—of a seismically active region that experiences some 300 small quakes a year, and of the stone-splintering frosts of nearly 70 degrees below zero Fahrenheit. The gorge we're climbing looks like a cleavage blasted out with explosives. The forest thins, gives way to wiry bushes and planes of slippery, shattered rock. Rain beats harder, and the wind comes unimpeded, chilling us through at every brief rest.

Just as the ordeal begins to seem endless, there is a slow, painful scramble up one last pitch of talus...and unexpectedly we are astride a saddle between two peaks. Behind and far below, in the V of the cleft, lies the undefined blue sea-sky vastness of Baikal, with sunlight and cloud shadows playing on it—a different world. Up here there's a rock cairn, in which there's rumored to be a tin box with a paper to write your name on. We hunt for several minutes but can't find the box. Then, punished by fatigue and the weather, we just add one stone to the pile and turn to the other side.

Several hundred yards below us is an alpine valley, dotted dark with stunted cedars, curving away between the flanks of softer mountains in whose folds the snow still lies. Through that valley comes running a little brook, a streamlet you could step across at its smaller turnings.

"Please, Charles," says the Russian at my elbow. "Allow me to invite you to the Lena River."

A few miles up on those mountains' flanks are the glacial seeps and snow-melt rivulets out of whose gatherings the great river is born. But this is the place geographers classify as its source. Another hard day remains before we will reach the point for launching rafts, and four of our men—Big Sasha, Andrusha, Vladimir and his son Edward—have gone on ahead, hoping to gain a few miles more before stopping for the night.

In rain and cold, the other six of us drop down from the ridge to make our camp. Wood is scarce, the branches of the gnarled cedars tough as iron. Our fire is smoky and small. We bend over it, wet to our hides, exhausted. In such a place, in such weather, a fire is the light of hope.

We discover the first mistake, which was Misha's. Somehow, only dry oatmeal, one bag of raisins and another of dry granola— the breakfast ration—made it into the packs we carry. All the rest he put in the loads that went ahead with the others. Sasha's strong tea is the only good part of that unsatisfatory supper. Then we put up the tent, and find the second mistake, mine. Our two pack tents are identical except for size. The one for four, that might have held six with crowding, went on with Big Sasha. We're left with the smaller one, meant for only two or three.

It doesn't matter, Victor says, because the rain is finished now. The clouds have rushed away to the north, leaving a pale speckle of stars across a sky that in this season never quite goes dark. Cold wind comes raking down the barren valley, and a cuckoo can be heard calling from the facing mountainside. The Russians, and maybe others, say that the number of times the cuckoo repeats his two-note song without a pause will tell the hearer how many years of life he has remaining. I know I will be asleep in the tent before the song can end.

We finish the pot of tea, and four of us somehow find room to lie under cover. Victor and his son unroll their bags in the open, beside the last of the embers. The affection between them is clear.

They shared their porridge meal from a single bowl, and now mean to sleep pressed near together. The boy is so slight as almost to seem frail, but he is made from the same material as his father. He carried a massive pack, and climbed without complaint.

ↂↂↂ

T HE CLOSENESS OF THE tent filled up with the warmth of the others of us sleeping. I hadn't rested well for several nights. Too many vain questions had come crowding: *What if my legs failed me, and I couldn't make it to the ridge? What if I had to turn back, defeated at the very start, and let the others go on?*

Those doubts were answered now, and it wasn't a bad dream that woke me but a peal of thunder rattling among the peaks, and rain beating on the tent. I threw back the fly and could see that a new cloud mass had poured into the valley. Driven by the mounting wind, it rushed low overhead in the 2 a.m. twilight, alive with lightning pulses. The fire was cold, drowned. Victor was sitting against a cedar bush, his arms around Alyosha, one plastic poncho over the two of them.

"Come in," I called to him.

"Too many there," he answered. "Is okay." He meant to sit the night through that way, holding the boy. His nature, we would learn, was both tender and unyielding. He liked the hardship— liked the testing. And there was nothing in him of self-pity.

"Damn it," I shouted into the deluge. "Come in!"

Four pairs of legs were drawn up fetally to make a place, and the two of them lay crossways at the bottom. At the edge of sleep again, I could hear the infant river 30 yards below, its bends still banked with snow, tumbling over stones as it hurried to gather its thousand tributaries and race the short, short summer to the polar sea.

TWENTY-SEVEN

JUNE 27, CAMP DISCOURAGEMENT.

We reached here at noon, with only three or maybe four hours' trek still ahead, and lingered over our midday fire. A thing seems easy—and, forgetting the immensity of the wilderness you're afoot in, you're taken off your guard.

So now we're back again tonight, in this same place. It happened like this.

The high valley of the headwaters, where we'd made our first camp, was lovely in morning sunlight. The storm had blown out, and the cuckoo was calling through the cold morning. We made a late and lazy start, following the little river's course, descending gradually through a dapple of mountain sun and cloud shadow into the zone of trees and greenery again.

It was queer, amid such beauty, to feel an ache of sadness. I should have been experiencing elation, but the country reminded me of forests and high meadows in the Front Range of the Colorado Rockies when our girls—and we—were young. Who would have guessed that the sense of irretrievable loss could follow one even *here?*

The way was mostly along game trails, and though it passed up and down across ridges it was good walking and not too punishing. There was a great deal of sign—hoof prints and droppings of deer and elk. And the green splatters left by a diarrheic bear who'd grazed too much. But no bears or other animals were met. And not one tick was found on any of us. It began to seem pointless even to check.

Shortly before midday we came to a curving ravine filled with snow that had compacted to ice—a great floe of it several feet thick, and blue as the sky—and stopped to fill our canteens where the melt ran from it in clear rivulets, as from a tap.

Then we arrived at this place. Evidently it was where the ones who'd gone ahead had spent last night. The ashes of their morning fire were not yet quite cold. We ate the damnable oatmeal, and set out again in bright expectation of what tonight would bring: two commodious tents, a decent supper with tinned meat, macaroni, candy bars, *no porridge!*

The afternoon began with a hard, steep climb that seemed end-less—my left calf and thigh cramping again. The animal track veered somewhat to the right, grew less distinct. The clouds had come back, spilling first a drizzle and then a steady, sullen rain. This last pull was taking longer than we'd expected. Finally we stumbled down a steep hillside—a mile-long hillside—to the valley's bend by the river where the other men, the rafts and the main supplies should be waiting.

It was the wrong valley. It was the wrong river, too small to be the Lena, from whose convoluted course we'd somehow strayed.

"Mistake!" cried Victor, furious at himself. "Bad mistake!"

The decision was to turn back to the noon camp, bitter as that notion was. So for three hours more in failing light we have retraced our way, arriving just at dusk at this place where we were at noon, having made no progress at all, lost another half-day, and gained nothing except a sense of how careful it pays to be when you are passing, even in good company, across some corner of one of the greatest wildernesses left on the planet.

By the end of this ordeal I'm exhausted, wet through, cold. The others are encouraging. They suffer as much, but they're younger.

A plume of smoke is spied rising through the rain beyond the last rise. It turns out Vladimir and Edward had started back toward Baikal, but when they failed to meet us on the trail knew we must be lost, so they'd decided to stop here again, make another fire and wait. They are carrying food, real food—beans and rice and noo-dles. With bellies full and wet clothes drying on sticks beside the fire, everything seems possible again. Tomorrow we will set out once more for the put-in place. And with two more to share the load, the going will be lighter.

⚜

THE MORNING CAME SUNNY, but no one trusted it.

In the first hour of walking we found where we'd gone wrong—where one game trail bent right and another, less distinct, swung left across a bog to parallel the river's course.

Two hard climbs were followed by sharp descents, then a long steady pull up a ridge, with the Lena below to our left, grown now into a substantial stream, audible in its rush over stones.

A pica whistled. "Mouse," said Little Sasha. He was trying to teach himself English a phrase at a time, and I could hear him ahead of me muttering his diligent repetitions: "Game trail... Animal trail... Animal game trail... Game animal trail."

Then, "This is useful plant...Useful plant."

The way his voice slid up into falsetto made him sound undeservedly silly, but he was a good and serious man. He stopped to gather bunches of wild onions for his pack—the mild, single-bladed kind and some of the spicy, two-eared ones with the red stem.

Now that we suffered less there was more opportunity to observe the country. And I was struck by the exploding vigor of life in a place whose season is so short: birds piping their urgent mating songs, beetles processing mulch and turning over leaves, ants building huge piles of chewed duff and bark, flowers erupting everywhere, mosquitoes multiplying in clouds—all risen out of the frozen death of winter to hunt, replicate, feed and be fed upon in a mortal race against time.

Approaching a long, high meadow we heard what sounded for all the world like a voice crying out in the distance. And after several minutes we came to the source of the racket. It was Andrusha, grinning and peering in confusion through his glasses. He said he'd been calling there for most of an hour. What preposterous faith, I thought, to stand somewhere in the endless boreal wilderness and cry unanswered greetings to friends who may be lost, or at least are late. The comedy of that raised all our spirits— that and knowing our march was near its end.

The trail passed out onto a knife-edged spine, falling away on the right into a dry, stony canyon and on the left to the river. Far below, through the trees on the river side, we could see a blaze of orange—one of the rafts inflated. Then the smoke of a fire, and the tent, with ropes strung up to the forest's edge and clothes drying. The camp had a look of permanence and incredible comfort. And all our packs, even Victor's, were suddenly weightless as we clambered over deadfall down the steep sidehill toward the gravel bar and the rush of noisy water.

❧

H ANDSHAKES AND EMBRACES. VICTOR drops his load with a groan. It's lovely here at a bend of the current—the river collecting in a deep green pool against the face of the cliff, then straightening and hurtling powerfully on. At the next turn several hundred yards below, the first of the great rapids can be both seen and heard. The volume and force of the flow, and the clamor of it, are astonishing.

The camp has a settled, companionable feel. But with the delays on Baikal, and another half-day wasted by our getting lost, there's no time to linger. It's early afternoon, with fine weather and no end of light, and miles to cover. The tents are down and rolled. The fire is watered. Little Sasha, Vladimir and the boys, Alyosha and Edward, carrying nothing but their personal things, say hasty good-bys and start up the hillside we've just come down. Traveling unburdened, they will try to make it back over the mountain ridge and all the way down to the lake in a single rush.

Four of us will travel on the orange raft. Victor and the video-grapher will be together in a rubber dinghy that, seen for the first time inflated, looks alarmingly small. Our load is aboard, in water-proof bags, tied down and covered. And Victor produces his sur-prise. In his pack, with everything else, he has carried a bottle of champagne and slyly chilled it in the river.

We bounce it first against the raft, and then against the bow of the rubber boat. "To the Lena," we say, and Victor opens the bottle and gives the first drink to the river. The rest foams into a metal cup we pass from hand to hand. The videographer is taping. The sound of the river fills the canyon like the shout of a rioting crowd. And then, with a scrape of metal paddles on stone, we're launched—hanging for a suspended moment in the circular swirl just below the pool. Then caught up and carried in the rush, the sound increasing, the cliff-face looming, haystacks curling, spray coming up and over, boulders flashing near. And we're through it.

"*Okay?*" cries Victor. "*Okay?*" And all of us are shouting. We've taken some water over the splash apron, but we're through and float-ing. The slanting fall of the river is dramatic, plunging down a crooked, cliff-lined chute. The growl of the next rapid already can be heard.

⚜

THEN THE SUN WENT out. The clouds came back and the hateful rain beat down in sheets. And the little mishaps began. Two swampings, with stops each time to get the water out and build fires to warm by and partly dry ourselves. And three punctures to be repaired.

The spintered stones of the canyon walls were like knives. Sometimes the force of the current hurled us irresistibly against them, and the raft would start to settle lower and would have to be dragged onto the bank, unloaded, patched. But first a shelter needed to be made against the rain, and a fire built and a flat stone heated to dry the rubber so the patch would stick.

And all of it took time. And the misery of everyone increased.

In good weather we might have traveled the night through, but now, with the rain, the light began to fail. After one last patching we rounded a turn and saw the boat ashore and Victor waving from the gravelly edge of a small island grown up in willow saplings. Everyone had had enough.

No dry wood could be found. Our poor fire gave off choking clouds of smoke, but little heat. Then we made one further, awful discovery. Of the decent food—the dry pasta and cheese, the canned tuna, the candy bars—practically nothing was left. In the mistake of packing, all of that had gone ahead to the put-in camp. And those who'd carried it, knowing the rations were supposed already to have been apportioned, had eaten what they'd found in their load. *Eaten nearly all of it!*

What remained for the days on the upper river were part of one soft container of peanut butter, two half-empty squeeze bottles of jelly, a pillowcase filled with cubes of dried bread sent by Victor's wife. Two bags of dry granola. And, of course, enough oatmeal for several natural lifetimes.

After the grim supper of porridge, I looked inside the larger tent where Victor and Big Sasha were bending with a flashlight over the map. As nearly as could be told, we had made only 10 miles, possibly no more than seven, in an afternoon and evening. At that rate, we could be as long as three weeks getting to Kachug.

"Today we learned," Victor said. "Today we were—" He searched with the flashlight in the pocket dictionary Sergei had loaned him. "— we were attentive." He closed the little book.

"*Zahftruh*—tomorrow—we will be more experienced."

But he could not hide the worry in his voice.

TWENTY-EIGHT

June 29, WILLOW ISLAND CAMP.

Wake to another day of driving rain, and misery ahead. In such conditions, morale will get to be a problem. Victor has said, whatever the weather, we will have to run late today. He's right. We must somehow make miles, a lot of them. We must keep the raft whole, and stay as dry as possible, and stop tonight at some place with good wood.

Morning goes well, with only one puncture. By the noon stop for porridge, all are damp and shivering. But the fire's warmth helps. I put on more clothes—heavy sweater, then windbreaker, then rain jacket, and a knit ski mask pulled down to protect face and neck, achieving a state of near-comfort. Then we push on through the leaden, dripping afternoon.

At first, when you travel such a river, the sound of each approaching rapid brings a surge of excitement and anxiety. And in the tent at night, on the edge of sleep, you hear the one that will be the morrow's first test. But as one stretch of furious water or hairpin bend succeeds another for hours on end, all gotten through without any great episode, the awareness of risk gradually lessens. Just as a wind on a treeless plain is voiceless until it is caught in the shell of the ear, the force of moving water cannot really be appreciated until it smites you.

The miles slip by. As Victor promised, today we're more experienced.

But not luckier.

◌⁂◌

THE PLACE SEEMED NOT much worse than dozens of others we had passed.

The current at the turn pinched down between a car-sized boulder and the canyon wall, and coming out from there exploded directly against and over another great rock partly submerged. Our raft hung for an instant atop it, began to tip, then came free and spun away into the stretch of unobstructed water below.

"Canyon almost finished," cried Big Sasha, who was paddling in the bow. "Hard part finished."

Seconds passed—seconds only.

Then, above the thunder of the river, we heard a shout from behind, from the chute we'd just negotiated. The rubber boat had gone under, only one end of it showing in the foaming hole below the second rock. I could see the videographer swimming in the icy race. But not Victor.

Things torn loose from ties were coming past us in a rush— Victor's coat, our cooking pots, one of the yellow waterproof bags, the pump for inflating the boat.

But still not Victor.

The water had pulled him under and held him there, pinned between boat and boulder, for what he later said he guessed might be the rest of his life. It let him up for one desperate breath, then pulled him down again. Finally he and boat were spat out together from the hole.

He was trying to get to the bank, swimming first, then stumbling, the videographer going back to help him as we caught the swamped boat and, dragging it behind, made the bank ourselves. The current had carried us a hundred yards beyond. I could see Victor in the shallows fall, get up and fall again, both hands holding his left leg. Then the videographer was with him, and we others were running through the forest in their direction.

"A *fire!*" we could hear the videographer shouting. "Get a fire going! Victor's hurt."

In the wetness, that seemed to take an eternity. Both of them were shaking violently. Victor's face was drained of color. That was the only time we would see in him anything like fear. And it wasn't so much fear for himself, I think, as the sudden fear of failing.

"Broke," he said, both shaking hands clamped fiercely around his upper leg. *"Broke."*

The fire burned a little higher. First he allowed his leg to be touched through the pants, to see if we could feel bone end. When we could not, he let us help him undress and spread his clothes on sticks in front of the fire.

The leg was not broken, only terribly bruised. On his left thigh was a swollen contusion the size of a melon and the color of uncooked beef. One of his hands also was badly scraped. But as soon as he saw he was only hurt, not really disabled, the shaking lessened and the fire's warmth began to bring his color back.

He was wounded, but we weren't yet stopped. Knowing that, he managed a thin little smile.

"Is *expedition*," he said, as if the word explained any hardship or discomfort.

And when his clothes and the videographer's had dried, he used vines and saplings to lower himself painfully down the rain-slick bank, wrapped his powerful hands around the oar grips and turned the rubber boat out into the stream to see what of our lost equipment we might recover.

⚜

I DON'T WANT TO seem to make too much of the difficulty of the upper Lena. I've read and seen enough accounts of rafting and kayaking to know that an expert would regard that canyon as easy going. But white water anywhere isn't to be taken lightly. And none of us, American or Russian, was an expert. What's more, our raft and rubber boat were old, marginal equipment for such a journey, although they were the best Victor had been able to find. And while there are many harder rivers, there cannot be too many places where one is farther from help if anything goes seriously wrong.

Had Victor's leg really been broken, or if we'd lost him in the hole under the rock, there'd have been no choice but somehow to continue on downstream to where we'd planned to meet the others. There wasn't any other way. But it's also fair to say we'd have been finished then. We couldn't have dreamed of going the remaining nearly 2,700 miles without him because, of all of us, he is by all odds the most essential to the expedition.

The waterproof bag we'd seen shooting past by is found caught on a stone and ripped, wetting everything inside, but at least it lodged there and is recovered.

The rifle also is found. As proof of the violence of water, its front and rear sights have been torn off against the rocks and the bolt is sprung in a way that makes the action inoperable. So we've lost our insurance against bears, on the chance any are met. But Victor is distraught for another reason. The carbine belongs to his Institute. And in a country where such weapons are feared by the government and tightly regulated, it may be impossible to replace.

"Did we lose the camera?" I ask the videographer.

"No. I'd just finished shooting, and put it in the waterproof box before we went under. The camera's fine."

There have been some tensions in our group. But he has shown courage and steady nerve in this first real crisis, and I'm grateful to him for it.

"You know what I thought when we went over?" he says now. "I thought, 'Well, I'm swimming in the Lena, in Siberia, and it's serious cold. But it isn't going to kill me.'"

The other things are gone—tumbling across the pebble bottom somewhere on their way to Kachug. Apart from the broken gun, our worst loss is the air pump. The one for the raft won't fit the air valve on the boat. And also our cooking pots, which means we'll have to cook porridge over fires in our individual bowls.

⚜

THE GOD OF THE River is capricious. He humbles you. Then, sometimes, he gives unexpected gifts.

The sun burst out in afternoon. The channel broadened, and we were borne along in an uneventful glide. Ahead of us swam families of ducks, brown-headed, wings chevroned in black and white.

The drakes fluttered up and circled while the hens, each with a fuzzy brood of five or six, herded their young out of sight under weeds at the bank.

For most of an hour, a large hawk had ridden the thermals overhead between the cliffs, traveling the river with us. Then we saw him fold, strike the water and lift heavily, carrying his catch on around a forested turn and out of view.

We noticed that. Remarked on it. It passed from mind.

Then we came to that bend, and rounded it, and with a scream and sudden beat of wings the hawk rose from the bank nearby on our left.

"*Rihbah!*" cried Big Sasha. And Andrusha echoed him. "*Rihbah!*" Fish!

On a stone at the river's edge, where the hawk had carried it to eat, was a trout still twitching—a fine big trout of nearly 20 inches, the kind some people put on walls. But we had better plans for it. Without discussion, three grown men were over the raft's side and splashing through the shallows to steal that bird's supper.

I don't know how long it takes a hawk to find and catch such a fish. But the River God gave it to us, and we felt no shame at all.

❧

A T HALF PAST 8 in the evening we call a halt and pull up on a muddy bank. The footprints of a large bear are stamped everywhere in the soft ground, and Victor examines the broken rifle again with regret. But no other reasonably level stopping place has been seen for the last hour, so we stay and make our camp.

Andrusha finds a foil plate in his pack and we use it to cook the trout, cut in six pieces, one for each. With Victor's dry bread cubes dipped in the fryings, and with the last of our peanut butter and jelly, it is the best meal we've had in several days, and the last good one in prospect for several more.

Ropes are strung to hang our sodden clothing, and a rough pole scaffolding built over the fire so sleeping bags can be at least partly dried. The rain stops and the evening lightens as the clouds break. Victor is in much pain. He has to lift and place the leg with his hands to walk. And the discomfort is sure to be worse tomorrow.

He and Big Sasha lay together the map squares that show the whole distance we have to travel. It is about one yard of map distance. The part we've accomplished in a calamitous day and a half can be covered with one hand. We will rise no later than 6 tomorrow morning, Victor says, aim at being away by 8, and spend at least 10 hours on the river, not counting stops. Along the way, we will look for what he calls a hunter's home—a rough trapper's cabin near the river, abandoned in this season—where he hopes we might find a pot for cooking and boiling our tea.

TWENTY-NINE

JUNE 30, MUD BANK Camp.

A happy discovery: somehow, the last of the oatmeal is gone. We breakfast on dry granola, then hurry to break camp and gain some miles.

More ducks, swimming ahead of us and behind. Some kind of huge grouse-like bird rises in the forest on our left and beats across the river to vanish among the trees on the other side. On the bank are the tracks of deer, elk and moose, but no creature shows itself.

The country is changing. The quakes and the winter freezes grind mountains into fist-sized pieces, and whole hill-faces have come sliding down hundreds of feet to form steep buttresses of rubble. So recent and violent does the breakage seem that you almost expect the landscape to change again, even as you watch. But the canyon walls are lower here.

The river is changing, too, although not noticeably slowing. It is wider, now, with longer stretches between the bends. And in places it divides into more than one channel, with islands of reeds and poplar saplings between. Today, for the first time, we are seeing a good deal of drifted-up deadfall, but we're nowhere blocked. Always the force of water has pushed at least one passage through.

A sad lunch of Victor's hard bread cubes. Only one brief

shower, and then a sparkle of sunlight on water.

Ahead is the blue of softer, rounded hills. How far are they away, and how many hours or days will it take us to reach them? And what's our rate of travel? Three paces on the river bank would make approximately 10 feet, and takes one second by my watch. That's 600 feet a minute which, multiplied by 60 minutes, gives 36,000 feet, meaning our progress would be just under seven miles in an hour. Then, looking ahead and estimating a quarter-mile's distance, I time how many minutes it takes to get there, multiply by four, divide by 60, and get an altogether different result. It doesn't matter. These arcane and largely useless exercises occupy the uneventful afternoon.

The clear sky means there will be no night, so we can travel late. We halt finally just before 9 o'clock, where the current washes in against a long, stony bar. While the others put up tents I'm able to catch two small grayling which we insist the oarsmen eat, since they are working hardest. Their hands are beginning to be in bad shape—Victor's and Big Sasha's the worst.

"The hands of a Russian scientist," Victor says wryly, showing his—the fingers bent like claws and palms raw where the blisters have broken. But after a day in the boat his leg pains him less. A man that fit heals quickly.

July 1, Stony Bar Camp.

Crisp, sunny morning. Light patchwork of fluffy clouds. Promise of a lovely day.

The mountains have receded on either side, opening the way across a marshy plain, bounded only by gentler, forested hills. Rapids are rare now, and of no consequence. The widening river has shallowed and slowed.

The videographer announces that his batteries have nearly run down, and the camera lens has stopped working properly.

"We have extra batteries, haven't we?" I ask him.

"Not here. The ones I brought got wet when we went over."

"Can they be dried?"

"I don't know. Maybe."

"Well, all we'll miss is this last part of the rafting. When we get to Kachug you'll have fresh batteries and the other lens."

He shakes his head. "It went in the river, too."

"You mean you *brought them both?*"

"Right."

In other words, when the expedition rejoins in Kachug we'll have the replacement camera that was flown from the States and hand-carried out from Moscow—but only one partly-functioning lens. I'm stunned at his risking our spare lens to no point. And furious at myself, the greater fool, for not having known and stopped him.

Where, after Kachug, can anything be gotten to us on the river, until Yakutsk which is almost at the Arctic? We'll see if we can manage with the one faulty lens. Or perhaps try to work another miracle by phone from Kachug. And if we can't, maybe I'll just send the videographer and soundperson home from there. I drift through this afternoon in a turmoil of anger and disappointment.

We stop at 8:30, according to Andrusha's watch, and put up one tent. Victor, when he arrives a half-hour later with the videographer in the rubber boat, is surprised to find us encamped. Andrusha's watch was wrong—and in fact wasn't even running. He's a peculiar little fellow, Andrusha. Each night, in a pitiful ritual, he opens and lays out to air the inner workings of his transistor radio which has never emitted one sound, and also carefully dries a four-foot strip of toilet tissue on a stick beside the fire. Maybe he does not understand the stuff is disposable.

Though it's really only a little after 6 o'clock, we decide to stay there anyway. The camp is at an especially pretty bend of the river, where the flow narrows below a deep pool. It's a good place, Victor thinks, to use what he calls his "square rod"—an illegal net—in the hope of catching trout. But sunken trees in the pool prevent it. And fighting the current to row back across, he tears out one of the oar-loops on the rubber boat. He and Sasha will try to stitch it with an awl and waxed cord from their repair kit.

Tonight, for the first time, the famous Lena mosquitoes are genuinely ferocious. We consult the maps only long enough to confirm we have no dependable notion of where we are, or how far

we must yet go. It could be one day more, or it could be three.
Then all dive for the protection of the tents.

The members of an expedition, I scribble in my notebook
before sleeping, *should be chosen more for temperament and good
sense than for their talents.*

July 2, Pretty Bend Camp.

We wake at 5:30, the mosquitoes gone and a fine clear day
beginning. There is a little porridge left, it turns out. And some
sugar to put over it is found at the bottom of Big Sasha's pack.
We're away by 7, leaving the pretty bend behind. An hour later
Victor gives a happy shout—*"Hunter's home!"* —and rows hard for
the left bank, where a tiny log structure can be glimpsed through
the birches and pines.

❧❧❧

T HE SPARENESS OF A lonely life hung all about the place. On one
side was the river, on the other a little clearing of meadow
grass, and beyond that the dark wall of the forest stretching away
forever.

In the center of the clearing was a slender pole made of a
peeled pine, with a rope for hoisting a signal flag to notify a helicopter of some emergency there below. At the clearing's edge was
a small, elevated platform, roofed with bark and badly deteriorated, for storing food above the reach of bears.

At the beginning of each winter some man came to that place
alone—about as alone as anyone ever could dream of being—to set
his traps for the sable and fox, then running his line, bundling the
pelts to be taken out in spring and shipped to Moscow to be auc-
tioned and finally made into coats to warm the shoulders of the
world's beautiful and rich.

The hut, with two small windows and a plank door, was made
of larch logs artfully dovetailed and joined at the corners, and
roofed with black tarred paper and bark-sided slabs of wood. It
seemed a minimal defense against the ferocity of the Siberian cold.

Its inside dimensions were three steps by four. There was a sleeping shelf made of sawn boards, a small table with one chair, a tiny tin stove for heat and cooking. The hut's floor was only beaten earth. It was low and dark and chilly—more a cave than a house. And the artifacts the man had left called up a picture of him and his winter isolation.

On the window ledge beside the table, in the light coming through the dusty glass, were an empty vodka bottle, a homemade candle in an open meat tin, an empty coffee can, a cigarette package also empty, a box with a few matches. On the dirt floor beside the stove, a hand ax leaned against some chunks of split wood, and hanging from the low pole rafters three plastic sacks, one containing salt, another flour, another some dry pasta, and also, suspended by a string, a spare glass chimney for a kerosene lamp.

On the table, an issue of *Pravda* dated June 1, 1990, lay open to page five and a story about pensions. Everyone, even a sable hunter, gets a pittance at the end, although it's nothing anyone could live on.

Tacked up on the log wall behind the chair was some kind of yellowed and stained document, with nails driven and bent to hold in place the pane of window glass that covered it. It was a citation, Victor said—a *Good Hunter* certificate for the years 1971 and 1972.

How is a life like that endured? Or could the man imagine any other?

Outside, on a shelf over the door, Andrusha had discovered two metal teapots, one with the handle broken. We took the broken one, so we would have something to boil our water in. And I wondered, a little guiltily, if the hunter would miss it when the snows began and the Lena turned to a winding road of ice and he came back to the silence and his loneliness again.

❧

N O MORE THAN A quarter mile farther on we hear ahead a rush of noisy water and meet our first bad obstruction—a mass of logs, all stripped of their bark and ground smooth by the violence of the river, hurled up in a tangled mound of drift that blocks the channel completely.

I guess it might cost us an hour or two in unloading, carrying around the place and reloading again. But Victor finds where broken pieces can be dragged aside to clear a narrow passage. Raft and boat, still loaded, are let through on ropes. And in no more than 20 minutes we're floating again.

The day has warmed. Big Sasha and Andrusha, shirts off to take the sun, have lost all will to work and lie dreaming at the front and rear of the raft, paddles across their laps, rousing only to fend off some sunken snag or avoid a collision with the bank. Raft and rubber boat drift side by side through the lazy morning.

"Listen," Victor says. He believes he hears a helicopter.

After a few moments we hear it too, a faint hum that resolves into the distinct *throp-throp* of whirling blades. It comes nearer. Then very near. The machine passes low over the river, across the opening between the trees, goes out of view, comes back, circles. Then just around the bend ahead we see it descend, the trees whipping and water churning at the river's edge.

It has landed on a large gravel bar. The four crewmen already are standing beside it, smoking, and out of the helicopter come Valera, Little Sasha, Sergei and Victor's son, Alyosha—they and we crying out greetings all at once and clasping hands. After the great stillness that has contained us, it seems a terrific clamor.

How near are we to where we're headed? Another day? More?

By running long, we might make it late tomorrow, Valera is telling Victor. Or by the middle of the day after, at the latest. But there's a problem. The level of the river is falling quickly. He has been in contact with the crew of the Zaria, which is waiting for us at Zhigalovo, some days beyond Kachug and the farthest point upriver it safely could be brought.

The Zaria's crew is worried about the water's depth. If it decreases more, they may have to retreat as far as Ust'Ilga, or even Ust'Kut, which would take us longer to reach. So time has become critical. It is urgent, Valera says, that we get to Kachug, resort our gear, and set off as soon as possible in canoes and hired native outboard boats to get to the Zaria, which will be our base for the next more than 1,500 miles.

What will we miss if we leave the river now?

Nothing, Valera says. They have seen this last small part from the air, as they came to try to find us. It's only more of what we're traveling now—wide and slow, with one kilometer no different from any other. Anyway, there isn't any choice. So our gear and the deflated raft and boat are flung and dragged aboard. All in hardly more time than it takes to tell it.

The rotors turn, the trees bend again in the wind and blown spray of the mechanical storm, and the helicopter lifts.

⚬⚬⚬

THERE'S A POWERFUL SENSE of dislocation that comes when different realities so suddenly collide.

In only moments, we had been plucked out of a place of eternal solitude, of unremembered time, and brought jarringly back into the world. I had to see that part of the Lena once again, to be sure of locking it in place so the days ahead wouldn't just blur everything.

On either side as we started back up the river I could see the hell of marshes spread on either side below—passable in winter, but impenetrable now. Then the last night's camp, the place at the pretty bend, fled underneath us. The canyon deepened, and I could see the stretch of water, if not the exact place, where Victor had been hurt.

Then, on a little flat beside a bluff, the camp we'd retreated to so miserably after a day of being lost.

Then our first night's stopping place, where the cuckoo had counted out our years. And the brook that ran on up from there in a diminishing trickle toward the snow seeps where it vanished among rocks and moss.

The helicopter's cabin door was open for making photographs—the engine howling and a gale whipping in around us as the pilot banked sharply to the left.

Straight underneath now was the treeless ridge of shattered stone we'd stood on, and falling away from that the gorge up which we'd struggled. Then the immense, modulated blueness of the magnificent lake, stretching away and paling to join the blue of sky. And, on a green spit directly below, a black speck that would be the cottage of Sunny Station where our climb began.

The pilot banked again, turning for Kachug. The door was closed, the racket less. The videographer, troubled by air sickness, sat with his eyes pressed closed, very still. Victor was writing in his notebook, and studying some documents Valera had brought for him to read and sign.

And I was thinking how far away we'd been, and how incredibly far it seemed we'd traveled—and what a little fraction that was of all the distance yet to go.

VI

Deep Into Summer:
The Middle River

THIRTY

O UR EXPEDITION IS REUNITED now, and we will have two days and nights in Kachug to prepare for the next part of the journey. The others hear our stories of the upper river, and have adventures of their own to tell.

Returning on Baikal toward Irkutsk, they were caught in one of the lake's great storms. But with a schedule to keep, they could-n't find an anchorage and wait for it to blow itself out, so the Yaroslavits slewed and pitched on southward through wind-whipped waves. Jennie lost her footing on the wet deck and was saved by a crewman from going overboard, and nearly everyone on the boat was desperately sick.

Now they have brought the mountain of cargo overland to Kachug, some of it in the red bus and the rest on a flatbed truck. And it and we are installed in the household of Clavdiya Petrovna Ovchinnikova. Amid the wreckage of a system gone wrong and an economy sliding into ruin, the provident still manage to make tidy, sensible lives. Clavdiya Petrovna's is such a life—or was, until our expedition came down upon her.

Her tiny wooden house with ornamented window frames and traditional blue shutters fronts on a dirt street near the edge of Kachug. A doll's house, spotlessly kept, with three cozy rooms, a kitchen, a closed-in porch. The door lintel is so low that even a small man must bend his head to enter. Ten steps across the door-yard is the summer kitchen, a small separate building used for cook-ing and eating when the weather is fine. There's also a shed garage, a little bathhouse and, at the end of a plank path, a privy no more or less horrid than any other we've seen.

All this is shut off from the street out front by a high wooden fence, which Victor, when he chose the place, valued because of the security it would afford our supplies.

On a scrap of land behind this little compound are Clavdiya Petrovna's potato garden, her greenhouse full of tomato and squash plants in bloom, and pens for the household's two pigs and five goats. Each morning, Clavdiya's mother, Galina Alexandrovna

Litvinova, opens the gate in the enclosing fence and lets the goats out to eat the grass along the road. In the evening, she steps out front and calls and they obediently return. She is a tiny, elfin woman in a red head scarf. Born in 1910 in a village not far from here, she can remember the war years, and walking through the dark mornings to work in the fields, with a bit of bread tied inside her dress to protect it from the hungry children. (That memory, she says, shames her.) After the war she came to Kachug and worked at a school, for which she has a small pension.

She cherishes the sweetness of this life. She helps Clavdiya water the garden and the greenhouse, and the goats are in her charge. In spring and summer, when the roadside grass grows rank, Clavdiya's husband cuts it with a scythe and Galina Alexandrovna gathers it up to be saved for winter. Clavdiya's grandson, Pasha, is a student in primary school, but school is dismissed now for the summer and he entertains himself by observing all these strangers with their amazing stacks of goods that have so suddenly appeared.

No doubt Victor is paying something for us to lodge here, but it can't be enough to compensate such clutter and confusion. Our supplies fill the garage and spill outside in a huge mound covered by tarpaulins. Our laundry is strung up everywhere on improvised lines. We bed at night on the floor in two of her rooms, with others in the summer kitchen and still more of us in the bathhouse.

It is wonderful to be under a roof and eating real food again, not porridge. The first night, we crowd around a table in the summer kitchen, the raft people especially wolfing the bread and stew. Victor pours vodka in the metal cups, making a toast to adventures still ahead. Then Volodya brings out his accordion and plays old Russian songs, singing in a sharp, clear voice. It's a fine moment, all of us together again and all safe, the light glowing warm on faces as we listen to Volodya playing.

There remain problems, of course. The replacement video camera came with our group from Irkutsk. But the lens that went in the upper river has dried all afternoon in the sun, and is a confirmed casualty. Also, the red bus must return from here to Irkutsk, so different transport—maybe a local bus—must be rented to take the bulk of our cargo as far as the road goes, or wherever we can load it aboard the first of our larger boats. We will go tomorrow with Victor to speak to town officials about the possibility of renting one. And the videographer will try to get through by phone late tonight to an American television crew in Moscow to see if another lens somehow can be gotten to us from the States.

(He and Victor, Volodya and Sergei do go at midnight into town, through a dark place between buildings, through brush, and climb a fence to a house where lights are on and they rap on the window. It's the telephone office, and miraculously the connection to Moscow is made.)

At the edge of sleep, in some small hour, I hear the red bus come back, but will wait until morning to know the news.

⚜

THE HEAD OF THE local Soviet, effectively the "mayor" of the town, was in a rage.

Some of his anger was generalized. He had many problems, we would learn, getting supplies for the town—especially supplies of food. Also, it was said that he'd supported one of the losing candidates in the Russian presidential election won by Boris Yeltsin.

At the moment, however, his fury was concentrated on the strangers who'd materialized before him, and on the unlucky woman, his secretary, whose mistake it had been to admit them.

What right had we to be there?, he demanded to know. *And what right to be in Kachug at all?*

He was a large, coarse-voiced man whose florid face grew darker by the moment.

We'd come by river, had we? How did we imagine we could travel the river without his permission?

Everything was approved, Victor replied evenly. Everything was documented. He opened his plastic folder with all the papers in it, stamped with their official seals. Licenses for the Lena headwaters preserve. Licenses for photography. Contracts with the Institute. The permission of the KGB for the whole itinerary.

Never mind any of that, the head of the Soviet cried, voice rising to a shout. And the two men sitting with him arranged their faces to match the scowl of their boss. *Kachug is my town.*

Sergei bent to my ear, interpreting.

"He says if we don't go from Kachug immediately he will call the militia."

"What's Victor saying?"

"He's telling the mayor that he wants to hire a bus or a truck."

The burly man snatched up his telephone.

"So," said Sergei. "He *is* calling the militia. Victor asks us to step outside."

From the spartan reception room, through the closed door, we and the nervous secretary could hear Victor and the mayor shouting at one another. After only moments three men in uniform appeared, and Victor was led away to the militia station, a small wooden building just down the street. We waited for him outside.

"Now," said Sergei, "you have seen an example of our local chieftains."

"Can he stop us?"

"No. He can only try to make problems."

"We sure pushed his button."

"It's what happens when people like that have a little power. You can never relax. They are everywhere. It is why I live as I do— as a night person, to be invisible, and not to be touched by any of this."

Somehow the commotion had attracted a small round man with a friendly face, who announced himself as Sergei Krotov, editor of *Lena Pravda*, the town newspaper. He was sorry about the unpleasantness.

"The brotherhood of journalists," he said, "must stand together."

If I could come to his office, he would write a story about our expedition and also tell me many interesting things about Kachug. But I explained that time was short. We planned to leave tomorrow, and we still had canoes to finish assembling and provisions to arrange.

The life of the provincial town circulated along the street under a beating sun. Then Victor came out of the militia headquarters. He was smiling.

"Everything is okay," he said. The commander of the militia had turned out to be a reasonable fellow. In fact, he had made a telephone call to help arrange the hire of a bus and a man to drive it. We could leave tomorrow as we'd intended.

Back in Clavdiya Petrovna's courtyard, the two canoes were finished. Good supper smells drifted from the summer kitchen. The departure hour was set for 9 o'clock in the morning, though we would have to rise earlier to transport everything to the river's edge.

The photographer was concerned about the cargo. Much of it should be left in Kachug, he insisted. He was worried, too, about these next two days in canoes and native boats. What chance would there be to photograph villages we might pass along the river? It was villages, and the people lived in them, he meant to concentrate on.

If he didn't want to travel by river to Zhigalovo, I said, he could ride in the bus with the equipment and stop when he cared to. Then no village would be missed. It seemed temporarily to satisfy him.

Clavdiya Petrovna's manner in the evening was detectably lighter, merrier, as she saw her ordeal ending and the prospect of her household becoming her own again.

❧

THE RIVER FLOWS SILVER and fast under a bright morning sky, but from behind the hills to the north and west a rank of clouds approaches.

Our two canoes are in the river, one with a motor on its square stern, the other with the motor attached to a bracket at the side. A long, grassy meadow sweeps up from the water's edge, and some of the townsfolk passing on the road have stopped on foot, or stand with their bicycles to witness the departure.

Two native boatmen are waiting, and they seem amused at our sleek little craft and tiny motors. Their boats, which they also speak of as "canoes," are seven and one-half meters (more than 24 feet) long, hand-built of heavy aluminum-nickel aircraft sheeting, and driven by 30-horsepower engines from which, as from all others we saw in the country, the engine cover has been removed. These canoes look crude and ponderous, but we will find how swift and nimble they are—and also how *stable*—although starting the old motors requires an eternity of winding and yanking.

Loading is complicated by a herd of cattle that has come grazing along the meadow and into our midst. Two adolescent bulls begin a snorting, head-butting match, stepping over and around our gear. The crowd of people on the hill above has grown.

"It is necessary to have a photograph," Victor announces. "Before every expedition of the Russian geographical society, the photograph is a tradition."

So we are arranged in a line at the river's edge, with the canoes behind—our number made larger by the two boatmen, Mikhail and Anatoli, the driver of our new bus (an orange one), his small son, and several onlookers who insist on having their pictures made with us. It's necessary to retreat far up the hillside to fit so large a company in the frame. There is a rustle of camera shutters as the occasion is amply recorded.

"This moment is historic in more than one way," Victor says, a bit formally. "We also salute our American partners on their national day." Until that instant it had occurred to none of us except him that this is the Fourth of July.

The last gear is stowed. Those going overland climb the meadow to the bus. The side-mounted motor of the red canoe is started, and Valera and Alyosha, Victor's son, take it out into the current. We've decided the boy, who was so uncomplaining on the hard climb to the headwaters, can travel with us as far as Lensk.

"Keep your weight to the left side," I say, Sergei calling out the words in Russian above the engine hum. They are unacquainted with the relative instability of American-style canoes, or the additional balance problems presented by a side-mounted motor. I think they have understood, and I've turned to start the other engine when a sudden collective shout rises from the throng up by the road.

Valera at the helm only meant to turn the red canoe back upriver toward us—but swung it with a flourish too sharply to the weighted side. They are in the water, the canoe floating bottom-up, the motor buzzing briefly then going silent as men and canoe pass away from us downstream. They are plucked out without loss, except to pride, and retreat to the bus to get dry clothing from their duffels.

✺

THE YOUNGER BOATMAN, MIKHAIL Kuzmuk, removed the spark plug from the drowned engine and was pulling the starter cord to pump the water out. And I, meantime, was pawing through the operator's manual—written both in Japanese-English and Japanese-French—hoping to find other useful suggestions.

In case of an accidental immersion, the manual said, the engine should be taken to the nearest Yamaha dealer for a thorough cleaning and lubrication.

By my reckoning, the nearest dealer might be somewhere around Sapporo, Japan, if not Tokyo.

Kuzmuk dried the spark plug and replaced it. But the little engine would not start. Its innards were wet. Valera and Alyosha came down from the bus in their dry clothes and all stood aimlessly around as Kuzmuk pulled some more. The morning was drawing on. The river at Zhigalovo was falling. And the crowd of people up there on the hillside had grown larger, witness not only to our historic expedition but also to a diverting spectacle in a town, and in a time, when amusements were all too rare.

Sergei Orlov, our interpreter, bent close.

"Victor says we must go," he whispered. "We can try the motor at the next stop. But now we must go. As soon as possible! In order to be away from this place *before the people begin to laugh.*"

The red canoe, less motor, was heaved aboard one of the native boats, occupying but the front half of it. And we were away at last, rushing between steep forested hillsides to the valley's first sharp bend. Then on around it, leaving Kachug and the memory of our shredded dignity behind.

THIRTY-ONE

O UR CANOES AND TWO native boats delivered us to Zhigalovo and the meeting with the first of our main expedition ships, but not without more misery on the way. The clouds that rimmed the hills as we left Kachug soon mounted up, darkened, and spilled a relentless cold deluge. Except for the last morning on the upper river and the sunny spell in Clavdiya's courtyard, rain had come to seem the constant feature of this country and of all our days.

The orange bus paralleled our route, and at a place where the rough road dipped down beside the river we stopped all together to build a sputtering driftwood fire and make an afternoon lunch of soup and tea. Before the rain put out our lunch fire, the boatmen had revived the drowned engine. The rain came harder as the afternoon drew on. In the open boats we sat facing the rear, our backs to the wind and the wet, watching the hills and the river slip away behind. The Lena was wider now, rushing between small wooded islands, but very shallow, the pebble bottom flying past close underneath. Even in canoes the way was difficult. Often we had to step out in the shallows and drag until we found a passable channel.

The bus was met again at a village called Verkholensk, with the silver onion dome of its little church shining through the mist. The driver had come down with a ferocious ear ache and, dizzy with terror that a tick might have gotten in there, he went to find the village clinic to have it looked at. Then we pushed on, by road and river. The afternoon turned colder, and discomfort grew. The boatmen, Mikhail and Anatoli, gave Anne and Jennie their heavy leather coats with lamb's wool lining and collars of wolf fur. The boatmen faced the rain and spray hatless, gloveless, with their inner jackets unzipped. Winters they spent as hunters and trappers in the Siberian forest, and such weather as this was hardly worth their notice.

The late daylight went blue. We pulled the boats in to the steep grassy bank, and climbed to a shelf under the spread of a great larch, where the needle duff was dry as dust. The girls, the boatmen and I dragged wet branches into a pile, and Mikhail used the "big match"—a splash of gasoline—to start a fire. It ignited with a windy *whoosh*, and instantly there was warmth, bringing hope and possibilities. We stood drying, coats hung on the lower limbs, steam fuming up from them.

Then Victor arrived with the last canoe. And after him Sergei, coming on foot back along the muddy road, to say the bus people had stopped a bit farther on at a pretty place and a fire had been started and camp was being made. A quarter-hour more of wetness in the boats brought us to the meadow by the river where two tents already were up and there was a bustle of settling in.

Valera and Volodya cut saplings and made a framework covered with a tarp to sit under while things dried next to the flames. A third tent was pitched. Sleeping bags and pads were excavated from the chaos in the rear of the bus. Some preferred to sleep in there on the cargo mound.

✦

THE BUS DRIVER'S EAR still pains him fiercely, although he's relieved to know the cause is not a tick. His small son Andrei has come with him, and the boy is very worried and solicitous as the two of them cook potatoes in the fire, first directly in the coals then under an upturned pot. We distribute bowls so all can have soup, and the boatmen invite us to share pieces of raw, salted fish they've brought in a sack. We are now a mighty company: 12 permanent expeditioners, Victor's son Alyosha, the bus driver and his boy, the boatmen Anatoli and Mikhail, 17 in all. With our soup and tea, it's warm and companionable all crowded together under the tarp shelter in the smoke of the fire.

I'm uncomfortable with some digestive problem that has flowered this day into severe cramping and diarrhea, and have been eating Lomotil, which makes me sleepy and weak. Even so, it's a grand evening in our camp between river and forest's edge. For now it's possible not even to notice the rain. All drift away then to tents and bus, leaving poor Volodya to sit the night through by the fire for security. He won't mind, he says, unfailingly good-natured. He requires little sleep, and will be happy and dry in the firelight.

But comfort for him and the rest of us is brief. We wake in the night with wetness everywhere. Water runs rivers across the tent floors. Clothes folded for pillows, and the sleeping bags, and us inside them—all are a sodden mess. The rain beats down in slanting sheets. Violent wind has collapsed the tarp lean-to, drowned the fire, driven Volodya to cover in the bus. Anne, whose bag could not be located in the piled cargo, has wrapped herself in as many coats as she could find and sat and lain awake on a soaked foam pad, and probably will take cold from that. At first daylight the camp is a wreck. It's bad enough to end a day wet. Here, as on the upper river, we *begin* it wet.

The boatmen, who know this section well, say it may be possible to reach Zhigalovo by early afternoon, and we resolve to push on with as few stops as possible. Then, as if tired of testing us, the weather clears, the day is sunny and mellow. And by 1 o'clock we're all arrived on the gravel river landing below the town.

EVERYTHING HAD TO BE unloaded from the bus, since it and the driver and his son, the native boats and boatmen would go back to Kachug from here.

The spectacle of us and the immensity of our heap of goods attracted a crowd of villagers—a small crowd at first, but growing steadily. The Zaria swung up the channel and nosed ashore, and we began yet another sorting—personal gear in one stack, food in another, expedition equipment in a third. Victor and Anne took on supervision of the loading. Supplies that would not be needed immediately were passed up to Volodya and Valera on the roof, to be stowed under the overturned canoes.

The townsfolk looked on, the children merry and playful, the adults impassive. They were worn, hard-used appearing people, and Victor was concerned about the attention we'd attracted. He worried about pilferage. The crew of the Zaria was nervous, too—about the falling river. Already the water level was marginal. If it fell much more, they could be marooned there until another spring. It was essential, they said, that we make a start by 7 o'clock.

Immediately behind the Zaria's control deck were two small crew cabins. Behind those, along a narrow passage, were two more compartments—the one on the port side filled almost completely with our personal gear, the starboard one for food storage.

"Most of it's in there," Anne said. "Food we have extras of is up under the canoes."

"All right. As long as you can find it when you cook," said the photographer.

"We'll all be cooking," I told him. "We'll do it in teams, two Americans and one Russian to a team, on a daily rotation. Victor's working out a schedule."

The last of the equipment was heaved aboard, the rooftop cargo lashed down. And at 10 minutes past the hour the engine rumbled to life. The Zaria backed away from the gravel landing and swung its bow downstream with the current.

∞∞∞

I N THIS SHIP WE will travel dry and powerfully, if not exactly in comfort. Sixty-six feet sounds like a great deal of boat. But subtracting the wheelroom, the crew's quarters, the compartments taken up with our storage, the tiny galley and toilet and the engine room which occupies the aft one-third of the Zaria, the effective living space is reduced to the single large common compartment amidship.

Its dimensions are 10 feet by 17 feet, an area of 170 square feet in all for the 13 of us. That computes to slightly less than *one and one-half square yards per person*, a severity of crowding that, for prison inmates, no court would deem humane. In that cramped space for the next month—more than half the way to the Arctic coast—we will spend all our hours aboard, sitting, eating, working, sleeping. Anne and Jennie will sleep atop the long work table, Katie and I on the floor under it. The others will spread their bags, one beside the other on the floor the whole length of the compartment, like mummies in a museum storeroom. Sergei, for privacy, will withdraw at night to nest in one of the storage compartments atop the heap of personal duffel.

This first night, still plagued by a bad stomach, I'm uninterested in a meal, whoever cooks it. I crawl under the table and listen, half-awake, to the sound of the others eating. The bow of the Zaria grinds against the river bank and the engine stops. We are beached for the night at a place once called the "Hungry Cape," but later— in cruel irony—renamed Molodyozhni, "A Place of Youth." It's the site of one of Stalin's prisons, fallen into ruin now. Tomorrow we will take time to prowl there and hear, if we can, the echoes of its awful history.

The room subsides to silence. I feel Katie beside me on the floor. All are sleeping now, and the compartment bulbs are out, although the strong light of the far-northern night streams powerfully in upon us to illuminate our clutter.

Talis Bergmanis

Victor Gulevich leads the raft party on the climb to the Lena's source.

Talis Bergmanis

"Little" Sasha with reindeer moss.

Talis Bergmanis

"Big" Sasha, in the white water of the upper canyon.

Victor and his son, Alyosha, rest together on the climb.

Andrusha, in calmer water.

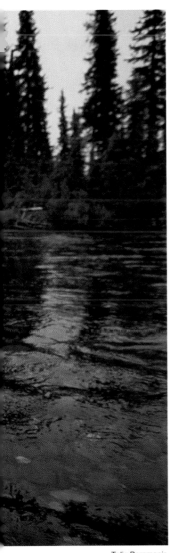

Talis Bergmanis

Talis Bergmanis

A lifetime of experience on her face: Clavdiya's mother, Galina Alexandrovna, in Kachug.

An expedition of children, many of them orphans, hoping to cross Siberia to Alaska.

Talis Bergmanis

The Author

Anne Gusewelle with a leader of the children's expedition.

THIRTY-TWO

VALERA, HIS DISFIGURED HAND thrust by habit in one jacket pocket, clambered ahead of our group up the high bank. Before us was a large meadow, reaching away hundreds of yards to the beginning of the dark forest. The morning was chilly, the meadow gaudy with purple and white spiked flowers and blue forget-me-nots. Rank grass, bent under a heavy dew, wet us to the knees.

The camp was established in 1947 to house 500 political prisoners, mostly peasants without blame for anything, also some with light criminal sentences for small offenses. They cut logs from the *taiga* and operated a sawmill, and a town of several hundred families grew up to serve the camp. The bakery, Valera remembers, was famous for its bread.

Stalin died in 1953. The next year the political prisoners were freed, the camp closed. It was reopened in 1959, for hardened criminals, then closed for the last time in 1964, and the village was ordered abandoned. Khrushchev had visited the U.S. and decided that the way of agriculture lay in large-scale corn cultivation. Thousands of such small places were designated as *non-prospective*—without a future—and their inhabitants were relocated by decree to larger farming centers.

"A fool's decision," said Volodya. And he knows, because his own boyhood village on the Arctic coast also was extinguished in that time.

For Valera, this meadow with its doleful history really was the place of his youth. He was born here in 1955, and it was home for the first 10 years of his life, until the relocation. His father was a guard at the camp. He wasn't a wicked man, or a political man. It was only a job. That was more than a quarter-century ago, and Valera has never been back until now. He led us through the wet grass to one of the few small wooden houses of the village still standing—vines and saplings prying at the boards, window sockets empty and dark, roof rotted in, the interior all ruin and clutter: a part of an iron bed, a broken pail, a legless chair. This was the house of his earliest memories. To see it now made him melancholy.

But this Hungry Cape, this Place of Youth, was not quite lifeless. For as we crossed the flowered meadow and passed through a gap in the fallen metal fence to the camp itself a solitary figure came to meet us. He and Valera spoke, peering at one another through the masks of years. Then Valera knew the face, and the man recognized him as the boy with missing fingers.

He was Nikolai Ivanovich Larionov, sole proprietor of this kingdom of beauty and remembered sorrow. He came with his family to live at the meadow's edge in 1938, and has seen it be two camps, then a village, and now nothing. When all the others left, he refused to go. Now his is the only living house for many miles around. There is no electricity, no store, no mail, no services of any kind, and life is very hard, Nikolai Ivanovich said. He is all alone, except for his four dogs and his cows that graze among the ruins.

But the great river runs by, with fish to catch. The pines at the edge of the forest whisper. The forget-me-nots and purple and white lupines and clover blossom in season. "I will live here and keep cows until the end of my life," this strange, lean man said, and seemed at peace.

"Do you get many visitors?" I asked him.

"Sometimes," he replied. "Usually from museums in places like Irkutsk." They come looking for relics from the evil time.

"Ever any Americans?"

"You are the first. And I have been here more than fifty years."

⋙⋘

NIKOLAI IVANOVICH WALKS WITH us. Past the wreckage of the sawmill. Past the derelict power plant, and the small iron cage that was reserved for special punishment, with metal doors and peephole, and an aperture through which food was passed. All toppled, twisted, fallen—like the whole mad structure that conceived the camp itself.

The largest building still standing is the main assembly hall. Movies were shown there, Valera recalls, and political lectures given, and sometimes the prisoners presented programs on a stage. Fading but still decipherable over the entryway is a painted slogan: *Only Labor Will Lead Us Into the New Social Order*. The old lie resonates with malice, hardly different qualitatively from the one it paraphrases—*Work Will Make You Free*—that is wrought in iron letters over the entrance gate at Auschwitz.

Inside, the floor is covered entirely with the dried manure of Nikolai Ivanovich's cows, who shelter there in bitter weather in a time when the wickedness of the lie is fully known.

⚜

A T EVERY SETTLEMENT VISIBLE from the river we turned the Zaria in toward the bank, one of the crewmen testing the depth with a marked pole, and would go ashore to see what we might find or learn, and to give the photographer and videographer some time to work.

In their poverty and general meanness of aspect, these places at civilization's edge all looked very much the same, numbingly dismal.

At a hamlet called Surovo, we did find a charming little church perched high on the bank, overlooking the Lena and the ranks of forested hills running off endlessly on the far side. It was built entirely of wood, even its onion dome. Like the hundreds of others that once served the Orthodox faithful along the river, it had been converted in the Soviet era to a place of political instruction, and finally abandoned altogether.

Inside there were a few tumbled benches, party slogans on a banner and on posters underfoot, one of them a trampled poster of Lenin. At the front, where the altar must once have been, was a crude film projection booth, and inside that a child's cap and an empty soda bottle. Folded on a window ledge lay a yellowing, 20-year-old issue of *Pravda* commemorating a half-century of Communist power.

Architectually the church was a treasure, and absolutely the only structure of distinction in that place. But it was succumbing to time, neglect and the severity of the Siberian weather. Was it their poverty that made the people of Surovo indifferent to this loss? Or something else—an emptiness of spirit, perhaps?

The question started a discussion with Sergei about the meaning of the words *city* and *town* and *village*. The difference has to do with more than simply size, we agreed. Cities and even towns may be collections of strangers to their past and even to themselves. But a village has heart, has a history that is valued, has collective memory.

Surovo, caring nothing for its little church, was disqualified as a village, we decided. Surovo was just *a place where people lived.*

Then the current bore us on to the next place called Konoshanovo, somewhat larger, where we were able to find a fresh supply of dark country bread, and also the miracle of a bath.

One comes upon such places—everything in them old, and built of weathered wood, their two or three dirt streets either quagmires or blowing clouds of saffron dust, depending on the weather. Defeat hangs over everything. The people's faces are lined with work and hardship. Women 30 years of age look 50. Men go and come ragged from their poor potato fields hacked from the forest's edge. Some of the people are shoeless.

The children are so beautiful they take the breath, and every slight bit of color or finery is lavished on them. But childhood lasts only a moment here. Everything that comes afterward is relentlessly hard.

In the squalor to be seen all about, and without amenities, not even running water, one assumes that the people must live in a condition of more or less perpetual filth. But the assumption is wrong.

Victor and Volodya climbed the dirt path from the riverbank and spoke briefly to a man they met passing. The man looked down at the Zaria, and at us coming out from the boat and stretching ourselves at the water's edge. He nodded, and went into a small shed building from whose tin chimney pipe smoke could be seen pluming up.

Victor and Volodya came back down to the Zaria.

"They are preparing our bath," Volodya announced. "The women will go first."

"Together?"

"Yes, all together. And after them, the men."

Inside the board shed was a spotless sauna, walled with bright birch boards, an iron cauldron of stones atop a wood-burning heater and a tub of water with a pail dipper to pour water on the stones, a bench to sit upon while steaming, and neat bundles of birch switches to be used in flailing oneself or serving a friend. In summer, in the absence of snow to roll in, there was another vat of cold water for the bathers to splash over themselves between their cookings.

Every village, we would discover, and almost every place of habitation—even remote forest farms—had at least one such bathhouse. The citizens of Konoshanovo shared theirs gladly.

"When people travel they have needs," said Volodya. "That's understood."

❧

WE ARE STOPPED IN the gloomy evening on an unpeopled reach of river above a series of small islands. Much rain today, and it continues without cessation. It's been 15 days now since we started north on Baikal from Irkutsk to begin our journey, and only two or possibly three of those have been rainless.

The downpour slackens to a drizzle, and Anne and Jennie flee the boat with me onto the silence of the shore. We drag wood from under a tangle of drift and make a sputtering little fire that smokes in the darkness and throws murky shadows against the dark wall of trees behind. Huddled beside it in rain jackets, we relish the stillness, the absence of voices.

The crowding can be borne—in fact, we've fairly quickly become almost used to it. But how, in such conditions, does one find any quiet inner space? How can we connect intensely with the gift of this place and this experience? Shore camping will help, when the weather permits. And time spent apart from the others, fishing. And most of all time like this just to sit, unspeaking, considering.

A shoe scrapes on the Zaria's deck. There's a rattle of stones as someone leaps ashore and a tall, angular figure approaches in the darkness. It's Sergei, come to say that this is the eve of the Day of River Workers. The main celebration will be tomorrow night. But we may be in Ust'Kut by then, the uppermost port on the Lena. The town will be rowdy and possibly dangerous with drunken river men. So the crew of our boat is making a little party tonight, and we're wanted back on board.

The captain, Valery Leonidovich Plenkov, is a large man, plain and silent—not so much taciturn, I believe, as agonizingly shy. But tonight he has had some drinks with his crewmates in his cabin forward, and takes another from the bottle of vodka Victor has brought out. Valera opens two small tins of meat to pass around. We all shake Plenkov's large hand and congratulate him on the excellence of his profession. He is 44 years old, and all of his working life has been spent on Siberian rivers, the Yenisey and the Lena.

Both are very great, he says. "But the Lena is the most dangerous because its channel is always changing."

Has he lost friends to the river?

"Yes. Some," he says. "A river must be taken seriously."

That's all, but for him it has been an outburst of loquacity. He falls silent, then, and drinks with a purpose, not wanting to embarrass himself by talking more.

THIRTY-THREE

WE DRESSED IN THE half-dark, stepped carefully over the other sleepers, and went out into the splatter of another rainy day beginning. Below the islands a few hundred yards downstream the river might be running over graveled shallows, Victor said. It should be a good place to find fish.

We unlashed one of the canoes from the top of the Zaria and let the river carry us away from the sleeping boat. I have always loved the solemnity of that hour of morning, with the fishing about to begin and the possibilities all still unknown.

Fog wraiths drifted like torn gauze above the water, against the dark of forest behind. The only sounds were the soft splash of paddles and the voice of the Lena muttering over its pebble bed.

Between Kachug and our last night's anchorage Victor had several times seen the surface broken by feeding *taimen*, the great salmonoid of Siberia that can attain a size of 150 pounds or more. Maybe we would find one here. We beached the canoe on gravel at the lower end of the largest island and stepped out into the thigh-deep current—Victor in his rubber hip boots, I in blue jeans and tennis shoes.

The force of the water tugged at my legs. But in the fine excitement of the moment, its coldness hardly was noticed.

Fishermen are vain about their methods. The only argument between us had begun with him insisting that Siberian fish could not be taken except with very specific lures and methods, and my contending, just as heatedly, that fish were fish and could be caught here exactly as they were at home. Now was the chance to settle the question.

Victor tied on his hand-made fur mouse, and cast it where the current cut deep under the island's bank. Russian tackle is primitive—a stiff, heavy rod that must be swung in a violent arc to make the line feed out from a large, flat reel. I was on the opposite side of the island's gravel point, working a small spinner across the angle of the current.

No *taimen* were there, or none rose to his mouse at any rate, and he also changed to a metal spinner. Victor took two small pike and two trout, and I took four trout about like his, no more than ten inches but beautifully speckled and strong in the fast current. And in the end our silly little disagreement was washed away, forgotten. We were glad for one another's small successes, and glad to have shared that splendid hour where the river ran as it had for unremembered ages, through forest that had never heard the ringing of an ax, and where it was possible to imagine no fishermen had been before us.

We came back to the Zaria, whose whole company was awake now, and to the good surprise of pancakes made by Anne and Jennie and Valera on the morning of their day of cooking. The cakes were sweetened with jelly from our plastic squeeze bottles, and Volodya, who surely loved food more than any of us, ate them with eyes pressed shut, while emitting soft, reverential groans of happiness.

I was sorry we hadn't gotten fish enough for a decent meal for the whole group.

"It's plenty," Valera said.

And while I watched, horrified, he hacked them into

chunks—bones, tails, heads and all—and threw them in a pot along with some potatoes and an onion. For lunch, he said, we'd have *oooh-hah.*

Oooh-hah, Sergei explained, was a kind of traditional Siberian fish stew.

The pronunciation of the word suggests, with good reason, the sound of retching.

❧

THE LENA TODAY, AS yesterday, is quite broad, often as much as 75 yards across, and swift but very shallow—so shallow in places that one can walk across it and not be wet above the waist. The stony bottom flies under the Zaria and takes the captain's heart. Had we lost even one more day in the mountains of the upper river, our boat would have had to retreat to Ust'Kut and wait for us there, costing at least a week.

The valley, too, has broadened perhaps a mile now between the crests of the two lines of bounding hills. The *taiga* is lovely in its changing shades of green. First emerald grass at the river's edge. Then light green willows and lesser vegetation. After that the yellow-green of white-stemmed birches. Finally the deep green of pines, and black of firs and cedars mounting up the steep flanks of the ridges on either side.

Pennants of mist and fog hang like smoke in the clefts and against the hill faces on a rainy day. It's as if the forest in this stretch of river smoldered with a thousand fires.

And then at midday we come upon an astonishment—an expedition a good deal braver than our own.

❧

WE FIRST SPIED A floating object far ahead of us in mid-river. Then drew abreast of it—a raft of truck tire tubes with a rough wooden platform built on top, a flapping tent of plastic sheeting, lines with laundry drying, tea water heating over a tiny, smoky wood stove at the rear.

Our mighty Zaria slowed, stopped dead, and turned back to inspect that comical conveyance drifting with the current northward. Aboard the floating tenement, whose dimensions were 10 feet by 15 feet at most, was a gang of people, most of them youngsters.

"Greetings from our expedition to yours," I shouted over to them.

I meant it for a joke, because theirs looked at best like a prankish and somewhat risky local outing. There was a bustle of activity. A tiny rubber boat was launched. A boy and an older man lowered themselves into it, and paddled over to us.

How many were on the raft? I called down to the man when they drew alongside. Twelve, he said. It seemed a great company for so frail a vessel.

And where were they bound for?

"Alaska," he cried happily. "Kodiak Island, Alaska."

Are you mad?

He ignored the question, and handed up his card, which identified him as Alexander Borisovich Rushnikov. He was one of the leaders of a four-year expedition following the route of the merchant-explorer G. I. Shelikhov, who pioneered Russian settlement in Alaska.

The expedition had 60 members in all, he said—mostly orphans and children whose parents, for one reason or another, had given them up. They meant to raft more than a thousand miles to Yakutsk, then strike eastward on foot through wilderness to the Sea of Okhotsk, and somehow voyage from there to America. Never mind whether Soviet authorities would let them out, or the American authorities let them in. Details must not deflect so magnificent an intention.

"Five more rafts of us are somewhere just ahead," he cried, handing us some literature before he pushed away. "You're sure to see them."

And we did. The strange flotilla was beached near the village of Omoloy several miles farther on. We went ashore with a case of granola bars. The rafters had a great pot of herb tea brewing, and pine nuts roasting over their fire. The principal leader, a young school teacher named Mikhail Nikolayevich Sapishev, and some of the boys dragged logs for us to sit on.

A guitar was brought out. Then another. Volodya went back to our boat for his accordion. The youngest expeditioner was only four. Most were in their teens, luminous with the beauty of that age—before life had quite begun to coarsen them with the hardness of its blows. Unselfconsciously talented, they passed the instruments from hand to hand as casually as anyone might pass a pen.

We sang together. Some members of both our parties even danced together. Effusive and slightly formal speeches were made on both sides.

I can't remember ever meeting a finer gang of young people anywhere, or passing a sweeter couple of hours. For that bit of time, our two expeditions were as close as one.

Did they really mean to reach Alaska in four years? we asked.

"Some of us might," they said. "All of us hope to."

It's only dreams that matter, after all.

The rain had stopped, and the low-drifting clouds were blowing out. I could have sat there with them the rest of afternoon and evening, drinking tea and listening to their music. But Victor and our boat crew still were nervous about the falling river. To be sure of having water enough to run, we had to be in Ust'Kut that night.

Volodya, dear Volodya, squeezed his accordion, struck up a lively Russian tune, and strode away down the shore like the pied-piper, all the rest of us following behind. Arms were around shoulders. Anne and Jennie and some of the young women were holding hands, making promises of the kind hardly anyone ever keeps.

The whole group stood together waving at the water's edge, singing a last song over the engine's growl as our Zaria backed away from the bank and turned downstream, the motorman feeling with his pole for the channel. Then we had to let the river carry us on.

THIRTY-FOUR

S OME OF THE AMERICANS have begun scribbling furious lists, setting forth
their demands: lights out at a fixed hour; make the boat's crew turn
down music; keep crew members out of our cabin. Katie is impatient—thinks I should make my own list. Anne and Jennie say I'm
letting the complainers "take over," to which I reply more sharply
than I need to. I have no desire for more wrangling.

Ust'Kut is a sprawling and wretched port town, announced by
a tangle of looming cranes, rusted scrap yards and log depots. The
Baikal-Amur railroad vaults the Lena here on an iron bridge on its
way to the Far East and the Pacific—the last surface transport,
except the river itself, to be met in nearly 2,500 remaining miles of
travel northward. Thus it's a crossroads of sorts, and has drawn to
itself the underculture of toughs and rowdies such places invariably
attract. Valera has been to Ust'Kut before, and finds it disagreeable.
Last night, an aerial bomb exploded above the river, releasing a red
flare that floated down by parachute through the rain. That seemed
to be the sum of the celebration of river workers. The rest would be
vodka and drunken men. Volodya took his shotgun from its metal
case and kept it beside him in the night, with one cartridge of
heavy buckshot, the other a solid slug. The gun was his father's and
is an old one, double-barreled with exposed hammers.

Work is difficult in our compacted common quarters. Today,
I've retreated to the privacy of the engine room, setting up my typewriter on the big engine itself which is cool after a night at anchorage. A bath has been prepared for us somewhere in the town, but I
stay to write and let the others go. Notes from the days since
Kachug have to be typed in the journal pages. And I need to write
the second of several dispatches to the expedition's sponsors. The
first was carried back to Irkutsk from Kachug, and on to Moscow to
be faxed to the States for distribution. I will try to do that all the
way to the end, wherever a courier can be found.

The short-wave radio brings in a forecast from Moscow,
promising bright weather for this part of Siberia. But rain continues
through the day, without a break. Volodya and Sergei have gone

prowling with the other Americans. Victor has a meeting with the head of the enterprise that owns our Zaria, to speak about our plans for the next thousand miles of river. By the schedule, posted on a wall, it's Katie's day and mine for cooking with Valera, and in late afternoon, with the journal caught up and the sponsors' notes finished, we dig out provisions from the food-storage compartment and start the two burners heating in the tiny galley. Then the others come back.

The airing of the list of demands turns dinner rancorous. Yes, he will tell the crew to mute its radio music, Victor says. And a general hour for sleeping can be agreed. But there is no way the crewmen can avoid passing through our quarters. It's the only way to the Zaria's one toilet, and to the galley, which they, too, have to use. In fact, he says, they also have complained to him that we spend so much time cooking that they sometimes have little chance to prepare their own meals, and must eat at irregular hours. So he's caught in between, impatient with petty grievances.

Afterward, both still drawn thin with our frustrations, he and I go out to stand under a shed roof of the pier.

HE SPILLED OUT HIS unhappiness, then, at the tensions festering on board. The discontent baffled and angered him. Maybe the Americans could not understand the difficulty of such a venture, or how complicated his part in it had been. Or maybe it was the problem of having women on an expedition—although that did not seem specifically the cause. The main trouble, he said, was the lack of discipline and the endless discussion that resulted. Valera and Volodya are his friends, he said. But on expedition, his word is law and they must follow it without question or hesitation. Why should it not be the same between me and the other Americans?

Maybe it should be, I told him. Certainly it would be easier that way. But our traditions and our histories are different from his. We imagine—or I imagined, anyway—that such a journey ought to be a collaboration, with decisions taken collectively. It sounded foolish and unconvincing as I said it, even to me.

He shook his head. "At other times, maybe yes. Not on expedition."

His certainty was somehow humiliating.

"About my wife and daughters, there's something you need to know," I said. "Without them, I would not have done this. There would be no expedition at all. I mean that. I'd be back in the U.S. And you'd be sitting in Irkutsk."

He was startled.

"You can see how they've worked. They haven't complained once, or made any problem."

"No, not them. But some of the others—"

"I'll deal with the others the best I can. That's all I promise."

"All right. But we *must lead*—or it can fall apart."

Victor stayed out on the pier to talk a while longer with Sergei. I went in to my sleeping place on the floor, resentful and tired of the weight of it all. My wants weren't unreasonable, I was thinking. All I wanted was to pass down this great river to its end, learn some things, and have some experiences worth remembering along the way.

⚜

W E'RE AWAY IN THE rarity of a dazzling morning. First under a motor bridge, then the Baikal-Amur railway bridge. Beyond here, all the way to the Arctic Ocean, no spans of any kind have been flung across the Lena. The unsightliness of Ust'Kut is behind, and we're passing through forest once more.

The chart shows a village called Nazarovo not far ahead. But when we stop it's a broken, puddled, and all-but-unpeopled place, most of its inhabitants having long ago been relocated to a larger settlement farther on. An old man hoes a plot of potatoes beside his wretched house. A small boy of 10 years or so, spied at a distance, disappears around a bend of the muddy, rutted street. There's a log post office, which seems still to be in service. And log houses, mostly abandoned—their window decorations rotting and unpainted.

The one street of Nazarovo leads to the end of the hamlet, then bends out across a field of grain just coming into head. There used to be an old cemetery, a woman tells us, but it no longer can be found. It was a burial place of the pioneers—the first wave of Russians who came here in the early 1600s to try to carve a life out of the pristine *taiga*. But the markers fell or rotted. The memory of the exact location was lost, although in expanding the field the farmers still sometimes unearth a stone or a skull while plowing. She points to a grove of trees on a distant rise. Maybe we would care to see the "new" cemetery, whose dates are only from a century and a half ago.

Mosquitoes and biting gnats swarm up with ferocity out of the high grass. When reached, the cemetery is a weedy place of humble grief, enclosed by a fence whose gate is fallen. There's a rough plank table and bench—where people may sit, break bread, pour vodka for themselves and a glass for the deceased, and try to remember. A spotted cow prospects for forage among the vines and sprouts that have overgrown the site.

Most of the markers are wooden, some with a small laminated photograph of the person laid below. Many have been toppled by wind, or time, or possibly by the cow. Of the surviving monuments, the dominant one is an enormous stone slab five feet by seven—just a great uncut fieldstone hauled here and set on edge—with history engraved upon it by some patient hand.

Here gained eternal peace the members of six generations of the family Razdyakonov, which arrived here from the upper Volga, says the inscription at the top.

First named is Stepan Mironovich Razdyakonov, 1785-1854. What fierce, untouched beauty the wilderness must have presented to his eye. One has to wonder, also, at the vaulting dreams or the oppression that could drive a man to this edge of empire, and at the unimagined hardships he may have found here.

After many intervening entries, the last name on the enormous stone is of Praskovya Nikitichna, 1900-1982, *Mother of Seven Sons of the Sixth Generation*. And at the bottom corner, the usual travel plans of them all, and all of us: *From Here to Eternity*.

The view from the cemetery is down across a poor stand of wheat or rye, to a village moribund and going to earth. For what, those six generations? To what point? No Razdyakonovs are left in

Nazarova. And the silence here evokes no peace—only the sense of wasted time, and an ordeal without redemption at the end.

Tomorrow we will reach Kirensk, where the first of the Lena's major tributaries, the Kirenga, joins our river and swells its flow. Actually, by pushing directly on, we could be there tonight. But before Kirensk we've decided to stop, put tents on shore as a little relief from crowding, and see if we might find enough decent fish for something more palatable than another *oooh-hah*.

Victor tries fishing from the bank, Valera and the crew from the stern of the boat. Sergei and some of the other Americans take advantage of the warm late afternoon to bathe in the river. Anne, Jennie and I have gone out with our rods in one of the canoes, letting the current carry us down toward a forested bend.

We've hardly begun to cast our lures when, with astonishing suddenness, the sky goes dark.

⚜

T HE EVENING STORM CAME striding up the river between the shoulders of two hills. It advanced like a moving wall, sooty colored, with terrific lightning discharges lancing down.

The three of us were perhaps a hundred yards downstream from the Zaria, but any notion of catching supper was erased by the seriousness of that oncoming mass of darkness. I started the little motor and we fled back, dragging the canoe high on the bank just as the wind whipped its first violent patterns on the water.

Victor and Valera were up on the Zaria's roof, trying to get a tarpaulin over our topside cargo. Two others of us rushed to help. In an instant, then, the storm was upon us.

Unbelievable, such wind. The first raindrops driven on the blast stung like birdshot where they struck the skin. The lightning flashed nearer, and then was striking all around. Each of us had one hand locked around some metal part of the boat, the other in a death grip on the canvas. If let slip loose a fraction, it would be torn away and lost forever.

You cannot imagine a straight wind coming with such force. Sustained assaults of two minutes, three minutes or more. Then a lull of several seconds, in which we called out encouragement and improved our grips on boat and tarp. And then it would come harder by half again. Three such increases. At the last and worst, the sound was a sustained and monstrous roar. The air was white as milk, full of water and impossible to see through, all but pointless to try to breathe. It was as if the river itself had been lifted up and blown backward upon us, as indeed some part of it must have been.

Then it passed. The terrible dark cloud went on to southward, trailing its skirt behind.

In the vastness of that northern wilderness are born prodigious storms. I could not help thinking, afterward, of our young friends on their fragile rafts—two days upriver behind us, in the direction the cloud had gone.

❧

THERE IS NO MORE talk of tenting this night. We who've been outside towel ourselves and get on dry clothes. Supper's a companionable affair, and Victor pours one drink of vodka around—the limit he and I have agreed on, except for special celebrations.

Volodya takes out his accordion. And with occasional lightning pulses still flaring in the dark window behind him, plays and sings some of his fine old Russian songs. We're filled up with the music and the appreciation of being inside, safe and warm. Instead of being just a vexation, our physical closeness seems for this little time almost a comfort. It is one of those surprising moments of unspoiled congeniality that, though rare, are precious when they come.

Then Volodya, self-taught in music as in English—a young man who came from hard beginnings but has made much of himself—has played all the songs he knows, and a few he only half knows, and puts the instrument aside. The wind falls away to a whisper, and stops completely. And we sleep to the sound of rain pelting on the roof of the boat.

THIRTY-FIVE

I MIGHT SAY A few words here about the routine of our shipboard days which, except for some variations made necessary by work, fall into a dependable pattern.

Breakfast is at half past 8 o'clock, which means that by a little after 7 the two Americans and one Russian who have the day's cooking duty are out of their bags, dressed, and stepping gingerly over the other supine forms to take their turns in the toilet, get provisions from the food storage compartment and begin their labors in the galley.

Waking at that hour is easy. On fair nights, darkness never really comes—only a kind of blueness as the sun makes its brief dip below the horizon before rising again at 2:30 or so in the morning. By 6, the day already seems far advanced, and by 8, when the others have begun stirring, sunlight floods in as hot and bright as noon.

If Anne and Jennie are cooking, their rising vacates the table. Otherwise, they must roll off and drag their bags into the places the cookers have left, to free the table top for laying out dry provisions—the granola, raisins, unsalted almonds and other fabulous delights. One of the food team attends to that. Another mixes a half-gallon of instant lemonade in a plastic pitcher, slices two loaves of our bread and locates the plastic squeeze-bottles of jelly. The third starts the two electric burners in the galley heating for any real cooking that might be planned.

The cook sets the menu, so on every fourth morning, when I have the duty, we eat pancakes made from the fifty-pound sack of bulk mix we've brought, using dried milk and powdered eggs. Once in a great while I vary that with biscuits, although baking them in our folding stove-top oven set over one of the weak burners takes so long that some of the Americans begin grumbling impatiently and the motorman of the Zaria, Vitaly Yambarshev, complains it is running down the boat's batteries. Our Russian companions are somewhat unsatisfied with any meal that does not include potatoes, and will cook them, fried or boiled, even as a garnish for morning pancakes or evening pasta.

While breakfast is being made, the others of our company roll sleeping bags and set our living space in order for another day. Victor's son, Alyosha, who still is with us and will go as far as Lensk, sweeps the whole floor of the compartment with a little brush. After the meal, one member of the kitchen team cleans and stows our metal plates, bowls and utensils. The other two go out for water.

Our Katadyn expedition filter is a wonder. It weighs only 12 pounds, looks and operates a good deal like a hand tire pump, and can produce up to four liters of drinkable water a minute. Sometimes we operate the filter from the rear of the boat, pulling up water with a bucket on a rope, and sometimes from the shore, putting the inlet tube of the filter directly in the river. Pumping forces the water under pressure through the pores of a ceramic cartridge inside the unit—pores so fine that they can remove dissolved minerals and even the most microscopic bacteria or other impurities. What comes out is odorless, tasteless and perfectly safe to drink.

As great rivers go, the Lena is astonishingly clean, except immediately below places of human settlement. But far as we are from medical help, we take no chances, filtering all the water we use, even for cooking. The Lena, as it grows larger and more powerful, carries a great freight of suspended sand that accumulates on the surface of the porcelain cartridge, making the pump hard to operate. So at least once during every use, and sometimes more than once, the device must be taken apart and the cartridge cleaned with a special brush. Coleman sent with us two plastic containers with spigots for water storage, one holding five gallons and the other two gallons. Filling them both, and cleaning the filter afterward, is a job of about 30 minutes. Our experience is that our party requires, for all purposes, about a gallon per person per day, so the filtering must be repeated again, usually in late afternoon.

Lunch is at 1:30, supper at 7:30, lights-out at about 11 o'clock—although, as I've said, the sun does not set until sometime after midnight, and even then darkness doesn't come. So "lights-out" really only signals an end of activity in our common room.

The rest of the time is spent either making miles on the river toward some place where we hope to work, or, if we're there already, spending hours ashore, talking to people about the history of that place, and about their lives, their occupations, their disappointments and their hopes for the future. The photographer and the videographer prefer to work independently, with only Volodya or Sergei along to interpret, and that's understandable. It is hard to record people going naturally about their everyday affairs when they have just been descended on by a gang of folks including not just Russian strangers but also the first Americans—often the first *foreigners*—they've ever seen.

On our days for cooking, Katie and I are able to use part of the quiet mid-mornings and mid-afternoons, especially when the others are off somewhere, catching up our journals, preparing packets of notes to the sponsors in the hope of finding some way to send them back. Those times are important. Only she has understood this dream from the beginning, and knows how hard it has been to get here. It has been hard for her, also, and we are one another's best allies against the discouragements and complications of the enterprise.

Our Russian companions also are diligent journalers. Bent over their notebooks, they put down their observations about the landscapes, the people and the character of the river itself—each according to his professional specialty. It is the greatest expedition any of them has made, or is likely to make, and they mean for nothing to go unrecorded.

Victor and Valera, in slack hours when they are not solving some problem with us, the crew, or the petty authorities in a settlement where we have stopped, pass their time in savagely serious games of chess, often with one or another of the crew members looking on and giving unwanted advice about the next move.

Sergei, the solitary, when his services are not needed retires to his nest atop the duffel in one of the storage compartments. Volodya, because of his English, seems to prefer passing time in conversation with the Americans. He is interested in naval history, and can recite the specifications of every major U.S. warship—its tonnage, an inventory of its armaments, the weight of a salvo from its guns. Battleships especially fascinate him. A friend in Kansas City sent with me an officer's baseball-type hat from the U.S.S. Missouri, splendid with gold braid and the ship's name. I will remember to give that to Volodya on August 3, a little more than three weeks from now, on his 30th birthday.

Jennie and Anne also are keeping journals, and I will depend on them to notice things that I have missed. The other Americans, when not working, pass time up front in the wheelroom, or napping, or reading books.

Those are our days. Evenings, after supper is finished and cleared, we take out the maps. And Victor and I, in consultation with the Zaria's captain, Valery, and with the aid of his charts, try to plan a destination for the next day. That's the moment I do not look forward to, for it's the time when disagreement is most apt to erupt.

Distances, the character of the river and the landscape, the location of marked villages (which sometimes no longer exist at all) and in some part the weather govern the decision. But there are other factors. The photographer insists that he must have the first hours of morning and last hours of evening in some inhabited place, because the light is best then, and it's the villages and their people that most interest him.

Victor, on the other hand, specifically wants *not* to stop the night in such places. Mostly his worry is security. He knows the hardship and grinding need along this river. And the fabulous treasure our cargo of food and equipment represents to people who must live in such poverty and isolation. Also the mischief that can flow from drunkenness—the disease of the Russian north that will only grow worse the farther toward the Arctic we proceed. What's more, Victor is an outdoorsman. He prefers unsettled places, the sense of the *taiga* pressing close, shore camping, the possibility of ending the day with an hour or two of fishing, both for pleasure and for the pot. And all those preferences of his I share.

So in endless discussion and attempts at conciliation, a plan must somehow be brokered out. Then we lie down on the floor in our sleeping bags, body pressed against body, light still pouring through the windows, feeling others clamber over to take their last turns in the toilet, trying to remember we used to know an easier way to live. And sleep a few hours until the next day's cooking crew begins to stir and it is time to do it all again.

Enduring is not so hard. What's harder is to remember how rare, how priceless, is the chance even to be here. There are whole days when I lose sight of that entirely. Then, at some unexpected moment, the richness of adventure will come back to smite me with amazing force.

☙❧

K IRENSK, A TOWN OF 17,000 souls, materialized out of fog on the Lena's right bank like an antique tintype, a vision of something out of place and out of time. The immediate impression was of isolated communities I'd seen 30 years ago in the interior of Africa. Blantyre, perhaps, in what used to be Nyasaland, or stations huddled on the banks of the Congo or the Zambezi—some very old outpost from which the colonials had departed, leaving it to run slowly back to earth. Except here the colonials remained to administer the decline.

In 1630, at the start of the decade when determined European penetration of Siberia began, a band of Cossacks led by a man named Vasily Bugor arrived at the meeting of the Lena and the Kirenga and built a cabin on the high ground commanding the bend of the larger river. The next year, that prospecting band was followed by another, whose leader is identified only as Galkin, and the cabin was replaced by a log fortress.

The Cossacks were the outriders of empire, coming independently first, propelled by adventure and greed, and then in the service of the Czars. The great south-to-north Siberian rivers—the Ob, Yenisey and Lena—were their highways of exploration. The tributaries, like the Tunguska, the Angara, the Kirenga, Vilyuy and Aldan, were the lateral water roadways between. Throughout the vastness of the north Asian wilderness, water was—and except for planes and helicopters still is—the only means of access, especially in summer, when thaw turns much of the interior to a hell of bogs and biting insects.

The Cossacks took tribute in furs from the indigenous people, and began the practice of agriculture to supply their forts. But actual conflict was rare. The local people were hunters and trappers, and when oppression was felt they simply retreated deeper into the *taiga*.

Nothing remains of the log fort of 350 years ago. The town's post, telephone and telegraph building now occupies that site on the prominence looking down on the bend of the Lena. In 1775, a year before American independence, Catherine II granted Kirensk the official status of a town.

Our escort and recounter of this history was a pretty, dark-haired woman, Natalia Alexandrovna Ankudinova, who was introduced as the director of the town museum. I apologized for our arriving unannounced, and taking so much of her time. Sergei waited until she was walking a bit ahead, out of hearing, then bent to whisper something almost as sad as the rest of the history she had to tell.

"The truth is," he said, "she has no place to go, no place to work. There *is no museum*—only the title of director."

After the Cossacks came Russian merchants to build their hewn larch-log houses and stores along the embankment of the river, many of which have survived to this day, still solid and in use. The wood of the larch tree endures well in the harsh winters, but in summer, which sometimes brings long spells of parching heat, fires are an ever-present danger. They kindle somewhere in the *taiga* and advance, wind-whipped, upon the town. Last year fire claimed a dozen houses.

An even worse threat, until it was abandoned only in 1990, was a Brobdingnagian scheme by the authorities in Moscow to somehow divert the flow of some Siberian rivers, including the Lena, to Central Asia for irrigation. It would have meant the end of Kirensk, said Natalia Alexandrovna. "There would have been here no river, only swamp."

The town's life, in this century, has been grim.

In 1912, there was a two-month strike by river workers in Kirensk. When the strikers went to present a petition to the authorities, the Czar's soldiers turned their guns on the crowd and 250 were killed, 270 wounded.

More than 1,500 of the town's men and boys died in World War II, and here, as everywhere in Russia, the conflict is remembered with a mix of pride and unassuaged grief.

Kirensk lay on the route from Alaska to Krasnoyarsk, north-west of Irkutsk, used from 1942 through 1946 for flying planes contributed by the U.S. to the Soviet war effort. The flight was long and hazardous, the route little-known, and as many as 30 of the planes crashed along the way. Only three years ago, the wreckage of one of them, a bomber named the "Boston," was found in the forest less than 20 miles from the town. The remains of the crew were brought to Kirensk and buried. Locals have tried to recover as much of the plane as possible, with the thought of creating a memorial, but there's no money for the purpose and no support from the state.

Several years ago the town had a small but memorable bit of luck. Alexei Kosygin, long-time Soviet prime minister, spent three years of his young manhood in Kirensk. Local people attending a party congress in Moscow approached him, reminded him of that, and through his intervention were able to get a satellite TV receiving station, allowing them a glimpse of the wider world, or as much of it as state broadcasting authorities permitted them to see.

From the hill above, the town had a derelict charm. The fog had cleared, and people circulated among the old buildings, along the dirt streets and broken sidewalks. On the other side of the river, a newer part of Kirensk has been established, and a ferry churned back and forth, taking passengers to the far bank, bringing others back and discharging them at the floating boat station, green-painted, with a spindled veranda all around, the town's name in white letters on a sign above. It was a vision out of Conrad, frozen in time a century ago.

There was something else Natalia Alexandrovna wanted to show us. Not so much *wanted* to, as felt she should. We trudged after her through the suddenly brutal midday heat, up through a miserable quarter to a cluster of brick buildings on the high ground, where the last of the town backs up to the gorge of the Kirenga River just before its meeting with the Lena.

The old building into whose courtyard Natalia led us was the office of an abandoned distillery, and in the 1930s was the local headquarters of the dreaded NKVD. This spring, someone exploring in the basement noticed an odd thing about the floor. Some of the bricks looked to have been laid by a craftsman's careful hand. But another section was the work of an amateur. On April 17, not quite three months ago, the bricks of that section were taken up, and Kirensk was shocked by a ghastly discovery.

Under the bricks were 83 bodies, all in a state of remarkable preservation because of the permafrost—the zone of never-thawing earth—that underlies much of this part of Siberia. Through an oversight by the murderers, one of the bodies still bore identification papers. A list with that name on it was located among old papers of the secret police. Working from that, and by deduction, it was possible to identify with fair certainty the victims, all fellow townspeople who had disappeared without explanation in 1937 and 1938.

Few of them died of gunshot wounds, Natalia told us. Most had broken skulls.

Just then a woman coming out of the adjoining building, another of the distillery's brick structures converted now to dismal apartments, accosted us in the courtyard. Rimma Alexeevna Glotova, she said her name was. She appeared to be in her 50s, although with the hardness of life it often was impossible to know.

"In every town," she shouted, "there are good things and bad things! The things that happened in this house, the people of my generation were not responsible for and know nothing about."

The bloodshot little eyes in her bloated face seemed afire with defensiveness and anger. And she launched then into a long, dimwitted tirade, alternating between apology and resentment of our having come there—then changing, astonishingly, into effusive and obsequious greetings that ended, disgustingly, with her attempt to kiss our hands.

"Please," Natalia rebuked the woman. *"Please!"* And she led us quickly away from there, seeming sick with humiliation. Not all of us were well, either. Most of our party was getting, or just getting over, a stomach ailment. And the heat of the day was sapping. There was a ruined church she would have liked to show us, but we'd seen all we cared to of Kirensk.

"Are there other such burial places in the town," I asked her, as we went back down toward the river.

"None known," she said. "But people suspect. We continue to research and to look."

"What's the official attitude?"

"There is no interference, but no help either. They say, 'All right, well, you have found eighty-three. Now leave it alone.'"

Natalia and her mother kept a garden, and with the usual generosity of Siberians she wanted to share some of the produce. We hated to take anything, in a place that had so little. But she was determined that Anne and Jennie must go home with her, so she could send back to us some onions, radishes and cuttings of fresh dill.

I lay down for an hour in the hot cabin, waiting for them to return. And while I slept there, sweating, some of the others went to an ice cream parlor Victor had found near the embankment. When I woke up and discovered that, I was childishly and unreasonably piqued. *Ice cream*, for God's sake! No one makes it better than the Russians. And to miss a little amenity like that in the middle of a wilderness is like missing one's only chance at salvation.

So I asked Sergei to lead me back there alone. The place was called the "Fairy Tale" cafe. It must have closed shortly after the others left, because the door was locked and a hand-lettered notice said they were preparing for a private party.

I damned near wept with disappointment. But Sergei beat on the door with the flat of his hand, and after much pounding the curtain was drawn back.

"I have an American," he told the young woman through the glass.

There was the sound of bolts being drawn back, and a key turning, and we were admitted with much cordiality. We each had a plate of ice cream, and it was wonderful—the last we'd taste for another 2,000 miles. In fact, I had two plates. On the walls of the cafe were painted illustrations from traditional Russian fairy tales, tales far happier than any the town of Kirensk has to tell about itself.

THIRTY-SIX

L AST NIGHT, A FEW hours north of Kirensk, we stopped where a gravel bank rose steeply from the river's edge all the way to the forest—an unappealing spot, impossible for putting up tents. We cast our lines for the better part of an hour, but the place also was barren of fish.

There *must* be fish there, Victor insisted. But catching them in Siberia required very specific methods, and he repeated once again his declaration that the problem was our technique. That was nonsense, of course, because he'd caught nothing either. In fact, the only fish of consequence we'd taken—the grayling on Baikal—had risen to our lures. I mentioned that, and it provoked some good-natured bantering between us.

Somewhere, without my registering the addition—it must have been in Ust'Kut—a fourth member has joined the crew of our boat. Valery Plenkov, the captain, is 44 years old, a quiet, solid man. The motorman, Vitaly Yambarshev, is 35, short and slim but heavily muscled as a boxer, with a small mustache, a stiff bush of hair and a Middle Eastern cast to his features. The youngest is the assistant motorman, Alexei Alexeievich Surayev, 30, a gaunt fellow who wears a perpetual hang-dog look, as if he'd just come from a tongue-lashing or a beating, but friendly and capable.

The new man's name is Yuri Yanovich Gnas. He's 38, riding with us as co-captain, and his duty will be to spell Valery at the wheel. He's tall, vainly handsome, with a bit of a swagger in his manner. And though I can't put my finger on it quite, he's the only unlikeable one of the four. It isn't that he's disagreeable, but he smiles without meaning it while his eyes look through and past you. His interest is mainly in himself, and the women he might attract.

And he has brought a bit of the local wildlife on board. I noticed her yesterday, when she came down to our mooring at Kirensk to flirt and be flirted with—just past being young, hair bleached yellow-blonde and wearing a frilly summer sun dress, a creature more extravagant than you might expect to see on a wilderness river. It's clear she shared his cabin last night, and she's with him in the wheelhouse when we make a late start this morning after waiting for fog to lift.

The river, its volume nearly doubled by the addition of the waters of the Kirenga, flows between and around islands now, so the helmsman must use a chart to keep to the true channel. And we have begun to meet traffic of more frequent and larger boats. On the middle and lower Lena, in this short season of navigation when she is free of ice, there is a frantic rush of commerce, delivering to the isolated towns and settlements along the river the equipment and staple goods they will require for another year, and carrying out whatever they produce—mostly raw materials.

Traveling both ways, upstream and down, big boats are seen in growing numbers: great barge tows of coal and ore and logs, ships riding low under cargoes of fuel oil and liquified gas. Using his radio-phone, our captain, Valery, hails one of these. It slows its engines so that it just holds against the current, and our Zaria comes about. A small motorboat is lowered from the tanker and, with a young seaman in it, crosses to us to fetch Yuri's lady.

Regal as a crenolined princess entering a carriage, she lets herself be assisted into the idling boat and borne over to the larger ship to be transported back to Kirensk. Hers is an occupation, like any other. And while not all river men require the service she provides, they respect and accommodate the needs of those who do, and honor her willingness to work.

Victor is indifferent to this transfer in mid-river. He has rejected Valera's offer of a game of chess, and instead has spent a good part of the morning working furiously with his fishing tackle, arranging his box of lures and spooling onto his reel new monofilament line from the supply I've given him. Evidently the gauntlet has been flung down on the question of whose methods will catch fish, and he does not mean to be unready when another chance presents itself.

⚜

CLOUDS BEGAN BUILDING TO the north and west, but then they blew away. The wind lay, and the evening turned warm and fine.

Our camp was at a place called the "Cheeks" of the Lena, where the valley pinched down to walls of looming yellow cliffs, a sheer cut worn through the foothills of the Patom Mountains by the great river in its ages of patient rushing.

I stood a bit apart, and took in the scene. Could this really be Siberia? The tents were on a spit of pale, flour-fine sand. Our expedition, all in swimming suits, lolled on towels in an hour of golden sun, getting up from time to time for dips at the edge of the water. The videographer was teaching Valera, Volodya and Alyosha the art of throwing a Frisbee. It might have been a scrap of beach tucked against a bluff somewhere in northern California.

Victor had rushed away immediately with his rod, skipping supper, to defend his honor as a fisherman. But he caught nothing. Jennie, Anne and I took one of the canoes a quarter mile upstream and let the current drift us down. Anne had one fish on—one that might have settled the question for all time. A *taimen* it may have been. That or a huge pike. We never saw it. The fish fought deep and powerfully. And just when she'd begun to raise him slightly, the line went slack. It hadn't broken. The great fish, whatever it was, had just come off.

The chance for shore camping allowed us all space, and blessed relief from one another. In the midnight twilight, the gasoline lanterns gave our sand bar the look of a settled place. The wake of a passing barge tow flung up a rank of lapping waves on our little shore.

The short-wave radio, its wire antenna strung between the side poles of the tents, told of Mikhail Gorbachev's meeting with Western finance ministers and his urgent plea for aid to prop up the collapsing Soviet economy. The ministers, according to the BBC, were sympathetic but not forthcoming with any promises of money.

Tomorrow, we'd decided, we would make an early start—5:30 at the latest—cook breakfast on the move and stop only for photography. If all went well, the crew said, evening would find us at the next great tributary, the Vitim River, and the town that bears its name.

V ITIM WILL BE WORTH remembering, if at all, only for two conversations. The first is with Mamont Stepanovich Oblansky, whose given name means "mammoth"—although he is of ordinary size and, at 73, rather frail except for his voice, which rings with the authority of a man who spent a lifetime in school classrooms and expects his pronouncements to be heeded.

We'd asked at the office of the local Soviet for directions to older people who might be able to tell some history of the town. The wooden building had the flavor of a country courthouse any-where: old wooden furniture, the lingering smell of some past fire, a door leaning against a wall waiting to be rehung, postings of work schedules, geraniums in pots, a room for having tea. A secre-tary gave directions to Mammoth's house, at the end of a broken street running along the high bank above the river.

Unannounced, we knock. And he, composed as one might be who every day received travelers from half a world away, admits us. His kind wife, Clavdiya Gregorievna, brings forth a plate of wonder-ful sugar cookies, little chocolate candies wrapped in foil (gotten from God knows where, or how) and a pot of strong tea. And Mammoth gladly talks.

In the middle of the last century, he says, gold was found 200 miles up the Vitim River to the south, and the boom town of Bodaibo was founded. People poured in then from other regions, from all over Siberia as far west as the Urals. Nearly all of them were men, "because women's work was of no value here." He sup-poses it was much like the gold rush in California. The gold-seekers went up the Vitim, using *taiga* paths, to find new strikes and work the diggings. Traders followed, but only as far as here, the junction of the rivers, to build their houses and deal in provisions, alcohol and women.

"The miners went up the Vitim to get their gold," he says, "then came back down to Vitim town to lose it." There was nowhere else for them to go. River commerce did not begin until the 1890s, when two Japanese steamboats were disassembled, brought overland by horse, and reassembled at Kirensk.

At about the time the gold rush was beginning, in the mid-1800s, Mammoth's grandfather was ordered into Siberian exile from his native Odessa, traveling on foot with a group of fellow unfortunates toward Irkutsk. But he slipped away, and made it to the Lena, to Kachug, and began his family there. "And that," says Mammoth, "is how my name happened to come to this part of the country."

His own parents came to Vitim 60 years ago, when Mammoth was just a boy. Since the age of 20, he has been a teacher of geography, and has watched the size of the town treble in his lifetime, to 7,000 now. Seventy-two men of the town were lost in the great war. It was Siberians, he says proudly, who determined the course of the war and defeated the Germans.

The town's main activity now is cutting timber from the forest, often rafting the logs north some 2,000 miles on the Lena all the way to Tiksi, on the Arctic coast, to be loaded on ships to Japan. He likes this place, likes Siberia, and especially, he says, he likes the climate which even in winter is "very nice"—hardly more than 60 degrees below zero. When he was in the army, he corresponded with a girl in Moscow who wanted him to come there to live. But he refused, writing back that he could think of no better place than Siberia.

He's retired, now, and in good health he says—although there's a blood pressure cuff on the table beside him. His view of most things is generally optimistic. A recent geological expedition found promising deposits of oil and gas not far from Vitim, and he sees a good future for the area. What Mammoth is not encouraged about is the growing social indiscipline, particularly among the young.

"Young people today are lazy. They will do nothing of any use, and also they are disrespectful. American moving pictures, if you ask me, are very bad for youth. I can tell you this—" He leans forward, his voice booming for emphasis. "Under Stalin, at least there was *discipline*."

"Maybe," I reply tentatively. "The cost, though, was pretty high."

"Yes, but if you put aside the wrong that was done, things were more orderly then."

Mammoth is a kindly man, not vicious. But change has left him behind.

The other conversation, briefer, is in the house of Maria Maximovna Kazakova, almost an exact contemporary of Mammoth's—she'll be 73 in another month—and also a former teacher. She's given her whole life and all her labor to children, she says. There may have been 600 students in all, though she never thought to count them.

You can't go in any Russian house, however poor, without being offered hospitality. Maria Maximovna brings a cold pitcher of *kvass* for us to drink while she tells her life.

She was born in Kirensk, lost her mother at age 6 and her father at 14. She married in 1941. Ten months later the war began and her husband was taken in the first wave, leaving her about to bear a child. Three years later, she received the paper saying he'd been killed at the front. The document was official, but she could not believe it—could not accept that he was dead—and kept waiting for him to come home.

Twelve years passed, and she married another man. He was kind to her daughter, and later to her daughter's child. She taught for 32 years, and receives a pittance of a pension. But now her second husband is sick and nearly blind. And she, too, is an invalid—lower legs and ankles elephantine with swelling. They live in a wooden house built in 1900 for the local priest. Health is their greatest problem, and the difficulty of getting either care or medicine. Her grandson has come to work two years as an air controller at the tiny landing strip of the town, and has promised to help them as he can. But that is only for two years.

To lift her spirits, Maria Maximovna brings out her cache of old photographs. Most are of relatives on her husband's side, in the time before the revolution. They were *kulaks*—well-to-do farmers—special targets for liquidation during the brutal 1929-1934 drive to collectivize Soviet agriculture. I don't ask her, but I suppose a great many of them must have been killed in Stalin's day.

The photographs, all taken in a portrait studio and signed by the photographer, freeze forever in place a time and a way of life before any of those horrors happened. The women wear puffy satin dresses, the men frock coats and wing collars. All of them look very smug and vain, with no intimation of the future in their eyes. In

Maria Maximovna's box also are some old pictures of Vitim town. It
looked then much as it does now, except for the addition of light
poles: a tired, muddy and half-broken place.

What about the future, I ask her.

"I try to maintain optimism," she replies. "But this is a hinterland, far from the center. In the past, we have never been hungry.
We have never been rich, but we have always had work. In the time
to come, I don't know. My grandson is constantly telling me, 'You
haven't got *this*. You haven't got *that*. You've lived all your life and
you have nothing for it.'"

A wonderfully tactful and considerate young fellow, that
grandson.

THIRTY-SEVEN

S WELLED BY ITS SECOND major tributary, the Lena beyond Vitim flows
three-quarters of a mile wide, dark and muscular, the surface
creased by the current's power. Somewhere on the left bank the
taiga is afire. An acrid haze hangs over the route ahead and turns
the air blue for miles in every direction, biting the nose and eyes.

Much of this day will be lost pursuing a rumor of grim history.
We've been told there is an old prison camp of the Stalin era, with
a gallows still standing, near a village called Peleduy and we reach
the place in afternoon. There's a sign commemorating the establish-
ment of the town in 1933, and a statue of a river captain on the
river bank. But no such camp. It was at the other Peleduy, we're
told—Big Peleduy, which is several miles farther on.

Big Peleduy is all but derelict, though—a place of only six families and a ruined church. A little knot of people, a good part of the
hamlet's population, stands on the brow of the high bank and
watches us climb up. The wind keeps the mosquitoes off and brings
a bit of freshness. It's been uncommonly hot, they say, with no rain
here in more than a month.

The oldest woman in the group tells fondly of the time, before

1933, when Big Peleduy was a substantial settlement of "sixty yards"—by which she means 60 houses. Then the other Peleduy was carved out of the forest, and the people left for there. A prison camp? Not here, she says. She does remember when some German prisoners were brought through, and they stopped for a week in the meadow behind the village. But nothing was built, and then the prisoners were taken on to somewhere else. Who knows where?

The fire smell is stronger. The blue haze drifts thicker over the river, and Valery, the Zaria's captain, is concerned. There is no knowing how large the blaze in the forest might be. In dry weather, raging unattended, *taiga* fires have been known to achieve such size that smoke from them reduces visibility to zero, halting boat passage on the Lena for as much as a fortnight.

After another hour we reach what seems to be the worst place, where a great column of flame and ash billows up from behind the second rank of hills. Then suddenly we are beyond, the air startlingly clear again, wind carrying the smoke away behind. The place we've chosen for the night's stop looks, from the map, to have the double virtue of a small river, the Konyok, to explore and possibly fish in, and a village situated just at its mouth, although we will arrive there late and will have to defer our investigations until tomorrow.

ოჲჲ

A LL WERE OUT IN the first freshness of morning, but the village proved unproductive for the photo people. And the Konyok, more a creek than a river, was too shallow to be traversed more than a hundred yards, even by canoe.

There was one astonishing moment, just as we were turning to go down the little stream and back to the boat. From the wilderness to our right we thought we heard a sound of voices, mingled and indistinct, then growing louder. Then it seemed to be a single voice, gasping and stammering with rage.

Suddenly, through the all but impenetrable wall of under-growth there burst into view an apparition—a gaunt man in ragged clothes, with a wild growth of grizzled beard, a walking staff in his hand, a pack on his back and, at his heels, some kind of bristling mongrel dog as disreputable as himself.

Evidently those two were bound somewhere on foot through the *taiga* together.

The voyageur halted on the streambank, wheeled round and fixed us with blazing eyes. Then, as if deciding we weren't worth confiding the reason for his great fury, he lurched straight into the water to his waist, the dog swimming behind him, crossed the little Konyok, stumbled dripping up the bank and disappeared, ranting and cursing, into the forest on the other side.

What could derange a man like that, and send him plunging through the endless forest, shouting his anger to no audience but voles and trees? Maybe he once tried to lead an expedition.

⚜

THE PHOTOGRAPHER WANTS TO spend this night at Lensk, which can be seen just a mile or so ahead, its cranes angled out from the high bank on the left. Victor and the other Russians specifically *do not* want to stay moored at the town, and with good reason. Even before we reach the place, two motorboats of drunks have raced to meet us, orbiting the Zaria, passing bottles from hand to hand, showing off and importuning—coarse-faced idlers, stupid and malicious.

The solution is to work this evening and tomorrow in Lensk, but both nights, after the light for photography goes bad, to beach at some place a little way downriver. The day after tomorrow we plan to make a hard six-hour trip overland by rough road connecting Lensk and the diamond mining center of Mirnyy, on the Vilyuy River, and the day after that by helicopter to the Yakut town of Suntar.

Meantime, we seem again to have passengers. Somewhere, probably at Vitim, Yuri the Lascivious brought two young women aboard and he and the Arabic-looking motorman, Vitaly, evidently have kept them hidden in the crew quarters forward since then. I see them for the first time when we stop for bathing on a sandy island before going into Lensk. The girls are hardly more than children, beautiful and delicate as birds. They come back from bathing carrying great bouquets of wildflowers in their arms, and disappear with their keepers into the privacy of the cabins again. Valery, the captain, is a stolid family man and has no part in it, but understands how the loneliness of life on the river torments some men. Alexei, the motorman's assistant, is envious but painfully shy.

There'll be opportunity enough to prowl Lensk. The first impression, though, is of raw and relentless ugliness. A large sign announces that this is the 25th anniversary of the town's founding. It looks already broken and ruined in its youth. Volodya points to the first building we come to.

"It is the biggest restaurant in this town," he announces grandly. "Also the smallest. Also the most popular and the worst. In fact, it's the *only* one." Just past that is a rectangular block of flats, plaster siding flaking off, deteriorating with neglect and the weather. Two cows are held in by a fence to graze the little yard of the apartment building.

We go into a store to see what's offered. The shelves are empty, except for a few loaves of bread, some fur hats, two bridal veils, a dozen pairs of rubber boots and several stacked cases of Gerber's baby food. How in God's name—by what accident of commerce—did those manage to find their way to Lensk?

Thirty-six thousand people call this town their home. But why? How can life here even be imagined? For Volodya, who spent many years of his boyhood in such half-made places, the imagining is easy enough.

"People come for the advantage of higher pay, the chance to buy cars and other things," he says. "The government gives—or used to give—special privileges for coming to Siberia. Also there's the hunting and fishing. And most Russians do not sense cultural deprivation. It's hard to travel anyway. Few will ever leave the country. But in the evening, when they turn on the television," says Volodya, "they can see New York. They can see Washington.

"So people come here, and they say, 'I'll stay ten years, and then go back to where I am from.' And after ten years, they say, 'Well, maybe another five.' Then another five. And, in the end, they find they have spent a lifetime here." The evening wind whips up clouds of grit from the dirt streets and flings it in our faces, so that we have to press our mouths closed and squint against it as we make our way back to the boat.

In the blue evening of midnight, on the spit downriver to which we've retreated for the night, Valera and the boat crew are frying potatoes in a huge skillet over a driftwood fire. The chill of the great river breathes up onto the shore, but it's pleasant sitting on a log close to the blaze. Yuri insists I have some of the potatoes, which are peppered and cooked in oil. They're tasty, but I'm uneasy with his hospitality. There's something about him I neither like nor trust.

A small boat roars up in the gloom—two young game wardens in camouflage suits, with pistols on their hips, come to investigate the fire. They sit, too, and take the potatoes they're offered, plucking them from the skillet with knife points, almost without a word, as if the sharing were obligatory. Then they race off in their little boat to somewhere else, and the fire burns low.

The two young women are nowhere about. Evidently Yuri and the motorman dismissed them while we were taking stock of the town. Maybe they weren't really professionals after all—just two girls from somewhere wretchedly poor, desperate for transport to the brighter lights of Lensk. If so, I expect they'll find it a nastier place than the one they left, hardly worth what they bartered for their passage.

THIRTY-EIGHT

I N THE LIGHT OF a new day, Lensk is no less grim but at least there is a frail stirring of life and commerce. It's a port town, and the people and enterprises along this reach of the Lena depend for their sustenance on goods brought around the north coast of Europe and Asia and upriver from the Arctic by ship.

Boats of all sizes, and all conditions, are tethered in the current, ranging from the small outboards that are the "automobiles" of the river—the only practical transport from one settlement to the next—to coal barges and container ships waiting to unload. A quarter-mile-long raft of logs from the forest slides by on the river's far side, guided by a tug, riding the current north.

One of the great cranes is at work on this Sunday, its dinosaur neck pivoting out over the water and pausing while men below attach cables to the load. The videographer is up in the machine's cab, filming the crane operator, a woman in a red dress and purple heels, as she manipulates the controls to lift, pivot and deposit the goods on the pier. A dozen or so people have come down to the river to stand on the high quayside and pass time watching the unloading.

The vessel below is a refrigerator ship, but it also carries an array of deck cargo. There are eighteen cars, most of them humble Ladas—some new, most used, one quite comprehensively wrecked—which the crane is unloading now, plucking them up delicately and setting them ashore. There also are several large bundles of truck tires. But what fascinates me are the new toilets, huge crates of them occupying the greater part of the deck. Lord knows, Siberia—like all Russia—needs them desperately, since it's virtually impossible to find one anywhere that's not broken or somehow inoperable.

By counting the number in a crate, and the number of crates stacked atop one another in one small section of deck, then extending the calculation to the whole area they take up, I'm trying to determine how many there are. The number I come up with is *nineteen thousand two hundred* new toilets. I've worked the multiplication in my head, so the figure isn't altogether dependable. But anyway it's a lot of toilets—more of them, I'd bet, than you'd be able to find in working order in all of Siberia east of Novosibirsk. Where will they all disappear to? How long before they're broken like the rest? I can't help thinking of the violence that awaits them.

In the little crowd on the quay is Vladimir Nikolayevich Ostanin, a burly, gregarious fellow who is glad to meet someone from another place. With Sergei's help, I talk with him while we watch the crane work. He is 38 years old, and came to Lensk after the army. He's in business for himself, buying used trucks from other parts of the Soviet Union and bringing them by ship for delivery in Siberia, though it turns out that none of his are in this cargo. He says he likes Lensk well enough.

"It's a friendly place. Everybody knows everybody. You can walk in the street at night. People here might beat you, but they won't kill you. And I can take care of myself." From his stature, one can believe that. "But as for life," he says, "it's only work and television."

From the unloading pier, we pass through a scrap yard of rusted pipe and machine parts into the maze of the *balki*, a compacted area of wretched, cobbled-together wooden shacks lying between the riverfront and the main part of the town. The *balki* district is a feature of every new settlement across Siberia—a warren of rough habitations tacked together for temporary shelter while the town was being built. But in Lensk as elsewhere, with the eternal shortages of everything, especially of housing, the *balki* has matured into a permanent slum. Mostly it shelters new arrivals while they wait for lodging in one of the modern apartment blocks which, though dreadful to look at, are warmer and more convenient.

Children play games in the twisted alleyways that thread between the shacks, or peer out around gateposts in the rough board fences that enclose dooryards. Even here, the provident try to make some kind of life, building greenhouses covered with plastic sheeting to grow tomatoes and planting potatoes in any scrap of dirt not taken up by shack or winter woodpile. The district is reminiscent of the squatter settlements that huddle at the edges of cities in Africa or Latin America. It isn't that the cities are so grand—just that this is so much *worse*.

We spend a half-hour there, wanting to get a sense of it but feeling a bit ashamed to gape too long or obviously at the circumstances of people so unlucky and ill-used. Coming out again on the main street that bounds, and confines, the district, we turn back toward the boat and supper.

A YOUNG BOY APPROACHED to hand us something folded shyly in his hand. It was a lapel pin, with the name of the town on it. Russians are passionate traders and givers of pins. We thanked him for it.

"No," he said in his schoolroom English. "That lady." And he pointed.

We turned, and the small woman waved from the other side of the road. In a place where people from the outer world so rarely come, our foreignness was noticeable as a uniform.

We crossed to thank her. She was a stout little woman, with a head-scarf framing her sweet, round face and a smile that showed several silver-metal teeth. Where were we from?

"From the *U.S.A.?*" That amazed and pleased her. She'd never seen an American before.

We asked where she lived.

"In there." She pointed back into the maze of shacks. She was glad we'd seen it, she said, and glad that we had made pictures there. "Maybe if you show to the world how it is necessary to live in the *balki* some good will result. Maybe the officials will have to do something."

"Can we see your house?" the videographer asked her.

I would not have suggested it. There's a softness, a kind of reticence about intruding in people's most private matters, that has always disabled me as a journalist and of which I am not proud. With time, when I've come to know people, I can do it. But I can't ask outright for access to their lives. In that, I think, photojournalists are abler—perhaps because a machine, the camera, is interposed between them and their subject.

Anyway, he did ask. It made her ashamed, she said, to invite anyone to such a place. But, yes, we were welcome to see. And she led the way down one of the alleys. "That's not my house," she said as we passed a dismal shack. "Mine is worse than that."

The little woman's name was Anastasia Kiriollovna Simagina, and she told us her story as we walked. She was 45 years old when she came to this raw new place—before Lensk was even officially a town— to work as a clerk in a shop. The authorities assigned her a place in the *balki* while she waited for a flat in one of the regular apartments.

She is 74 now. And still waiting.

Turning a corner in the alley, she opened the fence gate into a few square yards of beaten earth where a woolly black dog and orange cat were sharing food from a single bowl. The door of her house was fastened with an enormous iron padlock, and inside that was another door, also locked.

The interior was sparely furnished but clean. One room was her kitchen, with a masonry stove for heat and cooking, and near it a cot on which she slept. In the other room were a sofa, table and chair, dressing table. On the wall, for decoration, she'd hung several small carpets of poor quality that she brought with her half a lifetime ago when she came here from the Central Asian Kazakh Soviet republic.

She has a little pension. Her days are passed visiting friends and drinking tea. She has tried to make a life, but the place she must live in is broken, decaying around her.

"Do you see?" She pointed in despair at the floor, rotted through and sagging open to the winter's awful frosts. "And here." Another cavity beside her cot. "And the wall here." Also eaten through by rot. She's tried to patch the place with cardboard and a piece of tin. But those do not turn the wind.

"Only the stove chimney holds the ceiling up," said Anastasia Kiriollovna, with a little laugh. Then her lips trembled. The sudden tears came.

Food isn't the problem. She gets the same ration as the rest. The biggest problem is shelter—shelter and firewood. She doesn't know how she can live another winter. She has gotten too old to cut firewood, and cannot afford to pay someone to do it for her.

She has a friend who got a flat. But somehow, her own name does not seem to move up on the list. She goes repeatedly to the local authorities—goes almost every week—but they are tired of seeing her and only tell her to come some other time.

"I'm an old woman now, and no one cares."

I tried to think of some encouragement to give.

"At least you're not alone. You have your dog and cat for company."

"Yes," she said. And the smile burst through her tears like

spring cloud-shadows changing. "We are a household. But go tell that there is an old woman in Lensk, and *this* is how she must live."

I wondered afterward if our talking with her might somehow complicate her troubles, since the prying of foreigners with cameras in the *balki* was unlikely to go unnoticed.

The videographer was annoyed by the question.

"How could it be worse?"

And of course he was right.

⚜

WALKING BACK ALONG THE high river bank toward our Zaria I'm assailed by a young man from Afghanistan who grasps at my sleeve as I pass. He has heard me speaking, and supposes I am English. American is even better. He has been traveling for seven years in all the Soviet republics, he says. Now he would like to go to the U.S.

Fine, I say. But that's not an easy thing to do. And why ask me? How does he imagine I can help him?

He wants me to come with him to his home, so he can cook for me a typical Afghan meal. I don't *want* a typical Afghan meal! I only want to be free of his entreaties—and the misfortune and need at every hand. I walk away and leave him sitting on a bench beside the road.

This evening there's another little miracle, of the kind that has enabled us to get this far. A small man from the Institute, one of those who went with us to the train in Moscow, comes into our crowded compartment on the boat just as we're finishing supper. He has arrived by helicopter from Irkutsk, after first taking the overnight plane from Moscow. And he is carrying a lens for the video camera—expressed to Moscow from Denver—to replace the one that was ruined in the raft accident in the mountains. It will improve life for the videographer, who has been working since then with only one partly-operable lens.

The courier also has a note from Tishkov, asking for instructions about the expenditure of dollars for our air passage back from the Arctic at our journey's end. I'll type an answer to send back with him tomorrow. He also can carry back another bundle of expedition notes, which the Institute will fax to Patrick Dolan's office in Kansas City for distribution to the sponsors.

We fix the man a plate of food, macaroni with canned tuna in it and the inevitable boiled potatoes. Victor and his team would like to talk with him, to get the political news after a month out of touch. But the messenger is exhausted. He has been traveling most of two days without rest, and will start west again in the morning, as soon as he can find a helicopter going out. It's sleep he wants now, and we get one of our extra bags from the storage cabin.

He looks around the compartment, sees how we live, and, being no fool, takes the bag outside to sleep on the Zaria's roof.

THIRTY-NINE

VALERA HAS SPENT NEARLY the whole day trying to find transport—any sort of vehicle that can accommodate our number and negotiate the primitive road to Mirnyy. He comes back, finally, with a small bus of the kind we've used before, and we're away by 6 o'clock in the afternoon, our gear for two days and a dry meal for the trip in our packs.

Victor has spoken from the expedition's very beginning— vehemently and often—of the awful havoc being wrought in the forest by ungoverned timber exploitation. But in the mountains at the Lena's source, because the area was a natural preserve, the forest was untouched. Neither has any serious damage been seen as we've passed from Kachug onward. Like huge, dark-pelted animals asleep in the Asian sun, the hills that channel the river roll endlessly away, furred with birch and conifers. Except for the occasional town or small settlement of log houses huddled at the river's edge, no sign of man's hand can be seen.

It's only by leaving the river and traveling into the forest itself that the tragic truth is discovered.

The sand-dirt road leads out of Lensk, bound to the north across a quick, bright little river. Almost immediately we begin to meet a string of heavy vehicles—fuel tankers, log trucks, flatbeds carrying bulldozers. We slow at the road's edge to let them pass around, raising suffocating clouds of orange dust that billow through the open windows of our bus, crusting eyes and mouths, covering everything. The big machines run all through the long daylight in the summer's brief frenzy of production.

Logging trails are cut at right angles into the *taiga*. The roadside is littered with broken and discarded truck tires, and with increasing frequency we pass directly by—or can see at greater distance—clearcut wastelands, the earth churned by metal treads, with no evidence of reforestation, and other tracts of standing trees charred black by fire. At intervals between are the logging camps and sawmills, dismal clutches of rough barracks amid a clutter of machinery, with dirt landing places for helicopters.

Doomsayers like the writer and militant conservationist Valentin Rasputin, whose home is not far from Irkutsk, have pronounced Siberia spoiled forever—already exploited beyond any hope of healing. Others say that the forest region, greater in expanse than the whole continental United States, is so vast that it hardly has been scratched, much less fatally damaged. A traveler can't know the absolute truth. But what's certain is that behind the river-bordering collar of uncut timberland, the loggers are furiously at work.

And not just Russian loggers. The Japanese and Koreans are said to be cutting logging roads in from the Arctic coast across the fragile tundra, with no regard at all for the environment. And an American company has built a timber-loading platform on the Pacific coast that a Soviet environmentalist described as the largest he'd ever seen. He was horrified, he said, by what its sheer scale implied about the company's intentions. Unlike the Koreans and Japanese, American timbermen have come with the promise of a tree-for-tree replanting program. But in so harsh a climate, where the time from seedling to maturity is between a century and a century and a half, the promise is meaningless for the next several generations.

American environmentalists speak of the Siberian forest as an ecological resource on the same order of global importance as the rain forest of the Amazon basin. The estimates they and their Soviet colleagues have developed suggest that the *taiga* is being depleted at the rate of about 10 million acres a year. What we are seeing on this overland journey north to Mirnyy is only the merest hint, then, of a process that is sure to accelerate as the Soviet economy continues its collapse and the desperation for hard-currency earnings worsens.

For timber, as for other bulk products, the Lena is the highway to the sea and to the world. Two hours away from the river the logging activity seems to lessen, then finally stops. The trees are being cut in the most convenient terrain, and we have passed beyond that. In a pretty stretch of forest, where a small iron bridge crosses a clear, fishy looking creek, we stop to dig food from packs. Evening is coming on, though, and the mosquitoes that swarm in clouds through the windows of the halted bus are unbearable.

So we push on to Mirnyy, arriving before midnight. It's a company town of 30,000, built and operated by the state diamond mining enterprise Yakutalmaz to house and provide supporting services for the work force that digs and processes the stones. The twilight view of the place is stygian—the road descending through an awful *balki* district strung out along a succession of green sloughs over which milky vapors drift and curl, before ascending to the main part of the town. Over everything, dominating the largest buildings of Mirnyy and even the topography of the hills around, are the manmade mountains of tailings from the pit.

But we arrive, then, at the Zarnitsa (Heat Lightning) Hotel, an oasis of high civilization. All right, maybe it isn't a Ritz-Carlton, a Sheraton—or even a Red Roof Inn. But after the best part of a month on the floor of the Zaria, our perspective is skewed. The rooms have showers, and toilets that actually work. There are carpets from Soviet Asian republics on the floors, light fixtures, real beds. The hotel people are wonderful, and open the buffet on our floor so we can eat: smoked salmon, breaded cutlets, fresh tomatoes, boiled eggs, cakes and cookies. Several members of the expedition, mainly Sergei, can be heard crying out loudly at dinner that they never mean to leave this blessed place.

Afterward, we pass the filter from room to room so tap water can be pumped for drinking in the night and filling our canteens. Finally, there's the incredible, obscene luxury of clean sheets and a mattress, of space from the others and of being clean oneself. Tomorrow we will see the mine.

❧❧❧

I N 1947, A SINGLE diamond was founded embedded in an earthen bank of the Vilyuy River 60 miles or so from here. Then, in a tributary of the Vilyuy, were found rubies, which are diamonds' companions. The search was on.

From that tributary, a creek led to this place. Ten years later, in 1957, a party of prospecting geologists made their night camp along the creek. They noticed a fox's den nearby, looked inside it and found there the "blue earth"—the diamond-bearing deposit. They rushed to the nearest outpost from which they could send an encoded message. "*The Peace Pipe is lit,*" it said, "*and the tobacco is very fine.*" The discovery set the Soviet Union on its way to becoming the world's fourth-largest diamond producer after only Australia, Botswana and Zaire.

Our Russian companions had sent word ahead, asking if we might meet with the head of the mine. Evidently the communication went astray or was ignored, for the director wasn't in. And that was our luck, because instead of the director—an administrator and bureaucrat—we met with Igor Victorovich Tikhonov, head of production for the Peace Pipe mine.

Igor Victorovich is a shortish, square-set man of 55, with an open smile and huge enthusiasm for his work. He came here as a young graduate of 23, only two years after the strike was made, and watched a small city grow up where only creek and forest used to be. He lives on a street named for his father, who was the Peace Pipe mine's first director.

Standing together on a wooden platform at the rim, we looked down into the vast open pit he's spent half a lifetime helping to create.

"They believed diamonds must be here," he said wryly. "In the beginning there is theory. *But then you must dig a hole.*"

Four shifts of miners working around the clock, 365 days a year—even in winter when the terrible cold encumbers workers in protective clothing and causes steel machine parts to break like glass—have moved 200 million cubic meters of earth and rock. The Peace Pipe has reached a depth of 464 meters, more than a quarter mile, and the pipe has been tested diamond-rich to 1,200 meters.

"There's not another open-pit mine in the world with such steep walls," said Igor Victorovich. "It is an engineering feet to mine so steeply, forty-eight to fifty-one degrees, preserving the width of the pipe without cave-ins or compromises to safety."

The scale was disorienting. Giant scoop shovels working below and the 40-ton trucks creeping up the spiral ramps looked absurdly small, smaller than a child's toys. The town, perched near the rim on the far side, was reduced almost to insignificance by the pit itself.

Although his age entitles him to a pension, Igor Victorovich continues to run the mining operations.

"My father retired, stopped working," he said, "and a few years later he was dead. He could not stand leaving the work."

From here, and from later mines Yakutalmaz has established farther north, the diamonds all go to Moscow and then to London to be sold. Most are for industrial use. The best of the gem quality stones are kept in the Kremlin's diamond reserves.

I asked him if he could foresee a time coming when an enterprise like this one, instead of forwarding its whole yield to Moscow, might be able to market all or part of its product, accumulate hard currency and, in effect, actually profit from its operations.

"We are hoping," he replied. But the truth is he doesn't concern himself much with those matters. He's an engineer, an *excavator* he called himself, with a fierce smile. And he looked out with unguarded pride across the awesome cavity.

"It's one of the few such things in the whole world," he said. "To me, it looks very nice."

I commented that he'd changed the landscape in a way that might even be visible from space.

"Yes," he said, "I've seen the photographs made by satellites. It can be observed quite clearly from there."

THE DROUGHT IN CENTRAL Siberia has worsened, and so many *taiga* fires are burning in the Mirnyy district that all the helicopters based at the town's air field are in use carrying crews to protect the town. For the short flight to Suntar we have to crowd instead into the smaller cabin of an Antonov-2. This little single-engined biplane, first built in 1947 and unchanged in its design since then, is the pack-mule of the Siberian outback, still unbeatable for its reliability.

The pilot circles twice over Mirnyy, gaining altitude. The Peace Pipe mine is, if anything, even more stunning from the air. For the next three years, the washing plant will be reprocessing only old tailings, recovering stones missed the first time through. Mining has been suspended while the upper sections of the mine are widened in preparation for driving the pit deeper into the earth. Meantime, the great pumps have been shut off and the lake of water at the mine's bottom already is a hundred feet deep, brilliant turquoise blue, reflecting sky and clouds.

Suntar, with its 4,000 inhabitants, is the largest Yakut village on the Vilyuy, with almost no ethnic Russians living in the town. We'd thought we might be able to find there some remnant of the culture that once prevailed over an area larger than all of Western Europe.

The first sound after landing on the village's one rough dirt strip in the hammering heat of mid-afternoon is the sound of the videographer retching behind the plane. Air sickness is his curse. But, to his credit, he always works hard—leaning from the plane or helicopter door, secured with a safety strap—until he feels the queasiness coming on. Then he has to sit very still, eyes pressed closed, until we're on the ground and he can find a place to empty himself.

So complete is the ethnic homogeneity of Suntar that there's a feeling of having been set down somewhere in Mongolia itself. The Yakuts are small people, some incredibly tiny—fine-boned, handsome, ruddy-complexioned. We're curiosities in the village, objects of furtive, sidelong inspection by the people as they go about their affairs. By tradition that is centuries old, the Yakuts are herders and horse breeders—unadapted to crop farming, with no taste for manufacturing work. The few stores we look in seem poorly stocked, though with a fair supply of tin cookware and saddles. A majority of the people on the one principal street are women, children and the aged. The men of the village, we're told, are many miles away with the horse herds on their summer pastures.

There's nothing more to see and no reason to stay. The heat is all the more staggering for being so unexpected—at least 90 degrees—in a zone where the permafrost, the eternally frozen earth, is only a meter and a half under our feet. On the way back to the plane, we stop for the photographing of a Yakut cemetery, the markers made of metal rods welded in haunting spires and cones that rise in a spidery tangle against the pale sky.

Volodya remembers that on the Arctic coast, where he spent some years of boyhood, the permafrost was only four *inches* below the surface. There dynamite had to be used to blast holes for burying the dead. While the photographer works, Volodya speaks with sadness of the generally poor condition of the native people, a subject he has studied. The Yakuts in Suntar and other villages like it have severe health problems, and medical treatment is not readily gotten. The ailments that defeat them—the most chronic being alcoholism and tuberculosis—are the same ones he understands plague the Indians in the U.S. Vodka is hard to get, and prohibitively expensive in such places. But many make home brew of bad quality, with injurious and sometimes fatal result.

Airborne toward Lensk, the Antonov's pilot peels off his shirt and flies stripped to the waist. Some of the expedition's members are asleep. The videographer's face is pale as a marble statue, and his eyes are shut, too, though he isn't sleeping.

The fires cannot be seen. But the pall of smoke from them lies like a blue filter over the hills and the endlessly spreading forest a thousand feet below.

From Lensk, Victor's son, Alyosha, will leave us tomorrow to go back to Irkutsk and prepare for the beginning of his school term in August. He is a fine boy, always cheerful and uncomplaining. Already you can see plainly in him the strength and decency of the ones who raised him. He has been good company, and we all will miss him.

FORTY

ALYOSHA STILL IS WITH us. Because he'd originally planned to return to Irkutsk by road from Kachug, he did not bring with him his internal passport, without which no Soviet citizen can purchase a ticket for air travel even inside the country. They went to the Lensk air field, but the clerk refused to make an exception. So Alyosha's passport will have to be sent ahead of us to Yakutsk, and he will try again from there.

In the absence of real night, one has to discipline oneself to sleep. Otherwise time gets confused. We stopped at the beginning of twilight yesterday at a steep, stony bank an hour beyond Lensk. Some of the others were settling into their bags and the ship was going quiet, but I needed to make notes. So I took my sleeping bag and a lantern and went out alone on the bank, cleared stones to make a sort of level place, lit the lantern and built a fire for companionship and for comfort against the river's chill.

I wrote for an hour. Then Sergei came out to the fire. And after him Victor and Valera, who brought a piece of pork fat, a knife to cut it with and part of a loaf of dark, sour bread to put the pieces on. Then the motorman, Vitaly, with a pot of tea. Twilight deepened to dusk, and time passed unnoticed. The motorman took his empty teapot and went back on board. We were talking about the strangeness of life, and how remarkable it was to be in this place together. Then we spoke some about books, and Victor told his fondness for the stories of Hemingway and Jack London—especially Hemingway's stories about the young Nick Adams. We talked about fishing and hunting, and winter camping, the things that men—some men—do outdoors.

Victor looked down the bank at the silent boat, where the rest of our party was sleeping. He understood how troubled several of them were by the uncertainties of every day. "Some of them are just not *expedition* people." Didn't say it in a blameful way, but simply as a fact to be dealt with.

I knew he could not be speaking of Katie or Anne and Jennie, because they'd borne everything without one word of questioning or protest. And I reminded him of his worries earlier about the problems of having women on such a journey. "So what do you think about that now?" I asked.

"I think," he said slowly, "that we all are trying very hard not to fall in love."

Valera said nothing, but for him, certainly, it was true. Who could not have noticed the amount of time he spent with Jennie, or the way his brown eyes softened when he looked at her? Or, for that matter, her fondness for him. It was friendship now. In time, it could be something else.

The fire burned down, and the sky was turning paler blue again. We all shivered inside our coats from the dampness of the hour. I looked at my watch, and it was nearly 5 o'clock in the morning.

Today I'm paying a fearful price for that lost night of sleep— smitten with fatigue, stomach cramping either from the motor- man's tea, no doubt made with unfiltered water, or from the pork fat Valera brought to the fire. Also a cut on my left forefinger has gotten infected, and the finger is badly swollen. No one has yet been seriously ill, but we begin, all of us, to be burdened with an accumulation of small infirmities.

We stop at a marked village, but find that like so many others it is derelict and all but abandoned. The name of the place is—or was—Kochegarova. One house seems to be occupied. A man is nailing up the boards of a broken fence, his hammer blows ringing in the stillness, while a woman and a gang of children work in the little vegetable garden the fence encloses. In the yard of the house there's a fire, with a tea kettle on the grate over it.

The man and woman are Yevegny Ivanovich Shestakov and his wife, Raisa Mikhailovna. They live in Olekminsk 90 miles farther downriver, but have come with their eight grandchildren to spend the summer here. The house, though far gone in neglect, still can be used in the warm season. It's the same house in which Raisa Mikhailovna grew up, long ago when Kochegarova was a lived-in place. Sometimes they also come in the fall to pick berries.

Except during winter, when the river is frozen to a highway that can be traveled by trucks, the only way here is by boat. Raisa's sister, who lives in another village a little farther on, comes occasionally to bring them bread and other things they need. It's good here, they say, away from people. Being pensioners, they can stay as long as it pleases them to—they came a month ago, and will stay six weeks more. Their grandchildren love the country in summer.

Apart from a few other houses worse broken than theirs, the only thing to see in this ghost village is the monument to the sons of Kochegarovo lost in the great war. The marker bears 19 entries: 11 Pshennikovs (Raisa was a Pshennikov), six Kopilovs, one each of two other families. There were others killed, says Raisa, but somehow their names were not recorded.

On toward Olekminsk, the character of the river decidedly changes. Nearly a mile wide and so shallow the crew must follow the channel markers carefully, its surface is oily smooth as it flows around and between a succession of low, dark-forested islands. On the left, its course is bounded by hills and *taiga*. The right bank is defined by a miles-long series of immense sand dunes, as vast as the dunes of the Sahara, formed in that unimaginable antiquity when much of Siberia was the floor of the primordial sea. We slow the Zaria while the videographer tries to film the dunes, but the vibration of the engine, even at idle, makes it difficult to steady the camera.

We beach for the night on a sandy spit. I put up one of the small tents and Katie, Jennie, Anne and I all unroll our bags inside, away from the crush of the boat. The BBC on our short wave radio brings us the day's news. A powerful evening wind has risen, and we lie down to the sound of a sand blizzard beating at the side of the tent.

⚜

T HE COSSACKS IN 1635 built their log fort near the mouth of the Olekma River, where it flows into the Lena. And over the ensuing centuries the town of Olekminsk grew up—a place of substantial wooden buildings with an appearance, by Siberian standards, of neatness and prosperity.

Among the builders of the community were the Russian "Old Believers," who began arriving in the middle 1800s, hoping to find-in Siberia relief from religious persecution by the Orthodox church. They were a hard-working and thrifty people, who accumulated much property and wealth, built fine houses, and incurred no little jealousy from other Russian settlers and from the local Yakut population.

The migrants also included a more peculiar sect, the *Skoptsi*, whose prosperity was based on small families and closely-held ownership of land and business. Theirs was a draconian brand of family planning: men, after fathering two children, submitted to castration. Nothing remains of the faith, now, except a church no longer in use and a few log houses and granaries still standing, looking to be the most durable structures in the town.

Much of what we were able to learn about the place came from Tatiana Larionova at the local museum. Unlike Kirensk, which had only a museum director, Olekminsk had a museum as well. Tatiana was a lovely Yakut woman in her 30s, fine-boned and serious. For centuries after they rode up out of Mongolia on their stout, long furred little horses, hers were the dominant people from here to the Arctic region. Subsequent waves of Russian immigration have made the Yakuts a minority in the republic—365,000 of the total 1.1 million population of Yakutia, or 33 percent, down from 43 percent only a little more than a decade ago.

In Olekminsk, a town of 12,000, almost everybody knows everybody, Tatiana said, so there are no problems in relations between ethnic Russians and Yakuts. But she is active nevertheless in the movement to revive traditional culture—teaching her own children to speak the Yakut language, encouraging young people to visit the museum and learn about their heritage.

"It's too early to know if it can be done. But at least now it is permitted to try," Tatiana said. "*Perestroika* has come—maybe you have heard of it."

The little museum was intelligently organized, its exhibits appealingly displayed. They ranged from the ponderous skull of a prehistoric bison once native in the region, to a typical room in a Russian settler's home. The rough plank table in that room held a little Singer sewing machine.

In the section dealing with more modern times, she wanted us to see a display celebrating a war hero, Ivan Nikolaievich Kulbertinov. *Olekma*, the name of the river and root of the town's name, means "place of many squirrels," Tatiana explained. Siberian squirrels were valued for their pelts, and Yakut hunters made it a practice to shoot them only in the eye so as not to spoil the hide.

Ivan Nikolaievich was drafted into service as a sniper in the war against Hitler, and became the Yakut equivalent of Sergeant Alvin York. From 1943 to 1945, he accounted for 252 Germans. Their deaths, one supposes, must have been sudden and painless. If he could see their eyes, they were finished.

She also wanted to take us to see the Old Believers' church, a monument to the World War II dead and another to the Russian Revolution. She was prettily dressed, the day was a blistering 95 degrees, and I didn't want to inconvenience her.

I asked if those places were far.

"There are no distances for Yakuti people," she replied. "Since the beginning of time, we have been measuring the Earth with our footsteps."

On the way, we met on the street a local official who was a friend of Tatiana's. He insisted that we come into his office, and we had to sit, prisoners for most of an hour, while he leafed dully and determinedly through an enormous ledger, reading aloud from its pages endless statistics which I pretended to copy down in my notebook while trying not to go to sleep, or maybe faint, from the tedium and the heat.

The man was chief of the department of economic planning and forecasting for the region.

He had it all at his fingertips in that ledger: the numbers, rounded off to the nearest thousand, of cows, pigs, horses and reindeer; tons of meat and milk produced; numbers of hectares in grain, in hay ground and grazing land; the proportion of cabbages—90 percent—among vegetables grown. The book was inches think, and I was afraid he would read it all.

One figure I did write down. Last year's total value of agricultural and non-agricultural products, he said, was 31.3 million rubles. Later, back at the Zaria, I divided that by the Olekminsk region's population of 31,000 people. It came to a per capita annual product of just over 1,000 rubles—or about $37 at the current rate of exchange.

This year, he said, would be worse. Drought had cut prospects for the crops, and price increases all across the Union, especially for food, had made life difficult, with no corresponding increase in incomes.

"In my opinion," he said, closing the great ledger at last, "for at least the next four years, until the new economic policies show a result and wages can be raised, life will be harder before it gets easier. People must be prepared for that."

The most useful information I got came as an aside.

Somewhere in his recitation he'd noted that the average potato yield for the region was nine tons per hectare. But if we cared to know about growing potatoes, we might want to stop at the village of Uritskoye tomorrow and ask for a man named Ivanov—Anatoly Stepanovich Ivanov.

He was the champion potato grower of all Yakutia, and a fellow worth talking to.

⚜

E VENING FINDS US AT an attractive place for camping, where steep *taiga* runs down to a level shelf at the river's edge. Mosquitoes are voracious—they seem to grow larger and more numerous the farther we progress. We're slapping the bugs and struggling with tents when one of the crew comes to say he'd heard from a boatman in Olekminsk that bears lately have been a big problem on this stretch of the right-hand shore.

Volodya has a solution to the problem. He proposes to fire several blasts from his shotgun into the air, and leave the expended shells distributed around the campsite. The smell of burnt powder, he says, will certainly keep any bears away. We all stare together into the shadows of the forest, which suddenly are unnaturally mysterious and dark. Our one rifle, broken in the rapids in the mountains, is wrapped in canvas in the storage cabin. Volodya's stragegy, while resourceful, seems unconvincing.

Wordlessly the tents are rolled up again and, mosquitoes humming after us, all retreat for another night on board.

FORTY-ONE

THE WIDENING AND SHALLOWING of the river has begun to present severe problems. At times, the only passable water is in midriver, or at a bend where the current cuts deep alongside a bluff. Many of the smaller settlements seem to be on the gentler rise of the far bank, reachable only by canoe. And if the wind happens to be blowing up a heavy chop the canoes can be a risky affair. Then the place has to be passed by, and we wait for one of the boat stations—barges, with houses built atop them—anchored in the channel.

Luckily, the village of Uritskoye, with its 389 souls, has such a station. Our Zaria is made fast to it, and with the surface reasonably tranquil we unload a canoe and motor to carry us across the shallows to look for the champion potato grower.

The village was founded in the middle 1600s, and its fields have been farmed in a single crop, potatoes, from that day to this. In the middle of the last century, a man named Ivanov was sent here, a political exile. He grew potatoes and died here, as did his son after him, and his grandson as well. That's how lives pass in such small places, wrapped by the forest, on the banks of the great north-flowing river. The headstones in the cemeteries record the dates of lives that left no mark.

But in 1981—a year in which fertilizer was available and the rains came on time—Anatoli Stepanovich Ivanov, great-grandson of that first exiled settler, achieved his fame. From a field of 55 hectares (140 acres), he produced an average of *31 tons* of potatoes per hectare (25,000 pounds per acre)—more than three times the usual yield in the district. The amazing harvest was achieved with the help of only six other people, his wife and four sons and his wife's brother.

The authorities plucked him from the bank of the river, flew

him to Moscow, made him a Hero of Soviet Agriculture and award-
ed him an Order of Lenin. Covered with honors, he's a man to be
reckoned with. Regrettably, he can't immediately be found.

An aged Yakut woman sitting on her doorstep and smoking
her clay pipe says we should ask the village authorities his where-
abouts, but the head of the Uritskoye Soviet is away. Then another,
friendlier woman comes along. *Why see officials anyway?*, she says.
Why not just go to the man directly? She leads us to his house, a
cottage with flowers in the lace-curtained windows and a fine
growth of cucumber vines inside the board fence. Alas, Anatoli
Stepanovich has gone fishing in the river, his wife reports. It's 5
o'clock in the evening, now. If we come back at 10 or 11, it's likely
he'll have returned.

So we're passed to yet another guide, described as the "substi-
tute" for the absent village leader. This vessel of temporary authority
is a portly young woman whose features are arranged in an expression of studied solemnity. It's her opinion that we must see the village museum, and she delivers us there, into the hands of a stylish,
coiffed lady in a flowered summer blouse and irridescent skirt. She's
the village school mistress, also the establisher of the museum, and a
person in the habit of commanding absolute attention.

She brings two tiny wooden class chairs, of the size meant for
7- or 8-year-olds. Sergei and I are instructed to squat down upon
them. He, especially, is a comical sight, bony knees folded almost to
his chin. Pacing before us, armed with a pointer, she commences a
lecture about the pictures on the wall of this room that is not so
much a museum as a shrine to Uritskoye's other famous son
besides the potato champion.

*Moyisey Solomonovich Uritsky (Moses, son of Solomon), born
to a family of wealthy Jewish merchants in the southern Ukraine,
was educated as a lawyer at Kiev University, got involved in revolutionary activities and in 1902, at the age of 29, was sent to exile in
this village beside the river, which since its founding under
Catherine II had been known as Chekurka.*

Sergei, following her with narrowed eyes as she paces before
us, interprets *sotto voce*.

He remained here for only two years, from 1902 to 1904. But the impression he made on the villagers was profound. He wasn't a doctor, but this was the hinterland, the frontier, and the people knew nothing at all of medicine. So he tried to help them with their health problems. They regarded him almost as a saint.

"He was a murderer," Sergei adds softly.

He also helped them with other problems. He helped the mail line horse couriers argue for fair pay. He helped peasants in their disputes with landlords.

The pictures—and she must have nearly every one of him ever published—are indicated with the pointer. A few are actual photographs. Others are prints cut from newspapers. Still others are images of poor quality reproduced on a copying machine. They reveal a weak-chinned, petulant, somewhat arrogant face, the mouth drawn down at the corners—a face that was later somewhat improved and strengthened by the addition of a beard. The eyes look out through small, round, wire-rimmed glasses of the style favored by revolutionaries, then and now.

I try to change the subject to the history of the town itself, but she ignores that. This is *her* museum, of her making. She's neither a wicked woman, nor a stupid one. But her mind is deformed by her devotion to the man about whom she's speaking, and the history of which he was a part. Undeflectable, she plunges on.

Uritsky's activities among the peasants angered the local authorities, who moved him first to Olekminsk, then to a village called Nakhtuisk. There he met a beautiful girl. The pointer traverses to a clutch of photographs of a young woman. *But the girl had tuberculosis. She died in his arms, and she was the one love of his life.*

Christ, is there no end to it? Sergei and I are sweating on our little chairs, dizzy from the heat and from the monotonous recitation, which is delivered with a smile that is at once ingratiating and defensive.

After enduring many exiles, Uritsky finally escaped, fled to Europe, and lived in Switzerland where he helped to prepare the Revolution. He was the closest associate of Lenin—

"The architect of our disaster," says Sergei.

—who made Uritsky chairman of the Petrograd CHEKA.

"The organization of official terror," notes the voice at my ear.

When the revolutionary government moved to Moscow, he remained in Petrograd to control the city. He was killed by a counter-revolutionary on August 30, 1918, the same day that Lenin himself was wounded by an assassin's bullet.

You can sense her regret at the way this unlucky coincidence deflected public attention from Uritsky's death and thus robbed him of his full measure of fame. Although two years later, in 1920, the name of this village was officially changed from Chekurka to Uritskoye in his honor—an event that passed unnoticed except by map-makers and the few people who lived here.

"You see? It's a madhouse," groans Sergei. "This country is truly a madhouse."

⚜

THERE WAS NO KNOWING how much more she intended to tell us, how long it would have taken, had not the potato grower, Anatoli Stepanovich, just then been produced in the flesh. Somehow he'd been tracked down at his fishing, made to dress uncomfortably in a suit, stiff collar and necktie and led breathless before us, as one might present a prize steer.

He was a small, friendly seeming man of 55 years, face creased and sun-browned, hands rough from a farmer's work—a decent, hard-used little fellow with a slight facial tic when he spoke. We escaped from the woman official and the school teacher and went out together to see his field, where the year's potato crop was just coming into bloom.

"Look at this ground," he said, squatting to snatch up a handful from between the rows. Dust-fine, it rode away on the wind. "It's nothing but sand. The life has been taken from it."

It was true, he said, that the great crop of 10 years ago won him honors. But he shrugged bitterly, deprecatingly, at that. "You can't eat medals." And it also brought him grief. Certain people, especially the agricultural bureaucrats of the distict, actually were angry.

"Here am I, with only six years of schooling, and I make such a yield—more than they have achieved even on their experimental farms. And they do not like it. So they tried to make talk that I had more than fifty-five hectares. They came three times to measure my field, and each time it measured a little *smaller* than fifty-five hectares."

Some of the worst resentment came from farmers in his own village. But he knows that jealousy is natural. He also knows those men, and how they farm.

The crop is harvested by German-made machines. The German machines are good, he said, unlike the Russian ones. Just as American irrigation systems must be better than the Czech water cannons farmers here are obliged to use. But even a good machine does not get the whole crop. Some farmers go over a field only once and call the work finished. Anatoli Stepanovich and his family go out afterward and spend many days digging and sacking by hand the potatoes the machine has missed. They do it for pride, he said, since there's no difference in income for good farmers or bad.

"When I made such a big crop, I received nine hundred rubles for my year's work. That's all—nine hundred rubles." His voice grew louder and his tic more pronounced with the agitation of remembering that.

"The government *stole* it from me!" He shook his head vehemently, and looked out across the field that ended at the dark line of the forest.

This year did not promise to be a good one for Uritskoye. In a normal season, the field would have been white as snow with bloom. But after six weeks without rain, the plants were short and had not yet even closed over to shade between the rows.

He crouched to dig with his hand in the earth, exposing some potatoes just forming, the size of a robin's egg. I brushed the sand off one and bit into it. It had the texture of a water chestnut, but not yet much taste.

August would be the critical month, he said. He would water the field two times, and in August the potatoes would make most of their growth. But it would not be a large harvest in any case.

Each year, he said, he urges the village authorities to allow the clearing of new areas, so the tired fields can be rested. But it hasn't happened. And it *won't* happen, he believes, until the system of the country is changed at its root.

"Farmers should have their own land," he said bluntly. It was as simple as that. "They should own it, and get the results of their labor. Then this would not be a hungry country. Yields would double. We could grow enough potatoes here to feed the whole district."

I asked him if it was risky to be heard proclaiming such ideas.

"Once it was dangerous. And not all my fellow farmers feel the same way. Some are against me. But now political conditions are changed."

"*Really* changed?" I asked.

"Yes, really. I believe it. And I think ownership of the land will come, although it will take time."

That's how it seemed to him things should be, anyhow. And as the all-time potato growing champion of the largest of all the Russian autonomous republics, he had no hesitation at all about telling even a passing stranger exactly what was on his mind.

WHEN WE FINISH IN the field, there's one thing more Anatoli Stepanovich wants me to see. He stops at his house to get a drinking glass, then we walk together to a grassy pasture slanting to the river. A little stream, clear and icy cold, rushes down the hillside. The stream never freezes, he says, and people of the village can use it all through the winter, even when the river is covered with ice.

There's no sweeter water anywhere, he says. He rinses the glass, dips it full, and hands it to me to drink.

There are cows in the pasture, which is dotted with their dung, both old and fresh. But he's a fine little man, who has given me his time. *Well, what the devil*, I'm thinking, *it's only one more diarrhea. Anything for art.* So I tip the glass up and drain it. The water is sweet as he promised, achingly cold—and afterward, though I'm resigned to the worst, it produces no unfortunate effect.

Returning by canoe to the boat station in mid-river, we find that a Yaroslavits, of the type we took up Baikal, has tied up to the opposite side of the barge. Its crew is drunk and mean-spirited. They've been swaggering up and down outside, shouting insults and proposing to make trades for vodka.

"Give us those Americans, and we'll show them!" one of the drunks is shouting as we lift the canoe to its place on top and lash the tarpaulin over it.

It is more addled bravado than actual malice. As we pull away, the noisy one jumps down into the outboard boat tethered behind their ship, unties the rope and makes a show of following us. But he has 30 horsepower. We have 900. Valery, our captain, pushes the throttle forward. And our Zaria leaves the braying lout behind like a greyhound taking leave of a pig.

FORTY-TWO

WITH EACH DAY OF northward progress, now, the wind increases. And the wind is both a blessing and inconvenience. On the one hand, it keeps the clouds of insects off. On the other, it blows up ranks of waves that come at us against the current, slowing progress and making use of the canoes on the main river all but impossible.

The vistas are broad and magnificent. A pale growth of willows lines the banks, and behind them is a band of birches with the startling white brush strokes of their slender trunks. Then the coniferous forest. Shoulders of hills fall in clefts, revealing a forested valley rising behind to other shoulders, other clefts, higher and farther valleys. Those views are powerfully inviting. One has a longing to enter in, with pack and gun, and probe into the forest as far as legs and courage allow.

The same with the streams emptying in. We have been trying to find one up which we might explore a little way. But they are mostly shallow in this season and impassable beyond the first hundred or two hundred yards. Early this morning, for example, we stopped at a tiny hamlet named Markha, at the mouth of a tributary of the same name, looking on the map to be a stream of some importance. We beached the Zaria on a gravel bar a bit up from the cluster of houses. At that early hour, the day's wind hadn't yet risen so we unloaded a canoe and in two trips several of us were ferried in to Markha. The photographer and videographer went in the first load. By the time Victor arrived with Anne and me, they'd decided the village was of no interest photographically and wanted to move on.

Agreeing to meet Victor on his return at the little Markha's mouth, we followed a path around a slough toward where we thought the river must be. It was shady and cool in the forest. Bushes hung heavy with bright red berries, and a family of Capercaillie—a hen and her young—scuttled ahead of us without flying. The Capercaillie *(Tetrao urogallus)* is the largest member of the grouse family, a bird of the northern pine woods and an interesting creature. The male, when displaying, resembles the American wild turkey, although slightly smaller. Hunters stalk him in the mating season by creeping forward as the bird is calling, when he is momentarily both deaf and blind.

The path did take us to the stream a quarter-mile in from its joining with the Lena, but in the dry midsummer it had shrunk to a few small pools linked by a rivulet that soon disappeared entirely into the gravel bed. We crossed to the far bank, and beat our way through undergrowth and saplings back to our meeting with the canoe. The mosquitoes in the forest were a plague.

That is the disappointment of our small explorations—and perhaps of most explorations. Scale is deceptive. The eye takes in views of great breadth and idyllic beauty, and the mind, uncritically, tells you to follow there. But the same landscape, measured on the smaller scale of one step after another, is entirely different. I'm not sure which is the illusion and which the truth.

Talis Bergmanis

Village in mud time, middle river.

Talis Bergmanis

A totem of his oppressors, Stalin and Beria, carved from a native log by Yuri Panov, who was exiled to Siberia 50 years ago for a political comment.

Talis Bergmanis

Yuri Panov.

Selling tomatoes.

Talis Bergmanis

Talis Bergmanis

A smile for strangers passing.

Talis Bergmanis

Fragile flowers, in a land where childhood is brief.

The Author

The pillars of the Lena, towering giants of stone.

The Author

Valera Sherstyanikov and Jennie Gusewelle.

꧁❀꧂

IN OUR ABSENCE, THE crew of the boat had caught a great quantity of small perch which they put in a bucket in the galley, waiting to be chopped for a stew. The smell of ripening *oooh-hah* pervades that whole quarter of the Zaria, dominating the atmosphere at breakfast.

The map showed another tributary, larger than the Markha, running in from the right not far ahead. The river was the Tuolba, and a short way up it was marked a village where Victor believed we might find a group of Evenk people still living their traditional life.

In Yakutia—as in the whole of Siberia—nearly four centuries of colonization have made Russians the ethnic majority. The Yakuts, or at any rate the militant nationalists among them, nevertheless regard the Russians as interlopers and would like to establish an ethnic republic of their own on the territory. But to the Evenks and the Evens, the true indigenous people who have dwelt in these mountains and forests from time immemorial, it was the Yakuts—expanding their dominance into the Lena basin as late as the 12th and 13th centuries—who were the usurpers and original oppressors.

That suggests, in a small way, the muddled equities that complicate any attempt to unscramble the Soviet egg.

We stopped at the farming settlement of Sangyyakhtakh, a place of 2,000 people, on the Lena's bank opposite the mouth of the Tuolba, to ask about the feasibility of ascending the lesser river. There was a man who could answer the question absolutely, we were told, and Victor, Valera and I waited while he was sent for.

Vitaly Mikhailovich Petrov was a stocky, bronze-skinned man with an open face but a solemn and somewhat guarded manner. He was startled, I think, to see an American in that place. But he warmed when he discovered our interest in the Tuolba was real.

Two things he told us straight-off. First, in this dry season the small river would be hard to travel, even with canoes. Much of the time the boats would have to be carried. Although it was less than 20 miles away, it would take as much as three days to reach and another three to return from the place marked on the map as Alekseyevka—longer than we could afford.

Second, Victor's information and the map itself were more than 30 years out of date. Even if we were to go there, we would not find the community we sought. And he told us why.

In the middle 1950s, when the decree went out from Moscow that small settlements should be abandoned, it meant more for people like Vitaly Mikhailovich than simply a change of location. It was the end of an ages-old way of life. His name is Russian—the gift of the governing race. But his people are the reindeer people and hunters of the northern forest. He's a man filled with sadness, because he remembers the good time of boyhood at that place on the Tuolba.

Russians gave the settlement its name, as they gave him his. But the Evenki people had used the place "for all time." It wasn't a village, really. The Evenks were wanderers in the *taiga* most of the year. It was just a place of humble log houses to which they came in the hardest frosts of more than 60 degrees below zero. And where they gathered again in their time of festival, when the first leaves were on the trees, to celebrate the passing of winter and arrival of the gentler season. It was the time of marriages.

He was 15 when the abandonment order came. Some families, to escape resettlement, fled north through the forest to the region of the Aldan River. Others, Vitaly Mikhailovich's among them, were transplanted to this farming town beside the Lena. In violent dislocation, deer herders and fur trappers would be made to follow a plow.

He is 44 years old, now. "It is very hard," he told us—not of the work, but of the sadness. "You may say that everything is lost."

Does nothing at all survive? I asked him. Nothing of the old ceremonies or traditions?

"I hunt," he said. "I hope my son can hunt." He has one son and three daughters.

"In this neighborhood we still have moose, sable, the noble deer, bear, wolves in great numbers, wolverines, lynx, and muskrats, which were brought a long time ago from America and have begun to be established. But the otter are finished, hunted out, and also the musk deer. Each year you can notice the game becoming more scarce.

"It used to be," he said, "that an Evenk did not ever take meat with him when he went in the *taiga*. Now, if he did not take meat, he might starve."

There are more fires in the forest now, Vitaly Mikhailovich said. The authorities blame them on thunderstorms, but in his boyhood the storms did not set fires. Then, you could go for a thousand miles and see no sign of men. Now there are helicopters everywhere, and the motorized sleds—snowmobiles. He is afraid, in time, no wilderness will be left.

"Still," he said, "if you are born in *taiga*, you cannot live without it. If I cannot go to *taiga* in the autumn, I actually grow ill. But to travel safely in the forest a man must have a rifle. The government does not allow the owning of a rifle—only a shotgun with a smooth bore. We must have the right. Who could use a rifle against a government? Who would even use it against a man? I would not."

Vitaly Mikhailovich is chairman of the local Evenki community, a minority of about a hundred people in this mostly Russian town. With the coming of greater political freedom, his family and several others are attempting to revive their abandoned forest outpost and re-establish there the traditional life. They would like to create a kind of reservation, he said, where nature would be respected and from which the uninvited could be kept out.

Victor asked what his wife and children thought of that.

"They would go," he replied.

He seemed a fine, serious man with a grand and perhaps impossible dream, and I wanted to leave something with him. I got from the box on the boat one of the fine skinning knives we brought as gifts. He admired it with a hunter's eye, and tried its edge with his thumb. Then, because an unregistered knife, like a rifle, is feared as an instrument of possible anarchy, he had to hide it inside his shirt.

"I'd like to come this way again sometime," I told him. "To fish, or maybe hunt together."

"I'd like that, too," he said. "You will find me not here but at Alekseyevka." He spoke it like a promise he hoped the hearer might believe.

❧

SUPPER IS LATE, BECAUSE just at sundown we come upon a crew of five men making hay from wild grass beside the river, across from a village called Isit. The grass grows tall and thick in the long daylight. Their equipment makes 45-pound square bales, tied with twine, and they get about 100 bales to the hectare, although this year, with the drought, it could be less. They have to make hay for the 300 cows of their village.

"It takes a lot, about 100 bales, to keep a cow," one of them says. "We live in a place where there are three months of cold and nine months of *very* cold."

The men seem happy. They are friends, and it is good work, and they catch plenty of fish to eat. They just moved to this place today, but already their little camp has a settled look—three tents, a rough table, a cooking fire with a pot hanging over it and laundered clothes spread out on the tent ropes. They began cutting hay in early July, and will continue north along the river, working until September's first hard freeze. When they finish a meadow, they stack the bales and cover them with bushes before moving on. In autumn, when the Lena freezes solid, they will come back and transport the hay across the river on the ice to their village. As we talk, the mosquitoes worsen, though the hay men seem unbothered by them. A cloud of cotton fog comes rolling down and fills the channel of the bright little stream that runs behind their camp.

The Zaria leaves there in twilight, pushing on to find a good place to beach for the night. Studying the map later under the cabin light, I reckon that we are a bit past the river's midpoint, with Yakutsk, the largest town on the Lena, still most of a week ahead. Beyond there, it's said, the river will become more dangerous. And habitation will grow even thinner as we approach the Arctic zone.

FORTY-THREE

I T'S BEEN A DAY of cold rain, strong wind, and heavy waves cresting white with froth—*waves with sheep*, the crew calls them. Victor's map indicates a village with prehistoric paintings or carvings on a cliff nearby, but the village lies across a shallow and the condition of the water gives no hope of trying to get to the place by canoe.

There's nothing to do but go on to where we plan to stop the night, a place that is called, depending on the translation, the Lena Pillars, Poles or Piles. We reach there in mid-afternoon, not quite prepared for the magnificence of the formation that we find. Along a stretch of nearly 20 miles, massive, free-standing stone columns rear up 500 feet and more from the river's edge.

Volcanic dikes thrust up in great antiquity through the bed of the primal sea have been liberated from the surrounding sedimentary rock by the relentless carving action of wind and frost. One is an Easter Island face. Others are long-necked dinosaurs. Still others stand shoulder to shoulder like platoons of armored titans guarding passage along their river.

The weather has worsened steadily. We'll wait the night here, and as long after as we must, for the storm to pass and conditions for photography to improve. I go out with Katie, Anne and Jennie, all bundled in our heavy coats, for a preliminary exploration along the boulder-littered shore. Katie and Jennie walk only a little way, then have to turn back. Both have gotten a bug and feel bad stomachs coming on. Anne and I decide to climb up among the enormous creature-rocks—up where the wind whips at our coats and the river is just a leaden shine directly below.

After the lower pitch of talus, a thick moss carpet over the stones makes climbing easier. Up close, the faces of the pillars resemble the careful work of dry-stone masons, cracked and fissured, covered over with crusty red-orange lichens and also a kind that is flat and circular, with smaller ones around it, like a hen and her chicks. Massive as the structures are, they also seem strangely delicate. The impulse is to whisper, on the chance that a careless word could start one stone slipping, then more, until you and the pillars were sent crashing down hundreds of feet together to the shore below.

I go as high as acrophobia comfortably allows. Then Anne encourages me on, scrambling on hands and knees. Until we come at last to a wonderful overlook, between the pillars to the river, with green moss all around us and niches in which we imagine it would be splendid to hunker a night through the storm—to camp up there, and prowl among the giants.

Tomorrow we'll explore the area more, but now I'm afraid the others, especially the Russians, will worry. Coming down is faster and easier than I'd expected. No one else, we find, has left the ship. Katie and Jennie both are under the table, miserable and eating Lomotil. There's nothing we can do to help them, so Anne and I go out again, drag driftwood for a fire to sit by—the wind whipping and waves beating—our backs chilly but our fronts warm. Alyosha comes out to join us. Then Victor to be with him. Anne has brought some potatoes in her pocket and we roast them in the fire, burning them down to cindery black lumps that are surprisingly tasty inside.

Supper will be late again, Victor says. Volodya also is cooking potatoes, fried. But in our small skillet he has to fry five batches of them to have enough, and with the slowness of the stove it will be after 9 o'clock before he's finished.

❦

ALTHOUGH THE SEASON IS drawing on, we have progressed so far north—above the 60th north latitude, in the zone of Arctic days—that in summer, except on storm nights, real darkness never comes. The sun dips briefly from view, there is an interval of twilight and then the sudden dawn.

I woke once at 2 o'clock in the morning, and could see the rock giants looming above us, already brushed silver by the light. Then I slept again, and got up with the rest of the boat still quiet, crept over the tangle of bags and bodies, and closed myself in the four-by-four-foot galley to transcribe notes from yesterday.

There was a cold draft around the one small window, but the stove warming tea water made the cubby comfortable. It was July

22, the first morning of my 59th year. I wondered what that land-mark would bring.

What it brought was a glorious day. The storm had cleared entirely, leaving the sky vast and blue, dappled with fleecy ranks of clouds. The air warmed until there was only a faint edge, hardly more than a memory, of chill.

Katie and Jennie still were in misery under the table. Of the 13 of us, Russians and Americans, only one, the boy Alyosha, had not been sick at least a day—some several times. Most of the ail-ments have been digestive, and often quite severe, in spite of our filtering all the water we've used.

Valera stayed behind, ostensibly to start preparing the midday meal but really, I thought, to be with Jennie in her distress. All the others of us climbed up among the pillars, even higher than Anne and I had gone the day before, all the way to the top and the plateau that lay behind. The videographer bounded fearlessly from one exposed perch to another, and was able to film a ship between two of the stone columns as it passed along the sparkling blue immensity of the river below. The photographer seemed happy, too, waiting for a cloud to pass so that he could capture the amaz-ing formations in just the right play of light.

How many men, I was thinking, have had the luck to greet a new year of their lives in such a place?

On the way down, we passed through an area of low blueberry bushes. The berries were small, and many not yet ripe, but they were sweet to mouths starved for fruit. Victor filled his cap with enough of them to put over our dry cereal for tomorrow's breakfast.

⚜

IN AFTERNOON, WITH THE wind fallen and the river running fairly calm, it's possible to use canoes again. On the left-hand bank, where the flow divides around an island, there's supposed to be a village and another chance to find petroglyphs close by.

On the stony shore we meet a friendly man about my age, a young woman who looks to be his daughter, and some small ones who must be grandchildren. They've just finished doing laundry in the river. Behind them, in a sloping, grassy basin between the water and the steeply forested hills behind, are several houses, most in good repair, but no other sign of life.

That's because it really isn't a village any more. It used to be, the man tells us. In fact, it was the place of his birth. Then, of its hundred families, 40 men went away to the great war, and more than half of those did not come back. That began the death of the village. The policy of the 1950s finished it. His father tried to stay on here, the man says, but life was too difficult and in the end they took him to live with them in Yakutsk.

Now the man and some others are trying to revive the place. They have built 10 new houses, and have repaired some others and some barns. The land here is very good, he says, naturally alkaline. It will grow anything. It's even possible to grow cucumbers without a greenhouse, because the steep hillside catches the sun and the dampness that rises from the river, and creates—he actually uses the word—a kind of *microclimate*.

The people who arrived in a past century to plant their houses in the wilderness weren't fools, and it wasn't for nothing that they chose this special place. The fools were the ones in Moscow who didn't know, or care about, its virtues.

The father is dead, now. But they come here in summer to plant potatoes, and live in the old house as a kind of *dacha*. In the fall, they come back again to dig their crop and pick berries. Or sometimes, he says, they come just to do nothing. Once there were many fish in this part of the Lena, but now you must go up the tributaries, sometimes for many miles, to find them. The fishing is like many other things here in Siberia, he says. It *used* to be good.

As for the petroglyphs we're looking for, he tells us, there's only one—a small rock painting of a moose. He remembers seeing it as a boy, somewhere on a cliff in that direction—and gestures indefinitely to the south. But he doubts that he could find it now.

⚜

THE NIGHT'S ANCHORAGE WAS at a quiet bend, with a small hay meadow atop the bank. All through the day there'd been a great stir in the main compartment, and especially in the little galley, from which I'd been excluded.

I went to put up one of the large tents in the meadow, and when I came back the compartment was transformed.

The table had been pulled out from the side to make a real table again, instead of only a sleeping and working shelf, with chairs and folding canvas stools arranged so all could sit around it.

Katie and Jennie were recovered enough to join the group, although not to eat much. Then, to applause and cheers, the feast was brought forth. Several days before, Victor had traded sugar, tobacco and vodka to some boatmen near one of the villages we'd passed for several slabs of smoked sturgeon and part of a haunch of moose. The excellent sturgeon was our first course, a rich moose stew the main one.

Then Anne got from the galley two chocolate cakes she'd made in the folding stove-top oven, and had decorated, using bits of colored candy, with my name and the numeral 58. Because of the slowness of baking anything, her cakes had been the project of half a day. All this was washed down with a bottle of sparkling red Bulgarian wine, one glass for each. And after that, Victor brought out one of his bottles of vodka, made from the waters of Baikal, he said, and far the best in all the country.

He proposed two toasts. The first was to my "great age" and to the remarkable fact, evidenced by this expedition, that I was still going. The other was serious. "When people sit together to eat," he said, "they must be friends."

Responding, I recalled that it would be a month tomorrow since we left Irkutsk, and that we'd come more than half our journey, with still another thousand miles to go.

"We began as strangers," I said. "Now we're separated only by the small inconvenience of language."

We invited the boat crew to join our toasting. The day had been a good one, and the meal of real food had lifted all our spirits. Even Katie and Jennie were able to eat a little. The mood was festive, and the tensions among us were far from mind.

꧁꧂

A FTER THE PARTY, THOUGH, the photographer spills out his discontent.
"How am I supposed to be getting any pictures when we're
missing all the villages?"

"The fact is," I tell him, "we've stopped at every village we
could get to."

"But it's always at the wrong time. I never get the morning
and evening light there. And look at the way we have to live." It's
true, of course, that the conditions have been hard. Hard for him,
and for all of us. "I'd rather be in a motel in Kansas," he says. "The
mistake was ever getting on this boat in Zhigalovo. If it had been
up to me, I'd have waited until they put in bunks and dividers. Or
until they got another boat."

"You'd have waited the whole summer," I reply.

"All right. Then I'd have waited."

The man is wonderfully gifted, but the things that discomfit
him—the loss of control, in a situation where we must depend so
much on the judgments and resourcefulness of others; the uncertainties that a journey like this one involves—are things I can do
nothing about.

"I've never been this disagreeable for this length of time," he
says now. "If I'd been anyone else on this ship I'd probably have killed
me before now. So to make it easier for everyone, I'm thinking of
leaving the expedition at Yakutsk, flying to Tiksi and waiting there."

The proposal astonishes me. However uncomfortable the conditions, and whatever the working difficulties, I believe we're obliged
to the sponsors to try to travel this river to its end. I tell him, though,
that he's not a prisoner. He can go if he must. But what he needs to
understand, as clearly as possible, are the terms of his leaving.

"You're in the middle of Siberia," I tell him. "The only way to
Tiksi is by plane, and you'll have to buy the ticket with whatever
personal money you're carrying. Tiksi is a closed town, and our permission to be there is only for certain dates. You may have to
explain to the KGB why you're there early, and I don't know if
they'll let you stay."

The complications strike him silent.

"Then there's the question of how you get from there to Moscow. I've paid the Institute for the air tickets, but we won't have them until we're in Tiksi. And the tickets from Moscow to the States are for a fixed date—another month from now. Those can't be changed.

"I'll be concerned about your safety, but once you go I can't be responsible for that. Finally, and it's not a small point, you won't have an interpreter. Because we can't spare either Volodya or Sergei from the expedition to look after you along the way."

Those are the facts, and I lay them out as dispassionately as possible.

"Now, if you think you can handle all that, I won't try to stop you."

I go outside, then, to where the videographer is filming the oddity of a splendid, peach-colored sunset and the rising of the enormous full moon over the black rim of the forest, *both in the same quarter of the sky*. The celestial mechanics at this latitude are eternally confusing. The sun does not so much pass across overhead as describe an elongated loop above us, with the lower edge of the loop taking it briefly out of view.

Sleep is wonderful in the tent. The breeze off the hay meadow is refreshing through the net side panels. It is good to be off the boat.

FORTY-FOUR

TODAY'S WEATHER IS AS foul as yesterday's was lovely. The river runs a chop that sets up a hard vibration in the boat, sending provisions sliding off the table. We mean to stop at a town called Bestyakh, but discover it has no boat station. So we go on to the next place, the settlement of Moksogollokh—squatting atop a mud bank so high it seems almost a cliff. Over the bluff pour foaming rivulets of what must be sewage. The lower shelf, where the Zaria is beached, is a horror of broken glass, frayed cables, shards of splintered wood, small outboard boats both serviceable and abandoned, and a jumble of rusted metal sea containers, each with a giant padlock, in which the local fishermen keep their motors and other equipment.

We climb a steep path up into the town. The faces are a mixture of ethnic Russian and Yakut, mostly Russian. Far down a road at the end is the belching smokestack of some enterprise. At a kiosk, two women are selling radishes, green onions and umbrellas. Some of the buildings are old, some more recent. All the later ones are elevated on pylons, and the pipes that carry heat and water through the town also are raised, wrapped in insulation, coiling among the buildings and looping high across the road like exposed intestines.

The buildings and pipes are elevated to give separation from the earth and protect the underlying permafrost. It is an expensive way to build, but less expensive than *not* making such provision. The evidence is clearly seen in the old buildings set flush against the earth, allowing their radiant heat to destroy the support of the frozen ground. Comically swaybacked, with windows and doorways all leaning toward the center, they have sunk away into the bottomless ooze.

It does not take long for curiosity about these more northern settlements, especially the larger ones, to fail utterly. The forest villages we've passed, even the abandoned ones, or maybe especially those, have been in handsome settings, with the river, a green clearing, the *taiga* pressing in behind. But the people who built there did so with an eye for their surroundings. By contrast, these newer towns vie with one another in their relentless hideousness— raw, stricken places where the spirit cannot live.

The people do not, amazingly, look wretched. Most appear scrubbed, a few almost stylish. But they do look worn by their lives, as indeed they must be, eyes uncurious and flatly staring at and through the strangers who have come among them. It is hard to believe such settlements can be in any way productive. They are abominations whose names you do not care to know, and which anyone with initiative or imagination enough to leave would not long remember being from.

Painted on a building side is a heroic mural of a workman in a hard hat, holding fat stalks of wheat. We need bread, but it's a use-less search. Store Number 1 is out of loaves. Store Number 2 is closed.

At the town's north end, at the rim of the bluff just above where our boat is beached, can be seen a wooden fence with con-certina wire atop it, and a flimsy tower that supports a shack with a porch. It's a prison, Volodya tells us, not for political offenders but ordinary criminals who are allowed out during the day to work in the town. *Prison...town...* Can they even detect a difference?

We descend to the awful beach and flee away from there, a few miles on to a less horrid village called Pokrovsk, where the Zaria is put ashore for the night. It is raining harder as evening deepens. The low clouds actually give a sense of darkness coming on. Lights shine yellow from the windows of the little houses, although strangely no smoke can be seen pluming up from any of the chim-neys.

The wind worsens in the night, with a hard rain pelting. Several unmanned motor boats float by, torn loose from their moorings. Twice the captain, Valery, has to start the boat, back it into the river, then reposition it on shore to keep it from being damaged by beating against the rocks.

❧

I WOKE IN THE STILL compartment, in my place beside Katie under the table, with the sharp ache beginning in my lower left back, just over the hip.

If you've ever had that misery, you recognize it forever after-ward without any need for a physician's diagnosis. They say a kidney stone is the nearest thing a man can experience to a woman's pain of childbirth—though you have a good deal less to show for it.

I suffered my first attack 27 years ago, in terror, at an oasis in the Sahara on the caravan trail between Morocco and Senegal. Since then there'd been 23 more—all passed without surgery. This one would be the 25th. And it was the emergency I'd feared worst during our medical planning for the expedition because, except for the Demerol tablets my doctor prescribes to carry when I travel, there was no provision that could be made against it.

I got up without disturbing the others, swallowed two tablets, and retreated to the galley to transcribe notes and make a start on the next set of dispatches to the sponsors before the pills sent me off to dreaming.

The ship began stirring then, and I rolled under the table onto my bag beside Katie.

"There's a problem," I told her.

"What is it?"

"A stone," I said quietly. There was no use advertising it, since there was no help anyone could give. "I've taken the Demerol, and we'll see how it goes. Right now it's manageable. I should be asleep before long."

"What will you do?"

"I don't know." Even if the ureter is blocked completely, it's some time before there's risk of damage to the kidney on the affected side. How long I wasn't sure—but a day or two, anyway, I thought. Possibly longer.

"We'll be in Yakutsk tomorrow at the latest," I told her. "Maybe even tonight. We'll see what the situation is then. The worst, I guess, would be that I'll have to try to find some kind of flight out from there."

Katie told the others only that I wasn't feeling well, and I lay through the first part of morning in a state between waking and sleep—hearing breakfast go on around and above me; hearing the engine start and then slow twice for attempted landings at settlements that proved impossible to reach because of a shallow shoreline and more waves with sheep.

I was reckoning the possibilities. It wouldn't end the expedition, because undoubtedly Victor could take it on to Tiksi. There was no choice, anyway, since our group was to fly back to Moscow from there. The worst case was only that the journey might be finished for me—that I would miss the last third of the river, the Arctic coast, the elation of having done what we set out to do. A bitter prospect, considering the chances of my ever passing this way again.

The Demerol wore off, and the discomfort was no worse. So I got up and dressed.

The waves were higher. The bow of the Zaria hammered hard against them. There was no hope now of stopping anywhere, and Victor and the crew already had decided to make straight for Yakutsk.

The cranes of the port came in view in early evening. There are said to be 1,800 ships of our Zaria's size or larger plying the middle and lower Lena during its short season free of ice, and a good share of those appeared to be at rest in the area of the quays, either loading, unloading or waiting their turns.

Here, where the river would again grow larger and its currents more treacherous, we'd have to trade our vessel for one of deeper draft. Meantime, during several days ashore, there'd once more be the novelty of real beds. Volodya stayed on the boat to guard our cargo, which we would remove in the morning. We took only personal gear to the hotel, which was modest by any ordinary standard but seemed a wonder of luxury after the boat. All the rooms were single and small. They had functioning toilets, though, and the miracle of a shower.

Victor arranged for a dinner to be laid for our group, but I hadn't any appetite. Just the small activity of transferring to the hotel had aggravated the pain of the stone. Katie offered to wait with me in the room.

"No, go on and eat," I told her. "I'll work a while and see how it goes. If I have to, I'll take some more Demerol."

"I'm worried."

"I know. So am I."

But it helped to think about something else. I spread out on the small bed the pages from the notebook handwritten in the boat's galley at the beginning of the day, and started to type the dispatch for the sponsors, which Alyosha would carry back to Irkutsk.

I'd just finished a passage on the diamond mine and begun an entry about the potato farmer, when I was brought back from the river and into the room by a sudden, startling awareness of the *absence* of pain. I stood, then, and walked around cautiously. The discomfort hadn't just decreased. It was gone entirely, which meant that the stone had moved past the point of narrowest constriction. And a quarter-hour later, at 7:40, I was delivered of the thing—a fairly large one, black in color, not of gem quality but lovely to my eye.

It's an ailment without convalescence. When it's done, you pick up your bed like Lazarus and walk, and unless an infection sets in or there's a companion stone, the episode is finished. Katie's face registered surprise when I joined her and the others at the table.

"You're better?"

"I'm rid of it," I told her. "And hungry."

The hotel food was plentiful and good. Victor ordered a bottle of vodka brought to the table, but I didn't know how alcohol and the painkiller would mix. Anyway, the relief I felt was rush enough. Because I absolutely believed now that I would see the river to its end.

FORTY-FIVE

THE COSSACKS CAME IN 1632 (how alike all the stories begin!) and built their log fort first on the right-hand, or east, bank of the river. Fifty years later the *ostrog* was moved to the left bank, which was less subject to flooding. And from that, over the next three centuries, a community of 220,000 people has grown.

Yakutsk is many times over the largest city on the Lena, and capital of the autonomous republic of Yakutia—a place less lovely by a good deal than, say, Irkutsk, but tidier than Ust'Kut and nowhere near as wretched as Lensk. The weather in winter is almost unimaginably brutal. Not far from the river in northern Yakutia is what climatologists speak of as the "cold pole" of the planet. At a village called Oymyakon, 400 miles northeast of Yakutsk, the record low is minus-89.9 degrees Fahrenheit, the coldest ever recorded in a permanently inhabited place on Earth. Schools in Yakutsk remain open to 50 below zero. The permafrost in the area reaches a depth of as much as 820 feet.

One might think there would be slight concern, in such conditions, for anything except survival. But Yakutsk, besides being a port and a manufacturing town, also is the principal intellectual center on the Lena. The town has 19 scientific institutes and a plethora of museums—geological, historical, ethnic and so forth—more of them than time, stamina or interest will let us inspect.

Morning is spent at the boat, sorting and unloading cargo, and making our good-bys to our Zaria's crewmen, who will leave today on the journey back upriver to Ust'Kut. Victor's friend and contact in Yakutsk is a small, soft-spoken Russian man named Vadim Yuriovich Shamshurin. Now they, with Volodya and Valera, have gone off to arrange temporary storage of our gear and settle the matter of the next boat—the one that will take us to the river's end. That was supposed to be contracted already, but evidently some problem has arisen.

We also have to say farewell—again—to Alyosha, Victor's son. His internal passport was waiting in the mail here. Before the end of this day, he'll be away by plane back to Irkutsk and his preparation for school. Sergei accompanies the photographer and videographer in the city. And we're left in the relentless care of a young woman named Nadia, whom Vadim has engaged as our temporary interpreter and guide.

⚜

In the matter of museums, we discovered, Nadia was indefatigable. First was the geological museum. Then one of Yakut crafts. Then a historical museum. Then one that seemed to contain mostly photographs, including a great many of a Yakut folk singer who became involved in political activism and perished in one of Stalin's camps. Somewhere in the afternoon's march I stopped even pretending to make notes.

The custodians of all those places were unfailingly cordial, surprised and pleased to have American visitors, and proud of their collections, many of which were handsomely displayed. But there comes a time in the blur of such a day when the mind disengages, and one is able to think only of a chair, a meal, a bed.

The evening ended well, however. Nadia led our whole group to a little cabaret—yes, a *cabaret*, there in the middle of Siberia. The place was crowded with people seated at low tables, drinking vodka from purple glasses. And the entertainers were wonderful, two young women and a young man, charming and gifted.

They juggled and mimed all together. Then the young man played a set of haunting airs on the jew's-harp, which the Yakuts call the *khomus* and which is their national instrument. After him the girls sang separately. One's song was a humorous variation on an old Yakut melody. The other's was almost a ululation, strident and strangely metallic, rendered with an astonishing manipulation of the larynx that produced a hard clicking sound between the notes.

The cafe hushed absolutely as she performed. Listening in the darkness, there was a feeling somehow that the city no longer was around us—that we were out somewhere perfectly alone in the *taiga* and that what we were hearing was not really music at all, but the rattle of tree branches in a wind keening across an eternity of forest and ice.

Afterward, as I lay down in the hotel room to sleep, that sound still resonated in my mind.

The second day with Nadia there were no museums. Instead there were institutes. The first was the Institute of Yakut Language and Literature, where a meeting had been arranged. At the table were the director, whose specialty was languages; a white-haired man whose field was literature (he also was a literary critic), and a third man, small, square-faced and humorous, whose concern was ethnic traditions. All three, of course, were Yakut.

Theirs is of the ancient family of Turkik tongues, the director explained. And because Yakuts separated early from the other Turkik tribes, many of the very old words are preserved in their pure form, both in literary and everyday use. Yakuts began to write in their own language in the last century. And ethnic Russians, whose people had been so long in the region that Yakut was their first tongue—*bahynai*, they called themselves—also translated old Russian stories into the native language. In 1900, the first Yakut professional writer edited a book of his poems. A literary circle developed in the town, and by the time of the revolution about 40 books had been published in Yakut.

Even then, however, the tide of immigration from European Russia had begun to overwhelm Yakut culture and traditions. And the advent of Soviet power, with its policy of collectivization and its pressure for conformity, accelerated the process. Until after World War II, when the first modest revival began, the old ceremonies and festivals largely were ignored or forgotten—festivals like *Ysyakh*, the greatest of the celebrations, observed when the grass was renewed and hay-making for the herds began, which for Yakuts was the true beginning of the "new year."

"Now, for us and for other ethnic minorities in the Soviet Union, is a time of spiritual renaissance," declared the director. Until recently, Yakut school children were taught in their language only to the eighth form. Now it was the language of instruction through all of secondary school. And more books were being published, although the press runs were small. There's even a national literary magazine in Yakut, with a monthly circulation of 30,000.

"The sense of ethnicity and nationalism has revived. People here want more freedom," he said. "The question is how to regulate Yakutia's relations with the rest of the Russian Federated Republic, and with the government of the Union."

But if Yakuts must struggle to recapture the sense of themselves, others have it even harder, as I learned in another conversation later that day.

Nikolai Romanovich Kalitin was vice-president of the Association of Northern Peoples of Yakutia. The term "northern peoples," as the organization uses it, can be taken to mean *original* peoples—that is, the ones who were here before the Yakuts: the Evenks, numbering but 15,000 in all of Yakutia; the Evens, with 7,000, and members of even smaller groups of only a few hundred souls.

Nikolai Romanovich was an Evenk, and a friend of the local Evenk leader at the mouth of the Tuolba tributary, that fine little man with whom I'd left a skinning knife the week before. He was 50 years old, though his bronze Asian face—broad and flat—was unlined as a boy's.

For 20 years, he said, he'd worked with the local Soviet, "because it was comfortable and convenient to do that." But for the last two years he had devoted himself to the Association. It had created problems in his personal life, and even in his family life. He'd had quarrels with friends and former political associates, even though some of them were Evenks like himself. "They do not understand," he said, "that I am working for them and their future."

That work proceeds in small ways.

"There now is a special fund in the state budget for the reconstruction of communities that have suffered," he said. "But the trouble is getting any of the money."

The problems, both practical and cultural, are daunting. For example, the annual mortality among the native northern peoples is twice that for Yakuts. Of the 15,000 Evenks in the republic, only 1,500 can speak the language of their fathers. And of those, more than 90 percent are over 60 years old. The Association has created traveling schools to attempt to reintroduce the language among Evenk young people.

He was proud to say that his own son, who is 25, had made the decision to return to the traditional life, although it was unclear when or exactly how. He would like to do that himself, Nikolai Romanovich said wistfully. But the law against owning rifles must be revoked. And another law passed, exempting the traditional communities from state regulation so that they can manage their own affairs.

"Northern people need freedom in their lives," he said. "I have lived more than half my years in Yakutsk, but every weekend I go with my tent to the *taiga*. I am a hunter, and for the last 15 years I have been observing one bear. I think he now recognizes me by sight. But if any other man came the bear would surely kill him."

His tone suggested a profound symbolism in the relationship with the bear. But it struck me as an invention, a fiction. Just as everything else he'd said seemed shadowed by illusion and dreaming.

At one time or other, evidently, I'd mentioned to Nadia a wish to know more about gold production. So waiting at the hotel, when we returned exhausted from the day's many conversations, was a representative of Yakutzoloto, the state enterprise, founded in 1924, to control all gold mining in the republic. He was Vladimir Livovich Kuznetsov, deputy chief of scientific and technical administration for the giant company.

"You may ask me whatever you like," he said, a tidy, cautious man, eyes peering out slightly veiled behind tinted glasses. The truth was there wasn't a single thing—not one—I cared to ask him, but he told me anyway.

His enterprise employed 60,000 miners and, including support workers and families, was responsible for the lives of between 150,000 and 180,000 people in all. Yakuts are agriculturalists, and industrial work is not in their tradition, he said—though he himself was Yakut. Therefore most of the miners came from other republics of the Soviet Union, attracted by wages that were more than two and one-half times the pay of machine workers. And after retirement, at age 50 for underground and 55 for surface miners, they usually went back to their native parts.

(I was remembering, then, something a Yakut scholar had said earlier in the day. Yakuts would prefer there be no more Russian settlements at all, he'd told me—only camps, where men would be imported to labor for fixed terms, without their families, and from which they would be sent back at the end of their contract to make way for another "shift." In fact, he'd said, Yakuts would prefer that no further development came to the republic at all. Not roads. Not rail lines. Only such extractive industries as might be necessary to produce wealth.)

Gold, the Yakutzoloto functionary was saying now, was the biggest earner of foreign currency for the Soviet Union. But the price of extracting it had risen. About 10 years ago, environmental issues first began to be mentioned, and in the last five years, he said, the pressures have become very intense. Activists had succeeded in mobilizing public opinion, so that now a percentage of the revenues of the enterprise had to be set aside in a special environmental fund. Some of the plants even had been closed. It had meant a major increase in the cost of extracting metals. And whatever he might think of that as a man of the region and of his people, it was clear from his manner that as an official of the enterprise he regretted it.

After the gold man, we raced back to last night's cabaret to meet the three young musicians, who'd agreed to let us film them performing before the crowd began coming for the evening show.

Then, finally, dinner. And after that an interminable *komsomol* meeting with Victor, Vadim Shamshurin and some of the other Americans in Victor's hotel room.

⚜

THE DISCUSSION BEGINS AT half past 8 o'clock, and there are only three issues to be covered. First, Victor says, there is a crisis of finance. Nadia has presented her bill for her exertions on our behalf—for all the meetings of these two days and the time and transportation getting to and from them, and for an excursion in the city some others of the group have made. It comes to a very great sum. He is worried to tell us how great. *How much, exactly?* I ask him. As much as 2,500 rubles, he says. It computes to less than a hundred dollars. If that's the size of the problem, I tell him, we don't *have* a problem. We'll cover it out of pocket. He's relieved, but says he cannot help thinking it's a peculiar world, when an amount representing half a year's wage in one society is hardly worth notice in another.

The second item has to do with details about transport. We're to spend three days at the *dacha* belonging to Vadim's family— their summer house in the forest—on the far side of the river. The photographer plans to use part or all of that time to go independently to villages, but there are no such things as rental cars in Yakutsk, Vadim says. He will try to find a friend with a car to do it. There's a problem with arrangements for the boat, and it's obvious he's frantic with worry about that. But he will try to find a car. In the worst case, at his farm near the *dacha* he has an old military car, with four-wheel drive, which can be used.

Finally, we must collect the rest of our personal gear, along with tents, stoves and fuel and food for three days, from the house where Victor has stored the cargo, and take all that and ourselves to the ferry landing in time for tomorrow's first afternoon crossing. Victor says that will take two hours, and proposes to begin at 10 o'clock in the morning. But the videographer insists it will take three hours, not two, and an argument erupts. Victor is annoyed at the way even the smallest matter becomes the subject of haggling.

The others won't let go of it, though. Two hours or three? On and on the talk goes, circularly and to no point.

"I have an idea," I say finally. "Let's *do* it in two hours tomorrow—and *talk about it* for three more hours tonight." Victor doesn't understand it's a joke, and those who would rather keep arguing aren't amused. It's after 11 o'clock before the *komsomol* adjourns, with Victor disheartened, Vadim near a nervous breakdown, and the events of the morrow having assumed the dimensions of the landing on Omaha Beach.

The disputation is pointless. All we have to do is throw some gear aboard and ride across a river!

⚜

THE WOODEN RAMP WAS winched up and the ferry slid out into the flow, loaded full with trucks, cars, people on motorcycles and afoot, and our blue bus that Vadim had produced from somewhere.

It's an hour's journey to the far bank, the way threading among the many islands that dot the river in this part. The people in cars, plainly veterans of the crossing, lowered their seats to the horizontal and went immediately to sleep. But I spent most of the hour on the deck. Yakutsk had been warm and, in the main, tiresome. It was good to be back in a fresh wind and to smell the water again.

The ferry bumped against the far landing—only a notch in the sandy bank. The gangway was lowered, and the other travelers and their vehicles rushed down it and turned to the left, where I supposed there must be some village we could not see. We took the way to the right, a dirt track that was at first almost a road, but soon dwindled to a faint trace meandering through vast pastures and meadows, branching where it skirted mudholes and then rejoining again, a route as uncertain and indistinct as a crossing of the Serengetti.

The driver was immensely skilled, dodging some of the wet places and plunging boldly straight through others. Many times I was sure he'd doomed us, but he always chose his risks wisely. We'd traveled the better part of an hour, when we met a truck and out of it leapt Vadim and Valera, who'd evidently made an early crossing. I'm never altogether sure who'll be meeting us, or where, or how they'll come—by helicopter, as on the upper river; down the bank, as the messenger from Moscow had done at Lensk, or on some track like this across the outback.

From there onward, even Vadim was lost. For he rarely came by that route, usually crossing directly from Yakutsk in a small boat. He stopped at a hut standing isolated in an immense field of grass to ask the directions of a lovely, weathered Yakut woman, a herder's wife.

And not far past there the trail became something like a road again. Ahead of us, two Yakut men, one on horseback the other on a motorcycle, were driving a herd of cattle along the track. Our blue bus fell in step behind the cows, past a boggy lowland of drowned birches and an explosion of purple-pink flowers that looked to be a variety of Lythrum, which the Russians called by a name that sounded like *Ivanchai* (Ivan's tea?).

We stopped briefly at a roadside store, a little board building with nothing in it except some cigarettes of the poorest kind, all paper filter with an inch of tobacco at the end, bolts of rough cloth in red and blue, a few small onions and, mysteriously, a photo enlarger. The elderly storekeeper looked to be Russian, but the faces of the women in the line were all Yakut.

Then, after another few minutes' progress, the bus motor died, refused to start, and the driver ground the battery down to dead. The hood was lifted, and various of the men leaned importantly under it. But knowing it was useless, since none of them was a mechanic, the rest of us prowled among the bushes, grazing like bears on a profusion of wild currants just coming ripe. We should keep some in our hats for later, Valera said, because they were very nice when crushed in a glass of tea.

A chill crept into the air. Evening was coming on, which must mean that it was after 10 o'clock—my wristwatch had stopped working—and it had become clear that the bus engine was not going to start, no matter how many men peered earnestly at it. Never mind, Vadim said. It was only a bit more than a mile farther to the *dacha*. He would send a tractor back to pull the bus and those who preferred staying with the stricken machine. Anyone who cared to could walk ahead with him.

It was a pretty hour, the air blue and cool, with the mosquitoes not yet quite risen. And as we walked together he told me the reason for his sadness and great worry—so great he sometimes feared it might derange him or destroy his health.

It had to do with something more, of course, than just his immediate concern about the problem of our boat.

FORTY-SIX

V ADIM'S FATHER, YURI IVANOVICH Shamshurin, was a writer— Russian by blood, but in all other ways a pure Siberian, devoted to this wild country and to the folk tales that circulate among its peoples.

The hut where we'd be staying was his summer house, to which he brought his family in the gentle season of the year, and where he always worked best. In fact, in his final illness, when he was almost too weak to walk, his last stories were written lying on a sleeping shelf beside a window that looked out through the forest in the direction of the river.

Nearby was the *dacha* of another writer, a Yakut. Between them, there may have been a little of that jealousy that sometimes infects the natures of writing folk. But they'd had much else in common. They'd fished together, and shot ducks together on the pond in the forest not far away. And as far as such things can be really known, the two men were the best of friends.

Nearly 20 years ago, at the age of only 52, Vadim's father died of the effects of wounds suffered in the war, from which he'd never fully recovered. Not long after that, the Yakut neighbor sought to buy the Shamshurin *dacha*. He'd become a flaming nationalist, and said he wanted no Russians on what he called "kin ground."

Vadim's mother, Tamara Timofeyevna, turned the man's offer down. She didn't care to sell a place that had been so dear a part of her and her husband's life. She still came to spend the summers here, Vadim said, and would be waiting to greet us when we arrived.

But whenever she steps from the doorway of her hut, she sees nearby the house of a man who has become an enemy. And that enmity figures in Vadim's own story—a tale of bad faith, bad luck, bad blood and perhaps, in some part, bad judgment.

Vadim was a geologist by training, employed as the chief of his section at the Institute of Permafrost in Yakutsk, when in the 1970s his brother was found guilty of reading and distributing anti-Soviet literature. The brother was sent to prison, and his sins also were visited on Vadim, who was demoted to the rank of common laborer. He then left the Institute to work for several years as a sailor on the Lena.

A decade passed. And under Gorbachev the political climate changed. Laws were passed to allow private citizens to organize cooperative ventures. It seemed to Vadim that the need, and therefore the opportunity, lay in agriculture.

In October 1988 he received an allotment of 60 hectares of land near the summer house, and permission to establish there, with five friends, a farming cooperative. They bought 50 pigs for breeding. Then, with the next winter coming on and the sows heavy with young, the local authorities inexplicably withdrew use of the livestock shed that Vadim and his partners had made ready.

In a panic, with snow already falling, the beginning farmers cut trees and flung up a hasty, earth-covered and poorly ventilated structure. The piglets came, 500 of them. But in those crude and fetid quarters, 300 died. Discouraged, the other partners gave up and retreated back to Yakutsk. With his wife and three men he employed, Vadim next tried raising geese. The first 150 day-old goslings grew well, adapted to the severity of winter, laid many fine eggs. Encouraged, he decided to expand. He built a shelter for the geese. Only the roof remained to be covered. Leaving his employees to finish the work, he flew to Novosibirsk to bring back 5,000 hatchlings.

In his absence, again for no reason he could name, local officials ordered work on the shed halted. He returned—the date, the

5th of July, would be lodged forever in mind—to find the roof still uncovered. That night there was a torrential rain. Four thousand goslings perished.

Policies made in Moscow are not always, or maybe even often, greeted with enthusiasm in the provinces. A new set of authorities had come to power in the district, ones unsympathetic to the fledgling cooperative movement. They cut off sources of feed for Vadim's remaining stock, giving priority to state and collective farms, and denying him permission to grow his own.

His troubles were complicated by ethnicity, or possibly just personal grudge, when the writer neighbor began a campaign with local officials, and in the Yakut-language press, against Vadim and his struggling farm. That was the fatal blow. Vadim recently was told by the district authorities that he had three months to liquidate his operation.

His anguish as he told the story was plain to see.

"It's not easy," he said, "to give up something in which you have put so much of yourself." I asked who was mainly to blame for his failure—himself, the system, the local administrators, evil luck or the malicious neighbor? He shrugged.

"Blame? It's hard to say. It's like a cake with many layers." Part of the problem, he said, was simply that he was a pioneer. "For the ones who come after, it will be easier." What's more, he still had faith that cooperatives one day would let the country set a fuller table.

"People raised in the old system feel threatened by change. But in one year, two years, five years, the old system must die."

For the moment, though, the days melted from the calendar. And barring some miracle, his chance appeared to be lost.

❦

THE TINY LOG COTTAGE is wrapped close around by pine and larch woods, on a knoll looking down across a pattern of forest and mown pastures toward the silver-glinting ribbon of the Lena in the far distance. Tamara Timofeyevna crouches in her dooryard as we come there, feeding pine cones and wood chips into her samovar so that the tea will be hot to welcome us. Her features are refined and classical. She must once have been an uncommonly beautiful young woman, and in fact she is beautiful still, although she's embarrassed by the absence of several upper front teeth and covers her mouth shyly whenever she laughs or smiles, which is often.

There's no electricity—only candles and tall-chimneyed kerosene lamps for light. Water is carried by bucket from a pool in the spring branch that runs icy and clear down a crease in the wooded hillside. Nights can be crisp, but it is a fine time of year in Yakutia, after the worst heat of middle July, before September's frosts. The wild currants and blueberries have started to ripen, and the mushrooms soon will be coming.

We boil a great pot of soup on our camp stove. And the vast crowd of us, including Tamara, our expedition, Vadim's wife, who is Korean, his sister-in-law, and the bus driver, gathers around the table, faces brushed yellow by the lamp in the small, shadowed room. Then, sleepy from food and the hour, all retire—three to a porous shed in the woods behind, others to tents in the yard, the rest of us to plank benches in various cubbyholes of the house. Curtains hung at the open windows keep the insects out. Gathering clouds have brought a kind of dusk.

At the edge of sleep, we cannot help thinking how rare—how utterly astonishing—it is to lie down here in the Siberian forest, being made to feel so welcome and at home.

⚜

THE DAYS AT TAMARA'S cottage were idyllic and healing, with no argument, no endless discussion, no responsibility except the building of fires and carrying of water. Awake first in the mornings, I gathered pine cones and cut wood shavings to start the samovar heating in the yard. Then Katie would come out to join me, and soon Tamara. Some breakfasts we cooked on our gasoline stoves, and some on a grate over an open fire, squatting beside it in the chill of the hour.

Later, when the morning warmed, I set up my typewriter on a camp cooler to catch up on the job of transcribing notes from my pocket note pads into the loose-leaf book of the journal, trying to decipher my own scribblings. The journal now amounted to more than 100 single-spaced typed pages, and would be nearly twice that before our journey ended.

Vadim took me to the Yakut settlement nearby, where a family was building a new house. The larch logs, brought from the forest, were laid up green for the ease of working them, held in place with pegs driven in holes bored with a hand-auger and chinked with moss. The work, done in a way perfected over many centuries, was wonderfully exacting and a joy to watch. It would take three months—the whole of the summer—to build such a house, they told me. But it will stand for 60 years.

At the settlement store, we spoke with a man who relocated here with his wife and three children from his birthplace in Suntar on the Vilyuy River. He was one of five milkers at the nearby cattle collective, and was responsible for the milking of 23 cows. He missed Suntar, he said, because it was his home and a traditional center for Yakut people. But while it couldn't be proved, he and many others believed that chemical discharges into the Vilyuy from the diamond mine at Mirnyy were poisoning the river. Already, he said, some children had begun being born in Suntar with deformities. This place was not home, but at least the air and water here were clean.

Finally, Vadim wanted me to meet one of his neighbors, a Yakut friend. We went to the man's small, humble house, but had to wait outside while he prepared himself in a suit. Vladimir Simonovich Diakonov emerged finally, a tiny man of 57 years. They greeted one another warmly. One of Vladimir Simonovich's 10 living children had been named for Vadim.

He'd been a veterinarian for 16 years, head of the veterinary department for the local collective. Then, like Vadim, he'd seen an opportunity in these changing times, and had attempted to establish himself as a private farmer. At one time he'd had 80 pigs, but couldn't get feed for them, so he butchered 27 for their meat. The rest died. Recently, the local authorities had told him he could have 10 hectares for pasture and the growing of feed. But the agreement wasn't yet final. They refused to tell him when he'd get the land, or exactly where it would be, or how long he'd be allowed to keep it.

Except for a greenhouse outside his back door, full of riotous tomato and cucumber plants, nothing seemed to have come of his efforts. He was thinking now of buying 300 calves to keep through the winter, he told Vadim. But it was a reckless notion. How would he feed them? How could he plan anything, when the terms of his landholding were so unclear? As I listened to them talking together—a Yakut farmer and a Russian one—I could not escape the sense that the little man was plunging headlong, with not much except enthusiasm, toward a calamity as complete as Vadim's. So ethnicity was not the whole explanation. There was a degree of improvidence in these failures.

"I know how to work," said Vladimir Simonovich. "I *can* work! But I need a little help." His greatest lack was of transport, for he owned no vehicle of any kind. No doubt he and Vadim had discussed this before, without finding any solution. And now he turned to me.

"Can you help me get a truck?" he asked—asked it of a stranger from another world, who only happened to be passing along the river. It was a measure of his impracticality, and of his need.

When we left there, the afternoon was far advanced. Next to the lodging of his farmhands Vadim had built a bathhouse of which he was very proud, and he stopped there to order a fire built and the place prepared for the members of our expedition to wash themselves.

"You can see the conditions in which Russian farm workers must live," he said sadly—separating himself from their circumstance, or any responsibility for it, as if it were something ordained by natural law. Passing through the door into that broken, squalid place was like stepping back a century into a scene of peasant life written by Turgenev. One of the workers was Korean, the other two Russians—one of those a slight fellow in his 30s; the older one tall, sickle-jawed and sunken-eyed, with several days' growth of beard and a long fringe of stringy yellow hair hanging from the rim of his bald pate. All three had the look of beaten fellows, hangers-on in the death throes of a defeated enterprise.

The board floors were tracked and crusted with the eternal mud of the out-of-doors. Everywhere lay the fantastic clutter of men not only hopelessly poor but also too long alone. Dented cooking pans with dried matter hardened in them. Torn clothes. A paper package of Chinese tea. Ash trays full of the crushed paper ends of cheap cigarettes. Stale lumps of bread on a cracked plate. In every corner the filth and wreckage to which they'd become indifferent.

The only sign of modernity was a small black-and-white television, its volume either turned off or broken, flickering with the snowy, unwatched images of the Moscow channel. They must find living hard, I said—unnecessarily because it was so obvious. Yes, the gaunt one replied. The worst was that none of them spoke Yakut, and the local people would not speak Russian with them, though they knew it perfectly well. It was difficult, sometimes, even to buy small things at the store.

Vadim promised that we would find his bathhouse the cleanest one anywhere. And when all had washed themselves, we would have a feast of chicken at the *dacha*. The gaunt farmhand was dispatched with a handful of grain to entice a careless hen.

But the bath took a long time to heat. It was almost midnight when the last shift of bathers had finished. And the chicken feast turned out to be a poultry *oooh-hah*—the bird chopped into random bits with blows of a hatchet, flung in a pot and boiled to a tasteless mess of meat, potatoes and splintered bone. I had no appetite for it, and was content instead to sit outside by the fire while the others ate their late meal.

The scene, with lamplight glowing through the door curtain and falling in a yellow fan from the side window of the hut, was simple and sweet. I tried to fix that in memory, along with all the other details of the place. Then Victor and Vadim went back to the farmhouse, where they would sleep part of the night and leave early for Yakutsk. They hoped to settle the last details of the boat, load the cargo on it, and return sometime in the afternoon of the next day.

If the crowd of us had tried her patience, Tamara Timofeyevna gave no sign. Her disposition was unfailingly sunny. In the cool of the next morning she led any who would follow up a steep hillside and into the dark of the forest. Nimble as a girl, almost skipping, she sang as she walked—a lilting tune that drifted back to her followers in notes of delicious purity. We came to the reed-rimmed pond where her husband and the Yakut writer had hunted together. And as we stood at its edge, a band of Yakut horses, half-wild, with rolling eyes, thundered near, paused to inspect us, and with a sudden chorus of snorts, rushed away among the trees.

In afternoon we walked to a Yakut burying ground, also in the forest, where Tamara wanted us to see the *shaman tree*. Officially, shamanism is dead among the native peoples. In practice, however, something of the old beliefs endures. Beside the cemetery was a dead cedar, its great trunk twisted and branches gnarled. Affixed in the cracks in the wood, and tied to the branches, was a fabulous variety of objects, from ruble notes and kopek coins to bright ribbons, cigarettes, pins, toys and photographs—all left there to propitiate another of the many gods the Communists imagine they have slain.

⚜

THE DAY DRAWS ON. The sky is blue and deep, with only lambswool clouds drifting, so there will be no dark. But it's after 7 in the evening, and still no word of a boat. I climb with Katie, Anne and Jennie back up the path we took with Tamara in the morning. Small gray birds fly chittering from branch to branch, and the rich yellow and purple of lupines, the pink of wild rose, is all around.

The view from the brow of the ridge commands a long sweep of country both right and left. Below can be seen the roof of the little *dacha*, a thin curl of blue smoke rising from the dooryard where Tamara is firing up her samovar. Beyond, on to the west, lies a peaceful quiltwork—green meadows, paler mown fields stippled with haystacks, plump trees and copses throwing dark shadows. One could mistake it for the English countryside, but it isn't England. It is Siberia at the turn of August. A mile or more distant is the great river, running between emerald islands and rippled sand bars. Tranquil as a lake it seems to lie, painted rich bronze by the angle of the sun.

And as far as we can see there's no boat upon it.

I'm thinking that some part of me would not be disappointed if no boat *ever* came. We have to go on, of course. But whatever troubles or disappointments wait ahead, we will meet them restored by the serenity of this place. When Katie and I spread our bag on the straw mattress of the sleeping shelf in the tiny back room of the hut, the kitten is there again. It doesn't belong to Tamara. It just appeared from somewhere—shaggy haired and small enough, almost, to fit in the palm of one hand—and has come every night to nest in the indentation between our backs, reminding us how much we miss our cats at home.

In the last moment before sleep, I am thinking that for the rest of its life it will come to this door, hoping to find the bites of tuna and the gentle handling it received from the Americans who once passed this way.

cﾟↃ•ↄ

A HAND GRASPED MY shoulder. I sat up confused, and looked at my watch—then remembered it wasn't working.

It was Anne beside me in the room.

"What time is it?"

"Four o'clock," she said.

I was still partly in my dream, in which we were in Yakutsk and there were no boats to be found. It wasn't the authorities who had stopped us. There simply were no boats, which was a barrier that could not be surmounted. So we had failed, after all.

"What is it?" I asked her.

"Victor and Vadim. They're back."

"Yes?"

"They've come with the boat. Victor wants to leave."

"And it's what time?" I asked again, stupidly.

"Four—a little after."

"It's a crazy hour."

"I know. But Victor says we must go now."

Katie, who had heard, already was sitting up, pulling on her jeans inside the sleeping bag. And the last was begun.

VII

On to the Polar Sea

FORTY-SEVEN

WHILE VADIM AND ONE of his farmhands carry our gear around in a cart behind a tractor, Tamara Timofeyevna walks down with us from her house in the woods and out across a series of linked meadows toward the river. The grass is morning-wet. A herd of Yakut mares and their foals eyes us as we pass through and on.

The path is plain, and we tell Tamara we can find the way alone. But she insists on leading us. In more than 60 years not many foreigners have come to her door, and it might never happen again. Anyway, for all the nuisance we must have been, she seems genuinely to like us. She weeps when she says good-by, and stands waving at the edge of the trees beside a stream until we have crossed the last field and passed from view.

Tethered against the river's high bank is our new ship, the one that will carry us the last part of our journey, north past the Arctic Circle to the port of Tiksi on the polar sea. Her name is the Maxim Ammosov. She's 130 feet long, powered by two 140-horsepower diesel engines, and should be sturdy enough to bear us well through the high waves expected as we near the Lena's mouth. The river still has two major and more than 50 lesser tributaries to receive. Already it threads here among so many islands that its breadth cannot be seen. And by the time we have reached the coal mining settlement of Sangar only three days farther north, the braided torrent of the Lena will be more than 19 miles from one outermost bank to the other.

Victor, Valera and Volodya put our stored cargo from the Zaria aboard before leaving Yakutsk. The gear from Vadim's cart is passed down from the bank to the ship, and he and his man shake clenched fists aloft in a good luck signal as the ship swings out into the current. There's time, then, to take stock of our floating home.

The Ammosov must once have served to carry functionaries on their official rounds, for there is a kind of grand salon forward—a party room, with red and amber lights, no longer functional, mounted against the ceiling at one end. There's also a large tinted photograph of the man for whom she was named, a Yakut

Communist party boss who died (the cause unstated on the plaque under his portrait) in 1939, more than likely a victim of Stalin's purges.

The ship has been 33 years on the Lena, and if ever she was a queen, she's a tattered one now. There isn't a foot of her that doesn't show the scrapes of hard use and much neglect. But for spaciousness she's a wonder! The forward salon, larger by a good deal than our whole living space aboard the Zaria, will be our cooking and common room. A propane stove has been installed for us, with one functioning burner. And we will be able to sit and eat as a group at tables drawn together.

Aft, there are rough but serviceable compartments in which, after weeks of crowding, it will be possible to find a bit of privacy to sleep and work and think. The Americans lodge two to a compartment. Victor and his men each share a compartment with a part of our cargo. It would be more convenient to put all the foodstuffs in the big room forward, but Victor is afraid of theft. He does not have a very high opinion of the crew, and with good reason.

They're a scrofulous looking bunch, except for the mate, a former Red Army special forces man, and the youngest crew member, Andrei, custodian of the Ammosov's consumable liquid stores. Other than those two, all go perpetually shirtless. The style evidently is set by the captain, on whom it's not appealing. He's a squat, disheveled man with a roll of lard at front and sides. Although amiable enough, he peers out at the world from watery red eyes and smells more or less constantly of whatever it was he drank the night before.

Shortly after boarding, Anne and Jennie have made a ghastly discovery aft. The crew's regard for hygiene, it seems, is below even the prevailing standard. The Ammosov's one head, entered by an iron door next to the fantail, is a horror. The first two hours under way the girls are back there with buckets of water dipped from the river, mops, scrubbing powder and disinfectant, trying to make the place bearable. Victor and Valera, surprised and humiliated to discover them at their work, try to take over the cleaning. But the girls insist on finishing what they've begun. They don't mind sharing even the nastiest duties. The point is no one ought to abide such filth.

The whole first part of the day is spent at housekeeping, Russians and Americans working together to put the boat in a condition fit for living.

Until recently, Victor has learned, the Ammosov was the property of a state enterprise. When the former owners scrapped her, she was bought as salvage by her crewmen, who made minimal repairs, reworked the engines, and are attempting now to operate her as a cooperative on the river. They do not inspire confidence, these men or their boat. But it and they were the best Vadim was able to contract in Yakutsk. If they can manage to get us the thousand miles to the Arctic, we'll forgive the rest. Certainly the shirtlessness. Eventually, maybe, even the wretched toilet.

Already some in our group have been heard to speak a nostalgic word or two about the Zaria. Certainly she was cleaner and faster, her crew more agreeable. Still, morale has improved dramatically with the transfer to the larger vessel. Privacy is an incredible luxury. One cannot imagine, until one has done it, the irritation of living cheek to jowl with so many others every waking and sleeping hour.

At evening today, the photographer rejoined the ship at a village called Count's Bank—established by the Baron Ferdinand Petrovich Wrangel, 19th century explorer for which a Russian island and (with the addition of an extra "l") the Wrangell Mountains in Alaska are named. He'd spent a punishing day in Vadim's jeep, which had no brakes and a heater that could not be turned off. But he recounted the adventure with amused resignation. Maybe he is feeling happier about the pictures he has in hand. Or perhaps he has come to better understand the difficulties with which the Russians, and therefore we, must contend. The roads were wretched, and he'd managed to see only two settlements, those at a time of less than ideal light. Yet when I commented that Victor and Vadim had done the best they could, he readily agreed.

So we're bound for the cold sea and Tiksi, our expedition still intact, spirits better, optimism running a little higher. For the first time in several days my journal is caught up, all the scribbled notes typed onto loose-leaf pages. And I've begun another set of dispatches for the sponsors, though I haven't any notion how they'll be sent, or from where.

Waking to the gift of a second consecutive sparkling day, we make on toward Sangar. Volodya's father was a mining engineer, and he spent four years of boyhood there. He has sent word ahead, so a program will be arranged for our visit. At least on the water, there's relief from the heat. The breeze is fresh, the sky deep, the surface stirred to a light chop.

The Lena becomes progressively a vaster, wilder thing, running among numberless low, sandy islands with shoreline willow thickets and dark stands of pine on their higher ground. In spite of the river's breadth, the actual channel is complicated and small, navigable only by repeated sharp turns. In a meadow as we pass, Yakut men are gathering hay with a horse-drawn rake and stacking it with wooden forks. The country, except for blue hills or mountains at a great distance, is flattening. Fewer ships are met now, and fewer outposts of habitation seen as we penetrate farther north.

In early afternoon we reach the mouth of the great Aldan River, largest of the Lena's tributaries, draining a vast area that reaches eastward across the wilderness almost to the Pacific. The joining of their waters is dramatic—the Lena amber-colored with suspended sand, the Aldan chalky gray. We turn up the tributary and stop for the night at a village called Digdal. The motorboat is unloaded and several of our party go ashore at the settlement, which turns out to be uninteresting. Anne, Jennie, Victor and I cross to the far bank, and up the narrow course of an inflowing stream. The fishing is poor—one pike and six perch. But the return is splendid, through a sunset of the most brilliant orange, reflecting in the porthole glasses of our distant ship as if the Ammosov were afire inside.

I spirit our fish away onto the forward deck to filet them, and thus avoid another *oooh-hah*. Victor looks in dismay at what I bring back, wondering sadly where all the spines and heads have gone. One more evening's catch will make a dinner for us all.

The day's wind has fallen, and evening is breathless. We've taped netting of the finest mesh over the windows to keep the insects out. A pipe that circulates hot water from the engine under the bunks in the cabins cannot be turned off, so even with the ports open the compartments are stifling. Some of our people flee to the common room and spread their bags on the floor, but even there the heat and the flies keep them awake. I'm miserable with a cough and cold coming on, and between the moments of fitful napping am aware of a terrific commotion—a ruckus of some kind—somewhere on the boat.

It is, I will learn, the *woman*.

❦

WE'D BEEN SEVERAL HOURS aboard, after leaving Tamara's dacha, when it occurred to me that I was seeing more faces than I could account for. The mystery deepened when a woman and small child went past on the deck outside my cabin. Finally, I'd had to ask about it.

"How big is the crew, anyway?" I inquired of Victor. "And who the hell is the lady with the kid?"

"Crew is eight," he said.

"Are we taking passengers?"

It seemed that the Ammosov's captain, without consulting anyone, had agreed to transport the woman to Sangar. She and the child had concealed themselves below until the ship was under way, and Victor was annoyed by this deceit. If they made a problem, he'd warned, he would put them off. Maybe she thought it was a bluff.

The first night she managed to contain herself. But last night she was the problem—carousing until dawn in one of the crewmen's quarters, with loud music and laughter, and her piercing squeals of rapture and worse.

That was a regrettable mistake, because Victor is a man of his word.

Today, at the breakfast hour, the Ammosov shouldered up alongside a floating boat station anchored in the river many miles from anywhere. The gangway was swung out and lowered, and the woman, child and offending crewman walked it. How they would get any place from there I couldn't say. But they seemed in fine spirits about it all—desperately hungover, but smiling, waving jauntily, bidding the rest of us a courteous farewell.

I hoped some other boat would stop for them. I wouldn't want those three on my conscience when the Siberian autumn turns.

FORTY-EIGHT

S ANGAR PERCHES ON THE lip of the bluff above the river, and straggles eastward from there onto the lower flanks of a range of dark mountains rising behind, part of the southern end of the Verkhoyanskiy chain.

Coal mining towns anywhere seldom are pretty, but Sangar is a settlement of really breathtaking hideousness. That might be written off to the hardness of the frontier, except that the frontier is more than 60 years old. The town was founded in 1928, when coal was discovered under the mountains. Since then, miners and their families have come here from other parts of the Union, many from the Ukraine, to spend their working lives. And then they leave. There is nothing to keep them, certainly not the weather. Sangar experiences on average 218 days a year of snow cover. The ice on the Lena does not begin to break until late May or early June. By the first days of November, the temperature has fallen by nearly 100 degrees and the frozen river once more can be used as a road.

After three generations, the settlement of 13,000 souls still has the neglected, impermanent look of a company town: broken, muddy streets; stagnant mosquito-breeding water pooled greenly in the roadside ditches; wooden barracks-type housing. Three stores— Number 1, Number 2 and Number 3—whose shelves are all but empty. Some bread loaves in one. In another a few pairs of shoes and a sable hat, its price two months' wages. Grayness and grimness at every hand. We do not speak of these impressions to Volodya, who remembers being happy here and still has soft feelings about the place.

He is excited to be back. The program he's arranged is to begin tomorrow morning with a visit to the coal workings.

❧

Alexei Gregoreyevich Pata, chief technical engineer for the Sangarskaya mine, received us in his spartan office. He was a fine looking man of 37, who went into the mines at age 23 and worked his way up to his present position.

The mine, he said, produces 330,000 tons of coal a year, supplying not only the Sangar region but all the northern regions of Yakutia. By 1995, he hoped to increase production to 600,000 tons, but that would depend in large part on the labor supply. The native people are not attracted to industrial work, said Pata. Of the Sangarskaya's 400 underground miners, only five are Yakuts.

An experienced miner can earn 1,200 rubles a month, equivalent to $45 at the current exchange—several times the average Russian wage. In the past, attracting manpower was no problem. But that changed suddenly two years ago, as the economy went bad. We have seen the stores for ourselves. There's nothing to spend the money on. And unless the great crisis of shortages and prices can be solved, he foresees a problem keeping a labor force. What's more, during a time of worsening inflation, the price of coal has remained constant at 24 rubles (less than a dollar) per ton.

The miners, in four six-hour shifts around the clock, are working now at three levels, from 800 feet to more than 1,100 feet below the mountain, in seams of coal that are as much as 35 feet in thickness—"colossal" was how he described the deposits. The temperature below is a constant 41 to 44 degrees. In winter, the air from outside is warmed as it is circulated into the mine.

The Sangarskaya has recorded one death in each of the last two years, and injuries range from 30 to 40 annually, mostly from roof falls. Methane gas, the invisible killer of coal miners everywhere, is not a great problem in this mine, except when working in the deepest deposits, at the water level of the Lena.

Would he say then, I asked him, *that as coal mines go this is a safe one?*

Chief engineer Pata looked at me levelly as he answered. *"There are no safe mines,"* he said. *"As in your country, it is the most hazardous occupation."*

And on that reassuring note, he sent us to the pits.

Our escorts were Grigori Ilyich Rusak, chief of mine safety, a stocky, no-nonsense fellow of early middle age, and a small, refined-looking and genial older man named Ruslan Alexeyevich Ostapenko. Ostapenko was the oldest employee of the enterprise, and had been Pata's predecessor as chief engineer. He also was the longest friend of Volodya's father in Sangar, and it was through him the visit was made possible.

The first stop was in the dressing room—empty now, since the current shift of miners already had gone below.

We stripped to skin, and left our clothes on hooks. Then we pulled on freshly laundered white cotton trousers and tunics. Over those went an outer layer of heavier blue pants and shirt. Strips of toweling were wrapped around feet and lower legs, and feet thrust into knee-high rubber boots.

Suspended from each man's belt were batteries to power the lamp mounted on the hard hat, and also the emergency breathing apparatus, whose use the safety engineer, Rusak, demonstrated with great solemnity. The business with the mask produced a slight stirring of unease. Novice miners spend several months in the classroom before going underground. We'd spent part of an hour in an office. In that unfamiliar garb, with the various kinds of apparatus hanging from me, I felt as clumsy and unprepared as a gibbon in a space suit.

In a van, Rusak driving, we bumped up a steep graveled track to the top of the mountain, and from there the whole town of Sangar, with the great river running past, was spread directly below. A rough log shack sat astride the mine portal. The older man, Ostapenko, looked out across the folds of mountains with undisguised fondness for the wildness of the country. When they were digging this shaft, he remembered, a she-bear and her two cubs came every day and the miners always left food for the cubs.

"Now," he said, "we'll go down."

To reach the mountain's heart one has to ride singly on a primitive lift, something like a ski lift, with a small wooden seat, no larger than a tricycle seat, affixed to the supporting bar. The seats are spaced far apart on the cable. The lights in the shaft are few and faint.

Down one goes into the blackness and the increasing cold. Down between ancient timbers and wood-plank shaft walls, where frosty excrescences of ice have come pressing between the boards. You pass into the layer of "stone" permafrost—the never-melting earth—that in this region extends down more than half a mile. With each minute of descent the cold seems greater. There is the sense of being incredibly deep in the everlasting ice—down with the mammoth and the antique rhinoceros and the great-horned bison of the Pleistocene.

The glow of the next bulb is impossibly far ahead and below. There's a feeling of lostness and abandonment and peril, a suspicion that you've entered recklessly into a region where you weren't meant to go.

I could not help imagining how it must have been in the late 1920s, the mine's first years, with no air blown down from above, no light but carbide lanterns, only picks and shovels to break and load the coal, and horse- or man-drawn carts to take it out.

At the end of this plunge we stumbled off the lift seats, unprepared for the slant of floor, and made our way to a conveyor. The belt was running, but no coal was on it. So we followed Rusak and Ostapenko along a lateral corridor, then down again, and along another lateral. In a half-crouch we had to go, bending to clear the roof, hitting hats, clambering over and among and under broken and discarded pieces of metal, wood, cables—all the incredible clutter of a violent industry.

Arriving at the next level, we found men at work but no coal being mined there, either. They were repairing some enormous machine. The miners all were youngish men, in their 20s and 30s, friendly enough but clearly puzzled by our being there. I asked one of them, a blond-haired fellow who looked to be the oldest, how he liked the work.

Living conditions are hard, he said. And the coal they were working in now was "not so nice" —the seam only two meters thick, and lying on a steep incline. But when the coal was nice, it was good to see the production roll out. He came to Siberia intending to stay only a little while, he said, but now he cannot imagine what other work he would do.

I remembered the chief engineer saying that some months before there had been a one-day strike by the Sangar miners. Their immediate demands had been for increased pay and better food supply for the town. But in truth, the chief had said, the real purpose was to protest the failure of Gorbachev's economic policies.

"How are things for miners in the U.S.?" the blond one asked.

There was much unemployment and real poverty in many of the coal fields, I told him. And the once-powerful United Mine Workers union had become a feeble thing.

"Give us a little more time," he said, "and we will catch up with you in everything—even in unemployment."

The others in his work group had stopped to listen. As we spoke, we both observed the little courtesy I remembered from days I'd spent once with coal miners in Appalachia. Miners converse with their faces turned slightly aside, so their cap lamps will not shine directly in the other man's eyes. Until finally, by a lifetime of habit, they do that even when not underground.

"I understand this mine is for Boris Yeltsin," I said.

"You understand correctly," he replied, aiming his words into the darkness just to my left.

The older man, Ostapenko, turned his cap light on his wristwatch. The shift was nearly ended. We left the men with their broken machine, continued down that passage, across a lateral, then uphill for an eternity, and just as a claxon sounded arrived at the train of man-cars. The doors of the cars were no more than 18 inches wide and 40 high.

Each tiny compartment held four riders—two squeezed shoulder to shoulder on facing benches. We found places where we could. The man across from me was one of the mine's five Yakuts. The train started with a jerk and rattled and lurched along its track at what felt like a tremendous speed, seeming every minute about to derail, then stopped at another level and more miners crowded on. Upward we careened in nearly total dark, the racket deafening, and were delivered suddenly into blinding daylight and, unloading, went together to the showers.

VOLODYA IS IN GREAT distress. We've stayed so long below that the
schedule of the day's activities is wrecked. Among the things he'd
planned—and he'd planned too much—is a visit to a Young
Pioneers camp, the same one he remembered from his own childhood.

The children, 50 or so of them, have prepared a program of
singing, dancing and speeches, and have been waiting two hours
for the rude Americans to arrive. Their program is charming. The
camp director makes a speech, and at the end of the concert I'm
expected to respond. I praise their music and their patience. I
explain why we all look like something their cat might have
dragged in from the *taiga*. We're on expedition, I tell them, and
explain where we began and where we're going.

They've forgiven us. And suddenly we are celebrities, all writing our names in autograph books and on bits of paper thrust shyly
in our hands. Then away in another rush—Volodya still frantic at
our lateness—to the principal bakery of Sangar.

Three tons of loaves are baked there every day. Also pastries
and candy. But we've missed the action. The day workers have
gone, the night ones haven't yet arrived. The director is waiting for
us, though. She's a large woman in her 50s, stylishly dressed, with
an authoritative manner—a deputy in the regional government, and
one of only two women heads of enterprises in the town.

She asks my impression of Siberia, and of Sangar. And I reply
as truthfully as I can, knowing that she herself is a functionary in the
failed system. The surprise, I say, in a land of so many resources and
so many able people, is that life should be so relentlessly difficult.

Then I ask her, in turn, her opinion about the opportunities for
women. Of the 94 people who work in the bakery, she says, 55 are
women. "They care more for the success of their enterprises. And
women managers work better. They are better with their employees." She speaks with the absolute conviction of someone who has
thought the problem through and come to the unshakable conclusion that the world would be a good deal better off if men could
somehow be dispensed with altogether. Considering that her party
and her country have been run by men exclusively, it's a reasonable
proposition.

Unfortunately, Volodya says when we leave there, the hour has gotten too late for us to complete the day's schedule. There's no way around it. We'll have to miss the visit to the municipal cucumber farm. Dear heaven, the *cucumber farm!* Well, I tell Volodya, maybe somehow we will find the character to continue on our way along the river without having seen it.

We go back along the muddy, rutted main road of the town, down to the river front and back on board our Ammosov. I fall onto the bunk, which is on the ship's shady side. Shortly, then, I hear the engine start and feel us slip sideways from the bank and swing downstream with the current toward the estuary of the next great tributary, the Vilyuy River, 50 miles farther to the north, which is our destination for tonight.

FORTY-NINE

CONDITIONS HAVE GOTTEN HARDER. We all have about us a deteriorated and faintly desperate look. Our clothes are gray from too many washings in the river. The mosquitoes and biting flies are pestilential. Eyes are red-rimmed from nights made sleepless by insects, and dull from our other ailments. I left my good glasses on a gravel bar a couple of weeks ago. Yesterday, Katie's sunglasses went overboard while she was filtering water, in a place where the river was too dangerous to try to dive and retrieve them. I have two spare pairs of drugstore glasses. The earpiece of one is broken at the connection, so really I have only one serviceable pair.

The surprise to us all has been the temperature. In recent days, even at this latitude, the heat has been punishing. Our bread was found yesterday to be molding. I cut off the worst parts, and we have most of one loaf and part of another remaining. Except for the town of Zhigansk, three days farther on, there may be no place from here to the journey's end to lay in a fresh supply. Bread simply cannot be kept long in such weather.

We celebrated Volodya's birthday, his 30th, last night at the

Vilyuy estuary. Victor caught a fine big pike, which with the fish we'd taken the day before made an abundant meal for us all. I gave Volodya the Battleship Missouri cap, gold-braided with the ship's name, and Victor and Valera gave him a new pair of hiking shoes they'd brought with them all the way from Irkutsk. There were two bottles of champagne from the supply of alcohol the young crewman, Andrei, had taken aboard in Yakutsk. And two of vodka. Then, after the toasting, Volodya brought out his accordion, and Valera danced with Jennie to the accordion music. Valera is capable and tough, but with easy humor and a soft side to his nature.

From the Vilyuy's mouth, another day northward through blazing heat has brought us to an anchorage beside a large sandy island fringed with scrub willows, with pines inland from the beach.

The undergrowth of the island is alive with hares—incredible numbers of them, skittering through the low bushes and rank grass. The hares are the most wildlife we've seen in more than 2,000 miles on the Lena. In the sand at the island's edge are the tracks of a moose cow and her calf, and also the great dog-like prints of a wolf that followed them a short distance along the shore, only as far as where the larger creatures turned inland into a willow jungle. The hoof marks are close-spaced and unhurried. With such an abundance of hares, no wolf in his right senses would need to try so formidable an adversary as a moose with calf.

Because it is my night and Katie's to cook, I miss what turns out to be the finest fishing of the whole journey. Anne and Victor, prospecting up the shore, find a place where the edge runs out shallow for several feet, then ledges off suddenly into a great depth. They tell afterward how, when they cast their lures and brought them back in across the ledge, the great pike would come crowding up from below like packs of dogs. They come back to the boat with several fine ones, but the largest of all was lost. It broke Victor's heavy line as if it were a thread.

"A fish like a sheep," he says, holding his hands far apart and shaking his head with amazement. "A *sheep!*"

L AST NIGHT WAS TERRIBLE for all aboard. Anchored in the lee of the island, we got no breeze at all. And through that breathless stillness the insects came—mosquitoes and midges in humming clouds.

Nothing will turn them. Not window netting, not net suits, not any chemical known. Swatting does not frighten them. They simply dodge the hand or paper, then come straight on. It's said that farther north, in the tundra region which we will reach in only days, they can drive reindeer mad. They have been bad before, but last night was insufferable.

Fully dressed, smeared with ointments, wearing face nets, with towels wrapped around the nets, we drew our heads down inside sleeping bags, zipped the bags all the way up, and lay sweating and miserable. And still they found us.

The night was endless. Leaping from bed desperate at sunrise, I found it was only half past 2 a.m.

Swollen, bloody and exhausted, we gathered in the ship's common room at 8:30 for the day's first meal. The insect hum there was deafening, and breakfast was a somber affair. Jennie had been out early with Valera, and had come back with the finest pike caught yet. Victor and Anne, trying the ledge again, found it barren and hunted for berries and mushrooms instead. As soon as they were back aboard the plank was winched up and we swung out into the current. Immediately, it was a different world.

Breeze through the open windows swept the mosquitoes out, and the moving air off the water was almost cool. In three or possibly four more hours, according to the charts, we would reach the Arctic Circle, and we must celebrate our arrival there with a swim, Victor said. It was mandatory. Anyone who refused would be thrown in the river.

A RRIVAL AT THE CIRCLE is announced by the boat slowing, turning, then running in to nose against a shelf of sand. Two of the Ammosov's crew set off inland with a shotgun to see if they can find a pond with ducks. The captain and the others lower the ship's dinghy and go far up the shore to put out their net for the silver smelt-like minnows they catch at almost every stop, and arrange carefully by the hundreds—more like thousands—on the ship's upper deck to dry crisp in the sun and be eaten whole, like popcorn.

While they're away, all the members of our expedition, Russians and Americans, make the ceremonial swim. The water is cold, but bearable. And the air when we come out is warm. Even in August, one does not expect to be comfortable in shorts and T-shirt this far north.

Sometime tomorrow we will reach the settlement of Zhigansk, with only about 500 miles of river remaining. Another 10 days and this remarkable expedition will end. It seems a good time to speak of the equipment and other provisions we have brought, and how they have served us.

Our Russian companions were astonished and appalled by the immensity of our cargo. Including the full air container we shipped ahead, the two canoes and a large amount of fuel that followed a week later from Coleman's inventory in Europe and the goods we brought as checked baggage, it amounted in all to something over a ton and a half of food and gear. Moving that mountain from Moscow to Siberia, stowing it in limited space aboard, unloading and reloading it from ship to land vehicle and back to ship—all this has presented undeniable problems.

Yet this can be said: *Of all we brought, nearly everything has proved useful and in most cases indispensable.* For example, when preparing the ship in Yakutsk, the Ammosov's slipshod crew failed to check the butane tank for the stove, which turned out to be less than half full. So now, and until the journey's end, we're again dependent on our gasoline camp stoves for preparing every meal.

Food made up the greatest bulk of our cargo. We'd been warned of the difficulty of finding anything but bread along our route, and the warning was accurate. Along more than 2,000 miles of river, besides the fish we've caught, we have found three dozen eggs, an occasional cucumber, perhaps a peck of poor tomatoes, and wild onions and berries from the forest. Without provisions of our own, we'd have come close to starving. The griddle and stove-top oven, included almost as afterthoughts, have enabled us to vary the fare in ways that helped morale. On a gray day of the spirit, pancakes filled with blueberries picked ashore, or a cake on the evening table, can be an important lift.

Tents and other camping gear were essential on the upper river. In later stages of the journey, shore camping has provided huge relief from the heat and shipboard crowding. Nearly all of us, Russians and Americans, are nicked, bruised or scraped in some way or other. And we continue to suffer recurring ailments, mostly intestinal and respiratory. With medical care unavailable, the kit of drugs generously put together by Ken Hoff, my doctor friend in Rochester, Indiana, has been our help and our insurance.

For two months, every drop of water used for drinking or cooking, even for washing dishes, has been pumped through our Swiss-made Katadyne filter. The Lena is reasonably clean, as great rivers go, but without the filter it's sure that some of us, the Americans particularly, would have been disabled and in misery much of the time.

And in a part of the country where the least amenities are so rare, where shelves in village stores are so empty that even matches cannot be bought without ration coupons, the gifts sent with us by the expedition's supplier friends have been welcome almost beyond telling. Our store of presents included tobacco, cigarette rolling machines, cosmetic products and a limited number of fine hunting knives. To each person whose help or kindness we answered with a gift, we said the same: "Remember that one day some Americans passed this way in friendship."

❧

M EAL PREPARATION FOR SO many took longer on the camp stoves, so our dinner at the Arctic Circle—of the fish caught yesterday and this morning—ran late.

In the continuous roseate glow of the polar night, Victor poured a vodka toast to the accomplishment now almost within grasp. He stared out at the orange shine of the river that, from the reign of the Czars through the years of Stalin's terror, was the sad highway for political prisoners and exiles bound for the outer cold. Then he looked pensively into his glass before he spoke.

"In our happiness," he said finally, "we should not forget the people who passed this way against their will, and whose lives were lost in the terrible times."

The videographer went out afterward to set his tripod on the sand and record on film the sky-filling fire of the sunset-sunrise, which in summer at this latitude is a single, prolonged event. A steady breeze made the temperature pleasant, and blew the mosquitoes and midges away so they were not a problem in the cabins. For the first full night in many, we all slept well.

FIFTY

Escorted by a squadron of the graceful little gray-backed river gulls that have been our constant outriders, we reached Zhigansk at midday, and found an anchorage among some other boats in the inlet on the river's west side that forms a harbor for the settlement of 4,500 people.

On the south side of the harbor was the town itself. On the north side, across a pontoon foot bridge, was the air strip, and the old wreckage of a plane that had fallen short on its approach to the little field. Zhigansk, like nearly all the settlements along the Lena, was situated atop a high sand bank and was reachable from the harbor only by clambering up and over an immense tangle of logs heaped at the edge, awaiting transport to a mill. Siberian towns give little thought to first impressions.

But once past the log mountain and into the town proper, it seemed a pleasant place—neater and more prosperous than most we'd seen. Unlike the coal mining settlement of Sangar, which was hardly more than a camp for transients, this looked to be a place where people actually spent their lives. The store shelves were as empty as everywhere. But there was a tidy sports field, and the barracks-type buildings looked well kept, with brightly painted metal skirts around the pilings that elevated the structures above the permafrost. People walked with a lighter, quicker step.

Afternoon was spent in a ramble around the settlement, with a stop at the bakery to lay in enough fresh loaves to take us the rest of the way. The streets, of course, were the usual rutted, puddled ruin. The heaving and breakage from the awful freezes, followed by the summer's thaw of the topmost layer of the underlying permafrost, make decent roadways all but impossible to maintain.

The brevity of the gentle season limits the chance to repair breakage inflicted by the ferocious climate. And one must take that into account when judging the look of any of these Siberian settlements.

Apart from the others for a while, walking the muddy streets of Zhigansk for no real purpose except exercise, there was a sudden moment when I was able to imagine—really imagine—the winter in such a place.

It would be night, the long darkness of the always night, with the frost an incredible 70 below. Leaving the warmth and yellow light of your little log house and iron stove, you would plunge on foot into that night—the streets all level now with snow, no ruts, no quagmires of slush and mud, just the smooth whiteness that covered all. Snow deep on all the roofs, and banked halfway up the log sides. Snow beaten into trails where people had trod before you.

Maybe there'd be a shine of moonlight, or starlight. And you would walk quickly, in high boots, wrapped in warm coat, hat, gloves, muffler around face, passing alone and yet safe through the fearful cold and come to the door of a friend, where the stove was hot and the samovar bubbling.

I thought I could understand, then, why Siberians insist that the winter is the best time.

⚜

W̲E HOPE TO VISIT the herds of a reindeer collective, and our Russian companions spent the whole last half of yesterday trying to arrange it. But, as usual, everything was hard. The Zhigansk phones were not working. Victor was unable to reach the collective. He tried then to call Vadim Shamshurin in Yakutsk, to see if Vadim could get through from there. It was no use. The line from Zhigansk to anywhere was out. It was impossible even to telephone the air strip on the opposite side of the harbor, so Volodya made three round trips there on foot—two miles each way—to try to locate a helicopter and pilot.

Not until late, as we sat in the common room, drinking powdered lemonade and talking the last of evening away, did he come to report it was tentatively arranged.

It's half past 5 o'clock in the morning now—the town still lost in dreams, no sound of stirring on our boat. Today the full light has come later, and on the deck there's a feel—the first faint premonition only—of cooler days drawing near. Motorboats are strung out below all along the edge of the harbor—scores of them, all of the same design, and mostly of the same color, the lower hulls a saffron yellow, the decks and gunwales red. Cars are optional in such an outpost, but a motorboat is essential.

The stillness, unbroken and absolute, resonates in the ear. It is as if silence were something the wilderness spilled down out of itself to cover this place.

Then a rooster sings. The on-board generator of a ship a quarter mile away, at the far end of the anchorage, can be heard to start. There's a creaking and piping of gulls as they rise up, white sparkles, off the water. A dog prospects along the sandy edge. A voice laughs musically. Then three men together come down the steep bank, across the log barrier, and there is the banging of them getting their motor out of a shed and putting it on their boat. Their voices across a hundred yards are as clear as if they were only steps away—the cursing and rough talk and laughter of men out together in the morning. The motor starts, and its whine cuts a wake through the stillness. The day begins.

Breakfast is early. All are away on foot to the air strip by 8:30—over the log pile, down a rutted track, balancing on a plank across a bog, over the pontoon foot bridge, then up a steep bank on the far side and along a shady, mosquito-humming path between birches and low bushes of blueberries just coming ripe. Victor finds the helicopter pilot inside the small wooden building. Then the two of them come outside.

There's a problem, the pilot says. He is a large, capable looking man, Yakut and Russian, who speaks a little English. He has to deliver some people and cargo to the collective before transporting us to one of the herds at a distant mountain camp. Because of the extra weight of people and cargo, he can take only five of our expedition. I have to choose, and the decision is obvious enough. The photographer, videographer, soundperson and I will go, and Sergei to interpret. The others are disappointed, but it can't be helped. They turn back along the path to the harbor and the boat, and we follow the pilot out to his orange Mikoyan-8 that is parked, rotor blades drooping, on the tarmac behind the wooden building.

"I am required to give you a pre-flight briefing." The pilot fixes us with a solemn look.

"This is a helicopter," he says. And that is his briefing. He smiles puckishly, and we climb aboard.

⚜

T HE KYSTATEMSKI REINDEER COLLECTIVE is made up of 800 people and nine herds of deer totaling 8,000 head. The collective's name means "stay for the night with me"—but the aspect of the place does not tempt one to take up that invitation.

From the air, we could see a collection of small houses spilling down a hillside from an arid ridge to a small river that wound through a fold of the nearly treeless landscape. Our helicopter raised a hurricane of tan dust as it settled onto the sand airstrip atop the ridge, and was immediately surrounded by a welcoming delegation of women and children on foot and men riding motorcycles with sidecars.

The Evenk faces, burned brown by the summer, were of endless variety, from broad and flattened to very fine, almost aquiline, but all with the same high Asian cheekbones.

In what seemed a confusion, but really was quite orderly haste, crates and sacks were passed in bucket-brigade fashion from the helicopter and borne away on the shoulders of the men. Simultaneously, other boxes and bundles lashed in tarpaulins were being carried from a small shed with a wind sock on its top and heaved up into the machine.

Several of the riders left us there. Three new ones got aboard, one of them a friendly man wearing a hooded yellow rain jacket and carrying a guitar. We discovered he was the collective's veterinarian, outbound with us for a visit to the herds. In only minutes, we were airborne again and bearing northeast over a vast terrain of boggy tundra, spotted with lakes and ponds of every shape and size, then over a larger river, and up that watershed, between steepening hills, the hills becoming first low mountains, then real mountains up whose sides the helicopter climbed, between crags and through carved gorges.

The Antonov biplane and Mikoyan helicopter are only practical means of travel across the Siberian wilderness. And the men who fly them, although they wear the insignia of Aeroflot, the national airline, are true bush pilots.

Vaulting over a high saddle, with the moss-covered stones and the scrub pines flashing so close on either side that it seemed they could be touched from the window, we hurtled down into another drainage. There was a shout from one of the Evenk men, who pointed ahead and down. A herd of several hundred reindeer could be seen moving—wild deer, these, appearing not as individuals but a single furred, flowing thing—through the shallows and along the glitter of a mountain stream.

The pilot circled for photography. A little after that there was another, smaller herd, and he circled again. Then we were dropping down, treetops whipping on either side and geysers of water blown up as the helicopter settled onto the gravel of a shallow river bed.

We all climbed out, the Evenk men with us dragging their duffel after them, and several others came down the bank and waded out to help. The place was very high, sloping up to forest on one side, the sheer planes and jagged spires of the mountaintops rising on the other. The air up there was clean and sharp—colder than we'd expected after the heat of the last weeks.

There were handshakes around. The pilot got back in his idling machine, started the rotors turning, then rose in a cloud of spray and disappeared around a bend of the steep mountain river, the *throp-throp-throp* of the helicopter echoing away to silence among the peaks. And we followed the herders up to their camp.

A large tepee, with canvas covering a framework of 25 poles, each at least 15 feet long, was their common place for resting and eating. Around it at some distance were seven smaller tents of modern kind. A fire was burning, ringed by stones, and in a tree beside it hung the carcass of a mountain sheep one of the men had killed on a ledge of the facing mountains. He pointed up to the place. It was all but impossible to imagine how one might get there, much less carry a carcass down. The ram's horns, an impressive full curl, were wedged in a fork of the tree.

Six men and three small boys no older than 10 years were the herders of this camp, custodians of 1,200 animals. With the first spring thaw, the herd began moving toward summer pasture in the mountains, where moss is plentiful for grazing and the insects fewer. From then until autumn and the start of the heavy snows, men and boys will follow the deer over an unpeopled reach of wilderness, moving their camp every three or four days as the moss is eaten and the herd ranges farther on.

The veterinarian in the yellow rain jacket, who'd ridden with us, was Pavel Ilyich Vinokurov, a bright and friendly fellow. He'd been trained at the agricultural institute in Yakutsk, but he'd grown up in the village, had herded deer himself as a boy and knew the life very well. Now, in August, he said, this herd was about 200 miles from the village of the collective—most of a week away, if a man were to travel straight through on deerback, or 20 days' travel with the herd.

Foodstuffs for the whole summer are deposited by helicopter in the spring. From then until October, said Pavel Ilyich, there is one helicopter visit a month to each of the herds, to take or bring out people as necessary. Between times, the only means of contact in case of an emergency is a small short-wave radio.

The herders' provisions do not include meat, so they must find game as they move or else kill a deer, which they do not prefer to do because deer are the wealth of the people. They do shoot wild reindeer, said the veterinarian, because a wild deer might take some of the tame ones away with him. Also there are moose to hunt in some of the high valleys like this one on the little Ogonnyor River.

Pieces cut from the carcass of the wild sheep were boiling in pots set over the fire. A small, powerful man with a face out of the steppes of Asia, wearing a rough, olive-drab jacket, appeared to be the leader of the camp. He forked a chunk of meat from a pot and invited the visitors to share it with the herders in the tepee.

The wild mutton, which I'd expected to be strong-flavored and tough from boiling, was delicious, cut off with knives and eaten with fingers along with flat pan bread they'd made, washed down with draughts of black Chinese tea. From our packs we produced granola bars and candy for the boys, almonds and trail mix, and the miracle of all, one of the Bugler cigarette rolling kits, which we would leave with a cannister of tobacco and a supply of papers.

A live brown rabbit was tied to one of the lodge poles by a cord around its foot. I wasn't sure if the creature was kept for company or as provender. From another pole hung a calendar, with yesterday's page not yet torn off.

I asked one of them if the loneliness of such a life ever was troubling.

"Well, sometimes you think about the village," he said, but only as a fact, not with any melancholy.

Pavel Ilyich, the veterinarian, explored the idea further.

"For small boys," he said, "it is very interesting to be with the grown-ups and with the deer—to go hunting with the men. For children it is an honor, and they want only to be in the camp. They do not think of the village at all.

"A man knows that there are other possibilities," he said. "And when you are here, you may think of those possibilities, or even miss them. But then, when you are away, you miss this country. You miss the deer. *Because this life has been going on here for thousands of years.*"

Would we like to see the herd? they asked. And of course we would. Except for the wild herd spied from the air, the only reindeer we'd seen so far were a half-dozen tied to trees among the tents—the men's riding animals and some being treated for lameness. But the herd was grazing unattended in that forest that reached all the way to the Pacific Ocean. What was the chance they could be found?

Pavel Ilyich laughed.

"In a few minutes, no more than half an hour, you will see them."

The camp leader and two of the little boys saddled deer and rode away out of sight up the river bed. The herd is never really lost, Pavel Ilyich said. Although sometimes, after a bad storm scattered them, it could be necessary to ride for several days without food or sleep until they are collected again.

"The loss because of death is about five percent a year," he said, "mostly to wolves and bears. And to diseases—foot injuries, pneumonia and black flies. In the spring and autumn, when the wolves come, the herders must stay awake with the deer all night."

Females calve in their second year, and mortality among the calves is about 20 percent. In autumn, when the herds are brought back to the village, the weak or lame are sorted out, fattened, and killed for meat. In the springtime, when the new antlers are growing and are soft, the antlers of the males are cut off and sold to be prepared for medicine.

"For one kilo," he said, "the herders get 50 rubles. It's the smallest part."

The collective sells the antlers to an enterprise in Yakutsk for 500 rubles a kilo. The enterprise sells them to the Japanese for 1,500 rubles. And doctors there grind them to powder and sell them to their patients, an ounce at a time, for unimaginable sums. That's how it used to be, anyway, Pavel Ilyich said. But in the two years since the cooperative began harvesting antlers other villages have begun doing it, too. Already the market has broken, and soon there'll be no profit in it at all.

As he spoke, a clattering rush could be heard around the bend of the river, then the first of the deer came filtering through the trees, and after that the main body of them. They were of all colors—fawn and piebald and a surprising number pure white—a milling, steaming, snorting mass. Those weren't all the deer, the veterinarian said. Only about a thousand of them. A couple of hundred must have gotten separated, but would rejoin the rest by night. He went in among them to see if he could detect any injuries.

A rain began to fall. The deer had calmed, and were starting to bed among the trees above the camp. We all retreated to the big tent.

I wondered what the weather might be down below.

"They can call on their radio and ask," Sergei said. But the radio was broken. It stopped sending or receiving the day before. The videographer took the radio apart, cleaned some connections and reassembled it. But it was no use. The link between that mountain valley and the world was lost.

At first the rain was intermittent. Then it came in earnest, filling the afternoon and blocking the view like a curtain drawn. No plane, even a helicopter, could fly in such conditions. The temperature fell as the day drew on. We'd brought no heavy clothes, no sleeping bags. I was beginning to consider the possibility of a night spent wrapped in reindeer hides on the floor of the tepee.

In the gloom of the great tent, Pavel Ilyich took up his guitar, ran his fingers across the strings, twisted a tuning peg, then began to play—strange, lovely music in a minor key. His shy, clear tenor voice carried the melody an octave above the instrument. It was the music born of the loneliness of such camps over long, long ages—songs about nature, he said, and about love.

During a pause in the playing, one of the herders raised his hand, listening intently. The others listed, too. They could hear the helicopter coming, they said. And maybe it was true. But if so they heard it at some old, old level, with some ancient ear, because it was a full half-hour before the MI-8 came beating up the valley through a break in the clouds.

The big machine hovered, river blowing and trees bending, then settled. Its motor stopped and the other members of our expedition climbed out—*all of them.* Throughout the day my one regret had been that they'd been denied the experience of this place, and now they were here. Tea was made at the fire and offered around, and in the confusion I took the leader of the herders aside, with Sergei.

"It's a fine life you have up here," I told him. "And your work with the deer is important. This is to remember a day some Americans spent with you."

He took the skinning knife from its sheath and looked with a hunter's eye at how it was made. His surprise and pleasure were clear. He called one of the others to see, and each tried the blade's edge with a careful thumb. "Ah," they said in turn. "Horosho! Ochin horosho!" *It's very good.*

⚜

THERE'S NO KNOWING HOW long the break in the weather will last. The others have most of an hour in the camp, then the pilot is restless to leave. Below us, as we lift away, the six men and three boys are standing together at their fire, arms upraised in salute. Tents and men diminish to specks, then disappear, absorbed into the vastness of the wild country.

Passing over the last high ridge and down into flat tundra and bog terrain, we leave the clouds behind. The evening is splendid and clear. Every rivulet, puddle and pond is burnished by the lowering sun. And the Lena, as we approach and turn along it, is enormous and intricate—its many channels uniting and redividing, running away to north like a river of molten copper so hot it almost blinds the eye.

On the far side is the blue smoke plume of a wildfire burning in the *taiga*, the pall spreading like a fan as far as can be seen.

FIFTY-ONE

THE CRISIS WAS SUDDEN, unforeseeable, and serious. It could have halted us for good.

The Ammosov was pushing hard to clear the haze of the forest fire, and I was typing in my journal, when Sergei pushed open the cabin door.

"I think you should come," he said. "There is a problem."

"What kind of problem?"

"Well, a rather big problem. It's about the boat." He filled me in hastily as we went forward together.

Evidently, when the state enterprise sold the Ammosov to her crew, the registry entitling the boat to navigate the Lena all the way to Tiksi did not pass with the sale. When writing the contract at Yakutsk, it had not occurred to Vadim to examine the registry, and the Ammosov's disheveled captain failed to mention this essential detail.

He confessed it to Victor only moments before, when he'd been radioed by a patrol boat of the river police demanding to inspect our papers. Passage on the middle and lower Lena was regulated by a thin salting of such patrols. Victor was furious at the captain, because there seemed to be no way out. The police boat would be coming shortly, Sergei said. And the Ammosov would be found to be traveling a part of the river where it had no right in law to be.

Outside, from the rail, a gray boat with a floodlight and speaker on its top could be seen boring slowly through the murk. The Ammosov's captain came down from the bridge, having put on a shirt and tried to make himself more presentable.

"What are our chances?" I asked Victor.

"I don't know. I will try."

The other Americans went about their normal activities in their cabins and the common room. There was no use alarming them. The outcome didn't depend on us.

The police boat eased alongside, made fast, and we were boarded. Two young men escorted Victor and our captain over to the other boat. It was impossible to see what went on there. A quarter-hour passed. They came back on deck. Another man was with them. Victor was smiling. Our captain was babbling and laughing noisily.

One of the Ammosov's crewmen was dispatched to collect a great quantity of dried minnows from the top deck, which he passed across in a dishpan to the other boat. Meantime, the police commander had come on board, gone with Victor into our ship's storeroom and reappeared with a bottle of vodka in each hand.

"See if you can find out what's happening," I told Sergei.

He spoke briefly to Victor on the deck, then came back to report.

"Well, it's a piece of luck," he said. "It turns out that the head of the police is related to the captain of our boat. A rather distant relative, but *related enough*. So we're allowed to go on."

How would one express mathematically the odds of that happening on a 2,800-mile river in the middle of Earth's greatest wilderness?

After more pleasantries and laughter, the gray police boat cast off its lines, swung round in the current and went back through the haze in the direction from which it had come.

"What was that all about?" the videographer asked.

"Just some administrative business," I said. "It's settled now."

Maybe there would be other registry problems in these last days toward the sea, but if so we would deal with them as they came. We'd already dealt with many to get this far. That night we spent tethered to a fuel tanker, cabins acrid with the smell of oil as we took on our final load of diesel for the run to the coast.

*Tamara Shamshurina and Katie Gusewelle at the Shamshurin
dacha near Yakutsk.*

*Rooftop in the coal mining settlement of Sangar—
and a face from the past.*

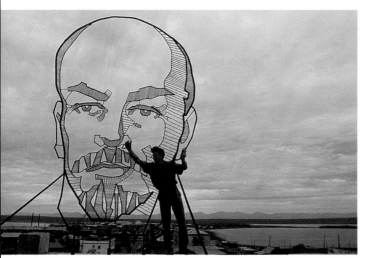

Talis Bergmanis

Talis Bergmanis

A young miner at the Sangarskaya mine.

The endless forest, late evening.

Anne Gusewelle

Anne Gusewelle

Forest detail.

Talis Bergmanis

Young Evenk reindeer herders, at their mountain camp.

Talis Bergmanis

Volodya Donskoi and the Ammosov, near midnight at the Arctic Circle.

The great Lena, pouring toward its end at the Arctic coast.

꙰

EVEN BEFORE YAKUTSK THERE was muttering about the shortness of the vodka ration—one or two drinks each in the evening.

"It's ours," said the photographer. "We paid for it. I say we should have it when we want it." But it wasn't ours. Victor, Valera and Volodya had saved coupons for six months to assemble the small supply. And it continues to be apportioned sparingly.

This morning, the videographer has castigated Victor—*indicted* him, is the word Victor uses—for being secretive about yesterday's episode with the river police. The problem arose without warning, was dealt with, is behind. It's impossible to see what use it would have been to involve the others, but nevertheless the videographer feels somehow that he was deceived.

It would have been Sergei who carried the details of that affair to the others. He has gotten moody and conspiratorial in recent days, withdrawing for long spells to his cabin, or sunning on the upper deck with the crisp minnows. I think he is frustrated by the inability to find an audience for his protracted mystical dissertations about himself, with which the other Russians never have any patience, and of which I've grown somewhat tired.

Victor is demoralized by the attack, and I do what I can to raise his spirits. For a time, I worried that the intermittent frictions were somehow my fault—the same mistake that Victor is making now. But we've done our best under the circumstances. And we are near enough now that I am sure we will finish. We will manage it even if the police put us ashore or this old boat falls out from under us. At least some of us will.

The character of the river has begun to change again. Islands are fewer, and there are not so many secondary channels. The main flow pours with great depth and power toward the north. On the right-hand side, much of the morning and afternoon, there have been towering banks of sandstone with a fringe of forest along their tops. A whole day has passed without seeing a village or settlement of any description. The race of man is spaced thinly on this sector of the planet.

For most of an hour in afternoon, we saw far ahead atop the bluff four geometric manmade objects. As we drew nearer, the shapes resolved into enormous concave rectangles, painted in alternate stripes of red and white—the antennas of a military communications post, manned by a detatchment of soldiers stationed there on the promontory above.

Now, at 8 o'clock of the bright evening, we are stopped against a shallow, rocky shore directly below that slope of scrub forest and sand that rises up 200 feet or more from the water's edge. Hardly had the engines stopped before three young men in a small motorboat came racing in from their fishing on the river and climbed aboard. They were young officers of the post, hoping we might have vodka and cigarettes they could buy.

Volodya has climbed the bluff to ask about the possibility of our visiting the place, and comes back down now to report his conversation with the commander of the station.

"I told him we were an expedition of Americans and Russians, and would like to see what is there. He said, *'Americans? Here?* No, no! It is impossible!' So I said to him, 'Why not?' And he thought about it for a minute, then he said, 'Oh, well, I suppose nothing is secret any more. *Bring* them.'"

Tonight is cool. Mosquitoes are absent. Some of the soldiers have come down and built a great bonfire on the shore, their figures silhouetted dark around it. From somewhere a man with a Husky dog has joined them. Before morning we will be inside our sleeping bags for comfort. The plan is to rise early, finish breakfast by 6:30, and climb to the top to learn how it is for young men who serve their country in such a desolate place.

WE HAVE MET THE ENEMY face to face. I can report that he is an uncertain, lonely lad whom you would not be able to distinguish, except for the green uniforms of scratchy wool, from the boys in the houses on your block in Kansas City or Buffalo or Minneapolis.

The complement of the post consisted of 26 soldiers, averaging 19 years of age and most just out of school; 12 young officers, five accompanied by their wives; several quite small children and one shaggy, friendly dog.

Arriving winded from our climb, we were met by Major Alexei Ivanovich Kuzminov, a cordial young man of 34, the garrison's commander. The post received few visitors, he said, and never any American ones before us. However he had seen Americans during a previous posting in Germany, and had found that they, too, were human beings like himself. In spite of being an army officer, he never thought of Americans as his personal enemies. Now he believed the agreements on disarmament had brought real change, and it would be possible to have more contacts, not just between governments but also between people.

The routine of the little camp is fixed, said Major Kuzminov. Two days a week, before breakfast, the men have a precision marching drill. In fact, they were doing that as he spoke, on a patch of flat ground among the temporary buildings.

First they marched in groups, then singly—raising high their legs and swinging their arms in the same exaggerated goose-step used by the honor guard at Lenin's tomb in Moscow. Except these were just boys, awkward, somewhat rumpled, of all sizes and shapes, looking sidelong at the visitors, the cheeks of some of them flushed red with both pleasure and embarrassment at being watched.

Two other days of the week there is physical training. And two days political instruction. Nothing special had been planned for us, Major Kuminov explained: "We are as we are." Perhaps we would like to see the mess hall. It was inside one of the prefabricated buildings, in a room only slightly larger than an ordinary living room. Boys not out marching were at the tables, and on the walls were river scenes the soldiers had painted.

The station was self-sufficient, the major explained. Food and diesel fuel for the generators were brought in once a year, and there was a three-year supply of dry food in reserve. The camp also raised pigs for meat. There was no doctor, but one of the soldiers with some medical skills was able to care for small hurts in the tiny two-bed infirmary. The bathhouse for the camp was a very fine one, built by the soldiers themselves.

The term of service here for a soldier was 18 months, and was not voluntary: "A man must serve where his motherland requires." For officers the tour was four to six years. His own native region was the Caucases, but he had been here three years now and was acclimated. One even got used to the isolation—200 miles to the nearest settlement of any size in one direction, 250 miles in the other.

Still, morale was the greatest problem. There were radios and a TV, so the men could know about events in the world. In the summer, they could fish in the river when off duty. But in the winter, when the frosts approached minus-60 degrees Fahrenheit, life drew in to the little cluster of buildings atop the bluff. Last winter, a bear that did not hibernate, and therefore was very hungry and dangerous, came around the camp and tried to break into the pig shed. They had to kill the bear.

The station had been in this place 23 years, said the major. And they were hoping now to replace some of the temporary metal buildings with more permanent ones. But supplies are as short as the season for working. In spite of its age, the post was a model of neatness. At the far end of one of the buildings was the barracks area, with the rows of beds all made drum-tight. Nothing was out of place on the small shelves between the metal bunks, or in the gear stowed in identical duffels in bins at the end.

"In such a situation as this," said Major Kuzminov, "discipline and order are necessary. Or things begin to come apart."

It was easy enough to imagine.

The major stopped for a moment at his office, at the other end of the long building. A large map on the wall showed, in great detail, this section of the lower river. I asked him what he thought of the Lena.

"I have never known so great a river," he said. "My feelings for it are—" He hesitated, reaching for the word. "— almost worshipful. When you live beside it, you see it in all its moods, wonderful and terrible. Storms that are violent, and create dangerous whirlpools in the current. Great stones breaking off and falling from the cliffs. I have *seen* it."

He shook his head, as if in an amazement that remained forever new.

As for the mission of the outpost, there were 26 such stations scattered over Siberia. All the communications for Yakutia north of the Arctic Circle passed through this one, using the great antennas to bounce the incoming and outgoing signals off the troposphere. Hundreds of messages could be sent and received simultaneously.

We followed him across a weedy field to the center of the station's electronic operations. Several young operators were sitting at the transmitters, and others were making adjustments to the banks of computers and other machines. The major asked one of the soldiers to get him the station at Tiksi, on the northern coast.

"Hello, Tiksi?" he said. "I have some Americans here."

A startled burst of Russian words came bouncing off the troposphere and crackled in the crowded room.

"That's right," said Major Kuzminov. "Americans. And I am sending them on to you." He grinned, put down the microphone, and led us back outside.

"The men want to make a picture," he said. "All of us together."

So we arranged ourselves, Russian and American expeditioners and a couple of dozen Soviet soldiers, their officers and their dog, on the grass at the edge of the station, with the huge antennas looming as a background. The soldiers who owned cameras had brought them from their barracks, and took turns recording the scene. We also made pictures.

Then, with some regret, we had to go back to the boat and let The Enemy get on with his work. Our descent was a careful one, using steps cut out of the face of the bluff. Several of the soldiers followed to the shore, but they did it in a breathless, vaulting lope down a sandslide in the center of the bluff.

They gave us a jar of blueberries they'd gathered from the *taiga*, and stood waving at the river's edge as long as we could see.

FIFTY-TWO

THE LENA HAS NARROWED now to a single channel, through which all its gathered waters pour northward in a mighty rush. This stretch is famous for dangerous winds and high waves, especially when the wind blows from the north against the flow. River men, we're told, speak of it as The Devil's Race, because it has claimed many boats and many lives. But our luck with the weather and the Yakutian summer holds. The water as we enter this treacherous part runs smooth as an evening pond.

The rigors of Siberian life can bring forth the best of a man's character and resourcefulness. Or it can break and degrade him. In the space of two days I have seen examples of both outcomes.

⁂

T HE EVENK FISHING VILLAGE of Siktyakh perched on a grassy shelf with the boulder-littered shore below and the dark of the forest behind. It had a cared-for, tidy look.

Vasily Nikolaiyevich Smirnov called down a greeting from the porch of his house, and invited Volodya and me to come rest for a while and talk. It was a commodious house by Siberian standards, and we sat together at a table in the kitchen.

The young man, 29, a fisherman and hunter, was of the Evenk facial type that is almost European. He was missing some upper front teeth on one side—common in a region where the trained practice of dentistry is rare. Siktyakh is a town of some 200 adults and even more children, Vasily Nikolaiyevich told us. And all the people there are Evenks.

"I was born here," he said, "and I will fish here all my life." He hoped to be as lucky as one man of the village who, though in his 80s, still was an active fisherman and hunter.

I asked him how keenly the economic situation was felt in his settlement. He was unable to speak for other places, said Vasily Nikolaiyevich, since this was the only place he'd ever known.

"But it's not so difficult here. The river and the *taiga* save us." Principally, he said, they catch the omul, which is eaten salted in summer, and in winter is frozen, sliced very thin and eaten raw.

"Winter is the best," he said. "Summer is too hot, but in winter there are many ducks and geese and moose for food, and under the ice there are more fish." Also in winter he traps the wild sable for its pelt.

"Of course, the life is hard. But I like it here. There is no better village than this one." Vasily Nikolaiyevich had two daughters, ages 2 and 4. He believed they also would live their lives in Siktyakh. "It is not a town whose children leave."

He was a fine man, cordial and proud. I asked him how often Americans had come here. He seemed surprised and amused at the question, as if the answer ought to be obvious.

"In my lifetime," he said, "none before you."

His wife came in, then—a pretty woman in a pale-flowered sun dress. Would we stay and take a tea? they asked. We thanked them, but it was two miles back along the stony beach to where we'd left the ship and we had to leave.

It was pleasant walking down to the river through the little settlement with its neat houses, neat board fences, laundry fluttering on the lines and the fences enclosing manicured plots of potatoes and onions. Plainly it was a village inhabited by other folk as capable and proud as the man we'd just met.

On the way to the Ammosov I picked up a stainless steel rod that was half-buried in the sand at the river's edge. A foot long and three-quarters of an inch in diameter, it may have been a part from a boat's engine, or perhaps the drive shaft from a motorcycle. Or maybe neither of those. But it was an artifact that felt satisfying in the hand.

We stopped last night on a broad beach backed by a rise of wild hillside, with a good supply of driftwood for our fire. The sky was cloudless, the dusk deepened to something like true dark, and the mosquitoes came out of the forest with a hum like a low-flying plane.

We dragged bleached logs down from the top of the beach and built our fire into a smoky inferno to chase them away before putting up tents.

This morning, two hours beyond our night's camp, we came upon another place of habitation. Its designation was Village Prilensk, but it was no village in any reasonable sense of the word. What met the eye were several large metal sheds, a dormitory-style building on a hillside, appearing to be derelict and abandoned, and scattered among these a variety of enormous machines, some whole, some broken and rusting.

The place had a failed, industrial look, except there was no suggestion of what the industry might have been or any sign that it ever had yielded a product. The earth all over this dismal area had been churned and rutted by the metal tracks of the machines. Little evidence of current habitation could be seen. The silence was profound. And all around was the watching forest.

The others remained on the boat. Volodya and I walked a bit farther on into the demented clutter.

"What's that?" I asked him uneasily. A faint crackling murmur was rising somewhere out of the stillness.

"A radio. Someone is playing a radio."

We followed the sound to its source—a squalid shanty just on the far side of a rise, where the hillside slanted through brush toward a murky creek. A bristling cur rushed forth to meet us. After an eternity of barking, a man stepped out in his underwear and silenced the dog.

Volodya made some explanation in Russian, and the man motioned for us to come in.

The interior of the shack was disheveled and spare. No criminal sent into exile could be asked to endure a meaner existence. Filth and odor were everywhere—food solidified in pans, mud covering the floor, broken things and soiled clothing heaped all about. Color magazine photographs of heavy-breasted women were nailed to the wall.

A second man lay on the bed, unspeaking. The first man pulled on a wretched pair of trousers and an undershirt. Evidently they'd been asleep at past 10 o'clock in the morning and the racket of the dog had awakened them. The man was sweating. Empty bottles lay on the floor by his bed. He spoke in Russian to Volodya.

"It is the base of a geological party," Volodya said. "They are hunting for diamonds. They have found the Kimberley deposit, the blue earth. But they have not yet found the volcanic pipe."

"How many men in the party?" I asked the man.

"Fifteen."

"We didn't see anyone else. Are they around here?"

"They're somewhere."

His name, he said, was Mikhail Alexandreyevich Prosayanikov.

He was 35 years old, and had been six years in this place. *Six years!*
It was unimaginable. The conditions, he conceded, were very hard.
If he told me how they have to work, I would not believe it. I said
for him to tell me anyway.

"Well, we dig a hole twenty meters (65 feet) deep and one and
a half meters (five feet) wide, down through the permafrost, to collect samples. For the man in the hole, loading a bucket to be drawn
up, it is very hot.

"Then the man in the hole and the man on top change
places," he said. "And when you come up the frost is fifty degrees
below freezing and your clothes could turn to ice on your body. It
is a dangerous moment." Surprisingly, he added, there is not much
illness among the men. "But you have to be careful."

Nothing about the camp, the shanty or the men themselves
suggested any capacity for carefulness.

Throughout this conversation the other man had been reading something written on a wrinkled scrap of blue note paper. He
was a huge man, and sometimes he got up from the bed and
prowled from one wall of the shack to the other, reading his paper.
Then he would lie down and read it some more. He never uttered
one word, or indicated in any way he knew we were there.

That one must be a pleasure to spend six years with, I was
thinking.

I asked the first man if he had a family.

"A wife," he said. "And a son eleven years. I can see them one
time a year."

He would try to find other work, but now the economy was
broken and there was little chance.

"We have *perestroika* one year, two years, three years. Nothing
happens. People are tired of waiting. The Communists have ruined
everything, taken everything."

The dog bristled at us again as we left. The huge, mute one
still was lying on his bed, fascinated by whatever was written on his
blue scrap of paper.

We walked without speaking back through the stillness of that
broken place and down to our boat, and for many hours afterward
they were on my mind, those two. I was remembering a story I'd

read once, about two men who went off to an outpost in some place at the outer margins.

They went with a purpose—to do business, as I recall. But they were too long away. The loneliness and the silence were overpowering. Something came between them. A rot of the spirit set in, and no good came of it in the end. The name of the story and of the writer were lost to memory, but it didn't matter.

I had just seen that story in life.

❦

THE DISTANCE YET TO go is measured now in days and hundreds of miles, instead of weeks and thousands.

Tired and frayed as we all have become, I've nevertheless begun to be oppressed and saddened by the foretaste of conclusion. The journal is as complete and careful as I can make it. And some of what we've seen and done together I will manage to put down and examine later in more deliberate form. But none of us—certainly not the Americans, and perhaps not even the Russians—will pass this way again.

Because even powerful memories blur, and because words can only evoke experience, not recreate it, a great deal must be lost.

FIFTY-THREE

DRUNKENNESS IS THE EPIDEMIC of the Far North. It savages a shocking number of those who live here—native peoples and ethnic Russians alike. And it has made the Ammosov's youngest crewman, Andrei, a capitalist at 21.

He brought with him from Yakutsk in the ship's stores a quantity of vodka, some poor-quality Russian brandy and several cases of a sweet Bulgarian wine. Their value has increased with each mile's progress northward. A bottle of vodka that was worth 37 rubles at midpoint on the river can be sold for 150 rubles—half a month's wage—as we approach the Arctic coast.

In this stark region, wrapped in snow and ice some 250 days of every year, the passion for blessed forgetting must be very great.

Word of the possible presence of alcohol seems to travel with something like the speed of the far northern light. The moment our expedition nudges ashore at some huddled village or wretched wilderness settlement, the seekers begin to appear. Already stuporous in afternoon or morning, they come stumbling down the bank on rubber legs, eyes moist, grinning foolishly, childishly, in their eagerness to do business with Andrei.

The disease afflicts men and women, young and old, impartially. Desperate and stinking, they swarm over the boat like locusts. Guards have to be posted at the entrances to our sleeping quarters and storerooms, since these ruined folk, besides being disgusting, are quick-handed thieves. The drunkest and most rowdy sometimes have to be dragged physically from the ship. Then we swing out into the current, leaving them howling and pleading on the shore behind us. And Andrei counts up his profits.

The spectacle today at the village of Kyusyur was practically riotous. Not only was there a milling throng trying to clamber aboard from the shore side, but also from the river's far bank more of them could be seen coming, gangs of men in small boats, converging like vultures on a road kill.

Volodya, with his shotgun near at hand, took up station in the common room. I stood at the entrance to the passageway leading to the cabins and storerooms. Tucked in my belt, inside my shirt, was the short steel bar I'd picked up on the beach at Siktyakh. Victor speaks of it as the "last answer" to such emergencies. I haven't had to use it, but would do so without hesitation to protect our people and our goods.

One of the drunks, snarling and coarse-faced, tried to climb the narrow ladder to the ship's bridge. The crewman who'd been in the army's special forces blocked the ladder at the top and flung him bodily back down. Many of the worst-debauched seemed to be women, and in some cases young girls. One, who could not have been older than 18 and who might have been lovely if her features had not been so slack with lascivious beseeching, lurched and fell repeatedly, until finally she had to be passed like a sack over the rail and lowered into the arms of her kinsmen and compatriots.

Then we took the Ammosov clear of that ghastly congregation, across the river and down another mile to a saddle between the hills of the far bank.

The place was near the original site of the native settlement of Bulun, where two members of DeLong's party, dispatched southward in search of help, wintered over and recovered from their ordeal—unable, however, to return to save their doomed companions in the frozen Lena delta.

But that upslanting meadow of grass and underbrush and wildflowers had other somber resonances as well.

Victor, shouldering into a clawing thicket, found what he was looking for—something he'd read about once in a book, but never imagined he actually would see. It was a small stone obelisk inscribed with the name and dates of Yakov Fedorovich Sannikov, 1844-1908.

Sannikov, he told us, was an untutored native, Yakut or perhaps Evenk, an amateur geographer and explorer of the far north who discovered several islands off the Arctic coast and for whom a strait is named on the maps. *Peace to Your Body* said an inscription at the base of the stone.

A few steps away, also buried in brush, was a monument to another explorer whose sacrifice did not gain him any fame. He was one Khariton Nosov, who died at this place on 10 September 1902, at age 26, while a member of a Russian expedition bound to, or possibly returning from—that wasn't clear—the polar region.

He'd been laid there, and the marker raised, *By His Shipmates.*

But the real sorrow that hung over that meadow, bounded by cliffs at either side and running up in a dapple of sunlight toward the scrub forest above, was greater and more recent than any of those others. The artifacts of it were the ruins of several fallen structures, dug partly into the hillside and roofed over to make crude living quarters. Remains of recent fires told that some of them still were used as shelters by hunters or fishermen caught by storms.

They were what remained, Volodya said, of a resettlement camp for Baltic people brought here as prisoners in the unimaginably brutal times during the last great war. There were many such camps along the Lena, and the people forcibly relocated there numbered in the hundreds of thousands. What followed was a horror that almost defies imagining.

The deportees scratched open the earth and planted seed, hoping to make a crop. They threw up their hasty lodgings against the coming of the Siberian winter, whose ferocity they only could guess. Then, before the crop was harvested, the order went out to the camps that the people should all assemble on the bank of the river. Ships were coming, they were told—American ships—to repatriate them to their Baltic lands.

Ships came, but not American ones. The people were herded aboard and transported still farther to the north, where they were deposited in barren places, without provisions and without shelter. The Arctic winter closed down around them, and in an agony of hunger and cold the greater part of them perished. How many? Who will ever know?

That's how we heard it recounted by Volodya and by others. In the last two years, with the shame of those terrible times no longer a secret of state, relatives of some of the dead had come here to Bulun, and to the more northern camps, a man in Kyusyur had told him. They opened many of the graves and took the bodies out—still identifiable, quite well preserved by the permafrost—and carried them in metal coffins back to the Baltic republics for reburial in native ground.

Volodya finished telling it. And we all stood amid the wildflowers of the hillside, smitten to silence by the enormity of the evil of that remembered time. A freshening breeze whipped at the grasses and eddied around the broken buildings, through whose empty windows we could see the shine of the water below.

Then, as we lingered there considering, the sun went out. The wind doubled and redoubled its force. A bank of sooty clouds rushed up the sky from the north. The river was whipped in an instant to rolling waves with combs of white, and the Ammosov's captain, drunk in afternoon, was sounding the ship's siren in a panic to be under way.

We raced down the meadow and along the shore, to scramble

aboard. The light had gone suddenly murky and low. The waves were like hammer blows against the bow, but they came straight-on so our boat breasted them without roll or pitch. All aboard her were pulling on heaviest sweaters and windbreakers.

It was the first autumn storm, come down out of the region of polar ice to blow the summer away. In no more time than this telling of it, the great river had changed from placid and congenial to slaty and forbidding. And the Arctic season turned.

FIFTY-FOUR

I T'S COLD, SITTING CROSS-LEGGED on the front deck, watching the last of the river pass, running the miles like sand through my fingers. I have to retreat to the cabin for an extra turtleneck, then come back outside. The others all are in the common room. I can see them through the window. Supper is being made, and I am glad it is not my night for cooking because I want to miss nothing out here.

The cold is the cold of the polar sea, foreteller of the months-long night that soon will be coming down.

In what's known as "The Tube"—this final reach from here to the beginning of the delta—the great river is pinched down between two converging mountain ranges, pouring deep and with enormous force along a channel no more than a half-mile wide. On the right-hand side, the east, the Verkhoyanskiy Khrebet presses in close, wild and barren and shattered, carved by time and the bitter frosts. The mountains' lower parts are speckled with a few stunted trees, then only the emerald tundra running up their flanks to where the scree begins. Some of the mountains are without even tundra vegetation, seeming to be only enormous heaps of flindered stone.

The far north of the Lena, above the 72nd north latitude, is different from anything I have ever seen. There is a sense of being at planet's end—a raw and fierce and somehow broken region. You understand very well how men could die here.

The plan is to find a sheltered place, if there is one, and wait out the night at anchor, so that we can finish this journey at our own pace, in some measured and considered way. I open the cabin window above my bunk to let in the cold. It is wonderful sleeping like that, warm inside the bag, with the top pulled up all the way around the face against the freshness, instead of against mosquitoes, which we left behind for good a day ago.

⚜

ENDINGS AREN'T ALWAYS AS you prefer them.
A hand closed on my shoulder. Volodya was bending over me in the cabin. I sat up on the bunk and he showed me his watch, which read 5:22 a.m.

"It is the last two miles before the delta," he said—softly, so as not to wake Katie across from me.

I pulled on my mackinaw over pajamas and went out with him on deck. The storm had worsened and the wind was blowing hard. The crew had been unwilling to try to make an anchorage, afraid of putting the boat aground on rocks. Volodya had sat awake through the night because it was our last on the river. Had I known, I'd have done the same.

Fear of wrecking had not interfered with the captain's drinking. At one point, for an hour and a half, he'd given the wheel to Volodya, with a caution to stay in the middle of the flow, and had gone below to sleep.

The *Stolb*, or Pillar—an enormous hump of rock, like the top of a submerged mountain—loomed ahead in the blue morning. That formation marked the end of the main river and the beginning of its branching into a vast network of lesser streams, most of them unnavigable, spreading in a great fan over hundreds of square miles and spilling the river's flow, as through a sieve, northward into the sea.

Volodya made a photograph of the stone hump.

"It's like a bear," he said. "A bear drinking." He believed there was a monument to the DeLong party atop the *Stolb*, but in such waves it was impossible to stop. Anyway, the place where the tragedy actually ended was farther north, in the delta itself, and it was possible we could go there a later day.

I could not help thinking, in that moment, how glad I was to be passing that place with all our party well, and our boat still sound under us, before the winter came.

The Ammosov bore hard to the right, between the rock formation and a shattered cliff, then farther right, entering into the largest of the Lena's many dividings. On either side was only stone and the emerald of tundra, luminous in that early morning hour. The others were waking, then, and starting to gather in the forward common room, lighting the stoves for tea—all bundled in heaviest coats, breath jetting up in frosty plumes.

As we've neared the end, the ship's crewmen, along with their more constant drunkenness, have become increasingly and unwelcomely familiar. We've made small gifts to all of them, and to the captain I presented a spool of monofilament line. Now every time I pass him he gives me another fish.

Slabs of pike are hung like pennants from every rail and cable, sun-curing and dripping oil.

The captain came again this morning, red-eyed and still recovering from his night, carrying a box of half-dried fish parts and also the head of Jennie's great pike, which he had kept up in the wheel room to stiffen and stink, its toothy jaws propped open with a stick.

I wasn't as grateful as I might have been, and tried to refuse the box. Then gentle Volodya spoke softly.

"He has nothing," he said of the captain. "Only fish to give." A whole life was in those words. A life of derelict men aboard a derelict boat, with drink and loneliness their companions, poverty their pay, and sorrow their destination. So I took the box, and thanked him, and he wrung my hand, breathing sourly in my face.

The wind seemed to lay a bit. The waves were smaller. The lowering hillsides of green tundra slid by. And at 11 o'clock that morning, Sunday, August 11, we arrived at the place marked on the charts as *Kilometer Zero*, where the Lena poured into Tiksi bay—emptied with such force and in such volume that it barred the sea itself from flowing in. A cup of water dipped from the bay was not salty, or even brackish, but fresh as it had been 2,000 miles before.

To the left, a bit inland from the coast, was where one boat of the Jeannette was blown ashore and the men in it saved by native villagers. Ahead, projecting from the right, a narrow spit of land ran across to partly close the entrance to the bay, and perched atop that were the few bleached and leaning wooden structures of the fishing village Bikovskiy. Beyond the point was only the pewter gleam of the Arctic Ocean.

What did I feel in that moment?

Not so much excitement as relief. Also gratitude, for the faith of others that had allowed us to make this expedition, and to Victor and Valera and Volodya for their resourcefulness and their companionship on the way. As much as anything, I suppose, what I felt was sadness. Perhaps that's to be expected when you've dreamed a thing so long, and then it's finished.

We made fast to a rusted, half-sunken barge at the shore of the bay, with the dismal hamlet of Bikovskiy strewn along the spit above and a litter of broken boats listing at the shore. I had to take my place then at the entrance to the cabins, with the "last answer" inside my coat. Because moist-eyed seekers—an army of them— came stumbling down from the village and across the listing barge and began to clamber over the rail onto our deck.

The seekers didn't care who we were or where we'd come from. They only knew that Andrei's pantry was open, and that in it was their only joy.

⚜

THE PARADE OF DEGENERATES lasts until evening, and it is tiresome. They come, make their purchases, reel away embracing one another and their bottles with powerful fondness. Then in an hour, sometimes less, they are back again. You begin to recognize the faces.

It is 15 miles across the bay to Tiksi, where we will have a week before the flight back to Moscow. Afternoon, when the bay was fairly calm, was lost because the crew had gone to their cabins and refused to be roused. By evening, when they reappeared, the wind had mounted again and the waves were rolling three feet high, with blown spray. Victor persuaded the captain to at least try a crossing. But after no more than a half-mile into open water, with the boat slewing in the troughs, the crew lost heart and turned back, managing to moor again with some difficulty to the derelict barge. So it seemed that we had reached Kilometer Zero twice in one day—first on a blowy but sunny midday, and again in the blood red of a storm sunset.

This morning was worse. I woke to an awful racket of crashing, and when I went out on deck the wind whined like a siren and the waves were running four feet, some cresting more than five. The dark, low line that was the bay's far side could not even be seen. A larger boat had secured itself to our windward side, so the Ammosov now was sandwiched between that one and the sunken barge, and that was the source of the crashing. Each rank of waves flung the ship against us, and us against the barge. Timbers along our side were splintering, and one was hanging loose. A few more hours and we could be beaten apart.

The engines were fired, and we slid free from that perilous confinement. Anchored several hundred yards out in the bay was a large oil tanker. We made for that, and now, with help from the tanker's crew, we're secured with hawsers to the great vessel's leeside, out of wind and wave. There is no real urgency to get across to Tiksi, after all. Sooner or later the wind *will* fall, the storm abate. And meantime we are safe.

The tanker's name is the Crocodile. Her captain has put the vessel's sauna at our disposal. The women will bathe first. While I wait for them to finish, I will heat a pot of tea water on the camp stove in the chilly common room, and write this journal through to the Lena's end.

FIFTY-FIVE

Y ESTERDAY'S CHANCE TO BATHE was followed by an invitation to dinner. We dressed in our best—our "best" being fairly disreputable after so long afloat—and clambered back across to the Crocodile, accompanied by Leontiy Arkhipovich Potapov, the Ammosov's captain.

A seaman ushered us up one flight from the deck, through a door into the tanker's living quarters, down a flight, along a passage then up again and into the captain's cabin where a beautiful table was laid. The captain and two of his officers were handsomely turned out in their dress blue uniforms with much gold braid. But the real host seemed to be Sergei Vasilyovich Pavlovski, a maritime inspector living aboard the ship—a genial man with sparkling dark eyes and a great drooping mustache, wearing a sport shirt.

There were slices of sausage, and loaves of fine, light bread baked in the ship's galley, and champagne to start. Then tasty cutlets and broiled fish, splendid light-fleshed *omul* fresh from the northern sea. More bottles were brought out, of vodka and brandy. There were toasts. Quite a lot of toasts. We praised the cook. She was brought up from below and presented to us, a pretty young woman of 21 named Natalia. Whatever other good fortune the men of the Crocodile might have, I told her, she was their finest luck. We toasted Natalia, and she blushed and went back to her stove.

The inspector, Sergei Vasilyovich, toasted Americans. He'd met his first one in 1968—a sailor who'd missed his ship in some European port. There were speeches. And more toasts. To friendship. To the greatness of the river. Katie thought of the Ammosov's captain, Leontiy Potapov, sunk low on the far side of the table, feeling left out, the master of a rickety tub in the company of greater men. So I proposed a toast to him—speaking of how he had brought us safely and with enormous skill from Yakutsk through the Devil's Race and the Tube to our destination at Kilometer Zero. I made it as elaborate and effusive as was possible without laughing, and he drew himself up straighter, greatly pleased.

Somewhere in that long confusion of eating and drinking it was decided that, rather than our risking the waves of the bay in our 130-foot vessel, we should let the Crocodile transport us around the outer coast to the port of Tiksi. She was an old tanker, her captain said, built in 1959. But she was well kept and sound, 360 feet long and 53 wide, with a displacement of 2,800 tons and a thousand horses of power. Waves didn't matter to such a ship as that.

But surely it was too great an inconvenience.

No, they said. It was decided. They would take us there
tomorrow. They had been a long while on board, and would themselves welcome a bit of time ashore. We toasted their kindness.
They toasted our graciousness in accepting their kindness. The
inspector, Pavlovski, insisted I had to go to his cabin and office
below to see pictures of his small son and his mother. He had a bad
heart, he told me, and was worried that because of the difficulty of
getting medicine he might not live to raise the boy. I presented him
a knife. He struck about desperately for something with which to
reciprocate, and finally gave me his razor, a plastic toy soldier and a
small tin of coffee.

I was ashamed to take anything. His life was so spare: a cot, his
desk with the photographs in its drawer and some papers on its top.
Several stacked books. But he insisted that I must. In the end I was
able to persuade him to keep his razor, then we went back up to join
the others. There still was some toasting going on, although my
memory of the specific subjects of these later ones is not too clear.
Shortly before midnight we crossed to the Ammosov—the hard
north wind still beating—and for some of us sleep came instantly.

Aboard the Crocodile, evidently, the party went on long after
that.

❧

I N THE STEELY LIGHT of 5 a.m. our cargo was passed up over the rail
and stacked on the forward deck of the tanker. Under a wintry
sky the waves were higher, the temperature lower—a hard silver
sun striking to metal the cold, cold sea.

Looking down on her from above, our little Ammosov seemed
frail and poor. Andrei, keeper of the liquid stores, a fellow with a
future ahead of him, wished us well. So did her captain, Potapov,
whose best, if ever there was any good, was all behind him. The former special forces man, Sergei, was up in the wheel room and
waved through the glass.

Then the lines were cast off and the Ammosov, her side rails
splintered from the battering against the barge and pieces hanging, turned away in the bay and made for the mouth of the river to

begin her long upstream march back to Yakutsk. Her engines made a tinny racket and a cloud of black smoke rose behind. Then we couldn't hear her any more. And when I thought to look again she was small in the distance, and just another ship.

The Crocodile at that hour had the feel of a ghost vessel. The man who met us on the deck, the third mate, announced himself as the only one awake besides the cook, and the only fit man aboard.

"But it doesn't matter," he declared with great confidence. "Because I can drive her."

And drive her he did—drove her twice aground on sand, managing both times to wallow the great vessel free and afloat again with violent reversings of the engines. The cook, meantime, was making breakfast for us, carrying platters of wonderful *blini* to be eaten with melted butter, plum jam and hot tea at a table just off her galley on the deck below.

After the second grounding, someone went to wake the captain. He rushed to the bridge, and though a trifle haggard seemed largely cleansed and restored by the emergency. Navigation near the Lena's mouth can be tricky, he said, because of its shallowness and shifting bars. He bent around the man at the helm to study the chart, then surveyed the shoreline to get his bearings.

Then he looked at the chart again and, with a cry of reproach, he *turned it right side up.*

⚜

TIKSI, CLOSED TO FOREIGNERS for so long, is a spartan place at water's edge, with no expectation of receiving people from another world, least of all Americans, and no place to put them if they come. It is an Arctic seaport, and also an air base in the first line of Soviet far northern defenses.

This is Tuesday. Our plane back to Moscow will leave on Sunday. The place Victor has found for us to stay meantime is next to the air base, across a mile of barren tundra hills from the town. The building looks like a hotel, and has a name, the Arktika, in great letters on its top. But it is no ordinary hotel, with dining room or other amenities. In fact, it is a lodging for Soviet air force men and their families.

We're on the third floor. Without elevators, all our goods— brought on a military truck from the port—have to be carried up. Jennie, Anne, Katie and I camp together in a room whose total furnishings are four single cots. The others are in similar quarters. Cold wind comes raking in around the windows. The floor is gritty linoleum. There are common toilets in the hall, one for men and another for women. But they are horrors. And the water runs only intermittently. The military families inspect us suspiciously, wondering what accident brought us here. We wonder, too.

But mean as the place is, I don't have it in my heart to complain because the day has been even harder for our Russian comrades. An hour ago, Volodya set off on foot across the tundra back into the town to see if he might arrange something of interest for us to see. Victor has found a way to heat tea water. Some of the others take a cold meal of tinned tuna and the last of our bread.

On Thursday, two more birthdays will be celebrated, Victor's 38th and Valera's 37th. That is not the exact day, but both are close and we will observe them together. I will give them the fishing rods and reels we brought to the river. Anne and Jennie are considering how it might be possible to make a cake.

Tomorrow I will sit with Volodya to prepare detailed translations of all the uses and dosages of the drugs and other items in our medical chest. All of our equipment will be left behind here to be divided between the Institute in Moscow and our partners on the river, except for the medical supplies, which we will give directly to our Irkutsk comrades. The rest is only valuable and unobtainable, but in this country now medicine is so rare as to be utterly beyond price.

T HE MAN FROM THE local Soviet appeared on the second afternoon, just before the supper hour. Victor came to our room, and when I opened the door the man was beside him.

"Sit down," Victor said, "so you won't fall down."

"What is it."

"They are saying we should move."

We'd taken our noon meal at the officers' mess on the air base. I didn't know how Volodya had arranged it, but it seemed to go well enough. The food was tasty, the servers pleasant, and the men of the Soviet air force had inspected us with only moderate curiosity.

Evidently, though, there was an officer on the base whose duty was to investigate accidents. After considering it, he'd decided we qualified as an "accident" and he telephoned the political authorities in the town.

"This place is not convenient for you," the man from the Soviet said. From the hardness of his expression, I could not believe our comfort concerned him much.

"It's all right," I said.

I was thinking of the equipment, and the stairs. We'd hauled our gear enough times that, unpleasant as the Arktika might be, one more move did not appeal.

"It's only for a few days," I told the man. "We'll stay."

"You don't understand," said Victor. "The truck is waiting outside."

So the mountain of our stuff was wrestled down and out to it. The man from the Soviet rode with us on the rutted track across the tundra to the town.

"This decision is not political," he said.

"We're not fools."

"It is only for your comfort."

"Right. But do you know what? It's late," I said. "You've caused us to miss our supper. And there's this funny thing about Americans. When we get very hungry, sometimes we get a little crazy. Sometimes even violent.

"Tell him that," I said to Sergei.

"It's not a good time to joke."

"Tell him anyway."

The hard-faced man gave no sign he was amused.

FIFTY-SIX

A S THE FELLOW PROMISED, our new quarters are more pleasant, although that plainly wasn't his concern. The two-story building is inside a fenced compound, its gate attended by guards. It is, we've learned, a place where senior officers stay when passing temporarily through. Several apartments are arranged around a connecting hall, each with one or two bedrooms for two persons and a small kitchen. The stove in our kitchen has an oven, so the cake for Victor and Valera can be baked after all and we will have the party tonight.

Volodya has arranged for me to meet the director of the Ust'Lensky State Reserve, covering 11,500 square miles of the Lena's delta—the world's second largest natural preserve after Antarctica, the director says. He is a small, cordial Evenk man named Sergei Larionov, and it's obvious he cares greatly for his work.

The reserve was created in 1985 by the Council of Ministers of the Russian Republic to protect the fragile area for generations to come, says Larionov. It is home to 46 species of endangered flora and fauna, and is a kind of crossroads of natural life—native Siberian species, Asian types carried northward by the river, and American types arrived on coastal currents from the east.

To guard such an immense area he has only eight people, the director says. But its very remoteness helps to protect it. Only a few main branches of the Lena can be traveled by boat, so helicopter is the enforcers' means of transport. In fact, he tells us, if the fog clears we may go by helicopter to see the actual place in the delta where the DeLong party perished, and also see the wild reindeer herds, which have increased from 60,000 to an estimated 85,000 animals since the reserve's creation.

The fog does not clear, though. With the turn of autumn weather, it has settled thickly upon this sector of the coast—an almost palpable blue murk out of which, from time to time, flurries of snowflakes fall. It is August 15, and already at 72 degrees 31 minutes north latitude, there is the sense of winter coming with a rush.

I also go with Victor and Volodya to a little marine museum in the town, whose keeper, an elfin white-bearded former ship captain, is an amateur historian. The first non-native people to come here were Cossacks who arrived in the bay from the mouth of the Lena in 1633. They called it *Burnt Bay*, and the hill behind it *Burnt Hill*, because inexplicably the coal deposits in the high ground above the site of the present town were burning when they came. The name of the bay was changed in 1878 to Tiksi, which, translated from the Yakut, means a waiting or resting place.

It was not until 1932, nearly three centuries after the first Cossack visit that the settlement itself was founded as a polar station. The permanent ice cap is only nine degrees of latitude to the north, and in this season floe ice is rapidly expanding south across what has variously been called the Lena Sea, the Yakutian Sea, the Tartarian Sea, the Cold Sea and, since 1913, the Laptev Sea of the Arctic Ocean.

The little captain is talkative and friendly. He asks if I might send him some kits for building ship models, and I must try to remember to do it. That's how he makes the endless dark of the winter pass.

⋘⋗

MISHA AND OLGA CAME on the afternoon plane from Moscow, to meet us at the end as Valery Tishkov promised they would. Suspicion and disagreement came with them, for almost immediately the hostility between Siberians and Muscovites boiled up again.

Our plan from the very start had been to leave the expedition's unexpended equipment and supplies behind here at Tiksi, for later use by Soviet expeditioners. The quarrel was over who would take possession of the goods—Misha and Olga, on behalf of the Institute, or Victor and his men from Irkutsk.

"It's supposed to be divided," I said. "Half to each. That was the agreement."

But each side was suspicious of the other. If the Muscovites took it all back with them, Victor said, the Siberians would never get their part. If it was left in the custody of the Siberians, argued Misha and Olga, the Institute would see none of it again. At issue were tents, canoes, motors, stoves, lanterns, sleeping bags and much else, including a quantity of remaining food, all with a value of perhaps $15,000—a stupendous treasure by Russian reckoning.

"You must make the division," Misha said.

"I won't do it," I told him. "There are two days before we leave, and I'm not going to spend them that way."

"But you *must.*"

"The hell I must! We've done what we meant to do, and now we're like some animal dead on the road, with the jackals gathering. I don't like it. And I shouldn't be in this position. The agreement said the Moscow and Irkutsk parties would divide the stuff according to a contract between them."

"Where did it say that?"

I got the paper from my duffel and put it in his hands.

"It says right here that you and the Irkutsk people would make a contract. So where is it?"

"There is no contract," Misha said.

"Well, that's not my fault. As far as I'm concerned, the agreement's breached. So I tell you what's going to happen. The equipment, all of it, is going to stay in Siberia until you and Victor's people make your own agreement. I'll give you each a note saying my expectation is you'll divide it equally, half and half. And then I'm finished with it. It's your problem, and I'm not going to talk about it any more."

And that's where it was left. Misha and Olga came back to my room that evening to share a pot of tea, and it was plain that they were wounded.

"I'm sorry it came to an argument," I told them.

"I know," said Misha. "But the part about jackals made me sad. It's not something I would like to be."

That was Thursday night. Friday the murk refused to lift, so the day was lost for anything but typing journal. Today began no better. Any hope of going to the delta by helicopter has had to be abandoned.

S O LITTLE TIME REMAINS. There is no use wasting the hours until tomorrow's plane shut in by walls. So taking tent and cooking pans and a bit of food, we go, six of us—Anne and Jennie and I, and our three Russian comrades—down to the harbor where the little white-bearded captain from the museum agrees to carry us across Tiksi Bay to a curve of barren coast, to spend this last night beside a fire in the tundra, remembering together the immense distance we have come.

The afternoon is raw, spilling cold rain. Ptarmigans with their nearly grown broods scurry ahead of us over the moss and through the low bushes, sometimes bursting into flight. Volodya leads the way, because he knows it well. He is going home.

The gift of memory is that childhood, provided it was rich in love, always is remembered sweetly. There used to be a village on that bend of the Arctic shore, home to 150 souls. Volodya spent four years there—his sixth through his 10th. His father was engineer of the mine that dug the coal that heated Tiksi. The gray wooden structure of the pithead can be seen at a distance inland.

Then, on that day in the 1950s, the government in Moscow which decided everything sent out its decree saying the village was useless and ordering it abandoned. Volodya's family was transferred upriver to Sangar. Time, the fierce northern seasons and plunderers have desolated the place.

He finds what is left of his house. Two doors stand sadly in their frames, but all the rest is fallen. He shows us what used to be the kitchen, and the room where he slept with his parents. He is 30 now, and he had not been back there until this year. It is just one more place, like so many we had seen along the river, emptied out and destroyed by such official pronouncements.

We pass the derelict mine buildings and climb two miles on up to the crest of the ridge, gathering mushrooms along the way, to where the view is unobstructed out across the cold ocean toward the top of the world. Then with evening coming we drop down to make our camp and build our fire in the shelter of a high bank where a bright little brook runs out of the naked hills and makes its last bend to the bay.

Firewood is easily gotten. Because beside the stream, along the shore of the bay and along the Arctic coast for tens, perhaps hundreds of miles is a collar of driftwood—beautiful sawn logs felled somewhere in the forest a thousand miles to the south, rafted up the Lena River, then carelessly lost in storms to be flung up in windrows and bleached silver. More logs than we'd seen in all our two-month passage. Enough to build a thousand new villages, or maybe a thousand thousand. All just *wasted.*

In the end, that has been the dominant impression: the incredible waste of everything—of resources, of time, of talents, of lives—by a system that has so brutally and relentlessly failed.

Valera cuts dry shavings from a piece of drift and nurses a flame to life. We all drag wood for the fire. In heavy sweaters and wrapped in our thickest coats, we sit beside it, making a stew of the mushrooms we have gathered, with potatoes and a tin of meat. The sky is low, and ducks are flying. Winter seems very close.

I'm tired to bone, and the stubborn cough that has plagued me the last fortnight has worsened, gotten painful. I should go to the tent and my bag, but I cannot make myself do that. If I miss this night, none like it will ever come again. All of us feel that way. Huddled close around the fire, touching, we are saying only a little but remembering all, the darkness of a real night vast outside the circle of our light.

It is a strange, uncertain hour between night and morning when Volodya, who'd spent all yesterday looking inward, suddenly speaks.

"People must have guns," he says, looking at me across the fire, the firelight shining on his glasses, hiding his eyes. "A gun in every house."

He is thinking of his boyhood, and of his parents' lives.

"Don't be crazy," I reply—startled, because Volodya is the gentlest of us all. "Look at the problems we Americans have had with too many guns."

"That's different. In your country, people keep guns to protect against crime. In our country, the danger is the government." He is thinking of his village as it used to be.

But things have changed, I say. After the reforms of these last years, surely the most terrible times are gone forever. I say it, really understanding nothing. Because unless one has lived this country's history, one cannot quite understand in a visceral way the awful suddenness with which the universe can take a fatal lurch.

Volodya shakes his head.

"Things have changed. And they could change again. Guns are necessary," he says again. "Or else the government can come at any time."

TOMORROW WILL BE SUNDAY, August 18.

The little captain will come for us at the shore of the bay to carry us back across. In afternoon, there will be tears spilled without embarrassment. Dear faces will be fixed a last time in mind. The plane will pivot on the runway and, still visible through its window, the three figures will stand at the edge of the tarmac.

Then the machine will roll forward, the figures blur and fall behind. We will lift out over the metallic ocean and, banking, find our course.

In only a few hours more I will know how foolishly as an outsider I have spoken. For in Moscow, our destination six time zones to the west, the final plans for the coup d'etat are nearly in place.

VIII

The Current Sweeps Clean

FIFTY-SEVEN

THE AEROFLOT JET BEARS us westward in time with the late afternoon sun, back across the Russia's oceanic vastness.

Traveling the other direction some 10 weeks ago on the Trans-Siberian Railway, toward Irkutsk and the expedition's beginning, we had seen the country at closer hand. The impression then, reinforced by all we have seen since and the people we've come to know, was of a land immensely rich in space, in resources, in capable and even gifted human beings—a nation fat with promise, but cheated by three generations of failed political experiment.

What can be seen now from the plane's window are only the glittering rivers, the sunset mirrors of lakes, the endlessly undulating Siberian landscape furred by the forests of the great northern wilderness. And, past the Ural Mountains, only clouds.

After months in the trackless outback, Moscow seems a miracle of order—a truly modern city, almost like any other city. A bus delivers us and our baggage from the airport into the city's center, to the Academy of Science's old hotel where this time we Americans all will be staying together. Worn ragged by hard weeks on the river, and by this final journey nearly twice the distance from California to New York, we eat in a buffet on one of the hotel's upper floors and fall in bed.

For two weeks, in changing weather, I've been plagued by this stubborn cough and by chronic exhaustion. Always before, though, sleep has healed. This night it *doesn't*. In the darkness of a small hour, I lie awake in worsening distress, aching in every part of my body, the cough dry and tight, a fever rising. And finally I have to admit it's something more and worse than just fatigue.

I wake Katie and try to dress. I can hardly stand from the bed, wobbly on my legs as a drunk. The fever by morning is 103 degrees. I'm not thinking coherently, and every movement is an effort. To go to a Russian hospital in these times would be foolhardy, maybe suicidal. Katie calls the U.S. embassy and they give her the address of an American-operated clinic just opened on the far side of Moscow. She helps me down to the street outside the hotel.

❧

N O TAXI WOULD STOP.
There were plenty of cabs running, but all of them were rushing past empty, taking no riders. I had seen that one time before,
in Cairo in the autumn of 1970, just before millions of Egyptians
poured into the streets in a spasm of fury and grief on the evening
Gamal Abdel Nasser died.

Katie stood in the edge of the street, waving urgently. And
finally a man in a car—just a motorist, not a cabbie—stopped. She
passed the address through the window on a slip of paper. It was a
great distance but, yes, he would take us there.

The ride was 40 minutes. And though my impressions may not
be too dependable, there was no particular sense of anything out
of the ordinary going on. Traffic passed as usual along the streets,
and pedestrians crossed with the lights. The Moscow Monday was
beginning.

The clinic was staffed by a young Canadian doctor and an
Irish nurse, and the cartons of medical supplies on their shelves
bore the reassuring labels of American manufacturers.

The diagnosis was pneumonia.

So recently had the little clinic opened that some of its equipment, including beds, had not yet arrived. I spent the day on a
gurney, with an IV needle in my arm. And whatever they dripped
into me from that bag was powerful, because by midday the fever
was falling and I'd begun to register things clearly again.

"Did you hear what's happened today?" I heard the doctor ask
Katie.

"No. What?"

"Gorbachev has been deposed. There's been a coup by the
army and the KGB."

"Who's in charge?" she asked.

"Hard-liners. Nobody really knows which ones."

"But the city seemed so quiet when we were coming here."

"Yes," the young doctor said. "It's *too* quiet."

The junta's radio announcement of its seizure of power had
come at 7 o'clock in the morning. Moments later, while we crossed

town toward the clinic, the tanks had begun rolling. The videographer recorded them on tape, rumbling along the street under his window at the Academy's hotel. Now he and the photographer worked, while I spent that first day of one of the biggest news stories of my lifetime immobilized on a medical cart.

There was nothing more Katie could do for me there, so we decided she should try to get back to the hotel before the streets were blocked completely. The clinic people told her a place where she might get a taxi, if any were to be found this day.

"Don't try to come back here," the doctor said. "If he's better by evening, we'll bring him in an embassy car."

Making her way to the hotel, Katie found traffic gridlocked. Halted at one intersection, she watched a column of tanks thunder through—37 of them after she began to count—followed by a great many armored personnel carriers. There is no other sound quite like a procession of metal treaded war machines moving as stately and implacable as doom over the paved streets of a major world capital.

By middle afternoon, the seizure of power by the Communist right-wing cabal seemed complete. Mikhail Gorbachev was a prisoner at his *dacha* in the Crimea. Boris Yeltsin had made his stand inside the Russian parliament building, crowds of unarmed political supporters around him, defying the usurpers in a way that all modern Russian history said could have but one tragic result. Official Moscow radio was broadcasting the junta's declarations. The country and the world were stunned at the apparent ease with which the takeover had occurred.

All this I was able to learn only second hand, lying on my clinic gurney.

"Put in me whatever you have to," I told the Canadian doctor. "I have to get out of here and work."

By evening, after another drip bag and one injection in my backside, the fever had come down three degrees, to 100. And I was on my feet again, if a bit unsteady. But it was not a story I would enjoy reporting. There's no pleasure in writing the obituary of decency, the epitaph of dreams.

Our friend, Volodya, had been right in what he'd said beside the fire two nights before. When the experience with democracy still is so new, so fragile, the destroyers can come again at any time.

The small lobby of the hotel was stacked with luggage. Crowds of men, mostly Asian, milled at the reception desk, waving pieces of paper and competing for the attention of the single clerk. All of them were foreign scholars who'd come at the Academy's invitation, trying now to get out of the country before the airport closed.

"Did you change the appointment with Tishkov?" I asked Katie in the room.

"It's for noon tomorrow. He'll send a car. Can you make it?"

"I think I'll be fine."

The charge for an office call at that clinic was $380. With the IVs, the day's bill was more than $800. In such a place, at such a time, real medical treatment is worth anything it costs.

FIFTY-EIGHT

THERE ARE SOME FINAL items of expedition business to be concluded with our official hosts, the Institute of Ethnography and Anthropology. Professor Valery Tishkov, my friend and the director, has arranged for Katie and me a small luncheon in the Institute's dining room.

We had meant for it to be a recapitulation—a chance to speak about the river itself, the glorious adventure of traveling it and some of what we'd learned along the way. But now only one subject is on anyone's mind.

Beside the elevators, as we ride down from his office, are posted notices of a public rally at the parliament building to support Yeltsin and denounce the coup. The feeling in the Institute, Tishkov says, is predominantly in favor of democratic reform—but even there, among intellectuals, the liberal sentiment is not universal. The conservatives who seized power yesterday are not without their base of support, he says at the table.

To begin with, there is the military. More than 95 percent of the officers are Communist Party members. Senior officers, particularly, support the hard line. They are older than their counterparts in the West, and crustily conservative. Then there is the KGB. And the local militias, which are not just police, in the sense an American understands, but a paramilitary force. Many of these people have a vested interest in keeping the party's power, and their privileges, intact.

Finally, he says, there's the older generation—pensioners, veterans' groups—people who have been seriously hurt by the worsening economic crisis, and who also are susceptible to the patriotic argument that the weakening of the center threatens to tear the Union apart.

"'We will not take responsibility before the future generations for dismembering a country that was built by a dozen previous generations'...That is the argument," says Tishkov, "and it has appeal to the hearts of many Russians." He lifts a slice of buttered bread—then hesitates with it halfway to his mouth.

"But I will say this. In my view, these hard-liners are *two years too late with their coup.*"

What, exactly, does he mean by that?

"Because now, for the Russian people, it has become the habit to discuss, to talk. That was not true two years ago."

Is he suggesting that the people will not be silenced?

"It depends if this junta will follow the example of Hitler and Pinochet."

Might there be a chance, then—just a chance—that the events of the last 30 hours could yet be reversed?

My friend shrugs.

"I am a historian," he says, "not a prophet. But I will say—again, just in my view—that these eight men are *kamikazes.* Do you know the word?"

I do. What force, though, does he think could bring them down? His answer is instant and unequivocal: "*Complete civil disobedience. They will be unable to rule.*"

Valery speaks of some events since yesterday. He recounts, with special delight, the comical news conference in which the conspirators tried to use the unfamiliar tool of media relations to give their action legitimacy, but only succeeded in making themselves look foolish.

President Gorbachev, according to vice-president Genady Yanayev, now acting in his place, was relieved for "health reasons." Whereupon a young Italian journalist piped up from the crowd: "Gospodin (Comrade) Yanayev, how about *your* health?"

Another question from the uncowed assembly: "You understand that you have made a military-reactionary coup d'etat, which is entirely unconstitutional. What do you expect for your action?" You could almost feel sorry for poor Yanayev, says Tishkov, the way the man's hands and his voice trembled.

Boris Yeltsin, from his stronghold inside the parliament building, has called for a republic-wide general strike. Valery, instead of his usual coat and tie, wore an open-collared shirt and windbreaker to the office today.

"If it were not for wanting to meet with you," he says, "I would have taken a day of vacation." As it is, he was notified in a telephone call from his wife a bit earlier that they will be spending this night—all night, if necessary—with other Yeltsin supporters at the barricades around the parliament.

That's where I plan to spend this evening, too.

⚜

K ATIE WAS AGAINST IT.
"You're sick. And no one else is going."

"There'll be a couple of hundred thousand people there."

"None of our people, I mean."

"I can't help that."

"You know there's a curfew? The driver refused to go. So did the interpreter. They say it's too dangerous. Tonight's when they say something is going to happen."

The junta had issued an ultimatum, giving Yeltsin a midnight deadline to surrender himself and the parliament building, or else be stormed.

"Yes, but that's where the story is."

"You don't have to go, though," she said. "I'm absolutely against it."

"That's the point, I *do* have to. A newspaperman can't just sit in a hotel room while the world changes. Either I go down there tonight, or I get out of the business. It's one or the other."

"Well, I oppose it."

"You know it's the truth, though."

"When will I see you?"

"Sometime after midnight. I won't do anything crazy. What time is our plane in the morning?"

"Valery's sending a van for us at 5 o'clock."

"I'll have to write before we leave."

In the hotel that night, Katie met a young Canadian man who'd arrived several hours before on a scientific exchange, only to find the country unraveling. During the day, several small units of the military had gone over to Yeltsin's and the reformers' side. But the junta's reserves were limitless. From the hotel window, Katie and the Canadian watched and listened as more columns of tanks rolled through the dark, all bound in the direction of the parliament.

What I saw I recorded in the short account I wrote for the paper.

Armed only with umbrellas and the desperate courage of people with everything to lose, Muscovites tonight are defying the junta that has claimed power in the Soviet Union.

Through the rain and darkness they stream—young couples holding hands, pensioners lame with age, whole families together. All of them bound for the place that has become the center of resistance, the parliament building of the Russian Federation.

Still besieged inside is Boris Yeltsin, the federation's president. He has denounced the coup d'etat, calling for the plotters to be punished. With Mikhail Gorbachev held somewhere in the Crimea, Yeltsin is the greatest danger to the junta.

They want him silenced. Getting him is the problem. His popularity in the capital and across much of the republic is enormous.

Yesterday, in the first day of this crisis, barricades were thrown up on streets leading to the parliament and great numbers of Yeltsin supporters—or simply opponents of the coup—began assembling.

By noon today, the gathering outside the building was said to be 200,000. By tonight, it must have grown to several times that.

You don't have to know the city to find the way there. In the metro or on any street in central Moscow, you only have to let yourself be carried with the flow.

There is almost a festive feeling among so many moving all together. Some of the young people carry guitars. Nearer the parliament, a few enterprising vendors circulate, selling pale little sandwiches of bread and cheese.

Then, nearer still, there is the sudden, startling clash of metal. Several young men are dismembering a construction scaffolding, hurling down the pipes for more barricade material.

And finally there are the barricades themselves, some built on foundations of overturned trucks or derailed trolleys—enlarged to bristling walls 15 feet high and more, with torn spikes of wood and metal projecting—all shiny-wet in the reflected light.

There is nothing festive about the barricades. They look like something seen in photos of an antique tragedy. They look too much like this country's bitter history.

Behind the barricades is the parliament building, white and bathed in light, with speechmaking going out over loudspeakers to that sea of people all around.

The hard-liners have threatened to send tanks and take parliament and Yeltsin by force. Maybe before daybreak they will.

But by midnight that hasn't happened. The people still are coming, standing through this rainy night to defend, in the only way they know, their fading hope of democracy.

And it is clear, if nothing else, how many of them the junta will have to kill to have its way.

To be altogether truthful, I was glad to have a reason to leave there and make my way back to the hotel to write. If the piece was done by early morning, it could, thanks to the nine-hour time difference, be published in that same morning's edition of *The Star* in

Kansas City. Otherwise it would have to be sent from Amsterdam the next day. If a bloodletting happened meantime, anything I wrote would be unimportant.

The 4 a.m. alarm, set to wake us for the plane, sounded exactly as the last words went on the page. It had taken three hours to get those 15 short paragraphs. I hoped they were the right paragraphs.

The phone connection through an operator in Finland to Kansas City—where it was just past last night's supper hour—went through quickly. A colleague there put the text into his computer.

We closed our duffels, checked the room a last time, pulled the door shut behind us and went down to the dark street.

FIFTY-NINE

THE VAN'S HEADLIGHTS REFLECT along pavement wet from the all-night drizzle. No pedestrians are abroad, and few cars. The city seems almost deserted as we pass along silent avenues and out into the countryside toward the airport.

Is it the stillness of exhaustion? Of grief? I am thinking of those fleets of ambulances positioned along side streets near the parliament last night, waiting for the tragedy that seemed certain to come. But Misha has no news, and the radio tells nothing. So we cannot even guess, at that hour, what if anything has happened.

As always, the Moscow international departures terminal is chaotic, with rubles to exchange, customs and passport control to clear, and lines—the eternal curse of lines—to wait in at every step. At least we are unencumbered. When we arrived in spring it was with a mountain of cargo. What each of us is taking back, besides personal clothing, is one metal cup.

At last, cocooned in comfort, we are borne away from the catastrophe we fear has happened, back toward the safer world we know. Breakfast is served—unlike any food we've found in months. The flight from Moscow to the Netherlands is short. The engine sound modulates. The plane tips down and the fine, meticulous geometry of the Dutch landscape slides beneath the wing.

In the Amsterdam hotel room, before sleep or anything else, we switch on the television to learn how terrible the night may have been in the place we've just left. Instead, we receive the news of a miracle we'd never dared dream of—an event unlike any in the whole history of the suffering Russian people.

At 1:30 that morning, while I was writing at the hotel, the junta's tanks had rolled.

Then hesitated.

Then, confronted by so many ordinary people willing to give their lives for a chance at being free, the tanks had backed away.

The coup d'etat had collapsed, the commentator was saying. One of the conspirators had killed himself. The others were fleeing and scrambling like rats to save their hides.

Brave Russian people, although beginners at democracy—with no clear idea of what it is, how it's gotten or how it's kept—had faced the reincarnation of the old tyranny squarely, eye to eye at the barricades. And tyranny had blinked.

❧

THE TELEPHONE BUZZED IN the room.

There was the premonitory crackle of the connection being completed, then the dear voices from the bend of a cove on the Michigan lake. I could see the blue sparkle of the water. I could see the faces.

"You're out of there," said Patrick Dolan, his voice singing with elation. Pauline was on the other phone with him.

"Just now—we just flew in."

"What an ending! You've seen the television?"

"We have it on here now."

Images of celebration were flashing across the soundless screen.

"Then you know it's over," Patrick said.

"Yes," I told him. "And we're coming home."

Talis Bergmanis

Moscow on the morning of August 19, 1991, at the start of the attempted coup by Communist hard-liners.

Talis Bergmanis

With newspapers closed and the radio silenced, Muscovites get news of the crisis from leaflets on a utility pole.

Talis Bergmanis

Tears, and a brave little pennant of hope, as the drama unfolds.

Talis Bergmanis

"Would you shoot your own people?" coup opponents ask a soldier peering sheepishly from his turret.

Faces without fear, at a mass rally outside the Russian parliament building.

Talis Bergmanis

An old warrior in the crowd.

Talis Bergmanis

A Soviet tanker, one of many who joined the coup resisters, flies a flag of the Russian republic from his machine.

Talis Bergmanis

An image of courage.

AFTERWORD

THE ORDEAL FOR THE people of the former Union was not over, of course. The events in Moscow on August 19-21, 1991, were only the beginning of a protracted, dangerous, and relentlessly painful process that continues to this day.

Now, through the window of my house in Kansas City, I can see Valery Tishkov in his warmup suit, out raking up leaves in piles and putting them in bags. He is in the U.S. to lead a workshop about ethnicity and regional strife in his country, and has taken the opportunity to spend a week with us. Part of the day he sits at the sunny table in the breakfast room, composing a scholarly paper about the disintegration of the Soviet empire and the huge numbers of internal refugees cast adrift in the process.

When he comes to a snag in the writing, he goes out in the sharp air to rake some more. Evidently the contrast between the leaf-litter of my yard and the tidiness of the ones on either side has not escaped him. It's surreal to watch a prominent Soviet academician doing my neglected yard work. I have tried to prevent him, but he says it clears his mind.

I have been glad to learn that the problem of the expedition equipment was solved satisfactorily. It was simply divided in equal parts with the Siberians, as I'd hoped and as was planned from the start. The greater problems now, says Tishkov, are the everyday ones of living. Shortages of even the most necessary goods are punishing. The inflation in prices has spun out of control. For the first time, when he departed for the U.S., he left his wife and son with an empty refrigerator in their flat. He will use the honoraria he earns in this country to buy medical supplies for his son, Vasily, who has been diagnosed with diabetes.

In the months since the expedition, although the lives of all of us have moved on, the feelings of luck and accomplishment upon reaching the river's end have endured. There also have been some afterthoughts.

I remember that autumn evening on the reconnaissance, when I first saw the Lena, how Sergei Orlov, who would be our interpreter, said as we walked together beside the river at Kachug that "*anyone who makes such a journey must come back changed.*" Were we changed? Each one would have to speak for himself. For me, the answer is yes.

The experience surprised and humbled me with the discovery that certain of the qualities of command useful in that kind of undertaking—the habit of authority for one—are qualities somehow alien to my nature. I am uncomfortable with control. My instinct is to do my own work, and let others do theirs. Therefore, while I gladly would take part in such an expedition again, I would want no part in leading it.

It also humbled me in another, more general way. That is, I understand more clearly than ever before how foolish is the notion of the solitary pursuit of dreams. We accomplish little alone. The dream itself may be personal, but the realization of it generally depends on the trust, the skills and sometimes the courage of others—and also, in some part, on luck. Our greatest luck was in the goodness of the Russian friends who made the journey with us.

We have gotten at least a dozen letters from Victor and the others, and have written long ones back. In one of his, Victor told how even office clerks and school teachers in Irkutsk were trying to learn the skills of trapping and hunting in order to provide. In another, he spoke of having gotten a small plot of forest land outside the town, where he and his wife and sons planned to build a log shelter and put out a vegetable garden as "emergency measures" against the worsening economic and political uncertainty whose end no one can yet see.

These conversations by mail help keep the memory fresh. Valery Tishkov's visit also has been satisfying.

Each day, during his time with us, the headlines have spoken of some new and more troubling aspect of the situation in Russia and the other republics. But he writes on—and rakes on. I can see him now, tying up the 14th large leaf bag and putting it with the others at the end of the walk, and I am praying some neighbor on the street does not make him a better offer.

Valery's determination to finish the tasks he's set himself reminds me of how Victor went about the challenge of our traveling the length of the river. The two of them strike me, in fact, as being alike in some important ways: strong, resourceful, absolutely to be counted on because they have a clear sense of the part that honor and obligation play in human affairs.

They are men, in other words, who in these critical times ought to be able to find common ground. Deep currents of history and experience have come between them, as between so many of the peoples of the fractured Union. And yet if something is to be built out of the wreckage of their nation, another powerful current—of need and shared purpose—will have to bring decent men like those together again.

It's a fragile hope, perhaps, but worth holding. There isn't any other.

Lena Reunion

W HEN WE SAID GOOD-BY to our expedition partners at Tiksi on the Arctic coast, there was no knowing if we'd ever meet again. We promised ourselves and one another that somehow it would happen. But who could say when or how?

The next two years were occupied, at my end, with writing and with the production of the television documentary of our journey together. As the project moved toward completion, I mentioned to Bill Reed, the president of KCPT Channel 19, the Kansas City public television station, and John Masterman, who had worked with me on the film, the possibility of bringing Victor, Valera and Volodya to this country. In a postscript to the documentary, they could tell about the current conditions in Siberia, the effect on lives there of the unraveling of Soviet power and the collapse of the economy, and about Siberians' hopes for the future.

Two corporate sponsors, Boatmen's First National Bank and the law firm of Watson, Ess, Marshall & Enggas, came forward to fund their visit. Trans World Airlines flew them from Frankfurt to Kansas City. Ford Motor Company provided a van for their ground transport in the U.S. A friend hand-carried the invitation to Irkutsk.

And the improbable hope became a fact. In October 1993, shortly before the documentary aired, Victor, Valera and Volodya arrived in Kansas City. They were with us until the day after Thanksgiving.

Six weeks is not time enough to see America. What we could do was show them some parts of it we love, and that we thought they'd find of interest. So after the television work was finished we crowded in the van—the three Russians and I, my wife Katie, and Pauline Dolan for part of the way—and took to the road.

The newspaper columns collected here recount some of our adventures together.

KANSAS CITY, OCTOBER 10.

In a rush, the foliage has begun to turn. Another week or two and, aflame with red and gold, the city and all that lies around it will be robed as if for celebration.

Our friends will be coming soon, from a place half a world from here. It will be their first time in America—their first time across a barrier of distance and dogma that for them, until now, was impassable.

The timing was circumstantial. But if I could have picked a season for their coming, this would have been the one.

The sky of autumn is the deepest and bluest, and the air the finest, crisp as Mosel wine. The sporting season will have just crested, with the World Series still fresh in mind and the football wars advancing.

All across the midlands, beyond the buildings and pavement, combines will be rolling over the swells of the land, gathering in the harvest, reaffirming—even after a season of tragic floods—the miracle of this country's ability to fill its granaries.

We'll travel some of America together, so they can appreciate the majesty of our landscapes and begin to understand the astonishing variety of cultures by which this society has been enriched.

Our friends will have arrived just in time to carve the pumpkin, and meet the costumed children at the door on Halloween. They'll stay for our fall festival of excess, Thanksgiving. And the day after that they will board a plane for home.

By then they'll have gotten a fair sense of who we Americans are, and this land we occupy, and the combination of luck and striving that shaped us.

What conclusions they might draw I can't begin to guess. Nor am I much concerned about that. They are fair minded. They know, from their own experience, that societies that claim perfection generally are the farthest from it.

We'll just lay out as much as we can before them, and let them see for themselves. Maybe one day I'll ask them what they've made of it all. Maybe one day I'll know what to make of it myself.

KANSAS CITY, OCTOBER 14.

The first plane bore them west across five time zones to Moscow, which to a Siberian is almost a different world.

The second delivered them to Germany. The third vaulted the Atlantic, the ocean invisible under a blanket of unbroken clouds.

They would have liked to see the Manhattan skyline and "the lady," as they called her, with her torch upraised. But the landing approach to Kennedy airport was from a direction that gave no satisfying view.

Cursorily their passports were examined. At Customs, they took the line marked "Nothing To Declare." That uneventfully they found themselves across the last of the frontiers that, for much of their lives, had separated the two most powerful, most dangerous nations of the planet—countries locked in a war of ideas and armed for war of a final and more terrible kind.

Now all that was changed, or changing.

One more plane carried them to the heartland. Then the lights of a strange city flashed by outside the car windows. It had been a prodigious and exhausting journey. But at last, in an unfamiliar house on an unknown street, in beds not their own, they were allowed to sleep.

Their names are Victor, Valerei and Vladimir. After you know them a bit—and men as fine as these are quickly friends—you may use the familiar forms.

Valerei, whose rather slight, wiry build hides amazing strength, becomes *Valera*. He wears a mustache, and his eyes are of a faintly middle Asian shape. He's a humorous, free-spirited fellow. And as someone who met him remarked, "When Valera smiles, the sun comes out."

Vladimir becomes *Volodya*. In his early 30s, he's the youngest by almost 10 years. Of the three, his English is the best. A gentle man, Volodya peers at the world through thick glasses. His manner is scholarly, reflective.

"I cannot help thinking," he said, "how many generations of our people have lived and died with only the dream of seeing

America. So this visit is not just for ourselves. It is for our fathers and mothers, our children, and maybe even our grandchildren."

He writes in his journal every night. He means to forget nothing.

The familiar for Victor is *Vitya*, but somehow it doesn't fit. Although he's wonderfully good natured, there's a dignity about him—an aura of command. He's the senior of the three in age and also experience, and he was the leader of the Russian expedition team.

He has the build of a fullback, and an athlete's fitness. I saw him carry a pack of nearly 100 pounds 20-some miles up a mountain. He travels the Siberian wilderness on foot in winter to research avalanche formations, often alone, with the temperature nearly 60 degress below zero.

Somehow the formal name, Victor, seems to suit better.

What else can I say about them?

They got our expedition down the great river to its end, solving countless problems along the way, including some that to this day, I'm sure, they haven't spoken about.

If I had to depend on three men to get my daughters safely through the South Bronx on foot at night, these would be the three I'd choose.

Now I'm the guide, and they're the ones on unknown ground. An adventure of several weeks lies ahead. Every experience and encounter, everything they see, will be entirely new to them.

It's possible that, through their eyes, we'll see the country freshly, too.

KANSAS CITY, OCTOBER 20.

Yes, the buildings are splendid. And the houses are commodious beyond need or reason.

And the roadways are fine. And the shelves of the grocery stores are fat with products no ordinary Russian has seen or tasted in years, if ever.

And gasoline can be had on demand, in any quantity.

And cars, for Americans, are a commonplace, not an unimaginable luxury.

The fields that lie out from the city, in this season of the harvest drawing down, are privately owned. No capricious bureaucrat can take a farmer's land or his crop or his livelihood from him.

We Americans go to bed at night knowing, within a fraction of a penny, what our dollar will be worth when we wake on the morrow, and what it will buy.

For Victor, Valera and Volodya—after so few days in this place—much of what we take for granted must seem powerfully, maybe even dishearteningly, strange.

They are scientists, geographers, two of them working toward their doctoral degrees. Until recently, all three were on the professional staff of the Institute of Geography in Irkutsk, part of the Siberian branch of the Russian Academy of Sciences.

Their salaries at the Institute were the equivalent of $12 *a month*—wretched in the best of times, but now, with the country in chaotic transition, the economy a ruin and inflation running wild, literally a starvation wage.

To survive, Victor and Valera have had to strike out in independent ventures, leading scientists and environmentalists from the West, mostly from Europe, on small expeditions on Lake Baikal and in the surrounding wilderness region.

It has been hard, but hard times impose painful choices.

The price of a loaf of bread—20 kopecks, or about one-half a cent when we were on the river together—has increased 600 fold. Earnings have not kept pace.

An ordinary pair of socks now costs two days' wages. A month's salary will buy one pair of blue jeans made in China.

By comparison, the opulence of this consumer society must be stunning. But my Siberian friends are thoughtful men. They know that what they see here is the product of history, and a measure of luck, and most of all a product of the different ideas around which our society has been organized.

So it's not the apparent surfeit of wealth they speak of. Other things interest them more. They have remarked on the cleanliness of the city, its streets, its neighborhoods.

Above everything else, they have been struck by the friendliness of the people.

Each early morning, often before the rest of the household has begun to stir, one or two or all of them have set out for tours afoot. It is the hour of joggers, and folks with dogs on leashes, and exercise walkers with elbows flailing.

"Good morning," these pedestrians call out in passing. And Victor, Valera and Volodya reply with the same words, mastered so that the accent barely is detectable.

"People smile," Volodya said at breakfast the other morning. "They speak freely to a stranger. No one is afraid."

That's how it used to be in their part of Siberia, said Victor—far from the crowding and the intrigues of Moscow. But with the worsening economic desperation, the breakdown of order and an accompanying increase in crime, that has changed in these last years.

"Now," he said ruefully, "if you meet someone you do not know, you look away."

"Maybe like New York," said Valera.

He does not know New York, except from an airplane window. But reputations travel.

E MINENCE, MISSOURI, OCTOBER 24.

Morning fog hung white along the valley, with only tree-furred hilltops thrusting above it like islands in a cotton sea. When it lifted, the sky was as cloudless and deep as the Siberian autumn sky of all their years.

I couldn't have ordered a more splendid day to ride the current with my Russian friends.

We had 18 miles to travel—six hours on the river, the canoe man reckoned, or eight if we loitered along the way. But in the chill of the day's beginning we paddled hard to warm ourselves and made the first six miles in just over an hour.

So the loitering began immediately.

We stopped on a gravel bar, where the rush of clear water on the far side bent hard against a limestone bluff. Valera and Volodya brought sticks of bleached drift from higher on the bank and Victor knelt to blow life into a little blaze of leaves and twigs.

"We tell in Siberia, must be only one match," he said. "Only one."

The twigs caught. The larger pieces were laid on. An hour we warmed there, hands outthrust to the fire. The stream muttered by over stones. Only one other canoe passed by.

"*Good morning*," Victor called out in Russian.

"And good-by," came the reply—also in Russian—from the young woman riding in the front.

"She understands!" It startled them to laughter. "She speaks!"

The canoe went on around the bend, and after it there were no others. The season was nearly finished, and we had that reach of river to ourselves.

Hawks wheeled above the rim of the bluff. Loosened by the frost, a rain of leaves spun down to ride the river with us.

Later we passed the red canoe drawn up at the edge, but the man and young woman were not in it.

By midday the air was springtime gentle. We stopped again and made another fire—not to warm beside but to make our lunch of venison and cheese and potatoes roasted in their skins in the coals.

Valera crouched at the stream's edge, turning over stones in the shallows. By the creatures he found there—small clams and other sorts of aquatic life—he judged the quality of the water to be, in his words, "very fine."

Except for the oak forest, this could be Siberia, said Victor. And the river reminded him of the one we'd traveled there together. It was very much smaller, of course, but with the same clarity and the sense of unspoiled country stretching away on either side.

The people in the red canoe came abreast of us again and turned in this time for a visit.

The young woman had studied a year of Russian in college. She would like to see Siberia. By all means, they told her, she'd be welcome there. Maybe sometime she could, she said. Then the current carried them on.

One languid hour stretched into two. Our loitering had become excessive. We had to pull hard to make the last half-dozen miles to the place where, with the afternoon just beginning to blue toward evening, the canoe man met us with his truck.

Back, then, in our log cabin at the Cedar Stone Lodge, on a hillside overlooking the valley and the town, we turned that day in mind.

It seemed odd, somehow, to try to put a price on such splendid time together. But for men from a country whose economy is shattered, where life is drawn down to a daily struggle for survival, the price of everything, even a loaf of bread, must be carefully weighed.

"May I ask," said Volodya, "what is the cost of it?"

"Of what?" I said.

"I mean, of the canoe. Of this place to sleep."

I added up the numbers in my mind. Two canoes for the day cost $60. The cabin for two nights $80. Somehow I would have to explain that, to an American, it seemed a modest expenditure— when for these good and capable friends that sum was the equivalent of *10 months'* wages as geographers.

And it shamed me to have to answer.

EMINENCE, MISSOURI, OCTOBER 25.

Even by country standards, the breakfasts that issue from Carole White's kitchen at the Cedar Stone Lodge are atonishingly generous.

For travelers from a land where food is both expensive and scarce, the meal that starts the day here must seem a miracle of excess.

Eggs fried to order, rashers of bacon, French toast for those who want it, biscuits, a bowl of peppery gravy, homemade cinnamon rolls—enough rich fare to plug the veins at one sitting, and an endless supply of coffee to wash it all down.

One family of 20 or so people, gathered from several states for a reunion, has filled all the rooms of the lodge, and Carole's serving help failed to show up this morning. But a friend from town has come in to assist with getting the hungry fed.

From high on the log walls of the vaulted main room, the stuffed heads of various native beasts look down on this spectacle of indulgence.

Yesterday the three Siberian geographers spent riding the bright, quick current of an Ozark river. Last night in the cabin, tired from the good day, we'd passed the hours in slow conversation.

Victor, Valera and Volodya had spoken of things seen and people met in the first week of their American journey, and of places yet to go. We'd unfolded the map and considered the route. And sometime before sleeping, the talk had turned to generations and their passing.

"Your mother and father are alive?" Victor had asked.

"No, both gone. And my wife's, too. Our children never really knew their grandparents."

"The same for my sons," he'd said. "My father died when they were very young. He died in my hands."

He had been a large man, and physically very strong. And formal in an old-fashioned way. He always wore his hat and a necktie, even when cutting wood. It was a heart attack that took him. Victor remembered trying to restart the heart, to somehow bring him back, even after the doctor had turned away. But of course it was no use.

I don't know what brought the memory back to him at just that moment. Except that part of friendship is being able to speak about your losses.

That was yesterday. Today, after breakfast, the three of them planned to go on horseback through the flame of the autumn woodland, up to a ridge where they could look out across the folded and water-carved splendor of the Ozark highlands.

We pushed back our plates with groans of satisfaction, drained the last coffee from the cups and went out on the porch of the lodge.

It was another fine morning, the sun bright and only a vagrant cirrus cloud or two across the whole breadth of sky. Several members of the reunion family were taking the air there, too.

Victor halted in mid-step. "That man," he said.

He was looking across the porch at a man who appeared to be in his 70s—a large man, with a long, strong-featured face.

Victor shook his head, as if to clear his vision.

"It is my father's face," he said.

And that is the gift of shared humanity. Wherever in the world the accidents of a life take us, we are apt to find there some remembered part of ourselves.

NEAR OSCEOLA, MISSOURI, NOVEMBER 1.

Our way led first through a meadow, then down toward a stream and across it on a path of stones, then up into a larger field.

The frost-burnt tan of wild grass was accented by clumps of scarlet sumac. Beyond lay the dark of the woods.

"Look!" said Victor, pointing. Three deer, startled by our approach, bounded up from their bedding places in the rank grass and disappeared into the trees.

We climbed an outcropping of stone at the top of the field. The view from there is fine in every season—eastward to yet another meadow, and south to the crest of a timbered ridge.

"Well," said Volodya, who'd been silent as we walked. "Now I see."

"See what?" I asked him.

"I see the difference of this country. I mean, the land is really yours. It's true?"

"Yes."

"And no one can take it from you?"

"The bank, maybe. But, yes, it's mine."

"And you can cut a tree if you like? Or do anything else?"

"As long as I own it. I did cut some trees here once. But I won't again."

"Why not?"

"Because I felt bad afterward."

We walked on, then, my three Siberian friends and I, each

with a gun on the shoulder—not because we intended to shoot anything, but because, traveling the country on foot in autumn, it just feels right to carry one.

The freedom to do that is, to them, another of the defining differences.

They are skilled outdoorsmen, these three. They live at the edge of Earth's greatest northern wilderness. Game is plentiful, and in a time of great economic need hunting could be one way to set a better table.

But Siberians, like other Russians, have been all but disarmed by the laws of a regime that for more than 70 years lived in mortal fear of its own people.

With considerable difficulty, it is possible to possess a shotgun, although the cost of one is prohibitive and ammunition is hard to find. To own a rifle is all but out of the question. Even a hunting knife must be registered with the authorities.

One of the great entertainments, as we've traveled together, has been to stop in places where sporting equipment is sold. They examine the skinning knives under the glass of the cases. They look at, and sometimes hold, the hunting guns.

They are knowledgeable about these implements. They handle them with caution and respect. *What they may not do is own such things.*

But in this time when so much in Russia is changing, I asked them, mightn't that change as well?

"Well, maybe," Volodya said. "Someday it could be possible. But I am afraid not for a very long time."

And that's how it will be, they believe, with other things also. With the land, for example. We spoke of that as we recrossed my fields toward the place where we'd left the car.

That very week, the news out of Moscow had told of a decree permitting private land ownership. In principle, it meant a dramatic break with the Soviet past. But my friends evinced no great excitement. They believe they know, in practice, how it will work out.

The policy made in Moscow will have little effect in the provinces. Local authorities will use their influence to acquire tracts for themselves. For ordinary people, there'll be nothing.

"If I go to those authorities and say I want to buy a piece of unused land," said Victor, "they will tell me, '*Oh, we are very sorry, but no land is free just now.*'"

The forests of Siberia lie across an area larger than this country, and most of the hinterland is unpeopled. Yet, incredibly, none of that vast territory will turn out to be available.

That's how my Siberian friends believe it will work out in the end, at any rate. In their experience, decrees may be nice but reality is something different. Theirs is the pessimism learned from a lifetime of promises broken.

KANSAS CITY, NOVEMBER 7.

The Siberians we met when we traveled the river there two years ago received us with warmth we found astonishing in people raised on Cold War dogmas, few of whom had ever seen an American before.

Most surprising of all was their generosity. Their existence was spare, but what they had they shared—a bunch of onions from the dooryard garden, a jar of blueberries picked at the forest's edge, a cup of tea, a loaf of crusty bread warm from the oven.

One military man insisted I take his identification bracelet to remember him by. I tried to refuse, but he was adamant. No gift could be refused.

Another gave me the holster for his pistol. If I'd asked, I believe he'd have given the pistol as well.

Each of those gestures I remember, now, as a little miracle. What sense of Americans will Volodya, Valera and Victor, carry back from their encounters here?

Impressions of the same sort, I'm sure. Because they have been greeted by hospitality so fervent as almost to be alarming.

They've been asked to dinner in homes, and invited out for so many evenings on the town that only their Siberian courage and great physical stamina has gotten them through it alive.

A friend took them on an outing to a place where blue jeans are sold, and outfitted them and their families entirely. Another made them a present of miniature tape players with earphones, and a stock of cassettes.

Another gave them a chess set to pass the evenings when they've tired of grappling with English. Still another sent each of them a sweater she'd imported from Peru.

A man appeared at the door with three toy soldiers his daughter had made. A perfect stranger called to say he wanted to buy them sweat shirts imprinted with some insignia of the town.

Victor had hoped to take home eyeglasses for his wife, since they're hard to get in Siberia. But he was daunted by the price. An optometrist friend made a pair to her prescription as a gift.

Barbers at the shop where I'm a regular invited the three in for complimentary cuts.

It just goes on and on—people appearing with food and presents, all meant to say, to these men from the far side of the world, *You're welcome here. We're glad you came.*

My Siberian friends were a bit uneasy at first. I had to remind them that Americans were only giving what they had—as Siberians had done for us, when we passed their way. On neither side was it done for any reason except the pleasure of the giving.

I remember, one night near the end of the river, when one of our companions—Volodya, I think it was—said pensively, "The pity is that we were lied to for so long about each other."

Now the lying is finished. And there seems almost a passion to celebrate the decency, the humanity, upon which—even after all that has passed—we can still find common ground.

PRATT, KANSAS, NOVEMBER 12.

The day started rainy, then the clouds blew away to eastward and sun burnished the autumn countryside.

The hardwood forest thinned, then ended entirely. The land mounted in long waves, the two-lane highway running off to a pale thread at the far horizon.

Wind gusts buffeted the van. In the rear seats, the men from Siberia had their faces to the glass, noticing every detail: hawks sitting broad-shouldered on fence posts, their downy chest feathers ruffling, eyes fixed on the ground; cattle in silhouette atop a ridge; the gleam of a brook running down a crease of hillside; a broken windmill; a derelict and leaning barn.

Then, cresting a last rise, we were atop the world. On every side the country rolled away and down to the end of seeing, with not a tree to interrupt the endless pelt of the prairie—no house or any other mark of man in view.

Nothing but the wind-swept majesty of that infinitude of land.

Earlier in the day, one of my friends had spoken of the difference he'd noticed between this country and his native Siberia. There, he'd said, people lived in isolated towns and hamlets, huddled islands of habitation surrounded on all sides by vast spaces.

He had the sense, by contrast, that Americans had spread out to tame and settle every bit of their country. Two days before, we'd spent several hours on the road. And in that journey he could not remember a time when at least one house, or more often several, couldn't be seen.

But that was before our route turned west. And now, in the silence as we drove, I almost could hear him revising that impression.

Today's road took us across the southern reaches of the Flint Hills, and the Russians were much taken by the austere beauty of that sea of grass, as anyone must be who passes that way, whether for the first time or the 50th.

It resembles for all the world that tawny lobe of the great Asian steppe that thrusts up from the south into their Siberian homeland, ending only where the northern forest begins.

An hour we rode, or longer, without a word spoken between us. Then Volodya leaned forward from the rear seat.

"Perhaps you are tired," he said.

"No, I'm fine. We'll go a while longer before supper." More empty miles slipped by. The voice from behind was heard again.

"By now you must be very tired, I think."

I understood, then. He'd brought his driver's license from Irkutsk, certifying his competence to operate any kind of vehicle from a motorcycle to a truck. He loved machines, and he yearned to take the wheel.

The highway was straight, now, and all but deserted. Volodya is a capable and careful man. Some things you do on faith.

I pulled onto the shoulder, stopped, and waited for him to come around. I don't know their religious affiliations, if any. But in the back seat, Victor and Valera were crossing themselves.

Solemn with gratitude and the importance of the moment, Volodya wrung my hand.

"It is very historic," he said. "The first Siberian driver in the American West."

He wasn't, I'm sure. But it was too fine a notion to puncture.

Tonight we're lucky to have rooms. The pheasant season is open, and the motels of Pratt are full of parties of hunters. They came in pickup campers, with dog crates in the back.

"Tomorrow," I told the Russians before retiring, "we'll see mountains."

"The big ones? Colorado?"

"No, smaller mountains, on the way to Santa Fe. But by the end of this week we'll be in snow."

SANTA FE, NOVEMBER 14.

Somewhere on the immense tableland of the High Plains southwest of La Junta, Colorado, the first dry snowflake brushed the windshield of the car.

The storm announced itself, then for a bit longer it waited. The next hour, on the long stretch of narrow, empty road down to Trinidad, the low, sooty sky dropped only misting rain.

Night came early. The light went out. The highway inclined upward toward Raton Pass, and the mist turned to snow again—a glittering presence in the headbeams.

By the next town, where we stopped to take on fuel, it was coming steadier. And beyond there, on the road over the Sangre de Christos to Santa Fe, it filled the world.

At first the darker vegetation at either side defined the pavement's edge. After that, whiteness enveloped everything. The snow began to cake on the windshield and the wipers. The lights bored through a tunnel of hurtling flakes, and the road's true location could only be guessed.

For 20 miles or so, a truck led the way, the rear lights of its trailer for company, laying a track to follow. Then the truck pulled off into a rest area, and we were alone again.

The three Siberians are no strangers to snow. Where they come from, winter lasts seven to eight months of the year. It's cars they are uneasy with. Valera does not drive at all. Victor has a license but no car—though he has constructed a garage to put a car in if he ever has the luck to own one.

Only Volodya has any experience to speak of, and even he is not truly at ease behind the wheel.

What alarms them isn't the snow, but the combination of it with an unfamiliar machine, a driver whose skills they can't be sure of, and an unknown mountain road leading through a whiteout to yet another place they've never been before.

In the rear-view mirror I could see them in the seats behind, all sitting up very straight, like men waiting to hear the sentence announced. Their faces were only shadows, except for the whiteness of their eyes, which were very wide.

Midway in that ordeal we saw a car's headlamps lancing up through the snow-curtain at a strange angle from below the road on the right-hand side. I braked, and eased onto what I imagined to be the shoulder. And waited with the emergency blinkers on while the three of them ran back to investigate.

It turned out to be two young girls, teen-agers, who'd driven off the highway, ending up in a drift on the slope below. Volodya cut his hand trying to help the others push their car out. It was no use. Then a truck came along behind, and also stopped. And my friends came back, snow to their knees. The trucker had called on his radio to the highway patrol. The girls, who were unhurt, preferred to wait there with the car.

"In Siberia," one of the Russians said, "we have no such patrol. In winter, if a traveler is in such a situation, it is necessary to extract the car or else that person might be—"

"Dead?"

"Well, not dead, perhaps. But seriously inconvenienced."

Getting stranded at 60 or 70 degrees below zero could, indeed, be inconvenient.

From there down to the valley and our lodging here we saw other cars and trucks strayed off the road and into ditches. But the plows were out by then, and the wreckers working, so we came on without any other stops. What should have been a three-hour trip over the mountain took nearly six.

When we climbed from the machine at the end of it, the congratulations I received were so effusive—shouts, handshakes and backslaps—that I felt like a bomber pilot who'd just brought his men safely through the flak.

This morning the sun is out and the snow already going. Last night on the road was a trial, but today I face an even harder challenge. How can one explain to a Russian, or to anyone, life in a town composed mainly of curio shops, small art salons and pricey boutiques?

FRIJOLES CANYON, NEW MEXICO, November 16.

The Taos Pueblo is more than 1,000 years old, and its people have managed to hold their ground against change.

"We plan to be here for another 1,000," a young woman of the pueblo told the three Russian visitors. "We will keep our ceremonies and our language alive."

It is a brave hope, which the visitors might be forgiven for disbelieving. In their Siberian homeland, indigenous cultures have been overwhelmed by four centuries of Russian migration. Among some smaller tribal groups, only a few dozen old people remember the ancestral traditions and still speak the native tongue.

For the young, the past is lost beyond recall.

This afternoon, under a low sky threatening to drop another snow, we have driven up from Santa Fe to Bandelier National Monument, and to this narrow, steep-walled canyon. Here, in the stillness of a raw winter day, one finds the mute proof of how complete, how final, a people's loss can be.

The number of families that lodged here in the forgotten past can only be guessed by the stone remains of their dwellings on the valley floor and the shelters they carved into the solidified volcanic ash of the canyon's side.

From that evidence, the population must have been several hundred, perhaps several thousand.

The archaeologists know that they cultivated squash and beans and primitive corn on the canyon floor, beside Frijoles Creek. Their stone tools and fragments of their pottery have been found. The petrogylphs they scratched into the walls of towering rock still can be seen. But that is all.

Their presence hangs powerfully over this place, and yet hardly anything about them can be surely known—what they called themselves, what gods they prayed to, what vision of the world they shared, what dreams and terrors animated their days.

Impenetrable, too, is the greatest and most haunting mystery about them. What natural calamity or enemy predation wrote an end to their habitation of this canyon? Where did they go from here, and what became of them?

There's conjecture, of course, but it's only that. Just the stones are left. The rest is gone.

Victor and Valera climbed the three pine-pole ladders to the largest cave shelter, high on the canyon wall, while Volodya made pictures from below. It was nearly twilight when they climbed back down.

"It is *wonderful* place," Victor said. "I would like to live here for long time."

That's what those people of the last millenium must have said when they first set eyes upon it. Possibly they imagined it would be forever.

But life is fragile, the margins finer than we suppose—for us, as for the people of the canyon.

Riding back through the dark, I was thinking of another place we'd visited earlier this day. That was Los Alamos, the science city, perched atop its nearby mesa, where man proved he could harness the fire of suns to make a danger unlike any known before.

The connection between the two—Los Alamos and the shelters where a nameless people once had lived—resonated powerfully. I suppose my Russian companions must have been turning in mind the same thought.

How long—most of our lifetimes—we had lived with the danger of an event that could leave, as the record of our passing, only our mute and tumbled stones. How easily it might have happened!

And now we were riding down a mountain together, reprieved from that terror, friends as near as friends can be, travelers in a changed world.

GRAND CANYON, ARIZONA, NOVEMBER 18.

They have seen the great abyss in the hard light of a winter morning sun. And in afternoon, when shadows more clearly defined the fabulous contours of its walls. And again at evening, when haze began to fill it, and the stone softened to shades of violet, pink and blue—the hour when the enormity of that rent in the planet's surface is best appreciated.

"*Today, the Grand Canyon,*" Volodya said. "It is the only time in my life I will speak those words."

They have photographed themselves, singly and together, standing at its edge. If time had let them, they would have liked to take a foot trail down to the canyon's floor and spent a night there, or longer, camped beside the Colorado River, listening to the power of it as it boiled past them in the dark.

They couldn't, though. There were miles to make, and other wonders of the land to see, and meetings to keep in other towns along the way. For Volodya, Victor and Valera, the memories of this day will have to suffice.

"I hope someday to tell about it to my grandchildren," one of them said. "I will show to them the pictures of myself in this place."

Now the night road carries us on. And there's no knowing how much farther we'll have to drive.

Two movie companies have come to shoot pictures against the backdrop of the desert's mesas and other fantastical formations, and it is said that every room from the canyon northward well into Utah is booked.

The motel parking lots are filled with California license plates and with the luxury motor homes of reputed stars whose names I've never heard and nobody will remember day after tomorrow. In one lodging from which we were turned away, the lobby was aswarm with loud-voiced young men with inch-deep winter suntans and ponytails.

And those are only the "grips," the "best boys" and such—the ones whose names are unreadable in the credits. The principals may be even more exotic. Hollywood, unlikeable enough for other reasons, tonight is preventing our finding a place to sleep.

One wonders what the Navajo people, whose land this is, make of all these theatrical invasions. The lights of their small houses, salted thinly across the parched and stony land, are like faint, lonely stars in the blackness that wraps the highway on either side.

An hour ago we stopped to stretch ourselves and take nourishment at a little roadside truck stop. It was a clean and cheerful place, operated and mostly patronized by Indian people. We ordered the specialty of the house, something called a Navajo Taco. It turned out to be delicious, served atop traditional Indian fry bread—another of those lucky hybrids, like Tex Mex and chop suey, that this mingled culture has produced.

Now we press on again, hoping to stumble upon some hamlet in which the legends of the silver screen and their retinues of flunkies might have overlooked a couple of rooms.

The three Russians riding with me are indifferent to the uncertainties of travel, which are not even to be compared with the difficulty of everyday life in the homeland they'll soon return to. All that will matter, in the end, are the experiences they store up along the way.

Often, in these days, something has called up a memory from the journey we shared two years ago when we rode the Lena's current together. But tonight their imaginations are filled with the canyon, and the great stream that carved it.

In the headlight beams, a bridge sign told that we were crossing that river farther to the north.

From the back seat, Victor's voice broke a long silence.

"The Colorado," he said, with an adventurer's longing, "is now the river of my dreams."

E STES PARK, COLORADO, NOVEMBER 21.

Selfishly materialistic.

That's how much of the world thinks of us. In embarrassment at all we have, it's how we sometimes think of ourselves. And yet how freely, how eagerly, Americans share.

In these last weeks, the outpouring of generosity toward our friends has been utterly astonishing—you might almost say *relentless*.

An insular people, and inward-looking.

That's another conventional image of Americans. And everywhere we've traveled the stereotype has been exploded.

In each town of any size where we've stopped, the men from Siberia have met speakers of their native tongue. Young Russians, some of them, here on student exchanges. And American scholars, who have devoted careers to Russian language and culture. And people whose business has taken them to that part of the world.

In every meeting they've been plied with questions—good questions, rising out of genuine interest in the political evolution and conditions of life in what used to be the Soviet Union, and in Siberia particularly.

The reputation of Americans as ill-informed and indifferent to world affairs has seemed, at least to the three visitors, ludicrously undeserved.

Finally, there is the notion—accepted uncritically by many in this country—that the natural beauty of the continent has been destroyed and the environment irreparably fouled by decades of carelessness and exploitation.

In certain parts of the land, without question, that's true. But traveling with the Russians, and seeing the heartland of the country through their eyes, I've been struck by *how much of the very best has been saved!*

There's nothing we've seen together that I hadn't seen before. But their enthusiasm gives a freshness to the experience, as though the visions were somehow new for me as well.

There remain great areas unspoiled, all but untouched. Even at the sites to which Americans and visitors have streamed by the tens of millions, there's proof of careful stewardship.

Not so much as a gum wrapper or a discarded soft drink can disfigured the famous landscapes of the West—the Grand Canyon, Monument Valley, the high reaches of the Rocky Mountains through which we passed.

Except for the concessions made to the needs of travelers— roads to drive, benches to sit upon and such—it was almost possible to imagine that one was seeing those splendid places as they appeared to the first explorers who passed that way two centuries and more ago.

As we near the end of our journeying together, I have the feeling that what I've shown my friends is not a country exhausted and despoiled, but one still rich in beauty and young in spirit, with some history still to make.

I don't say that vainly, but rather as a man humbled by a bit keener awareness of his luck.

KANSAS CITY, NOVEMBER 25.

Six weeks have gone by too quickly, as time does when it's usefully filled. Our visitors have been able to see only a fraction of America, but they've seen some of the best—the heartland, and the unchanging spaces of the West.

They came to experience and to learn, and they came unburdened by the dogmas that for so long disfigured Russians' and Americans' notions of one another. They are of the new breed, upon which their country's future, if it has one, must be built.

In a neighborhood tavern, a day after they arrived, some fellow who'd been too long at the watering hole made a comment, and might have made a scene. Other patrons of the place ushered him out with such quiet dispatch that the Russians will never know of it, unless they read it here.

During our travels, meetings were arranged at several colleges so they could have the chance to visit with faculty and students. The reception at every stop was astonishing. The evening programs were long. Sometimes they were on the eve of important examinations. But the audiences stayed until finally the questions had to be cut off by the organizers.

My friends are scholars, concerned about how change may affect the natural environment and the people of their native Siberia as the new Russia struggles to transform itself. My hope is that the contacts they have made here with colleagues in their field will lay a groundwork for further discourse and possibly cooperative projects.

Victor, Valera and Volodya have gotten a sense of the country's history that no book could give. They have stood on the very sites where the earliest dwellers in this land lived and chipped stones and loved and went to dust many centuries before the Europeans came.

They have seen the descendants of those people—custodians of memories that refuse to die, and proud in spite of losses beyond redeeming.

They have seen the towns and cities and the well-ordered, amazingly productive farms that now occupy the taken land, and perfectly understand that most of history is driven by needs and impulses not easily or fairly judged by the morality of another time.

Wearying journeys on night roads—ordeals that sometimes stretched into the small hours of morning—have taken them from one landscape to another in a kind of blur: from tidy cropland to heaving swells of prairie; from featureless semi-desert to Monument Valley in a region of sculpted stone; high up among the angled faces and snow-caped summits of the Rockies, then back across the High Plains again to where this long, exhausting and too-hasty exploration began.

Time and again they have remarked how graciously we Americans seem to behave—not just toward them, but toward *each other*. With an eagerness that has transcended handicaps of language, they have struck up conversations with everyone from university presidents to a woman trash-truck driver in an Arizona town.

At night, wherever the hour for stopping found us, they set down their recollections of the day in their notebooks before retiring.

The people of this country smile an uncommon lot, they say. Americans seem to them to be proud of what's been built here— proud of the results of all the striving by the people of the world gathered together to make a nation.

They have logged more miles than would seem possible in the time we've had. And they've eaten more hamburgers and French fried potatoes from drive-through windows than anyone ought to have to stomach in a lifetime.

But every time another fast-food restaurant has appeared on the horizon, what's heard from the seats in the rear of the van isn't a groan but a glad cry of thanksgiving.

"In my opinion," said Volodya, "it is the finest, the most valuable American contribution to the culture of the world."

It alarmed him, then, that he might be taken seriously.

"Is only joke," he said. But his devotion to the art form is real.

K ANSAS CITY, NOVEMBER 27.

It was hard letting them go, those three good men with whom we've spent nearly every waking moment of the last six weeks— harder still, knowing what they return to.

In the place they call home, the town of Irkutsk in eastern Siberia, the fierce winter will have closed down.

The Angara River will be frozen, as will the great lake, Baikal, although not yet hard enough to drive a truck across. Snow will cloak the mountain landscape. It will be sometime in late April or even May before the poplar buds begin to swell and the ground can be seen again.

And their country still will be in the near-mortal throes of a political and economic crisis whose end no one can predict.

Inflation is running at 25 to 30 percent a month, which means that during their absence, just since middle October, prices of most essential items will have increased by more than half. Yet the wages they go home to will be the same.

The three are scientists, well trained and experienced. They work hard, and they are in the prime of their careers. And after the collapse of the Communist system, that's the condition of humiliating distress in which they find themselves.

Astonishingly, they do not complain. They speak without bitterness, and sometimes even with humor, of the problems of making do.

"It is the price we pay for being free," one of them said.

That price gets higher daily. The ruble, which in a remembered time exchanged one-for-one with the U.S. dollar, has plummeted in value to 1,250 to the dollar. Victor would not be surprised to see it fall to 3,000 to the dollar before the next year ends.

"We will be like the Germans after the First War," he said. "We will have to carry money in baskets to buy one loaf of bread."

In some ways, the Siberians, so long isolated by distance from the rest of the country, are at an advantage. They have cultivated improvisation to a high art. They know how to make things last.

"In Irkutsk," said Volodya, "a twenty-year-old car is usual. A car only ten years old is practically new." If a part breaks, a replacement must be hand-made to fit.

And if everyday troubles were not enough, thievery and thuggery are on the increase—driven partly by the terrible need, and by the collapse of public order that came with the death of the authoritarian system. People walk the night streets even of provincial towns in fear. Anyone who leaves a flat untended for as much as a day is likely to find it emptied on return.

Before coming here, Volodya, who lives alone, manufactured and hung a door of quarter-inch steel plate to keep his lodgings safe.

But having said all this, the central fact remains: *they are free*— free in a way that, a few short years ago, they could not imagine being. The ease with which they received their passports to travel abroad is the proof of it.

Their journey was made possible by American sponsors. Otherwise, the adventure would have been unthinkably beyond their means. Who knows if they will be able ever in their lifetimes to make such a trip again?

Yet, after nearly 6,000 miles on the road, in the long silences as we rode the last of those miles together, I could sense their minds turning back, as any traveler's will. And they went eagerly to the plane that would carry them not just to troubles but also to their families and the place of their hearts' belonging.

In spite of the hardship it has put them through, they love their country—and in particular their native part of it. They believe that, in time, if not for themselves then for their children, something fine can be made of this chance at freedom.

Grand as the experience has been, *staying* never was in their minds. America may be a wonder. But Siberia is home.

A GREAT CURRENT RUNNING

was designed by Gene Funk,
digitally composed in New Baskerville and Frutiger 45,
and printed on Weyerhauser's Natural Cougar Opaque,
a neutral pH paper with an expected 300-year library storage life
as determined by the Council of Library Resources
of the American Library Association.
by
THE LOWELL PRESS, INC.
P.O. Box 411877
Kansas City, Missouri 64141-1877

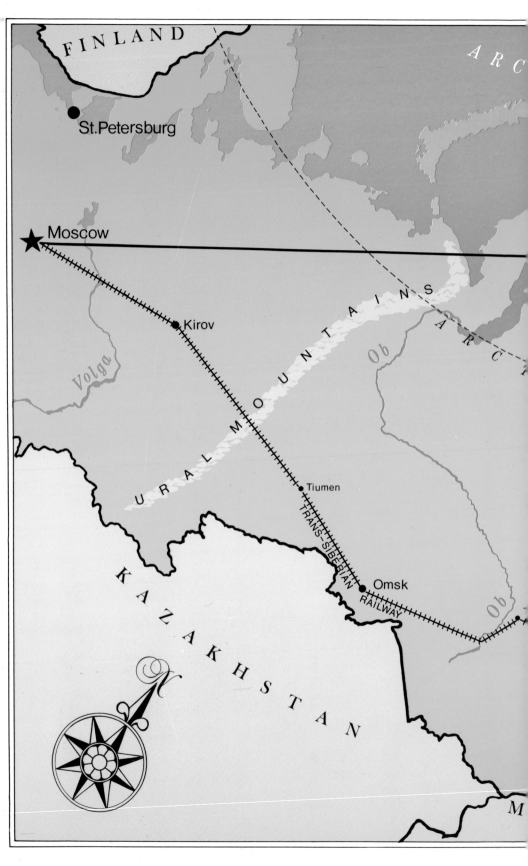